Place-Names in the Landscape

To my husband's memory

Place-Names in the Landscape

Margaret Gelling

J. M. Dent
London

First published 1984
First published in paperback 1993
© Margaret Gelling 1984

This book is set in 10/12pt VIP Plantin by
D. P. Media Limited, Hitchin, Hertfordshire
Made and printed in Great Britain by
Butler & Tanner Ltd, Frome and London, for
J. M. Dent Ltd
The Orion Publishing Group
Orion House
5 Upper St Martin's Lane
London WC2H 9EA

British Library Cataloguing in Publication Data

Gelling, Margaret
  Place-names in the landscape.
  1. Names, geographical—Great Britain
  2. Landscape—Great Britain
  I. Title
  914.1'0014   DA645

ISBN 0–460–86086–0

Contents

List of Maps

The final versions of Maps 1, 2, 3, 7 and 8 were drawn by Mr H Buglass of the Department of Archaeology and Ancient History at the University of Birmingham.

Abbreviations

COUNTY ABBREVIATIONS (the counties referred to are those which preceded the reorganization of 1974)

ABD	Aberdeenshire	FLI	Flintshire
AGL	Anglesey	GLA	Glamorgan
ANG	Angus	GLO	Gloucestershire
ARG	Argyllshire	GTL	Greater London
AYR	Ayrshire	HMP	Hampshire
BDF	Bedfordshire	HNT	Huntingdonshire
BNF	Banffshire	HRE	Herefordshire
BRE	Brecknockshire	HRT	Hertfordshire
BRK	Berkshire	INV	Inverness-shire
BTE	Bute	IOM	Isle of Man
BUC	Buckinghamshire	IOW	Isle of Wight
BWK	Berwickshire	KCB	Kirkcudbrightshire
CAI	Caithness	KCD	Kincardineshire
CAM	Cambridgeshire	KNR	Kinross-shire
CHE	Cheshire	KNT	Kent
CLA	Clackmannanshire	LAN	Lanarkshire
CMB	Cumberland	LEI	Leicestershire
CNW	Cornwall	LIN	Lincolnshire
CRD	Cardiganshire	LNC	Lancashire
CRM	Carmarthenshire	MDX	Middlesex
CRN	Caernarvonshire	MER	Merionethshire
DEN	Denbighshire	MLO	Midlothian
DEV	Devon	MON	Monmouthshire
DMF	Dumfriesshire	MOR	Morayshire
DNB	Dunbartonshire	MTG	Montgomeryshire
DOR	Dorset	NAI	Nairnshire
DRB	Derbyshire	NFK	Norfolk
DRH	Durham	NTB	Northumberland
ELO	East Lothian	NTP	Northamptonshire
ESX	Essex	NTT	Nottinghamshire
FIF	Fife	ORK	Orkney

OXF	Oxfordshire	SSX	Sussex
PEB	Peebleshire	STF	Staffordshire
PEM	Pembrokeshire	STL	Stirlingshire
PER	Perthshire	SUR	Surrey
RAD	Radnorshire	SUT	Sutherland
RNF	Renfrewshire	WAR	Warwickshire
ROS	Ross and Cromarty	WIG	Wigtownshire
ROX	Roxburghshire	WLO	West Lothian
RUT	Rutland	WLT	Wiltshire
SFK	Suffolk	WML	Westmorland
SHE	Shetland	WOR	Worcestershire
SHR	Shropshire	YOE	Yorkshire (East Riding)
SLK	Selkirkshire	YON	Yorkshire (North Riding)
SOM	Somerset	YOW	Yorkshire (West Riding)

OTHER ABBREVIATIONS

a.	*ante* ('earlier than')
acc.	accusative
Brit	British
c.	*circa* ('approximately')
Corn	Cornish
dat.	dative
DB	Domesday Book
E.	east
EPNS	English Place-Name Society
fem.	feminine
Fm	Farm
gen.	genitive
masc.	masculine
ME	Middle English
MS(s)	manuscripts
NED	*A New English Dictionary*, ed. J A H Murray and others, 1888–1933 (reissued as *The Oxford English Dictionary*)
N.	north
nom.	nominative
OE	Old English
OFr	Old French
OIr	Old Irish
ON	Old Norse
O.S.	Ordnance Survey
pers. n.	personal name

pl.	plural
poss.	possibly
PrCorn	Primitive Cornish
PrCumb	Primitive Cumbric
prob.	probably
PrW	Primitive Welsh
S.	south
sg.	singular
t.	*tempore* ('in the time of')
var. cos.	various counties
W.	west

The county surveys published by the English Place-Name Society are referred to as 'EPNS survey BRK' etc. Volume numbers are given when a county survey consists of several vols. paginated individually, but page numbers only when a several-volume survey is paginated consecutively.

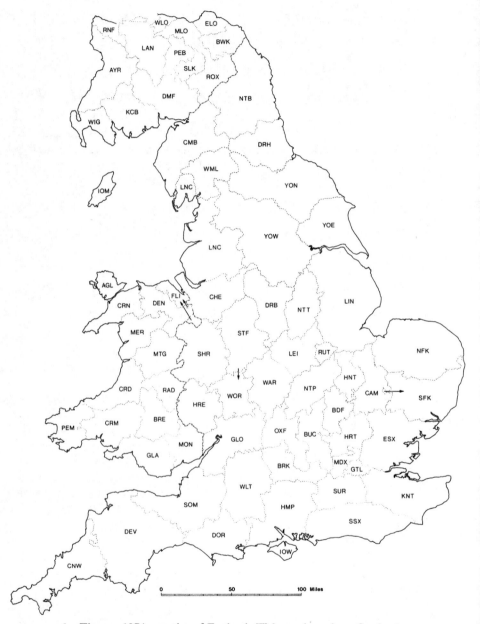

1   The pre-1974 counties of England, Wales and southern Scotland

Introduction

This book is the first large-scale study of the type of village-name which defines a settlement by reference to its topographical setting. In spite of their richness and variety, English settlement-names lend themselves to categorization, the two largest classes being the 'habitative', in which the main component is a word for habitation, such as **tūn, hām, wīc, worth,** and the 'topographical', like Claverdon, Knowle, Bothamsall, in which the main component refers to a feature of the surroundings. The two categories are not, of course, wholly distinct. Many 'habitative' names, such as Compton, Moreton or Waltham, have a first element which refers to topography, and occasionally, in a 'topographical' name such as Milborne, a landscape feature is defined by reference to a building. But the broad distinction between the two great classes is not obscured by this overlapping, and a study of topographical names can easily take account of the Compton type, and of the use of landscape terms as qualifiers in names belonging to other categories, such as Nazeing and Waldershare, which refer to groups of people named from a landscape feature. Such names are taken into account in the present study but (in contrast to earlier works) attention is concentrated on the **næss** of Nazeing and the **cumb** of Compton, rather than on the group of Anglo-Saxons known as 'people of the Ness' or on the institution called 'valley **tūn**'.

Topographical settlement-names have received less attention than other categories such as habitative names and those which refer to groups of people. Until quite recently they were regarded as later in origin and less informative for the historian. This was a mistaken hypothesis, belief in which obscured not only the historical importance of many of these names but also their intrinsic fascination. In order to understand why they were undervalued and comparatively neglected it is desirable to look briefly at the use hitherto made of place-name evidence by historians.

If place-names are considered as evidence for historical and linguistic developments in the Anglo-Saxon period, their dominant characteristics are abundance and ubiquity. It is these characteristics above all that differentiate them from the other types of evidence, archaeological and documentary, which are available for the elucidation of early English history.

Since the early years of the present century place-name specialists have been making this mass of material available to historians by providing etymologies based on the collection and study of early spellings. The proportion of the material recommended by place-name experts for the use of historians has, however, been quite small. Until recently it was felt that only certain categories of names had a specific historical message to offer. These were:

1 Pre-English names, important for estimating Celtic survival.
2 Names like Hastings and Reading, which refer to the descendants or followers of an Anglo-Saxon 'chieftain'.
3 Names like Wednesbury and Harrow which refer to pagan Anglo-Saxon religious sites.
4 Names like Wilsmere Down Fm in CAM and Hitcham in BUC, which were supposed (sometimes on inadequate grounds) to contain 'archaic' words or specially significant personal names.
5 Norse names, which are important evidence for the density of Scandinavian settlement in the Viking period.

Subsidiary interest was accorded to the distribution pattern of some common 'woodland' terms, such as **lēah**, **denn** and **feld**, since the creation of arable settlements in former forest was seen as an important part of the Anglo-Saxon colonization.

In the 1960s there was a reaction against the hypotheses which up till then had governed thinking about the historical significance of place-name evidence. An account of this reaction is given in my earlier book *Signposts to the Past: Place-Names and the History of England*. Much energy and ink was expended on demonstrating that categories 2 and 3 in the above list have a significance different from that accorded to them by the previous generation of scholars. It was also pointed out that the steady accumulation of information about Old English vocabulary and personal names had rendered the existence of category 4 open to question, and that the relationship of people like Hycga to settlements like Hitcham was not necessarily that of founding father or first English overlord. Some new categories of specially significant names, such as those containing OE *ecles* 'Christian centre' and *walh* 'Welshman', and those containing words borrowed by Anglo-Saxons from Latin speakers, were more clearly defined.

These were exciting developments, and the revisionist writing of the 1960s and 1970s has brought English place-name studies into the mainstream of contemporary work on the early history of England. With these events behind us, it now appears desirable to think about the future development of the subject. This future development will of course include the continuous labour of compiling county surveys for areas which are not yet covered in the English Place-Name Society's series; and if the end of the series were to be reached it would be desirable to produce new surveys for all the counties treated before the second world war, in order to provide detail on the scale of that supplied in the post-war volumes. But while, so to speak, painting the Forth Bridge, place-name scholars should be allowed and encouraged to consider the historical, geographical and linguistic significance of the material produced by their labours.

The necessity to revise earlier views about the significance of such categories as *–ingas* names and pagan names caused the new work of the 1960s and 1970s to concentrate largely on the same body of material as that which had been recommended by the pioneers of English place-name study for the special attention of historians. As noted above, this was only a small proportion of the great mass of material available, and, apart from the question of whether the selected names had been properly understood, there was perhaps a basic flaw in the approach which picked out for consideration exceptional or unusual items in a corpus of evenly distributed material. If place-names have specific historical messages to convey these may be written in the general mass rather than, or as well as, being concentrated in the exceptions. Even if this be not the case, the exceptions will hardly be properly understood without adequate study of the mass of material which forms their background.

The extent to which the general mass of English place-names was disregarded by early commentators can be quickly gauged by looking at the Introductions to EPNS county surveys. In the Introduction to the Warwickshire survey (1936), for instance, there are three paragraphs on names of heathen significance. These draw attention to a very small corpus, consisting of the village-name Tysoe, a ME field-name (*Grimeswrosne*) in Wolvey, and two instances of Harrow Hill, one recorded in 1800, the other a field-name supplied by contemporary schoolchildren. There is a paragraph on 'the surviving Celtic element' (again, a handful of names), seven paragraphs giving a complete account of Scandinavian names, and one on Norman French influence. Accompanying these there is one paragraph beginning 'The English element in the names of the county calls for little special comment', and in this only a few 'distinctive' items are mentioned. In 1952, charged with the task of writing an Introduction to the Oxfordshire survey, I had earlier Introductions of this kind as models and was led into the unfortunate remark 'The great majority of Oxfordshire place-names . . . are not in any way remarkable'. In spite of these dismissive utterances in EPNS Introductions, there has, of course, been a great deal of work on the commoner types of place-name; but it is probably fair to say, as a crude general statement, that the search for the exceptional, and the belief that a name had to be 'distinctive' or 'unusual' in order to be worthy of a historian's attention, have dominated English place-name studies for most of their course. A H Smith's monumental work *English Place-Name Elements* is more thorough and more reliable in its treatment of rare terms like *dus* 'a heap', *dūst* 'dust', *(ge)dwela* 'error, confusion, madness', *–dwostle* 'pennyroyal', *dyfe* 'hollow, valley', *dyfel* 'peg' (all from Part 1, p. 140) than it is in its treatment of words like **worth, tūn, lēah, feld**, where an enormous mass of material awaits analysis and study.

I feel that we should be looking at the general mass of English place-names and thinking about ways of organizing it so that we can appreciate its nature more clearly. And I think it best, for the first stages of this exercise, to concentrate on ancient settlement-names. A number of reasons could be given in justification of this, not least that it avoids the absurdity noted above of treating the village-name Tysoe as if it were of similar status to a modern field-name Harrow Hill. It has recently been estimated that *The Concise Oxford Dictionary of English Place-Names* (Ekwall 1960) contains about 19,000 items. Most of the names included are those of parishes and/or Domesday manors, though it must not be assumed that all parishes and Domesday manors are to be found there. The corpus of material assembled by Professor Ekwall in this great work was not selected on rigorously logical criteria. Some very 'minor' names are included, and some 'major' ones are left out. But the book certainly presents a representative collection of the ancient settlement-names of the country. Careful analysis and study of the material in the dictionary brings out a surprising wealth of information which was clearly not known to Smith, and was probably not appreciated by Ekwall himself.

It is clear that Ekwall did not quantify his material. Simple counting of some of the types of place-name in the dictionary has produced results which have been most enlightening to me, and a systematic statistical analysis of the whole book would be a valuable tool. EPNS surveys often include statistics for individual counties, but in the absence of overall figures place-name specialists have long been accustomed to use such terms as 'common', 'frequent', 'fairly frequent' when discussing words used in place-name formation. Professor Ekwall used identical expressions in his dictionary for elements whose occurrences in the book were in fact of quite different frequencies. He uses the word 'common' for **clif** (which occurs in c. 65 names in the dictionary), **land** (c. 95), **mere** (c. 105), **denu** (c. 170), **hyll** (c. 175), **feld** (c. 250) and **worth** (c. 250). 'Very common' is applied to both **well** (c. 250) and **ford** (c. 550). Some rather rare elements—e.g. **hȳth** which has less than 30 occurrences in the dictionary—are described as 'fairly common'.

A serious attempt to quantify place-name elements would obviously have to take into account the frequency with which they occur in minor names and field-names, as well as their incidence in the major settlement-names included in Ekwall 1960. Although this cannot yet be undertaken for the whole country, spot checks can be made in counties for which we have EPNS surveys. Such checks show that there are some elements which are used mainly or even exclusively in the formation of major settlement-names, others which are much more frequent in minor names; and these observations may be important for the correct appreciation of the significance of the word. Among words for habitations, *ærn*, *bōthl* (and variants *bōtl*, *bold*) and *stōw* may be instanced as terms only used in the naming of places which were, or later became, of some administrative importance. It follows that Much and Little Cowarne in Herefordshire are not named from an ordinary cowshed, and that Colerne (a large parish and ten-hide Domesday estate in Wiltshire) should be seen as more than a shed in which charcoal was stored. The interpretation of a number of topographical words discussed in this book—e.g. **hȳth, hyrst, trēow**—is affected by consideration of the extent to which they are used in major and minor place-names.

Statistical analysis is one of the ways in which the material in Ekwall 1960 might be marshalled to facilitate a clearer appreciation of its nature. Another approach is to arrange the names thematically, not only in the broad 'habitative', 'topographical', 'groups of people' classes, but in smaller ones within these. For habitative names this might involve such classifications as 'villages', 'hamlets and farms', 'single buildings', 'holy places', 'defended places', to which names could be assigned according to the meaning of their main component. Within the classes there could be further analyses taking account of the nature of the defining elements of compound names, whether personal names, descriptive terms, words like 'north' and 'south', and so on. In the present book, an exercise of this kind has been undertaken for the topographical settlement-names of the country, the seven chapters representing the main themes which emerged from a study of the whole corpus.

A full-length study of topographical settlement-names may help to redress an imbalance. A true appreciation of the early date and the importance of such names began to emerge in the 1970s, but prior to that they had been rated very low in the scale of historical interest. The attitude revealed in Sir Frank Stenton's early study of Berkshire place-names (Stenton 1911) was maintained by him, and by his associates, disciples and successors, for over half a century. In this work, on p. 17, he instances Welford, Boxford, Appleford and Burghfield as examples of names which are 'simply descriptive of the sites to which they refer'. On p. 19, after saying that 'Names of the descriptive type in general bear a very trivial character', he instances some—like Hendred, Woolley, Enborne, Goosey, Lambourn, Shifford, Swinford, Swinley and Catmore—in which the first element refers to birds or animals, and concludes that 'Oxford is only the most famous of many names in this quarter which carry a strong smack of the farmyard'. He is dismissive also, on pp. 12–13, about words for landscape features, regarding the choice of **hop** and **hōh**, in preference to other available 'valley' and 'hill-spur' terms, as governed by local dialectal usage, and concluding that 'It would be difficult to show that anything of historical or geographical significance underlies these facts'. On p. 23 he says 'The interest which belongs to names of the descriptive type is generally accidental and local'. In 1924, in one of his contributions to the introductory volume to the EPNS series, Stenton echoed his earlier views, saying that such names as Radford and Tilehurst 'are not, regarded singly, of much use as historical material' and that 'many place-names of this kind are intrinsically trivial'. In this 1924 essay he does, however, acknowledge that such names show that 'the Anglo-Saxons were remarkably sensitive to diversities of ground', and that 'they sometimes suggest interesting conclusions when they are studied in groups'.

The tide began to turn as regards appreciation of topographical settlement-names with the demonstration in the 1960s that other types so highly valued by Stenton, the *–ingas* and the heathen names, could not reasonably be regarded as the earliest in the English language. The true status of names like Burghfield and Woolley was hinted at by John Dodgson in his paper of 1966 attacking the *–ingas* theory, where he concluded: 'It might turn out that quite ordinary nature names such as *burna* "a stream", *lēah* "a wood", *feld* "open land" are the first to be used by settlers in a new land.' The possibility of regarding topographical settlement-names in this light was first systematically explored in the Introduction to the EPNS survey of Berkshire, which appeared in 1976, and an account of these developments and some further arguments in favour of regarding such items as Goosey and Lambourn as among the earliest English place-names can be found in Chapter 5 of *Signposts to the Past*. The hypothesis received the strongest possible support from Barrie Cox's paper (Cox 1976), which appeared too late to be cited in *Signposts to the Past* but is frequently quoted in the present book. Topographical settlement-names emerge triumphant from three methods of enquiry: they predominate in areas where the earliest pagan Anglo-Saxon presence is attested by archaeology, they predominate as names of parishes, and they outnumber other types in the analysis of English place-names recorded by AD 730.

Recognition of the chronological position of these names has brought them into the forefront of the subject for the first time. Now that they are receiving more careful attention it is becoming apparent that they are richly deserving of more detailed study from many points of view. They have much to contribute to linguistic and geographical studies, and they offer marvellous opportunities for imaginative contact with the Anglo-Saxons. They are never 'trivial'; the wolves of Woolley, the geese of Goosey and the swine of Swinford were matters of life and death to the Anglo-Saxons, and the choice of word to describe the settlement-site is as serious as any statement which our forefathers have bequeathed to us. It was a fundamental error on Sir Frank Stenton's part to describe them as 'accidental', and it is worth while to enquire into the reasons for this misconception.

During the compilation of this book I have become aware that two principles must be observed if the topographical vocabulary of the Anglo-Saxons as revealed in their place-names is to be studied successfully. Names must in all instances be considered in relation to the landscape, and each of the Old English words involved must be studied on a national, not a regional, basis. Stenton was led astray by failure to perceive these principles. He is impatient with the Anglo-Saxons for using **hōh** to designate hill-spurs in Bedfordshire but failing to use the term 'under similar circumstances' in Berkshire. The point is, of course, that 'similar circumstances' do not exist in Berkshire, where the Downs are not characterized by sharp projections of the sort to which **hōh** is applied in Bedfordshire and elsewhere. Names containing **hōh** are to be found anywhere in the country where the landscape has the appropriate feature. The use of the term in the Chilterns is illustrated by Fig.2, and it can be seen from that map that there is nothing 'accidental' in the occurrence of the word at certain points on the escarpment.

Some variations in frequency of elements are due to dialect differences, the rarity of **burna** in Mercian counties being perhaps the most notable example. But the irregular distribution of landscape terms in place-names is much more frequently due to differences in regional landscapes than to regional fashions of naming. The general picture which emerges from the study is of a people in possession of a vast and subtle topographical vocabulary, using certain items rather than others because of what Stenton called their 'remarkable sensitivity to diversities of ground'.

This vast topographical vocabulary includes many groups of words which dictionaries treat as synonyms. My study has convinced me that they were rarely, perhaps never, synonyms to the Anglo-Saxons. Just as the Arab has many words for 'camel' and the Eskimo has many words for 'snow', the Anglo-Saxon peasant farmer had many words for 'hill' and 'valley'. One of the advantages of the method adopted here is that the treatment of 'hill' and 'valley' terms in discrete chapters has necessitated consideration of all the common words in each category in association with each other. This thematic treatment enables it to be seen that many distinctions of meaning, such as that between **cumb** and **denu**, are common to the whole country, a point which has in the past been obscured by the regional or alphabetical nature of most of the reference books.

Sometimes the assembling of all instances of a place-name element, and the location of all of them on the map, produces a definition which, though obvious, has eluded previous investigators. The most striking instance is **wæsse**, where the facts assembled leave little room for dispute. Another is **ānstiga**, where the solution offered is not perhaps so watertight, but the description of the locations of the examples must at least be admitted to be highly detrimental to the hitherto accepted definition. In many cases besides these two words it will be observed that there is no equivalent modern term, and a lengthy periphrasis is required to translate the Old English word. There is not much left of the ancient variety and subtlety in the topographical vocabulary of modern English.

For some words, such as **hop, gelād** and **ofer**, which are either not evidenced at all in literary Old English or only recorded in a context which leaves the meaning vague, the place-name evidence is the main basis for discussion of the word; but this evidence has not been fully available to philologists because there has been no overall study of the topography of the place-names. I hope that the material assembled here will be useful in this way. It may also be of value for study of some words such as **dūn** and **mōr** which, though well evidenced in literary Old English, are of uncertain derivation.

It is not my purpose here to analyse the results of the investigation. A large amount of material is offered in the book, and I should prefer readers to draw their own conclusions about what is new or valuable in it. The exercise has transformed my own appreciation of topographical place-names, but I cannot predict what effect it will have on other people.

Topographical information has been taken mainly from the 1" Ordnance Survey maps of the post-war period. The series published between (roughly) 1950 and 1960 is probably the most convenient single cartographic tool the student of landscape history has ever possessed. Revisions of the mid-1960s onwards, by removing place-names and archaeological sites arbitrarily deemed obsolete or no longer of interest, have made the maps less valuable to the historian; and the new 1:50000 series, though a comfort to the eyesight, cannot be altogether recommended because it is a blow-up of the latest 1'. A most valuable additional tool is the David and Charles reprint of the 19th-century 1", on which the relief is shown by hachuring. Many of the discussions in this book hinge on the intricacies of surface relief, and some features which are not brought out clearly by the contouring of modern maps show remarkably well on the hachured maps. The main disadvantage of the modern 1" maps for this sort of study is the wide interval of the contours. Many names which are puzzling on a map with 50' contours are instantly explicable on a 2½" map with 25' contours. Study of the whole country on the 2½" maps has not been practicable, however, and in any case would not have obviated the main criticism which may be levelled at this whole enterprise, which is that topography should be studied on the ground, rather than on maps of any date, scale or quality.

This disadvantage, inevitable in a work on this scale undertaken by a single author, will be compensated for if the book succeeds in stimulating readers to undertake field-work. It is my hope that the type of investigation adumbrated will prove attractive to the non-specialist reader, and that large-scale participation will be provoked. If my suggestions are checked, refined, corrected where necessary, by people who live in the places whose names are discussed, a body of information will result which will be more valid than anything that might have been obtained by visiting sites. Visual appreciation of all but the most dramatic landscape features depends on, or at least improves with, familiarity; and the finer points of topography may require to be experienced in day-to-day living as well as being seen. If I have expressed myself adequately in the articles on such words as **halh, ēg, scelf, clif**, what I have written will be the starting point for local research which will prove satisfying to the non-specialist and enlightening to the expert.

The request for non-specialist participation in any branch of place-name study has to be accompanied by a warning that assumptions about the meaning of names must never be made on the basis of their modern spellings. It is essential to look up every name in a modern reference book before using it as evidence for anything. The glossarial index to the present book will serve for names which are specifically mentioned in this work. For others, Ekwall 1960 is the most complete reference book. Smith 1956, though requiring caution when a reader wants an opinion about a particular name, is by far the most comprehensive list of elements. The county volumes of the English Place-Name Society give the most detailed discussions available for most names.

The potential snares and pitfalls of modern spellings can be glimpsed from the glossarial index. Three names with the modern form Wellow have quite different etymologies, and a number of apparent doublets, like the two instances of Anglesey, Combs, Bulstrode and Burland, are actually quite different names. There is endless confusion between common final elements. But provided the necessary care is taken to obtain correct etymologies, detailed interpretations of topographical names are most likely to be successful if undertaken by people with an intimate knowledge of the area.

Abbreviations for counties are given after all names mentioned in the text of the book, and these counties are the ones which were operative before 1974. I realize that this will give rise to criticism and to some inconvenience, but I am convinced that historians whose work is based on regional studies must continue to use the framework of the pre-1974 counties. Modern students will have to familiarize themselves with the old units, or how will they know which place-name survey or which Victoria County History to consult? Series like the English Place-Name Society's volumes and *The Making of the English Landscape* will keep the old system alive for the local historian in the foreseeable future, and it is more important that new books should relate to earlier works on regional history than that they should give correct modern postal addresses. It may be illogical to recognize Greater London, but I do this because it has been with us much longer than Avon or Teeside, and because many people know that Harrow is north of London, therefore in ancient Middlesex, Barking east, therefore in ancient Essex, and so on. I have provided a map showing the ancient counties, and I assure young archaeologists, historians and geographers that any effort expended in relating this to modern administrative areas will be a useful part of their training.

1

Rivers, Springs, Pools and Lakes

Among all classes of toponyms, river-names have the highest survival rate, and in England they constitute a high percentage of the names which were taken over by the Anglo-Saxons from the British. Among the items passed on to English speakers are some which baffle Celtic philologists, and these may be still older names learnt by prehistoric Celtic immigrants from people who inhabited the British Isles in the Bronze Age. In addition to these fossils from pre-English times, there are many Old English river-names, and a sprinkling of Old Norse ones in northern and eastern Britain.

The use of river-names as settlement-names, sometimes with a suffix which was felt to adapt the river-name to its new function, as in *Rutunium* (near Whitchurch SHR, from the R. Roden), sometimes without modification, as in *Dubris* (Dover KNT), is well documented in the Romano-British period, and is likely to have been common in prehistoric times. The Anglo-Saxons also made much use of this manner of naming settlements, and when the river is a long one—as in the case of the Cray and Darent in KNT, the Darwen in LNC, the Colne in GLO, or the Kennet in WLT—the settlements which bear the river-name are likely to have been of special administrative importance in the early Anglo-Saxon period. When the river-name is pre-English (as in the examples just cited), there is an obvious probability that the Anglo-Saxons were continuing to use the name by which the settlement was known before they arrived, but this can only be proved when, as with Dover, the place is mentioned in Romano-British records. The Anglo-Saxons made much less use than Celtic speakers of suffixes for adapting river-names or other nature-names into names for settlements. The equivalent, in their language, was probably the addition of a settlement-term, such as **hām, worth** or **tūn**, to the river-name. Rotherham YOW, Leamington WAR, Taunton SOM and Tamworth STF, in which Old English words for settlements have been added to pre-English river-names, may be modifications of pre-English settlement-names, rather than new coinages for settlements which did not exist before the English arrival, or which had some quite different British name. River-names of English origin, such as Lambourn BRK, Collingbourne WLT, were also transferred to settlements, usually the more important ones, which lay beside the river.

The purpose of this chapter is, however, not to discuss river-names and their use as settlement-names, but to list the words employed by Old English and Old Norse speakers for rivers and other sources of water, and to study the use of these words in the naming of settlements. The OE place-name-forming vocabulary was particularly rich in words for different types of watercourse, and our understanding of the finer shades of meaning in these words must be limited. There is a distinction between terms only suitable for minor streams (**bæce, lacu, lād, læcc, rīth(ig), sīc**) and those which usually refer to more important ones (**brōc, burna, ēa, well**); but there are nuances regarding canalization (see **lacu, lād**) and intermittency of flow (see **burna, flōde**) which are difficult to pin down. The detailed behaviour, and the management, of minor watercourses was doubtless a subject of much concern to Anglo-Saxon farmers. The characteristics which caused them to use one word rather than another may often be no longer apparent, but there will probably be some instances where people with local knowledge can enlighten the philologist; and the presentation of most of the relevant terms in this chapter may provoke useful local investigation. About ponds, pools and lakes the Anglo-Saxons seem to have been less discriminating, since the most frequent term, **mere**, applies to features of very different size and character.

The ON contribution to the vocabulary for rivers, pools and lakes is relatively limited, but it is important to note that there are some ON river-names, such as Wreak LEI, Bain LIN, YON, Skell YOW, Gaunless DRH, in addition to those ON names which use common nouns (**á, bekkr**, perhaps **lœkr**) meaning 'river, stream'.

A substantial number of OE and ON place-names comment on the position of a settlement at the mouth of a river or at a confluence. References to river-junctions occurred in Romano-British place-names, this being the meaning of *Combretovium* and *Condate*. The commonest OE word for a river-junction is *gemȳthe*, which occurs uncompounded in The Mythe GLO, Meeth(e) DEV, but occurs most frequently as a first element in such names as Meaford STF, Midford SOM, Mitford NTB, and Mitton, Myton, Mytton in various counties. Eamont and the ON names Beckermet and Beckermonds also refer to stream-junctions. OE *mūtha* 'mouth' is used in place-names such as Charmouth, Dartmouth, Tynemouth, Weymouth, which resemble Welsh settlement-names in Aber– and Gaelic names in Inver–. ON *mynni* 'mouth of a river' occurs occasionally, as in Airmyn YOW, Stalmine LNC.

á ON 'river'. Several rivers in CMB, LNC, WML and Yorkshire have names ending in *á*, e.g. Beela, Brathay, Greta, Liza, Rawthey, Rothay. The word seldom enters into settlement-names, but it does occur in Aby LIN, Ambleside WML (from *á* and ON *melr* 'sand-bank' and *sætr* 'shieling'), and Ayresom in Middlesbrough YON ('at the houses of the river', containing *ár*, gen. of *á*). ON river-names in *á* were sometimes transferred to settlements in IOM, as Laxey, Cornaa. Ayton YON(3) is probably OE *ēa-tūn* (see **ēa**) modified by Scandinavian speech.

æwell OE 'river-source'. The Kentish form is **ēwell**, the West Saxon **æwiell**, **æwyll**. Alton DOR, HMP, WLT, Carshalton GTL, Aldon SHR. As a simplex name in Ewell KNT, SUR. For this and **æwelm** see Cole 1985.

æwelm OE 'river-source'. The Kentish form is **ēwelm** and the West Saxon **æwielm, æwylm**. Clyst William DEV (*Clistewelme* 1270 'source of R. Clyst'), Ewelme OXF, Ewen GLO (the source of R. Thames), Toller Whelme DOR. In Coundon WAR (earlier *Cundelma*) *æwelm* has been added to a British river-name identical with Cound SHR, Kennett WLT, Kent WML; the WAR name was presumably an earlier name of the R. Sherborne.

bæce, bece OE 'stream, valley'; used in midland place-names of a small stream flowing in a fairly well marked, but not dramatic, valley.

If the observations made under **bæc** about some names in East Anglia and about Burbage LEI, DRB, WLT be accepted, then *bæce, bece* is more limited in distribution than has hitherto been appreciated. There are a few instances in the south (Beckton HMP being one), and in the south west and the south midlands (e.g. Beachampton BUC), but the term is extremely rare in this large area, and there are some counties (e.g. BRK, OXF) where there is no trace of it in settlement-names, minor names or field-names. It has not been noted in the north, except for one possible instance in YOW. Examples are concentrated in SHR, HRE and CHE, and in these counties (and, to a lesser extent, in GLO and WOR) the word occurs in minor names such as Batch, The Batch, Beach, in a way which suggests that it had a continuous use in the local dialect.

In SHR, *bæce, bece* is the final element in the major settlement-names Colebatch, Pulverbatch and Welbatch, and it occurs in many minor names including Bache, Batchcott, Betchcott, Walsbatch and Woodbatch. In HRE it occurs in one major name, Evesbatch, and a number of minor names. In CHE there are the major names Betchton and Sandbach (from adjacent brooks), Bache and Comberbach. The word is rare in STF (Holbeche House in Himley being perhaps the only instance), and it has not been noted except in a few field-names in WAR. In GLO and WOR it is found in minor names and field-names.

In the east midlands there are four major names which contain *bæce, bece*. These are Haselbech NTP, Hazlebadge DRB, Cottesbach LEI and Beighton DRB. In the last name the word occurs in its stem-form (*bec–*), and there is the modern development of OE *–ct–* which has occurred in Aughton (from **āc**) and Broughton (from **brōc**). The term does not appear to enter into minor names in the east midlands, and this contrasts with the way in which it is used in the west-midland counties.

If it be accepted that *bæce, bece* is not the final element in Landbeach, Waterbeach, Wisbech, Pinchbeck, Holbeach, then it is absent or very rare in East Anglia, but a possible instance is Beccles SFK. Ekwall 1960 explains this as OE *bec-lǣs* 'pasture by a stream', and there is a tributary of the R. Waveney to the west of Beccles which resembles the streams described by this term elsewhere.

bæth, dat. pl. **bathum**, OE 'bath'.

Bath SOM derives from the dat. pl., the earliest genuine charter reference being *æt Bathum* in AD 796. A charter purporting to date from 676, which calls the place *Hat Bathu* 'hot baths', is not wholly genuine, but *æt thæm hatum bathum* occurs in a genuine charter of 864 and *Hatabathum* occurs also in one MS of the Anglo-Saxon Chronicle, so it can be accepted as an early form of the place-name. Bath is mentioned in the Anglo-Saxon Chronicle in connection with the coronation of King Edgar there in 973. MSS A, B and C call the city *Acemannesceaster*, adding 'the men who dwell in this island call it by another name, Bath'. MS F has *Acemannes beri* (substituting *burh* 'fort' for *ceaster* 'Roman town'). MS D has *Hatabathum*. The name *Acemannesceaster* only occurs in the annal recording the coronation, and in the absence of any confirmation in other records it is legitimate to question whether it was ever in local use. It may be a learned invention coined because of a feeling that a name meaning 'at the baths' lacked the dignity desirable for the scene of the ceremony. The inscriptions on Anglo-Saxon coins minted at Bath have *Bathan* or *Bathum*. The name refers to the elaborate constructions which made the waters of the hot springs available to the people of Roman Britain. In Bathamgate, the name of the road from Brough to Buxton, the dat. pl. is similarly used of the Roman spa which employed the medicinal springs at Buxton DRB.

It is possible that in other place-names *bæth* refers to constructed water containers, but this has not been demonstrated. It is not a common element. The following settlement-names have been noted:

Bale NFK, Bathley NTT (both with **lēah**).

Balking BRK. The gen. pl. of *bæth* has been prefixed to a stream-name *Lācing* 'the playful one' (Lockinge, also in the Ock valley, is named from another stream called *Lācing*). The stream at Balking has a number of roughly triangular pools along its course. Fuller's earth seeps into these, and they were probably constructed for soaking sheep fleeces.

Bathampton WLT, in Langford parish (second element **hāmtūn**).

Bampton and Morebath DEV. Bampton in this instance is *Bæthæmatūn*, 'farm of the dwellers at a bath'.

Bathe Barton DEV, in North Tawton parish. There is an 8' deep pit in a field near the farm.

Bathpool CNW, on the R. Lynher S.W. of Launceston.

Moorbath, N.W. of Bridport, DOR.

In the west midlands there is a recurrent minor name which may be from OE *dīc-bæth*, perhaps referring to a pool formed beside a causeway on the outskirts of a settlement. The best-known instance is the street-name Digbeth in Birmingham. Others are Digbeth Lane in Claverley SHR, Digbeth in

Stow-on-the-Wold GLO, *Dugbath*, a medieval street-name in Pershore WOR, and Digbeth, shown as a farm-name on the 1st edition 1″ Ordnance Survey map S.W. of Northfield near Birmingham (about where Turves Green is on the modern 1″ map). The earliest spelling noted for any of these five is for the Pershore street, *Dugbath* in 15th-century court rolls. Digbeth in Stow-on-the-Wold was *Duck Bath Street* in 1714, and these *Dug–*, *Duck* spellings do not favour derivation from *dīc* 'ditch, dyke'. For Digbeth in Birmingham, however, the earliest spellings are *Dygbath*, *Dyghbath* 1533, and the SHR name is *Digbath* in 1549, and these are compatible with derivation from *dīc-bæth*. Whatever the first element may be, the second is most likely to be *bæth*.

bekkr ON 'stream, beck', cognate with OE **bæce, bece,** is extensively used in some areas of Norwegian and Danish settlement, but the distribution is very uneven, both in northern England and in the east midlands.

In CMB and WML *bekkr* is much the commonest word for a stream in surviving place-names. It is common in Yorkshire, but less so in LNC. It is very rare in NTB and DRH, and not used in early place-name formation in those counties. In CHE there is only one possible instance in a field-name. It is common in NTT, but rare in DRB, and rare or absent in LEI. No place-name surveys are available for LIN, NFK and SFK, so the situation is not clear for this large area, but *bekkr* is certainly not common. In NTP, CAM, BDF and HNT *bekkr* occurs occasionally in field-names. A more detailed study of this patchy distribution might lead to some interesting conclusions.

bekkr occurs more frequently in stream-names than in names of villages and farms, but it is found in some ancient settlement-names. These include Caldbeck CMB, Hillbeck WML, Ellerbeck YON, Fulbeck LIN, Maplebeck NTT, Skirbeck LIN, Skirpenbeck YOE.

There are several instances of Holbeck. Ekwall 1960 translates this 'hollow, i.e. deep, brook', but 'stream in a hollow' seems preferable. The stream which gives name to Holbeck parish NTT runs between rocks called Cresswell Crags. The stream at Holbeck Fm in Southwell NTT runs in a well-marked valley; this watercourse is *holan broc* in an OE document of AD 958, so in this instance the ON word has replaced an English one. The stream called Holbeck near Ampleforth YON runs in a steep little valley, and so does the upper course of the stream which gives name to Holbeck on the south-west outskirts of Leeds.

Beckermet CMB and Beckermonds YOW are ON names meaning 'junction of streams'.

brōc OE 'brook, stream'. This is not one of the commoner elements in settlement-names, though it is very common in river-names and field-names, and probably more frequent in minor than in major settlement-names. It is rare in NTB and DRH, where **burna** is the usual term, and in areas (such as CMB, WML, parts of LNC and YON) where **bekkr** is particularly frequent.

The number of names containing *brōc* in Ekwall 1960 totals just over 100, of which nearly half have the word as first element.

Ekwall (1928, p. 53) considered that the sense 'marsh, bog', which is found in other Germanic languages, was the original one in English, and that the development from 'marsh' to 'stream' occurred on English soil; but Smith (1956, 1 p. 51) considered that there was little evidence for the sense 'marsh' having existed in OE.

Cox (1976, p. 66) found that *brōc* does not occur in English place-names recorded before AD 730, and there seems little doubt that it is not one of the earliest elements to be used in the coinage of English names. There are, however, a number of parish-names. These include Begbroke and Fulbrook OXF, Birdbrook ESX, Braybrooke, Bugbrooke, Cottesbrooke and Polebrook NTP, Budbrooke, Ladbroke, Tachbrook and Withybrook WAR, Carisbrooke IOW, Claybrook LEI, Ockbrook DRB, Sharnbrook BDF, Shottesbrooke BRK, Tilbrook HNT; so although *brōc* was not much employed before the 8th century, it must have been in use during the period when important settlements were still acquiring their English names. For the relationship of *brōc* to **burna** see the next article.

brōc is common as a first element, particularly with **tūn**. This compound has become Brocton STF(2), Brockton SHR (at least 5), and Brotton YON, but more commonly Broughton BUC(2), DRB(2), HNT, LNC(3), LEI(2), NTT, OXF(2), WAR, WLT, WOR, YON(2), YOW. Brockhampton DOR, GLO(2), HRE(2), HMP, Brockington DOR, and Brookhampton WAR, WOR(2), have *brōc* as first element. Other names in *Brōc–* include Brockdish NFK (*edisc* 'pasture'), Brockford SFK, Brockley SFK (**lēah**), Brockweir GLO, Brockworth GLO, Brogden YOW (**denu**), Brookthorpe GLO, Brookwood SUR, Broxfield NTB. As a simplex name *brōc* occurs once as the name of a river (R. Brook LNC) and occasionally as that of a settlement (Brook IOW, KNT, Brooke NFK, RUT).

The number of names in Ekwall 1960 in which *brōc* is the second element is too small to give a fully representative sample of the first elements with which it is compounded, so in the following analysis some items are included which refer to rivers, streams or minor settlements.

In major settlement-names the largest category of compound names in –*brōc* has as first element a word describing the brook, and this would probably be the most numerous type if the whole corpus were examined. Here belong: Braybrooke NTP, Claybrook LEI, Coalbrookdale SHR, Dearnbrook YOW, Fulbrook BUC, OXF, WAR, Holbrook DOR, DRB, SFK, Ludbrook DEV, Polebrook NTP, Sambrook SHR, Sharnbrook BDF, Shirebrook DRB, Skidbrook LIN. Black Brook and Small Brook occur in various counties.

Words referring to vegetation occur in Bilbrook SOM, STF, Ellenbrook LNC, Rushbrooke SFK, Sedgebrook LIN, Tarbock LNC, Withybrook WAR. Wild creatures are specified in Birdbrook ESX, Cornbrook LNC, Cranbrook KNT, Kidbrooke KNT, SSX, Sudbrooke LIN; and wild or domestic pigs in Swinbrook OXF. Cf. also Beversbrook WLT, Gosbrook STF, Midge Brook and Todd Brook CHE.

Use as a boundary is referred to in Marlbrook SHR, Meerbrook STF, Meersbrook DRB and Tachbrook WAR. Use for sheep-washing probably gives rise to Washbrook SFK. Millbrook occurs in BDF and HMP, and Skelbrook YOW also refers to a building. Superstition gives rise to Ladbrooke WAR, Purbrook HMP, Shobrooke DEV. Direction occurs in Sudbrooke LIN, Westbrook IOW, KNT; there are two settlements called Westbrook in BRK, but both are '(place) west of the brook'. Ancient river-names are rare in early compounds with *–brōc*, but such may be the first elements of Carisbrooke IOW and Colnbrook BUC. References to groups of people are also very rare, but Walbrook GTL is 'brook of the Britons', and Whitsun Brook, a stream-name in WOR, is OE *Wixena broc*, referring to the group of people who appear in the Tribal Hidage as the *Wixan*.

The category in which the first element is a personal name is not included in the analysis in Smith 1956, but it does exist, and it contains the major settlement-names Begbroke OXF, Budbrooke WAR, Bugbrooke NTP, Cottesbrooke NTP, Didbrook GLO, Forsbrook STF, Ivonbrook DRB, Ockbrook DRB, Tilbrook HNT, and possibly Shottesbrooke BRK.

burna OE 'stream'. Unlike **brōc**, this word does occur in names recorded by AD 730 (Cox 1976, p. 47); there are 5 examples. Other reasons for considering it to be an early English element are that it occurs with **hām** in some instances of Burnham (BUC, ESX, NFK), and is several times the final element in *–inga–* compounds (e.g. Bassingbourne CAM, Bathingbourne IOW, Collingbourne WLT, Hollingbourne and Sittingbourne KNT, Pangbourne BRK). Also it is more common in major than in minor names. It occurs in about 155 names in Ekwall 1960, most frequently as a second element. It is rare in field-names in all counties.

It has generally been assumed that in much of England *burna* was replaced at an early date by **brōc** as the common appellative for a stream, but that in the north the use of *burna* was reinforced by the cognate ON *brunnr* 'spring, stream'. This is not wholly convincing. The ON word appears to be very rare in English place-names. Ekwall 1960 points out that the original form of the OE word was *brunna*, and he considers that spellings such as *Brunne*, *Brunna* for Bourne CAM, LIN preserve this early form, and need not be ascribed to ON influence. Some names in areas of Scandinavian settlement may contain the ON word, but it is doubtful whether it was used so freely in place-name formation in England that it would have caused a resuscitation of an obsolescent English term. Nunburnholme YOE is likely to contain the dat. pl. of the ON word.

Study of the distribution of names containing *burna* suggests that the word remained in use as a place-name-forming term longer than has been assumed, and that its frequency was governed more by the racial affinities of the English settlers than by the date of the settlement. It should be noted that it is well represented in some areas of Wessex which lay beyond Selwood, where English names were mainly coined after the middle of the 7th century; this applies to DEV and DOR. It is noteworthy also that it was combined with *myln* to give the names Milbourne in NTB, WLT and WML and Milborne in DOR and SOM. Millbrook occurs in BDF and HMP, but appears to be the rarer name of the two. The water-mill is believed to have been a relatively late introduction in England, perhaps only becoming common in the 9th century.

The distribution suggests that *burna* was in fairly common use in Saxon and Jutish areas (England south of the Thames and MDX, ESX), up to the date of the English settlement in DOR and DEV and the date of the diffusion of the water-mill to the south west. It seems clear that it was already in common use in Northumbria before the Norse settlements, and it might have survived in the speech of north-eastern England and southern Scotland without the reinforcement provided by ON *brunnr*. It is very common in Yorkshire and NTB, and there are four instances in major names in DRH. It is well represented in LNC and WML. In CMB, names in *burna* lie to the east of the county, adjacent to NTB and DRH, with the single exception of Stainburn.

Names in *burna* occur occasionally throughout East Anglia and LIN. Among major settlement-names there are 4 instances in CAM, 4 in NFK, 3 in SFK and 7 in LIN. The term is also well represented in the area of the west midlands which formed the ancient sub-kingdom of the Hwicce (GLO, WOR, the western half of WAR), but in most of the Mercian counties lying between and to the north west of these two areas *burna* is extremely rare. There is only one instance in the counties of HNT (Morborne), NTP (Lilbourne), NTT (Winkburn) and OXF (Shirburn). It is similarly rare, with only one or two instances, in CHE, HRE, LEI, SHR. STF has 3 (Bourne Vale in Aldridge, Harborne, Wombourn), but they are all in the south of the county, on the borders of the Hwicce.

The main exception to the scarcity of names in *burna*, in those parts of Mercia which were not subject to Saxon influence, is to be found in DRB, where 10 instances occur in DB, making a sharp contrast with NTT, where there is only one. Possibly both counties had such names at an early date, owing to Northumbrian influence, but in NTT some were replaced by names in **bekkr**, owing to the Scandinavian presence being denser there than in DRB.

burna is sometimes used as a simplex place-name, the usual modern form being Bourne. A number of names which were simplex in DB later acquired prefixes: these include Eastbourne and Westbourne SSX, Bishopsbourne and Patrixbourne KNT. As a first element *burna* is compounded with **hām** in Burnham BUC, ESX, NFK, and occasionally with other elements, e.g. **hamm** in Burnham SOM, **tūn** in Brunton NTB(2), and *edisc* 'enclosed pasture', in Brundish SFK; but Burn– and Brun– can have other origins.

burna is most common as the final element of compound names. Analysis of the first elements of names in *–burna* in Ekwall 1960 yields the following results.

As with **brōc**, the largest category consists of a word describing the *burna* or its immediate surroundings. Here belong Brabourne KNT, Bradbourne DRB, Fulbourn CAM, Glusburn YOW, Harberton DEV, Harborne STF, Holborn GLT, Honeybourne GLO/WOR, Meaburn WML, Medbourne LEI, WLT, Melchbourne BDF, Morborne HNT, Newbourn SFK, Newburn NTB, Oborne DOR, Saltburn YON, Sambourn WAR, Shalbourne WLT, Sherborne DOR, GLO, HMP, Sherburn DRH, YOE, YOW, Shirburn OXF, Shernborne NFK, Slaidburn YOW, Sleekburn NTB, Stainburn CMB, YOW, Stambourne ESX, Washbourne GLO, Whitbourne HRE, Wimborne DOR, Winkburn NTT, Woburn BDF, SUR, Wombourn STF, Wooburn BUC. (For Winterborne, Winterbourne, Winterburn, see below.)

The categories in which the first element refers to vegetation and to wild creatures are roughly equal: again, this is similar to the compounds with *–brōc*. Vegetation occurs in Albourne SSX, Auborn LIN, Ashbourne DRB, Ashburnham SSX, Ashburton DEV, Ellerburn YON, Fairbourne KNT, Fairburn YOW, Golborne CHE, LNC, Hurstbourne HMP, Husborne BDF, Iburndale YON, Nutbourne (in Westbourne) SSX, Radbourn War, Radbourne DRB, Rodbourne WLT(2) and Selborne HMP. The 'meadow' names included in the last paragraph could be classified under this heading. Wild creatures are referred to in Barbon WML, Barbourne WOR, Broxbourne HRT, Cabourn LIN, Cranborne DOR, Cranbourne HMP, Enborne BRK, Exbourne DEV, Fishbourne SSX, Fishburn DRH, Hartburn DRH, NTB, Otterbourne HMP, Otterburn NTB, YOW, Pickburn YOW, Roeburn LNC and Swanbourne BUC. Sheep and lambs occur in Lambourne ESX, Lambourn BRK, Lamerton DEV, Shipbourne KNT; and pigs, which may be wild or domestic, in Somborne HMP and Swinburn NTB.

Personal names are not common with *burna*, in fact safe examples are only slightly more numerous than with **brōc**. They include Aldbourne WLT, Aldingbourne SSX, Bedburn DRH, Duntisborne GLO, Easebourne SSX, Nailsbourne SOM, Ogbourne WLT, Simonburn NTB, Tedburn DEV, Washburn YOW and Wellesbourne WAR. There are several others which may contain a personal name, as Hagbourne BRK, Ebbesborne WLT. Examples in which *burna* is added to an *–ingas* name are listed above. Englebourne DEV and Walburn YON also refer to groups of people.

The position of the *burna* is referred to in Melbourne YOE, Northbourne KNT, Nutbourne (in Pulborough) SSX, Sudbourne SFK. Westbourne GTL, on the other hand, is probably '(place) west of the stream', and Eastburn YOW '(place) east of the stream'. Tyburn GTL is considered to contain an archaic OE word for a boundary. Topographical features occur in Cliburn WML, Ditchburn NTB, Welbourn LIN, Welborne NFK, Welburn YON(2), Woodburn NTB. The use made of the stream is mentioned in the compound with 'mill' discussed above, and in Washbourne DEV. Ledburn BUC refers to a conduit. Calbourne IOW may contain a river-name. Holybourne HMP means what it says.

Some names (e.g. Auburn YOE, Gisburn YOW, Legbourne LIN, Leyburn YON, Melbourn CAM, Osborne IOW, Weybourne NFK) are obscure or ambiguous, so have not been classified. Kilburn DRB, GTL, YON probably all have the same etymology, but it is uncertain what this is.

The overall similarity between first elements used with **brōc** and those used with *burna* is striking. It seems likely that compounds using these terms as second element were originally coined for the streams, and only later transferred to settlements.

The final point to be considered is the size and nature of the streams referred to by the term *burna*. In some areas it is used especially of intermittent streams. This may be due to the influence of the appellative *winterburna*, which the evidence of place-names and of modern dialect usage in HMP and SSX shows to have been an OE term for a stream liable to run dry in summer. There are two rivers called Winterborne in DOR, which have given name to a number of villages, and other instances of the stream-name occur in Anglo-Saxon charter boundaries in KNT, SOM, WLT and WOR. As a village-name Winterbourne occurs in BRK, GLO, SSX, WLT, and Winterburn is found in YOW. There does not seem to be an ancient instance in Mercia, but Winterburn Brook in Stottesdon SHR is recorded in 1684. Compounds of *winter* with other words for streams are very rare indeed, but there is a Winterbrook in BRK and a Winter Beck in NTT. There are two instances of *burna* with *nīwe* 'new', Newbourn east of Ipswich SFK and Newburn-on-Tyne NTB. Both streams run in well-marked valleys, so cannot have changed their course. Perhaps they started to flow after the valleys had been dry for a considerable time.

Apart from this association with intermittent streams, which may have arisen from the compound *winterburna* rather than belonging to the word *burna* in the earliest period of its use, no clearly marked characteristics have been isolated. In some areas, such as DEV, WAR and BRK, it has been noted that there is an apparent tendency for *burna* to be applied to larger streams than **brōc**, but this appearance may be caused by the fact that *burna* was in use at an earlier period. The names of larger rivers and streams are more likely to survive without change, while smaller watercourses were frequently renamed. The brook from which Hagbourne BRK is named appears in some sets of charter bounds *haccanburnan* and in others as *haccanbroc*. The *burna* form must be earlier, as the settlement is named from it; and corresponding changes from *burna* to **brōc** may have taken place in the names of many small streams before the earlier names in *burna* had been recorded. In some counties, such as BUC and BDF, *burna* is used in names of settlements beside very small streams, so there is no question of the term having been originally restricted to larger watercourses. One of the five instances recorded before AD 730 is

Littlebourne KNT. Ekwall 1960 translates this 'small stream', but (while linguistically unexceptionable) this is not likely to be the meaning. Little-bourne is the most northerly of a string of villages (Bishopsbourne, Patrix-bourne, Bekesbourne) named from their position by the Little Stour river. As pointed out in Everitt 1977 (pp. 8–9), these names indicate that a large territory was called Bourn, this being the early OE name of the Little Stour. Professor Everitt suggests that the name Littlebourne implies that there was in early OE times an estate called Great Bourne, and that this can be identified with the parishes of Ickham and Wickhambreux, which lie on either side of the river, close to its original mouth. Stour must have been the name of the Great Stour, not of both rivers.

celde OE 'spring'. This is a rare term. The only major settlement-names which contain it are Bapchild and Honeychild KNT. Smith 1956 lists also the minor names Absol in Great Waltham ESX and Chillmill in Brenchley KNT; the former is a safe instance, but the latter is as likely to contain *cild* 'young nobleman'. Learchild NTB, which Smith classifies here but also lists under **helde** 'slope', is derived by Ekwall 1960 from **helde**, and this is more convincing.

ēa OE 'river'. This word and ON á are cognate with Latin *aqua*. *ēa* was the standard OE word for a river. On the whole it is used of watercourses of greater size than those denoted by **brōc** and **burna**. In the fenland of eastern England it became *Eau*, a development which appears to represent a combination of the OE and ON words with influence from French *eau*; hence such river-names as Eau and Great Eau LIN. In DEV and SOM *ēa* became Yeo (but there are rivers called Yeo in both counties which have different etymologies). Elsewhere, as a river-name, it appears as Ray or Rea, with R– from ME *atter e* 'at the river'. Romney Marsh KNT is named from a river called *Rumenea* in OE. Welney NFK is from OE *Wellan ēa* 'river of the spring'.

    ēa occurs in settlement-names as a first element, most commonly with **tūn**. This is the origin of Eton BUC, most instances of Eaton, and a single Yeaton in SHR, and probably of Ayton YON(3). See **ēg** for the instances of Eaton which contain **ēg** not *ēa*. Nuneaton WAR is another *ēa-tūn*.

    It is probable that *ēa-tūn* is more than a simple geographical statement. Unlike *brōc-tūn*, it usually refers to settlements on rivers big enough to have a number of settlements on their banks, any one of which would qualify for the name on geographical grounds. The compound could denote a village which performed a special local function in relation to the river. It is not a distinctive name in a wider regional or national context—for this it would be necessary to specify the river, as in Taunton or Leamington—but it could (like many other –**tūn** names) be an indication of the role played by a settlement in the economy of a multiple estate. Eaton Hastings BRK was probably within the great multiple estate of Faringdon which embraced land in BRK, WLT and OXF, and this place could have controlled ferry operations across the Thames for a group of settlements.

OE *ēa-gemōt* 'river-junction' is the source of Eamont WML and Emmott LNC. The WML name is *æt Eamotum* in the Anglo-Saxon Chronicle, and this spelling shows that it was originally in the plural. There are a few other compounds with *ēa* as first element: these include two instances of Ewood in LNC, Ewart LNC and Eythrope BUC. Ealand and Elland are discussed under **land**.

ēa is rare as a final element in settlement-names, but it does occur in Pevensey SSX and Welney NFK. Rivers of the status required for this designation had individual river-names, and it is these which are transferred to the more important settlements on their banks (e.g. Bladon, Thame OXF, Frome DOR, HRE, SOM, Blyth NTB, Roden SHR).

flēot, flēote OE 'estuary, inlet of the sea, small stream'. Smith 1956 says that in the majority of occurrences in place-names the meaning is 'estuary, inlet, creek', but this assessment and the discussion in Ekwall 1960 rather underestimate the number of inland examples, and do not take into account the use of the term in minor names and field-names in such counties as BRK and OXF, and the occurrences in Anglo-Saxon charter boundaries. It is possible that the meaning 'small stream' was current at an early date, but the sense 'estuary' survived longer.

The R. Fleet GTL was originally the lower end of the R. Holborn, but the name was later used of the whole stream. Other simplex examples are Fleet DOR (named from the channel cut off from the sea by Chesil Beach), Fleet on Hayling Island HMP (at the head of a creek), Fleet W. of Farnborough HMP (in an area dissected by small streams), Fleet LIN (E. of Holbeach, perhaps on an inlet of the sea when the name was coined). Northfleet and Southfleet KNT were both *fliote* in a document of c. 975, and the name refers to a stream flowing into the Thames W. of Gravesend. Byfleet SUR means 'beside the stream'; this is a marshy area with small streams draining into the R. Wey. As a first element *flēot* occurs with **hām** in Fleetham NTB and Kirkby Fleetham YON (the NTB village lies beside one of the small streams draining into Beadnell Bay, Kirkby Fleetham is by a tiny stream draining into the R. Swale, E. of Catterick), and it occurs with **tūn** in Fletton HNT (between two tributaries of the R. Nene).

As a second element in major settlement-names *flēot* is concentrated in YOE and YOW, with a limited distribution inside those counties. Six of the examples—Adlingfleet, Broomfleet, Faxfleet, Ousefleet, Swinefleet and Yokefleet—are on either side of the rivers Ouse and Humber, in the six-mile stretch E. of Goole. Marfleet is by the Humber, some distance E. of the main group, and Stillingfleet is 1½ miles N. of the Ouse, some distance to the W. Hunslet is by the R. Aire, on the outskirts of Leeds. The precise meaning of *flēot* in names which are not on the coast could perhaps be ascertained by detailed study of this area of Yorkshire, and the collection and study of occurrences in minor names and field-names in inland areas elsewhere.

There are a few compound names in *-flēot* among major names in southern England. Benfleet and Purfleet ESX are by the Thames estuary. Shalfleet IOW is at the end of an inlet of the sea. Longfleet DOR is beside Holes Bay. Herringfleet SFK is by the R. Waveney, N.W. of Lowestoft. The term is rather rare in the area round the Wash, but Wainfleet LIN is a notable instance, Saltfleet occurs further N. on the LIN coast, and Surfleet is in the marshes N. of Spalding.

Flitton and Flitwick BDF have hitherto been derived from a hypothetical OE *flīet*, a dialect form of *flēot*. Flitton, which early spellings show not to be a compound with **tūn**, was considered to be the dat. pl. of this word. This etymology is not now tenable because of the OE spelling *flittan*, which occurs in the will of the lady Æthelgifu, a document which came to light in 1942 and was published in 1968. The will dates from between 980 and 990, and *Flittan* must be accepted as the authentic OE spelling of Flitton. It cannot be a dative plural because the *-um* of that case is regularly preserved in other names in the same document. It appears to be the dat. sg. of an OE *Flitta* or *Flitte*, for which no etymology can at present be suggested.

flōde OE 'channel of water' has been considered on the evidence of boundary marks in Anglo-Saxon charters to be used of intermittent springs, notably those which burst out in chalk downs at intervals of several years. The term occurs in a few major place-names. Those noted are Cheselade SOM, Inglewood BRK, Princelett IOW and Winslade HMP.

funta OE 'spring', a loan-word from Latin *fons, fontis*. Place-names containing this word were listed, mapped and discussed in detail in Gelling 1978 (pp. 83–6). It was suggested there that the word was borrowed by early Anglo-Saxon settlers, or perhaps by Germanic mercenaries in the last century of Roman Britain, to describe a spring which was characterized by Roman building work, and was therefore felt to be different from the springs to which the normal OE term **well** was applied. Settlement-names containing *funta* are: Bedfont MDX, Bedmond HRT, Boarhunt HMP, Chadshunt WAR, Chalfont BUC, Cheshunt HRT, Fonthill WLT, Fovant WLT, Funtley HMP, Havant HMP, Mottisfont HMP, Teffont WLT, Tolleshunt ESX, Urchfont WLT, Wansunt (in Bexley) GTL.

kelda ON 'spring' is only found in northern counties and Scotland. It occurs as a first element in Keldholme YON, Kellet LNC, Kelleth WML, Kelsick CMB, and as a second element in Hallikeld YON, Threlkeld CMB. There are a number of instances in minor names in Yorkshire and LNC, including Calkeld Lane (in Lancaster) LNC, Cawkeld (in Watton) YOE, Creskeld (in Arthington) YOW, Trinkeld (in Ulverston) LNC.

kelda is cognate with OE **celde**, and Smith 1956 suggests that in place-names Keld–, –keld may sometimes be an ON adaptation of **celde**. This is very unlikely in view of the rarity and restricted provenance of the OE word. In the EPNS survey of WML(2, p. 186) Smith gives **celde** as the source of a ME field-name *le Chelde*, but this is probably an alternative way of spelling *Kelde*.

lacu OE 'small stream, watercourse'. This is not the source of Modern English *lake*, which was taken into ME from French. The OE word does, however, survive in southern dialects, or did until recently.

lacu is commoner in minor names, field-names and OE charter boundaries than it is in major settlement-names, which is natural in view of the trivial nature of the watercourses to which it usually refers. It was to some extent a specialized term for a side-channel of a river, and this sense is seen in the following settlement-names:

Bablock Hythe OXF, where Bablock was probably the name of one of the side-channels of the Thames;

Fishlake YOW, on a side-channel of the R. Don;

Lake WLT, S. of Amesbury, on a stretch of the Avon which has many side-channels;

Potlock DRB, S.W. of Derby, where the present course of the Trent may have been a side-channel;

Shiplake OXF, on a stretch of the Thames where there are side-channels;

Standlake OXF, on an arm of the R. Windrush.

Mortlake GTL is a possible example, though the tributary of the Thames, Beverley Brook, to which the name Mortlake has been considered to refer, is mentioned in charter boundaries by the name *beferithig* (see **rīthig**), and is not like the watercourses which gave rise to the above six names. On the other hand, the only surviving river-name containing *lacu*, R. Medlock LNC, is an ordinary tributary of the Irwell of similar size to Beverley Brook, and this suggests that *lacu* could be used of tributary streams as well as of side-channels and tiny watercourses.

Lacon SHR, near Wem, is from the dat. pl. of *lacu*. This is an extremely wet district, and 'at the drainage channels' would be an appropriate meaning. This sense would be suitable also in Lakenheath SFK. In BRK charter boundaries the senses 'side-channel', 'drainage channel' and 'very small stream' are all evidenced, the last being the most frequent.

lād OE, **lode** ME 'small watercourse, drainage ditch', also 'path'. This word and **gelād** are usually treated in place-name reference books as variants of the same term, and etymologically this is almost certainly correct. They have been treated separately here, however, because the use of **gelād** in a small group of major place-names seems sufficiently distinctive to be appropriate to treatment in Chapter 3. The two discussions should be considered together.

NED has entries for two modern English words, *load* and *lode*. These are stated to be spelling variants of a single term, the origin of which is OE *lād* 'way, course, journey, conveyance'. Under *load* are given meanings such as 'carriage, burden', while under *lode* are listed a number of specialized senses, some of which occur in place-names.

OE *lād*, ME *lode* (as distinct from **gelād**) rarely enters into major settlement-names. Whaplode LIN is probably the only true example. Lode CAM, although now a parish, was formerly a district of Bottisham. The term is mainly represented in minor names in the eastern fenlands and in SOM.

The first meaning given for *lode* in NED is 'way, journey, course (obs.); *dial*. a road'. The sense 'path, lane' occurs very occasionally in place-names. The clearest instance noted is Longload Lane in Middleton by Wirksworth DRB, and this may also be the sense in the only other DRB name to contain *lode*, Loads Head and Upper and Nether Loads W. of Chesterfield. *Milleslhade* (1301) in Wallingford BRK was the name of a road.

The second meaning of *lode* in NED is 'a watercourse; an aqueduct, channel; an open drain in fenny districts'. This is much the commonest use in place-names, which is the reason for including the word in this chapter. Whaplode LIN lies between Moulton and Holbeach on the slight ridge from which Holbeach is named, with fen on either side. The first element is thought to be an OE word *cwappa* 'eel-pout' (a kind of fish), and the *lād* may have been a partly artificial water-channel in which these creatures were found or were bred. There are a number of minor names containing *lād* in the fenlands of HNT (Crollode Fm, Fenton Lode, Yaxley Lode, Monks' Lode, Hook's Lode), and the term is common in minor names and field-names in parts of CAM. EPNS survey (p. 335) says that it is particularly frequent in the Isle of Ely, and that the watercourses are often artificial. Since there are no detailed place-name surveys for NFK and SFK it is not possible to say how frequently the term is used there. It has not been noted in ESX. There are several instances recorded in OE on the N. coast of KNT of a compound *gegnlād* (surviving in one example as Yantlet Creek near the Isle of Grain); as suggested in Forsberg 1950 (p. 29) this probably means 'direct lode', referring to a watercourse which provided a short cut between two areas of open water.

There are a few minor names in SOM, E. of Taunton, which probably contain *lād* in the sense 'small watercourse, drainage ditch'. *Sherwoldslode* occurs in an early boundary of Lyng, and Cogload and Curload are marked on the 1″ map near Lyng. Long and Little Load, N. of Martock, are in the next area of marsh to the E. The places lie on either side of the R. Yeo, and this occurrence of the name Load, which is recorded as *La Lada* from 1194, has been considered to contain *lād* in the sense 'river-crossing, ferry'; but it could equally well refer to one of the drainage channels of the marsh. Northload Bridge W. of Glastonbury stands over canalized streams.

In addition to occurrences in CAM, HNT, LIN, SOM, *lād* is found in a few names in OE charter boundaries in OXF and BRK. The statement in an OXF charter of 1005 that two weirs belong to Shifford 'one above the *lād*, one below' has been taken to indicate that *lād* meant 'river-crossing, ferry' (Forsberg 1950, p. 26), but it makes good sense to interpret *lād* as a reference to the Great Brook, a large drainage channel which runs into the Thames S. of the village.

A meaning 'river-crossing' has not been certainly established for OE *lād*. The use of ME *lode* to mean 'ferry', which seems to be confined to places on the R. Severn, is considered in the discussion of **gelād** in Chapter 3.

læcc, læce OE 'stream, bog'. This word (which must be related to lacu) is considered to be the ancestor of a dialect word *latch*, *letch*, used in the north and in the N.W. midlands of 'a stream flowing through boggy land, a muddy hole or ditch, a bog'. Neither the exact form of the word nor its meaning in OE are known with certainty, though it occurs in charter boundaries in GLO, WOR, WAR, STF. The place-name evidence suggests that it was current in all parts of England at an early date, but only survived in the north and north west.

læcc, læce is used as a river-name in R. Leach GLO, the river-name being subsequently transferred to the settlements of Eastleach and Northleach and combined with (ge)lād in Lechlade. The term occurs as a simplex place-name in Lach Dennis (S.E. of Northwich) and Lache (S. of Chester) CHE. It is the first element of Latchford CHE, OXF (in Great Haseley), Lashbrook OXF, DEV (in Bradford), and the second element of Blacklache LNC (in Leyland), Brindle Heath LNC (in Eccles), Cranage CHE, Shocklach CHE, Shurlach CHE.

læcc, læce is probably the first element of a series of minor names in DEV, ESX, HMP, HRT, SUR, WLT, in which it is combined with **mere** to give such modern forms as Latchmere, Latchmoor, Latchmore, Letchmoor; but some of these may contain *læce* 'leech'.

lœkr ON 'brook'. This ON word was cited in pre-war EPNS volumes as the source of Leake NTT, YON. Ekwall 1922 (p. 184) however, discussing Leck in Tunstall LNC, had expressed doubt about this on the grounds that 'the name is found so often in England', and more recently (as in Gelling 1970, Fellows Jensen 1978, p. 157) it has become customary to assign these names to an unrecorded OE *lece* 'brook', ascribing the –k of the modern forms to the influence of ON pronunciation and confusion with the ON word. The list of instances given in Ekwall 1922 consists of Leake NTT, YON, LIN, Leek STF, WAR. The WAR instance (cited also in Smith 1956 under *lœkr*) is probably a mistake. It occurs as a prefix in Leek Wootton, and is more likely, as stated in Ekwall 1960, to be *leek* the plant. With this example removed the distribution of the remaining items is appropriate to an ON origin. It might be preferable to consider the names as dating from the period of Norse settlement, with some of the ME spellings showing the influence of English speech. If this be accepted, there is very little evidence for the hypothetical OE *lece*.

mere OE 'pond, pool, lake'. This word occurs in at least 120 names in Ekwall 1960. The size of the feature referred to varies from that of a duck pond in southern counties to that of the extensive lakes of north SHR, CHE and the Lake District. The Anglo-Saxons do not appear to have felt the need of a different word for the larger areas of inland water. In so far as *mere* had a specialized meaning this was probably that the pond or lake was not part of a larger feature. For a land-locked bay of the sea, a wide estuary, or a pool in a major river, the Anglo-Saxons were more likely to use pōl, though there are some names (e.g. Almer DOR, Minsmere SFK, Kentmere WML, Wetmoor STF) in which *mere* is used for a wide place in a river. In Mersea ESX *mere* is probably used of the combined estuaries of the Colne and Blackwater.

mere is sometimes difficult to distinguish from *gemǣre* 'boundary' and *mere* 'mare'. It is often changed to –more or –moor in modern forms.

mere occurs as a simplex name in Meare SOM and Mere CHE, LIN, WLT. Mareham le Fen LIN is from the dat. pl. As a first element *mere* occurs in Marbury CHE(2), Mardale WML, Marfleet YOE, Marham NFK and Marholm NTP (both with **hām**), and Marland DEV, but the most frequent compound is with **tūn**. This gives Marten WLT, Martin HMP, KNT, LNC(2), LIN(2), NTT, WOR, Marton CHE(2), LIN, LNC, SHR, WAR, WML, YOE(2), YON(4), YOW(2), Merton DEV, NFK, OXF. Meertown STF was earlier a simplex name *Mere*. Delamere CHE is *mere* with French *de la* prefixed because the name usually occurred in the phrase 'forest of Mere'.

Analysis of first elements in compound names in –*mere* shows the largest category to be that containing a word for a wild creature. Here belong Almer DOR ('eel'), Anmer NFK and Enmore SOM ('duck'), Barmer NFK (?'bear'), Bridgemere CHE ('bird'), Catmore BRK, Cranmere SHR and Cranmore SOM ('heron'), Cromer NFK ('crow'), Eldmire YON ('swan'), Finmere OXF ('woodpecker'), Fowlmere CAM and Fulmer BUC ('fowl'), Frogmore BRK, DEV, DOR, HMP, HRT, Hurtmore SUR ('stag'), Ilmer BUC ('hedgehog'), Pickmere CHE ('pike'), Swanmore HMP, Tadmarton OXF ('toad'), and Woolmer Forest HMP ('wolf').

The second largest category refers to vegetation. This comprises Ashmore DOR; Buttermere CMB, WLT (an oblique reference to abundant grass); Dogmersfield HMP; Grasmere WML; Haslemere SUR and Hazelmere BUC; Oakmere CHE; Peasemore BRK; Radmanthwaite NTT, Redmarley WOR, Redmarshall DRH, Redmire YON and Rodmarton GLO (all 'reed'); and Rushmere SFK(2). Widmerpool NTT could contain 'wide' or *wīthig* 'willow'. Udimore SSX may be 'woody pond'.

A slightly smaller group has an OE personal name as first element: Badlesmere KNT, Bosmere SFK, Cadmore BUC, Colemere SHR, Egmere NFK, Ellesmere SHR. Gibsmere NTT, Imber WLT, Linchmere SSX, Monmore STF, Patmore HRT, Snosmeres SUR, Tedsmore SHR.

The category which has as first element a word describing the pond or lake is roughly the same size as that containing personal names. Here belong Blackmoor HMP, Blackmore HRT, Bradmore NTT, Colmore HMP, Falmer SSX, Fenemere SHR, Holmer BUC, HRE, Livermere SFK, Ringmer SSX, Stanmer SSX and Stanmore GTL, and possibly Tangmere SSX.

The only other category with many instances is that which consists of a word for a topographical feature. River-names can be included in this group. Here belong Dummer HMP, Ismere WOR, Kentmere WML, Minsmere SFK, Seamer YON(2) and Semer NFK, SFK, YON, Sledmere YOE, Sturmer ESX, Tusmore OXF and Wetmoor STF. Five names refer to domesticated creatures: Boulmer NTB and Bulmer ESX, YON, Keymer SSX, Peamore DEV. Three refer to classes of people: Fishmere LIN and Walmer KNT, WOR. Only Wickmere NFK has a habitative term as first element. Fimber YOE contains *fin* 'heap of wood'. Southmere NFK means what it says. Bridmore WLT is obscure.

The nature of the first elements suggests that many of the features referred to by the word *mere* did not appear to the Anglo-Saxons to provide immediately desirable settlement sites. Those most suitable for settlement are perhaps referred to in the 27 compounds with **tūn**. Where *mere* is the second element it appears likely that the compound was coined as a nature-name and was transferred to the settlement at a later date. Some of the settlements, e.g. Catmore and Peasemore BRK, Cadmore End and Holmer BUC, Anmer and Barmer NFK, Fimber YOE, Livermere SFK, are in areas where lack of water would be a serious problem; but the pools at these sites, while making settlement possible, would not provide the conditions for unlimited growth.

plæsc OE 'shallow piece of standing water'. Plaish SHR, Plash SOM, Melplash DOR. The only record of the word in OE is *Plesc* in a charter of AD 963, part of an estate of which the main part was Church Aston SHR. *Plesc* has been identified with Plaish in Cardington SHR. For Plush DOR Ekwall 1960 suggests *plysc*, which would be a cognate term with the same meaning.

pōl, pull OE 'pool', **pyll** OE 'tidal creek, ?small stream'. It is convenient to treat these words together, though etymologically *pull* and *pyll* are variants of the same term, and *pōl* is a different word.

A degree of confusion is apparent in the treatment of the three items in dictionaries and place-name reference books. NED says under *pool* 'OE. had also *pull* and *pyll* . . . the relations of which to OE. *pōl* are obscure, as are also those of the Celtic words: W. *pwll*, Corn. *pol*, Breton *poul* pool; Ir. *poll*, *pull*, Gael. *poll* hole, bog, pond, pit, mire, Manx *poyll* pool, puddle.' Smith 1956 and Ekwall 1960 treat *pōl* and *pull* as variants of the same word, the justification for this presumably being that spellings appropriate to both words interchange with each other in the early references to numerous English place-names. *pyll* is said in Ekwall 1960 to be a borrowing from Welsh, but in Smith 1956 to be a variant form of OE *pull*. Marple CHE is derived by Dodgson (EPNS survey 1, pp. 281–2) from *gemǣre* 'boundary' and 'OE **pyll, pull, pōl**[1], probably Welsh **pwll** originally.' More philological study is needed on all these terms.

pōl/pull is occasionally used of a harbour, as in Poole DOR, Hartlepool DRH. Skippool LNC was formerly a harbour, formed by the junction of two brooks near Poulton le Fylde. The *Pool* which became Netherpool and Overpool near Ellesmere Port CHE was described as a port in 1366. This may be partly the significance in Welshpool MTG.

In some names *pōl/pull* refers to creeks or coastal pools. N. and S. Pool DEV refer to a tidal arm of Kingsbridge harbour, Poulton (in the Wirral) CHE to the lower course of the creek at Port Sunlight, and Poulton (cum Seacombe) CHE to Wallasey Pool which was formerly a great tidal inlet from the Mersey. Poulton (in Awre) GLO is near an inlet of the R. Severn, and Poulton le Sands LNC is near the coast. Blackpool LNC referred to a peaty-coloured pool about half a mile from the sea, and Liverpool LNC to a tidal creek with thick water. Walpole NFK is in drained marshland by The Wash. Radipole DOR is by Radipole Lake, which opens into the sea at Weymouth.

Many names containing *pōl* are inland, and these must refer to pools which occurred on the course of streams, or at the junction of two streams. Such pools have been drained long since, and only people with local knowledge could usefully speculate about their exact whereabouts. A situation between two streams, or two headwaters of a small tributary, is seen in Poole (N. of Nantwich) CHE, Poolham (in Woodhall) LIN, Pulham DOR, Bradpole DOR, Cople BDF, Yarpole HRE. A situation by a small stream characterizes Poulton GLO, Pulham NFK, Hampole YOW, Otterpool (in Lympne) KNT. At Walpole SFK a large pool appears in times of flood in an ox-bow of the R. Blyth. At Wimpole CAM the 'pool' may have been converted into the ornamental lakes in the grounds of the Hall. At Polstead SFK there may have been a wide place in the R. Box, and at Claypole LIN a wide place in the R. Witham. Poole Keynes GLO is between the Thames and Flagham Brook. Pulborough SSX, by the R. Arun, is 'hill of the pools'.

Some places with *pōl/pull* names are in obviously marshy ground, as Pulford CHE, Pool (N. of Knottingley) YOW, but others, e.g. Polsloe (near Exeter) DEV, Poulton (in Warrington) LNC, Harpole NTP are not, though the second element of Polsloe (**slōh**) indicates that the ground was at one time wet.

Cornish *pol* (which means 'pit' as well as 'pool, stream, cove, creek') is used relatively frequently in Cornish place-names. Pool 1973 (p. 25) lists 9 instances in West Penwith. Polscoe, Polperro and Polruan are included in Ekwall 1960, but in Polperro and Polruan *pol* has replaced earlier *porth* 'harbour'; both words can mean 'cove'.

pyll occurs in a few names in the south west in the sense 'tidal creek'. Here belong Pilton DEV, SOM, Pylle (near Pilton), Huntspill and Uphill SOM. In OXF and BRK *pyll* appears to be used in field-names of a small inland stream, but this has not been noted in settlement-names.

rīth, rīthig OE 'small stream'. The short form is used as a simplex name in Ryde IOW, and in a number of minor names. As second element, *rīth* occurs in Chaureth ESX, Childrey BRK, Coldrey HMP, Cottered HRT, Fingrith ESX, Hendred BRK, Meldreth CAM, Rawreth ESX, Sawtry HNT, Seagry WLT, Shepreth CAM, Shottery WAR and Tingrith BDF. The longer form, *rīthig*, occurs in Cropredy OXF and Fulready WAR.

rīth has hitherto been considered to be the source of Reed YON, and to be the first element of Ritton NTB. Apart from these two possible outliers, however, the term does not appear to have been used in place-name formation further north than WAR, though there are a few possible occurrences in field-names in CHE. Reed YON is situated on Arkle Beck, which is a bigger river than is usually denoted by *rīth*, and Ritton NTB (N.W. of Netherwitton) is not on a stream. Alternative etymologies should possibly be sought for these two names.

sǣ, sā OE 'lake, sea'. As pointed out in Ekwall 1960 *sǣ* usually means 'sea' when used as a first element and 'lake' when it is the second element of a compound name. The meaning 'sea' occurs in Seacombe CHE, Seaford SSX, Seaham DRH, Seascale and Silloth CMB, and most instances of Seaton; but there are some *sǣ–*, *sā–* names in which the meaning is 'lake', e.g. Saham NFK, Soham SFK, Seacroft YOW, Seathwaite LNC and Seaton on Hornsea Mere YOE. In Seamer YON(2) and Semer NFK, SFK, YON, *sǣ* was glossed by **mere** when the sense 'lake' became obsolete. The meaning 'lake' is also seen in Haddlesey YOW, Hornsea YOE, Withernsea YOE. Meaux YOE (earlier *Melse*, *Mealsa*, *Mealse*) is derived by Ekwall 1960 from ON *mel-sǣr* 'lake with sandy shores'. ON *sǣr* 'lake' may enter into some other Yorkshire names listed above.

Soham CAM (*Sægham* c. 1000) is thought to contain a related word *sæge* 'swamp, lake'.

sīc OE 'small stream'. This term is used of such tiny watercourses and drainage channels that it is rare even in minor settlement-names and is only well evidenced in field-names, where it appears as Sitch, Sytch, Such, Sich, Seech. It is assumed in previous reference books to be the final element of the stream-name which gave rise to the village-names Gussage All Saints and Gussage St Michael DOR, but this may be questioned on the grounds that *sīc* is not likely to have been used of this watercourse, which would surely have been a **burna** or a **brōc**, or at least a **rīth**. Two stream-names in DEV, Gessage and Gissage Lake, are considered to be identical with Gussage. Ekwall 1960 suggests a compound of an OE *gyse* 'gush of water' and *sīc*. It is possible, however, that the OE noun-forming suffix *–ic* was added to a word from the same root as the postulated *gyse*, to make a stream-name meaning 'the gusher'.

ON *sik*, cognate with OE *sīc*, occurs in Sykehouse YOW, Kelsick CMB, and in minor names and field-names in the north.

vatn ON 'lake' occurs in Wasdale WML, Watendlath CMB.

wæter OE 'water, river, lake' occurs in Watercombe DOR, Waterden NFK, and is also used in some river-names, and in lake-names in the Lake District. It is most common as an affix, e.g. Waterperry, Waterstock OXF, Bourton on the Water GLO.

wæterscipe OE, possibly 'conduit' or 'reservoir'. The word is well recorded in OE, though not in a toponymic use. The quotations given in OE dictionaries suggest that 'water-supply' was the usual sense. NED mentions the OE word under the collective function of the suffix *–ship*, classing it with *burgscipe* 'municipality' and *folcscipe* 'nation'. *wæterscipe* occurs occasionally in minor names and field-names in southern and south-eastern counties. Watership Down HMP is presumably the pasture belonging to Watership House, W. of Kingsclere. Watership House lies higher up the valley of the tributary of the R. Enborne on which Ecchinswell is the main settlement. Brocket Park near Welwyn HRT was *Watershepe* from 1235 to 1482, and *Watershipp* is still recorded as an alternative to *Brockethall* in 1612. The R. Lea has been landscaped into broad pools here, and it looks as if there is a generous supply of water. The term occurs again in HRT as a field-name in Sawbridgeworth. There are several field-names from *wæterscipe* in ESX, but EPNS survey (p. 592) does not give the location. A surname *atte Watershype* has been noted in SSX in 1332.

well, wella, welle OE 'spring, stream'. The West Saxon form was **wiell, will, wyll** (–a, –e), and the west midland form was **wælla**. It is sometimes difficult to choose between the meanings 'spring' and 'stream', but 'spring' is certainly much more common in settlement-names. This is the commonest of the terms discussed in this chapter, occurring in at least 280 names in Ekwall 1960. It is poorly represented in names recorded before c. 730 (Cox 1976), and may not have become the usual term for a spring until after that date.

As a simplex name *well*, *wiell* or *wælla* occurs in Wall under Heywood and Walltown SHR, Well KNT, LIN, YON, Wool DOR, Outwell and Upwell CAM, Coffinswell DEV, Wells NFK, SOM, and Welham (dat. pl.) NTT, YOE. Some of the names which survive in singular form were originally plural. As a first element the word occurs with **burna** (Welborne NFK, Welbourn LIN, Welburn YON(2)), **beorg** (Welbury YON), **bý** (Welby LIN), **cumb** (Welcombe DEV, WAR, Woolcombe DOR), **dūn** (Weldon NTP), **ēa** (Welney NFK), **ford** (Welford GLO, NTP, Walford HRE, SHR), *haga* 'enclosure' (Wellow NTT), **hōh** (Wellow LIN), **hop** (Wallhope GLO, Wallop HMP, SHR), **lēah** (Woolley SOM), **tūn** (Welton CMB, LIN(3), NTP, YOE), and **wīc** (Welwick YOE).

Analysis of first elements in major settlement-names in *–well* reveals that the largest category consists of adjectives or nouns which describe the physical nature of the spring or stream. There are about 75 such names, and the following first elements recur:

'black' (Blackwell DRB(2), DRH, WOR)
'broad' (Bradwall CHE, Bradwell BUC, DRB, ESX(2), SFK, STF, Broadwell GLO, OXF, WAR)
'cold' (Belchalwell DOR, Caldwell YON, Caudle GLO, Cauldwell BDF, DRB, Chadwell ESX, LEI, Cholwell SOM, Coldwell NTB(3))
'foul' (Fulwell DRH, OXF). Brightwell BRK, OXF, SFK contrasts with this.
'hollow' (Hollowell NTP, Holwell DOR, HRT, LEI)
'loud' (Ludwell DRB, OXF, WLT)
'red' (Radwell BDF, HRT)
'shallow' (Scaldwell NTP, Shadwell GTL)
'stone' (Stanwell MDX, Stawell SOM, Stowell GLO, SOM, WLT)
'white' (Whitwell, DOR, DRB, HRT, IOW, NFK, RUT, WML, YON(2))

The next largest category of first elements consists of personal names; this contains from 36 to about 45 examples. Here belong Adwell OXF, Askerswell DOR, Badwell Ash SFK, Bakewell DRB, Banwell SOM, Bawdeswell NFK, Berkswell WAR, Bracewell YOW, Brauncewell LIN, Cadwell OXF, Chatwall SHR, Chatwell STF, Cobhall HRE, Crudwell WLT, Dodwell WAR, Dowdeswell GLO, Dunkeswell DEV, Epwell OXF, Etwall DRB, Fradswell STF, Gabwell DEV, Harswell YOE, Hemswell LIN, Loddiswell DEV, Mongewell OXF, Netteswell ESX, Nunwell Park IOW, Offwell DEV, Ogwell DEV, Pedwell SOM, Perdiswell WOR, Shotteswell WAR, Sizewell SFK, Sopwell HRT, Tideswell DRB, Wirswall CHE. There are other possible examples, and the frequency of personal names with this element contrasts with their scarcity in names containing **brōc** and **burna**.

Other categories of first elements are much smaller, the largest being words for vegetation (25) and for wild creatures (19). Vegetation is referred to in Ashwell ESX, HRT, RUT, Boxwell GLO, Bunwell NFK, Elmswell SFK, Feltwell NFK, Haswell DRH, SOM, Heswall CHE, Muswell Hill GTL, Nutwell DEV, Ridgewell ESX, and a group of names meaning 'cress spring or stream'—Carswalls GLO, Carswell BRK, Caswell NTP, OXF, DOR, SOM, Crasswall HRE, Cresswell DRB, STF, and Kerswell DEV(3). Wild creatures occur in Andwell HMP, Barwell LEI, Cornwell OXF and Cranwell LIN, Crabwall CHE, Crowell OXF, Greywell HMP, Hartwell BUC, NTP, STF, Hauxwell YON and Hawkwell NTB, SOM, Roel GLO, Snailwell CAM, Swalwell DRH, Tathwell LIN, Tranwell NTB, Wigwell DRB. The only certain reference to a domestic animal appears to be Titchwell NFK.

Springs are associated with superstitious or religious beliefs in Dewsall HRE (St David), Elwell DOR and Holywell LIN (*hǣl* 'omen'), Halliwell LNC, Halwell and Halwill DEV, Holwell DOR, OXF, Holywell HNT, KNT, NTB ('holy'), Runwell ESX and Rumwell SOM (*rūn* 'secret, council');

and perhaps also in the group of names which has 'seven' as first element—
Seawell NTP, Sewell BDF, Showell OXF and Sywell NTP.

Smaller categories refer to topographical features (e.g. Backwell SOM,
Bitteswell LEI, Bywell NTB, Harwell BRK, Hopwell DRB, Orwell CAM,
Pickwell LEI, Scarthingwell YOW, Shorwell IOW), direction (Astwell NTP
and Eastwell KNT, LEI, Norwell NTT, Southwell NTT, Westwell KNT,
OXF) and position on a boundary (Marwell DEV, HMP, Shadwell NFK,
YOW, Shawell LEI). River-names are very rare, but here belong Kentwell
SFK, Wiswell LNC and a few other possible examples. Groups of people are
referred to in Churwell YOW, Clerkenwell GTL, Gagingwell OXF, Maiden-
well LIN and Maidwell NTP, and Sunningwell BRK. Watchingwell IOW
contains an earlier place-name *Hwǣting* 'place where wheat was grown'.
Buildings or construction works are seldom mentioned, but cf. Burwell CAM,
LIN, Lewell DOR, Wyville LIN, Yarwell NTP. Pipewell NTP and Thatto
LNC may have had a conduit, and Trowell NTT perhaps had a bridge made of
a tree-trunk. Smith 1956 recognizes a category in which the first element refers
to a vessel for water. This is a likely interpretation for Bedwell HRT, Bidwell
BDF and some minor names which Smith lists. The first element, *byden*
'vessel, tub, butt', also occurs three times with **funta** (in Bedfont MDX,
Bedmond HRT, and a minor name Bedford Well in Eastbourne SSX). Can-
well STF could refer to a cup and Wherwell HMP to a cauldron, but *canne* is
perhaps used of a valley, and *hwer* could refer to the behaviour of the springs at
Wherwell. Hardwell BRK means 'treasure spring'.

This analysis is not exhaustive, but it covers the greater part of the material.
Some names (e.g. Barnwell NTP, Britwell BUC, OXF, Camberwell GTL,
Chigwell ESX, Herringswell SFK, Howell LIN, Letwell YOW, Shelswell
OXF, Tinwell RUT) are obscure or ambiguous.

2

Marsh, Moor and Flood-plain

To people migrating from the northern coasts of Europe the marshes of south-eastern England cannot have appeared unfamiliar or exceptionally daunting. The Anglo-Saxons had a rich vocabulary for marshes, and a number of words for the slightly raised areas which provided dry settlement-sites from which the marshlands could be exploited, and these two classes of place-name elements—words for marshes and words for marshland settlements—are discussed in this chapter.

There is some overlap between words used for marshland settlements and those used for settlements on hills and in valleys. An **ēg** may sometimes be as high as a **dūn**. The seclusion which caused some sites to be called **hop** in the sense 'cultivated ground in a fen' may have seemed comparable to the seclusion of some valley settlements in mountainous country in the Welsh Marches and round the Pennines, where **hop** is certainly a 'valley' term. The suggestion made in this book about the use of **bæc** in Holbeach and other names in East Anglia could have brought the word within the scope of this chapter; but it has seemed best to treat **hop** under Valleys and Remote Places (Chapter 4) and **bæc** under Hills, Slopes and Ridges (Chapter 5). There is also some overlap between the use of **ēg, hamm** and **holmr** (all in this chapter), and that of **halh** (included with **hop** in Chapter 4).

Some of the names discussed in this chapter may go back to the earliest period of English name-giving. Those containing **ēg** are likely to be among the earliest names in any district, since this is the commonest English word in place-names recorded by AD 730. If it had continued to be used after 730 with the same frequency as in the earliest-recorded names it would have been a much commoner element than it is. It was probably the obsolescence of **ēg** in the sense 'dry ground in marsh' which caused a number of other words (**dūn, hamm, halh, hop,** ON **holmr**) to be pressed into service to describe this type of settlement-site.

There is no way of ascertaining from the place-names whether the lowland areas called **fenn, mōr** or **mersc** were mostly derelict when the English first saw them, or whether the Anglo-Saxons used these words in naming flourishing pre-English settlements whose economy depended on the management of wet land. The first element of Weald Moors SHR and Wildmore LIN (OE *wilde* 'wild, uncultivated, desolate') implies that these marshes were in need of reclamation; and such areas, even if they had been carefully managed during the Roman period, would revert to bog very quickly if neglected. The lowland Mor(e)tons, however, and most of the Marston/Merston/Morston settlements are villages of the type which are likely to have been established in pre-English times. Most OE settlement-names probably refer to pre-English villages and reflect a change of language rather than a change of settlement-pattern, but this is not necessarily true of ON names, particularly the rather rare topographical ones. When a settlement bears an ON name referring to marsh it seems reasonable to suppose that new reclamation of marshland took place in that vicinity at the end of the 9th century. ON words for marshes are **kjarr**, **mosi** and **mýrr**.

The most important OE marsh terms used in major settlement-names are **fenn**, **mersc**, **mōr** and **mos**. The question of whether these words had specialized meanings and were used of different types of wet land must be left to investigators who are willing and able to carry out local geographical studies. Other words, like **slæp**, **slōh**, **soc**, **sol**, **strōd**, **wagen**, **wemm**, occur so rarely that the general translation 'marsh' seems unsatisfactory, though it may be impossible for the modern observer to discern the precise circumstances which led to the use of a rare term instead of a commoner one. It seems clear that **wæsse** was a highly specialized term for land in the flood-plain of a meandering river. The nearest modern English equivalent seems to be northern dialect *haugh*, which is discussed under **halh** in Chapter 4.

There are some marsh terms which are not included here because they are only used in minor names and field-names. One of these, **cwabba**, has, however, been included because Quob HMP appears in Ekwall 1960. There are also some notable 'one-off' place-names which refer to marshes. One such is Thurrock (Grays, Little and West) ESX. The most convincing explanation of Thurrock is that it is a transferred use of an OE word which means 'bilge of a ship'. Deeping LIN is a very early type of name in which the suffix *ing* has been added to OE *dēop* 'deep' to give a name meaning 'deep place'. Later names which only occur once are Marr YOW and Thirsk YON, from ON words for a marsh, and Bray BRK, a post-Conquest name which means 'marsh' in Norman French.

cwabba OE 'marsh' is the source of Quob in Titchfield HMP. All the instances from field-names and minor names cited in Smith 1956 are from southern counties, but the term occurs commonly as far north as SHR, where there are many names in Quab– and Quob–. There are a few instances in minor names and field-names in CHE, where the modern form is Wobbs. Elsewhere it occasionally becomes Squabbs.

ēg OE 'island' (West Saxon *īeg*) most frequently refers to dry ground surrounded by marsh when it occurs in ancient settlement-names. It is also used of islands in the modern sense. In names of late OE origin it sometimes means 'well-watered land'. In the northern tip of DRB and regions north of that it may be necessary to postulate other meanings, such as 'hill jutting into flat land' and 'patch of good land in moors'. Even without these suggested innovations, the use of *ēg* in settlement-names overlaps with that of **dūn, hamm, halh** and **ness**. Some low-lying settlements with names in **dūn** (e.g. Mundon ESX) look to the modern observer more deserving of names in *ēg*, but there may have been a subtle distinction which is difficult to see now. If it be accepted that Holbeach and some other fenland names contain the locative of **bæc**, this term also encroaches on the meanings of *ēg*. On the E. bank of the Severn estuary **hamm** appears to be used rather than *ēg* for farms in very low ground, and there are other areas where **halh** usurps this function. There is, however, very little use of *ēg* for land in a river-bend, Bungay SFK being the only instance noted, and the meaning 'land between rivers' sometimes adduced for *ēg* is not clearly established.

There are about 180 names containing *ēg* in Ekwall 1960, and the element is not very common in minor names or field-names. In view of this moderate frequency, it is remarkable that *ēg* heads the list of OE terms in names recorded by c. 730 (Cox 1976, p. 58). There are 19 instances, and even when some allowance has been made for the liking of early saints for island bases it must be concluded that *ēg* was more commonly used in place-name formation before AD 730 than in the centuries after. As with many of the settlement-names in **dūn**, the sites of villages with *ēg* names are often the likeliest places for colonists to choose, and it might be worth the archaeologist's while to look for continuity of settlement from pre-English times.

Smith 1956 says 'the element is widespread'; but the distribution is not, in fact, even, nor is it entirely dictated by geography. Names in *ēg* become less common north of a line from the Mersey to the Humber, and the true frequency in these northern counties is difficult to determine. Early spellings of possible instances show confusion between *ēg* and other elements, and reference books give diverse origins for a number of names. In YOW, for instance, the possible candidates among major names are Arksey, Bardsey, Hessay, Embsay, Methley, Pudsey and Wibsey. Ekwall 1960 accepts four of these as names in *ēg*, but ascribes Hessay to **sǣ** 'lake', and Methley to **lēah**. EPNS survey considers Hessay and Methley to be probably *ēg* names, but rejects this for Embsay, Pudsey and Wibsey, for which Smith prefers 'enclosure' or 'high place'. My own feeling is that Arksey and Bardsey are safe examples, Hessay is probably an *ēg* since the 50′ contour makes an appropriate feature, and Embsay, Pudsey and Wibsey are not certain to be *ēg* names but may be so if the senses 'hill jutting into flat land' and 'good land in moors' are allowed. Methley, on the other hand, seems to me more likely to contain **lēah**. One of the possible CHE examples, Aldersey, is ascribed in EPNS survey 4 (p. 82) to **gehæg** 'enclosure'; but the site is appropriate to *ēg* in the sense 'dry ground in marsh', and the spellings with *–hey(e)*, *–hay* are not so numerous as to compel acceptance of the alternative etymology. This high degree of uncertainty in northern counties should be borne in mind when use is made of the analysis offered in this discussion.

The use of *ēg* for places in high situations, which is partly the cause of this uncertainty, is found in the northern tip of DRB. Edale, Abney and Eyam are fairly close together near the YOW border. Abney village stands at over 900', and Eyam at over 800'. EPNS survey considers that *ēg* in these names has the sense 'land between rivers', but this is hardly the dominant characteristic of the sites. If the 'islands' could be seen as isolated patches of good land in moorland, this would be a sense-development similar to that postulated for **hamm** in some names in the south west.

Some other sites in DRB and counties further north suggest a meaning 'hill-spur'. Cold Eaton DRB is on a spur overlooking the R. Dove. Little Eaton, N. of Derby, has a clear 'hill-spur' site, though the name may refer not to this but to the large area of river-meadow overlooked by the village. At Corney CMB the hall and village occupy a long promontory with wet ground on either side. Bardsea LNC (S.E. of Ulverston) is on the tip of a hill which juts out into flat coastland. Tebay WML, which is a high site, lies near the tip of a hill-spur which overlooks a river-junction, and the name could refer either to the hill-spur or to the flat area where the rivers join, which was probably meadowland.

In counties south of DRB, however, names in *ēg* mostly belong to low-lying settlements. The counties with the greatest number of major names in *ēg* are NFK(15), CAM(13), SOM(13), LIN(11), SSX(8) and BRK(8). There are 11 in ESX, but 4 of them (Brightlingsea, Canvey, Mersea and Osea) are 'islands' in the modern sense, so the term is rather poorly represented in this large county in the sense 'dry ground in marsh'. SHR and WLT have 7 examples, and CHE, DRB, GLO, OXF and SFK have 6. There are 5 in BDF, GTL and WOR, and 4 in BUC, HMP, KNT and NTT. YOW has 3–6. The counties of HRT, LEI, NTP, STF, SUR (excluding part of GTL) and YON have 3. In spite of being fairly frequent in GLO, SHR, WOR and CHE, *ēg* is rare in the west midlands as a whole, with only one instance in WAR (Binley). There are 2 major names in HRE, one of which, Eye near Leominster, has a perfect site. Kinnersley SHR is another perfect site in the Weald Moors, but *ēg* is not much used in the marshes which characterize the northern half of the county. Wales has 2 examples, Saltney FLI and Eyton DNB, both on the R. Dee. (Some coastal islands, such as Anglesey and Bardsea, contain the corresponding ON word.) There is only one major name in *ēg* in the counties of CMB (Corney), DRH (Hartlepool), LNC (Bardsea) and WML (Tebay), and the word does not occur at all in major names in NTB or YOE. Southern counties in which *ēg* is rare are HNT (only Ramsey) and MDX (only Yeoveney in Staines).

The element dies out in the south west, after being frequent in SOM. In DOR it is used in the name of Brownsea Island, but not in settlement-names. There is one minor name in DEV, and the EPNS survey for that county says (p. 677) '*ēg* is practically unknown in Devon, and is not found in Cornwall'.

As regards distribution within areas, there are a fair number of isolated ēg names, but there are some noteworthy clusters. The densest concentration is in N.W. BRK and the adjacent part of OXF. Charney, Goosey, Hanney, Pusey and Tubney are parishes on the R. Ock or its tributaries, Cholsey and Hinksey are parishes on the R. Thames, and Mackney is a hamlet near Cholsey. Witney and Chimney OXF can be counted with this group, Witney being one of the few instances which have developed into towns.

In CAM the 13 instances fall into four geographical groups:

1   Thorney, Whittlesey, and Eastrea in Thorney; Ramsey HNT can be counted as one of this group.
2   Manea, Coveney, Stuntney in Ely, and Barway in Soham (it should be noted that Ely contains *gē* 'district', not *ēg*).
3   Denny in Waterbeach, Horningsea, Anglesey in Lode, and Quy.
4   Wendy and Shingay, to which Eyeworth and Sandy BDF are fairly close.

Most of the fairly numerous CAM minor names containing *ēg* are associated with these groups. Gamlingay CAM is classified as an *ēg* name in previous reference books, but spellings with *–heia*, *–hey*, *–hay(e)* are early and quite frequent, and the nature of the site and of the surrounding place-names suggests that OE *gehæg* is more likely, perhaps in the sense 'woodland enclosure'.

Clustering of names in *ēg* may be observed in some other counties, especially SOM and NFK.

The simplex name Eye occurs in HRE, NTP and SFK; and Ebury in Westminster GTL preserves the name of a place called *Eye*. Eyam DRB is from the dative plural. Rye SSX and Rye in Stanstead Abbots HRT mean 'at the island'. As a first element *ēg* occurs most frequently with tūn, becoming Eyton (on Severn, Upon the Weald Moors, near Ford, and probably Eyton near Baschurch) in SHR, but more frequently Eaton, in which form the compound occurs in BDF, CHE(2), DRB(3), LEI and STF. It is necessary to distinguish between Eaton from *ēg-tūn* and Eaton from *ēa-tūn* by study of the early spellings. Sometimes the evidence of the spellings is confirmed by the topography: Church and Wood Eaton STF, for example, could not be from *ēa-tūn*, as there is no watercourse deserving of the term ēa. In other instances, however, the settlement called *ēg-tūn* is on a patch of slightly raised ground in the flood-plain of a river, and there may have been early perception of the two possible etymologies, causing interchange between the spellings appropriate to each one. Other names in which *ēg* is the first element include Edale DRB, Emstrey SHR and Eycote GLO.

There are more than 150 compound names in which *ēg* is the final element, and it seems possible that nearly half of these have as first element a personal name. There is one feminine name, in Adeney SHR, one Celtic, in Chertsey SUR, one ON, in Maxey NTP; and Haxey LIN may also contain an ON name. A very small proportion—not more than 12—of the personal names are dithematic, like *Ælfrīc* in Arlesey BDF, *Beornrǣd* in Bardsea LNC and Bardsey YOW, *Beadurīc* in Battersea GTL, *Baldhere* in Bawdsey SFK, *Beornmund* in Bermondsey GTL, *Beorhtrīc* in Brightlingsea ESX, *Cyneheard* in Kinnersley SHR, *Mæthelhere* in Mattersey NTT and *Wilheard* in Willersey GLO. There is a high proportion of monothematic masculine names, and this is consistent with the hypothesis that most settlement-names in *ēg* belong to the earlier rather than the later centuries of the Anglo-Saxon period; but as always a devil's advocate could claim that some of these supposed monothematic personal names are significant words. In studying a list of supposed compounds of *ēg* and personal names, an obvious precaution is to look for recurrences of the same name. In accordance with this principle, Bilney, which occurs twice in NFK, and Binley WAR, which is shown by early spellings to be identical, are here taken to contain *bile* 'beak' used in some topographical sense. Although three occurrences with the same personal name are highly suspicious, two may be allowed to pass if no likely alternative etymology is available. The double occurrence of Mackney BRK and Makeney DRB is here accepted as coincidence. Olney BUC had a near doublet in GLO: there was a place near Deerhurst called *Olanige* where King Cnut and King Edmund made peace in 1016. (*Olanige* is cited in Ekwall 1960 under Alney in Maisemore GLO, but this is a mistake.) For Tiln NTT and Tilney NFK there is an alternative to derivation from a personal name; this pair may contain an oblique case of the adjective *til* 'good, useful'. Some other compound names in *ēg* may be suspected of containing words rather than personal names even without the suspicious circumstance of repetition. Cholsey BRK, though here accepted as a compound of *ēg* with the personal name *Cēol*, could be 'island of the keel', perhaps because its outline reminded people of an upturned boat. Horningsea CAM could contain *Horning* as a hill-name rather than a personal name. Blankney LIN and Molesey SUR could refer to a horse and a mule rather than to men called *Blanca* and *Mūl*.

When some allowance has been made for my admitted bias towards personal names, it still seems fair to assume that the following compounds in *–ēg* have as their first element a masculine personal name which is either monothematic or a shortened version of a dithematic name: Abney DRB, Alney GLO, Badsey WOR, Bardney LIN, Binsey OXF, Blankney LIN, Bodney NFK, Bolney SSX, Brownsea DOR, Cadney LIN, Chebsey STF, Chedzoy SOM, Chimney OXF, Cholsey BRK, Colney NFK, Cooksey WOR, Costessey NFK, Cuckney NTT, Dengie ESX, Doxey STF, Epney GLO, Gedney LIN, Godney SOM, (Gate) Helmsley YON, Impney WOR, Kempsey WOR, Lindsey SFK, Lulsley WOR, Lydney GLO, Mackney BRK, Makeney DRB, Molesey SUR, Nailsea SOM, Nunney SOM, Oaksey WLT, Olney BUC, Osea ESX, Osney OXF, Partney LIN, Patney WLT, Pewsey WLT, Pitney SOM, Pitsea ESX, Poultney LEI, Romsey HMP, Tebay WML, Tetney LIN, Titsey SUR, Torksey LIN, Tubney BRK, Whittlesey CAM, Wintney HMP, Witney OXF, Yeoveney MDX.

Leaving aside the apparent specialization of the type of personal name used to qualify *ēg*, if it be accepted that personal names of some sort make up nearly half the number of first elements in such compounds, it follows that *ēg* can be classified with **dūn**, **feld** and **ford** as a topographical term which had a quasi-habitative meaning.

All other classes of first elements in compounds with *ēg* are small. The largest is that consisting of terms which describe the island. Here belong Bilney NFK(2) and Binley WAR (see above), Blakeney, GLO, NFK ('black'), Bradney SOM ('broad'), Caldy CHE ('cold'), Henny ESX ('high'), Horningsea CAM (see above), Langney SSX and Longney GLO ('long'), Muchelney SOM ('big'), Palstre KNT ('spike'), Sandy BDF ('sand'), Stanney CHE ('stone'), Stickney LIN ('stick'), Stuntney CAM ('steep'), Turvey BDF ('turf'), Whitney HRE ('white'). Some of these could be considered to contain personal names, but most are probably descriptive. There is another 'stone island', in CAM—Stonea in Wimblington—and this has recently been identified as a slightly raised area in the Fens where Roman builders deposited masses of stones.

The next largest category (though only because two of the names recur) consists of words for vegetation. Here belong Kersey SFK, Minety WLT, Pusey BRK, Ramsey ESX, HNT, Sessay YON, Stiffkey NFK, and Thorney CAM, GTL, SOM, SSX. Hessay YOW probably contains *ēg* with the gen. sg. of *hæsel* 'hazel'. Domestic creatures are referred to in Goosey BRK, Hinksey BRK, Horse Eye SSX, Horsey NFK, SOM, Oxney KNT, NTP, Quy CAM, Sheepy LEI, Sheppey KNT. Wild creatures occur in Bawsey NFK (gadfly), Corney CMB, HRT (cranes), Dorney BUC (bumble-bees), Hannah LIN and Hanney BRK (wild birds), Hartlepool DRH and Harty KNT (stag), Iltney ESX (swans) and Selsey SSX (seal).

A topographical feature is referred to in Barway CAM, Coveney CAM, Wendy CAM and Winchelsea SSX. Beckney ESX 'island of the beacon' can be included loosely with these. An earlier place-name or river-name is used to define the *ēg* in Campsey SFK, Charney BRK, Colney HRT, Lindsey LIN, Middlezoy SOM. The position is commented on in Eastrea CAM, Medmerry SSX, Middleney SOM, Modney NFK, Southery NFK and Southrey LIN. Boveney BUC means 'place above the island', and Eastney HMP means 'place in the east of the island'.

Types of people are referred to in Athelney SOM, Denny CAM and Wallasey CHE; and Bungay SFK, Hilgay and Wormegay NFK, and Shingay CAM probably contain –inga–.

There are 11 names which are ambiguous or too obscure to be classified. These are Anglesey CAM, Arksey YOW, Bunny NTT, Canvey ESX, Eisey WLT, Fleckney LEI, Hackney GTL, Hillsea HMP, Kelsey LIN, Manea CAM and Pentney NFK.

The corresponding ON word, **ey**, is used in the names of coastal islands in the west of Britain, and round Scotland (where it frequently becomes –a, as in

Foula, Staffa, Flotta), but is probably to be reckoned with little, if at all, in inland settlement-names. Barrow-in-Furness LNC contains ON *ey* because Barrow was originally the name of a small island now joined to the mainland. Haxey LIN is considered in Fellows Jensen 1978 (p. 154) to contain the ON word, but the addition of ON **holmr** 'island' to Haxey which resulted in the name Axholme is easier to understand if the name was, at least in part, OE.

ēgland OE 'island' is rare in place-names, but two instances, Nayland SFK and Nyland DOR, are major settlement-names. Both acquired *N–* in the ME period, from the dat. of the definite article in the phrase *atten eilande* 'at the island'. Both are islands in the modern sense, not in the senses mainly evidenced for **ēg** and **holmr**.

At Nayland SFK the village is on the edge of an island made by two arms of the R. Stour. At Nyland DOR (S.W. of Gillingham) the two settlements lie between the R. Cale and Bow Brook.

fenn OE 'fen' has an uneven distribution in settlement-names, and is very rare in ancient names in the districts now known as The Fens. There appears to have been an early use in ESX, then a preference for other, synonymous, terms until a considerably later date. Perhaps *fenn* was brought back into use to replace **mōr** when the meaning of that term was restricted to 'barren upland'.

Fenham NTB(2) is from the dative plural. Fenham near Holy Island refers to the same marsh as one of the two instances of Fenwick in that county. Fenham in Newcastle upon Tyne adjoins the great common called Town Moor. Apart from these two instances of the dative plural, *fenn* only occurs uncompounded in minor names and field-names; and in major settlement-names *fenn* is more frequent as a first than as a second element. Both *fenn* and the adjective *fennig* are occasionally used as affixes.

The East Saxon form *fænn* is the first element of Vange and Fambridge, and the second element of Bulphan ESX. N. and S. Fambridge are on either side of the Crouch estuary, and *fænn* was probably the name of the district. The north bank of the R. Thames in London appears to have been called *fenn*. The OE bounds of land granted to Westminster Abbey refer to *bulunga fen* near the Abbey and 'London fen' near Blackfriars Bridge. Fenchurch is named from this stretch of marshy ground.

Moving west from ESX, there does not appear to be another major settlement-name containing *fenn* until Fencott OXF, but the term becomes commoner in the west midlands and the south west. Moving north from ESX, names in Fen– occur in LIN and occasionally in Yorkshire, and the word becomes relatively frequent in NTB. Two instances of Fenton, in HNT and NTT, are outliers of this distribution pattern, and there is at least one minor name, Fancott in Toddington BDF, in the gap between ESX and OXF.

Fenton occurs in CMB, HNT, LIN(2), NTB, NTT, STF and YOW, and there is a lost *Fenton* in Yeldersley DRB. This is sufficiently frequent in relation to the small corpus of names in *fenn* to be considered a compound appellative, and these places may have had a special function connected with the fen, rather than the name being a simple geographical statement. In Fencott OXF and Fencote HRE *fenn* is used to qualify **cot**, in Fenhampton HRE it qualifies **hāmtūn**, and in Fenwick NTB(2) and YOW it is used with **wīc**. The only other compound with a habitative term appears to be Fenby LIN, which may contain ON *fen*.

Major names in which *fenn* is the final element are Bulphan ESX, Edvin HRE, Mason NTB, Matfen NTB, Mousen NTB, Pinvin WOR, Pressen NTB, Ratfyn (in Amesbury) WLT, Swinfen STF, Warne DEV and Wervin CHE. Five of these have personal names as first element.

Macefen CHE, said in Ekwall 1960 to contain *fenn*, is derived by Dodgson (EPNS survey 4, p. 37) from Welsh *maes y ffin* 'boundary field'.

hamm OE 'land hemmed in by water or marsh (perhaps also by high ground); river-meadow; cultivated plot on the edge of woodland or moor'. These translations are controversial. Three articles on this element have been published since 1960. These are Gelling 1960, in which the three main senses given above were put forward, with the suggestion that 'land almost surrounded by water' was the earliest sense of *hamm* in English names, that the sense 'river-meadow' developed out of this, and that 'enclosed plot' was a late OE meaning. The second was Dodgson 1973, which accepted my suggestions for the senses of *hamm* in broad outline, but put forward an elaborated classification as follows:

hamm 1	'land in a river-bend'
hamm 2a	'a promontory of dry land into marsh or water'
hamm 2b	'a promontory into lower land, even without marsh or water; perhaps hence land on a hill-spur'
hamm 3	'a river-meadow'
hamm 4	'dry ground in a marsh'
hamm 5a	'a cultivated plot in marginal land'
hamm 5b	'an enclosed plot, a close'
hamm 6	'a piece of valley-bottom land hemmed in by higher ground'

The third was Sandred 1976, which entirely rejected my conclusions of 1960, and claimed that *hamm* was a term for a man-made enclosure, and that there was no firm evidence for any specialized topographical use.

Dr Sandred's conclusion seems to me misguided, but he makes an important correction to my 1960 article. Previous to 1960 it was considered that while the basic sense of *hamm* was 'something enclosed', the word had been influenced in its sense-development in place-names by another word, *hamm* 'bend of the knee' (modern *ham*), which is derived from a different root, meaning 'crooked'. In 1960 I was carried away by my topographical findings (which seemed, and still seem, to demonstrate that 'land in a river-bend' and 'coastal promontory' were the earliest meanings of *hamm* in place-names) to such an extent that I suggested that the place-name term was actually a transferred use of the anatomical term, rather than a separate word meaning 'enclosure'. Dr Sandred points out that *hamm* 'bend of the knee' is feminine, while the place-name element (which is generously represented in charter boundaries so that its grammar can be studied) is clearly masculine, so must be a different word.

There is, however, no need to throw out the baby with the bathwater. The baby in this instance consists of the topographical studies made independently by myself and by John Dodgson, which led us to the conclusion that *hamm* is mainly a topographical term in place-names, and that 'land in a river-bend, promontory of dry land into marsh or water' are the earliest senses. It is unlikely that two place-name specialists could have imposed on the material a pattern of topographical usage which does not really exist. Attempts to demonstrate a relationship between a place-name element and certain types of site founder very quickly if they have no basis in fact; and it is apparent that *hamm* is used in place-names quite differently from other words, such as **worth** and **tūn**, which also mean 'enclosure' but which did not develop any specialized topographical meanings.

One respect in which Dr Sandred's arguments are unsound is his use of material from charter boundaries to establish the original meaning of *hamm*. He does not recognize that boundaries are sometimes later additions to 8th and 9th-century charters. None of the examples he gives is likely to be earlier than AD 830, and this instance from 830 is a marshland name, on the edge of Romney Marsh KNT. Dr Sandred amalgamates evidence from this early set of boundaries, and others which he mistakenly considers to be early, with the evidence from the more numerous 10th-century boundaries. Many of the 10th-century references, as was carefully pointed out in Gelling 1960, indicate a meaning 'enclosure for keeping animals or for growing crops'. Dr Sandred also cites the reference in Ælfric's *Lives of Saints*, dating from c. AD 1000, to a *wyrtigan hamme*, which means 'garden plot'.

The charter boundaries and the writings of Ælfric are evidence for the meaning of *hamm* in the OE language in the 10th century; but it is legitimate to look at major place-names, particularly those in southern and eastern England, for evidence bearing on its meaning in the 5th to 9th centuries. Study of major place-names containing *hamm* suggests that there was a sense-development from meanings associated with water and marsh to meanings appropriate to enclosures in wooded country or moorland. In this last sense the word appears to have been used for isolated patches of cultivated land round the moorland areas of DEV and in some woodland areas in BRK and HMP. This was apparently a temporary meaning, which did not oust the earlier association with water, since *ham* is used in modern dialects of flat, low-lying land by a river.

There are four unequivocal occurrences of *hamm* in place-names recorded by AD 730 (Cox 1976, p. 49). These are Farnham SUR, Fulham GTL, and lost places called *Athom* near Muchelney SOM and *Hammespot* in Romney Marsh KNT, and these are all marsh or river-side sites. The masculine word *hamm* means 'enclosure', but it may well have been influenced by the feminine word *hamm* 'bend of the knee', and so have seemed especially appropriate to sites where the land jutted out like a bent leg into the curve of a river, or into the sea, or into a marsh. The meaning 'river-meadow' is a natural early development from the 'river-bend' sense. This meaning is not quite as common in major settlement-names as 'land in a river-bend', but it is at least twice as common in minor names, and is much the commonest meaning of *hamm* in charter boundaries, despite the evidence referred to above for a sense 'enclosed plot in marginal land' in some areas. Cf. Hooke 1981 (p. 217): 'every reference to a *hamm* in the boundary clauses of Worcestershire that can be located lies beside a stream or river and often within a well-marked bend.'

Major settlement-names which certainly contain *hamm* and which refer to places in river-bends or at river-junctions are: E. and W. Ham GTL, Ham SUR, Holme Lacy HRE, Hampreston DOR, Hammoon DOR, Hamsey SSX, Hampton GTL, Hampton Bishop HRE, Hampton Lucy WAR, Birlingham WOR, Buckingham BUC, Chippenham WLT, Culham OXF, Evesham WOR, Fulham GTL, Inglesham WLT, Passenham NTP, Pensham WOR, Twickenham GTL, Wellingham SSX, and Wittenham BRK. Names which refer to settlements on coastal or estuarine promontories are Hamworthy DOR, Southampton HMP, Bosham SSX, Dittisham DEV, Iham (now Winchelsea) SSX, Northam HMP, and Topsham DEV. A promontory of dry ground jutting out into marsh forms the sites of High and Low Ham SOM, Ham near Berkeley GLO, Powderham DEV, Witcham CAM and Wittersham KNT. In Hamp in Bridgewater SOM, Ham near Creech St Michael SOM, and Burnham SOM, the meaning may be 'dry ground in marsh', referring to a very slight rise. The 1″ maps for the Severn estuary and the adjacent marshes of Sedgemoor and Wedmore show a fair number of farms with names in –ham and simplex names such as Ham or Holme Fm, and it is likely that the determining factor in the sites of these was the presence of a small patch of firm ground.

The more general sense 'river-meadow' is suitable for a number of major settlement-names in sites less distinctive than those listed in the last paragraph. Here belong Barkham BRK (and perhaps Barkham SSX), Benham BRK, Churcham GLO, Cuxham OXF, Damerham HMP, Eynsham OXF, Farnham SUR, Feckenham WOR, Fernham BRK, Harrietsham KNT, Highnam GLO, Kingsholme GLO, Littleham (near Exmouth) DEV, Marcham BRK, Shrivenham BRK and Woodham BUC.

There is a series of *hamm* names along the rivers Brede and Rother in SSX in country which has been so much affected by drainage that it must be difficult to decide whether they originally contained the word in the sense 'land in a river-bend' or 'river-meadow' or 'promontory of dry land in marsh'. These names are Methersham, Kitchenham, Northiam, Padgham, Ockham along the Rother, and Snailham, Icklesham and Lidham on the Brede. Other names along the south coast, such as Westham and Hankham near Pevensey, and on other streams, such as Beddingham on the Glynde and Stoneham on the Ouse, cannot be easily classified because the topographical evidence is obscured by drainage. Dodgson 1973 should be consulted on these (most of them are not in Ekwall 1960): he classifies some as 'promontory of dry land into marsh or water', and says, e.g., that Snailham 'is a very prominent example of a promontory *hamm*' and that Beddingham 'in olden days . . . would have been on the south shore of a tidal estuary creek, and on a tongue of land between Glynde Reach and a creek'. The sense 'promontory into marsh' is certainly well represented between the Rivers Rother and Brede.

The evidence put forward above for the association of *hamm* with sites dominated by water or marsh could be multiplied greatly by the consideration of minor names and field-names, which are not included in this discussion. In field-names 'river-meadow' is probably the commonest sense, though more precise uses may sometimes be discerned. Foxall 1980 (p. 19 and Plate 2) finds that Ham in SHR 'usually means land in the bend of a river; a shape suggesting the inner part of the knee'.

On looking at the material after a long interval since 1960 I feel that John Dodgson's suggestion for a meaning 'a piece of valley-bottom land hemmed in by higher ground' (his *hamm* 6) is helpful for classifying some instances in major names. I should like to adopt this etymology for Ham WLT, Ham (near Cheltenham) GLO, Cheltenham GLO, Chesham BUC, Dyrham GLO, Georgeham DEV, Portisham DOR and Todenham GLO; but I should like to add to Mr Dodgson's solution the suggestion that *hamm* was felt to be appropriate for places enclosed in particularly well-watered valleys. This suits Chesham BUC, for instance: the valley is too narrow to admit of broad expanses of river-meadow but the name Chesham Moor, S. of the town, indicates marsh. At Cheltenham GLO numerous small streams rise in the escarpment to the E. of the town. Portisham DOR occupies a small valley in an escarpment, and two small streams rise in the village.

A major settlement-name in *–hamm* which has not been listed in the preceding paragraphs is Tidenham GLO. Tidenham stands on a promontory on the W. bank of the R. Severn, and much of its large parish consists of this great feature, which rises to 778', and separates the gorge of the R. Wye from the Severn estuary. It is tempting to see this as a dramatic instance of the sense 'promontory', but there are complicating factors. A document of AD 956, which gives a survey of the manor, speaks of land 'outside the *hamm*', and this suggests that we are here dealing with an artificially rather than a naturally 'enclosed' site. Another complicating factor is the southern end of Offa's Dyke, which runs above the Wye till it approaches the peninsula of Beachley, then crosses to the Severn at Sedbury Cliffs, leaving Beachley outside. The Dyke could be thought of as making an 'enclosure'. To take this as the meaning of *hamm* in Tidenham would postulate a very late origin, after AD 800, for the name, but it is by no means impossible that this great estate had a British name until then. It is called *Istrat Hafren* 'Roman road by the R. Severn' in charters of c. 703 and c. 878 in the Book of Llandaff.

Several problems remain to be considered. One is that posed by settlement-names in DEV which probably contain *hamm* since the other possible component, **hām**, was obsolescent when English names were formed in that county. This problem is connected with that of the charter boundaries in which *hamm* is used of man-made enclosures that have no connection with water or marsh. Another problem—the most difficult of all—is that of how to distinguish names in *hamm* from those in **hām** when there are no diagnostic spellings: and related to this is the question of how far north in England the element *hamm* is to be reckoned with.

All the place-names mentioned so far either have early spellings such as *–hamm(e)*, *–homm(e)*, *–hom(e)* which provide sound evidence for derivation from *hamm*, or are simplex names (Ham, sometimes corrupted to Holme) which must derive from *hamm* since **hām** is never used in that way. There are enough names of both types in DEV to show that *hamm* is common in that county. In addition to names mentioned above, Abbotsham (*Hama* in DB) and Brixham (*Brisehamme* in DB) are certainly from *hamm*, but these two have not been mentioned in preceding paragraphs because they are difficult to classify on a topographical basis. Abbotsham could be described as on a promontory, but the site is probably not sufficiently distinctive to warrant this special term. There are other major settlement-names near Abbotsham—Northam, Littleham, Parkham—which do not have distinctive *hamm* spellings, but which are not likely to contain **hām**, as it is improbable that **hām** (if it was still in use at all) would be so productive as far west as this. The best solution for these, and for a considerable number of minor names in –ham all over the county, might be to assume that they arose during the period when *hamm* meant 'enclosure for agricultural purposes'.

It was pointed out in Gelling 1960 (p. 153) that many of the DEV minor names in –ham belong to isolated farms or small hamlets in situations where there can be no special reference to water. Many are on the fringes of high moorland, and could result from a comparatively late breaking in of marginal land. A group of them (Didham, Callisham, Gnatham, Dittisham) occurs near the S.W. edge of Dartmoor, and there are others (Winsham, Viveham, Fernham, N. of the R. Taw, and Frizenham, Smytham, Craneham, S. of it) in high ground in the N.W. of the county. The choice of the word *hamm* for these isolated settlements could have owed something to the appearance presented by a farm in marginal land. The cultivated fields would stand out by reason of their greenness, and this comparatively lush appearance in the drab moorland could have suggested an association with green meadowland in the lowlands. If the element did have this sense 'cultivated ground' in DEV, this might explain the use of the word in the district-name South Hams, which refers to a large area in the S. of the county between the R. Plym and the R. Dart, and its use in a charter of AD 833 which says that a woman 'withdrew into Domnonia and took her part there in the place called *Derentunehomm*'. The farmland round Dartington might have been called *Derentunehomm*, and South Hams might be the cultivated lands south of Dartmoor.

The use of *hamm* in DEV place-names deserves attention from local historians. If it be accepted that there was a middle/late OE sense 'cultivated plot in marginal land', some of the names could be clues to an expansion of settlement in the 9th century. Otterham CNW should be considered as one of the names for which this meaning is suitable.

A few minor names in other counties (e.g. Ham Green in Mathon HRE, Ham Fm in Barham KNT, Tedham Fm in Horne SUR) can be classified with the DEV names just discussed. Otherwise this use of *hamm* for isolated patches of enclosed ground is best evidenced in 10th-century charter boundaries. Examples in N. HMP and S.W. BRK are cited in Gelling 1960 (pp. 151–2). The bulk of the charter-boundary evidence for this sense is in that area, but a meaning 'isolated patch of enclosed ground' probably occurs also in charters for other areas. It suits *hamm* in the phrase 'thæs leas and thæs hammes be northan thære lytlan dic' which occurs in a charter of AD 944 referring to land between Fox Hill and Newnham Hill, N.E. of Badby NTP (*leas*, from *lēah*, and *hammes* are gen. sg., following the verb *geunnan* 'to grant').

It should be noted that in charter boundaries names spelt –*ham* are usually regarded as being from *hamm*, since there is no possibility that a large number of ancient settlement-names containing **hām** were to be found on estate boundaries.

The EPNS survey of DEV has a summary of the evidence for the date of English settlement on p. xviii of the Introduction: 'It would therefore seem that the Saxon occupation of Eastern Devon may have begun very soon after the year 658, that the Saxons reached Exeter before the last decade of the seventh century, and that the west and north of the county were opened to them by the battle of 711.' Recent studies of **hām** have concluded that that element was not likely to be used for place-name formation after the 7th century. Cox 1973 says of STF: 'It seems clear that apart from the extreme south-east settlement in the county did not begin until the end of the pagan period. This explains the absence of names in **hām** which we associate with the period c. 400–650.' Dodgson 1973 says: 'In the three south-eastern counties the **hām** names record a process which took place in the fifth and sixth centuries. In Cheshire they mark an English "take-over" in the seventh century.' In the light of these conclusions (which are based on careful and thorough studies) it seems fair to make very little allowance for **hām** in DEV place-names even when dealing with examples for which there are no early spellings indicative of *hamm*. The insoluble problem remains of how far, in counties where English names arose much earlier, so that there is no reason to exclude **hām** on grounds of date, we are justified in sometimes preferring *hamm* to **hām** in names which have no distinctive spellings.

The evidence of some names in the midlands for which there are OE –*hamm* spellings shows that an undoubted *hamm* name may appear in ME with nothing to distinguish it from a name in **hām**. This is true, e.g., of Cheltenham GLO, Buckingham BUC, Birlingham WOR, Chesham BUC. In fact it is probably more usual than not in major names in *hamm* in the midlands. Comparable examples (e.g. Farnham SUR) are easily found in the south, though ME –*hamme* spellings are probably rather more numerous for major names in the southern counties. In Gelling 1960 it was pointed out that Passenham NTP and Buckingham BUC, which are both in sharp bends of the Bedfordshire Ouse, are shown to be –*hamm* names by OE spellings, whereas Blunham, Biddenham, Bromham, Pavenham, Felmersham (BDF) and Haversham, Tyringham (BUC)—which are similarly enclosed by loops of the river lower down its course—cannot be claimed as names in *hamm* because there are no OE spellings available, though the ME spellings are not evidence against *hamm*, since only –*ham* occurs in post-Conquest sources for Passenham and Buckingham. The HRE names Ballingham, Baysham, Bodenham and Lulham may be suspected of containing *hamm* 'land in a river-bend', though there are no spellings which positively support this. The suggestion that *hamm* may be postulated for some names which have only post-Conquest spellings because the sites closely resemble those of better-recorded settlements which certainly have names in *hamm* was treated seriously in Cox 1973 and Dodgson 1973. Cox omitted a number of items from his distribution maps of names in **hām** because their sites seemed more appropriate to *hamm*. Of Oakham RUT, e.g., he says 'most likely a name in *hamm* . . . set on a tongue of land formed by the arms of two streams'; Isham NTP 'is a typical *hamm* site'; the BDF names in bends of the Ouse are given as '?*hamm*', and Southam WAR as 'probably *hamm*'.

Dodgson 1973 takes a good deal further the attempt to identify *hamm* names for which there are no decisive spellings. His Appendix III contains a long list of names in KNT, SUR and SSX 'more likely to be from OE –*hamm* than from OE –**hām**.' These are selected mainly on topographical grounds, but some account is taken of status. The entry for Chimhams in Farningham KNT, e.g., says '*Chimbeham* 1203: OE *cimb* "edge". The first el. refers to the brink of a steep-sided valley. The position of the place is eccentric in relation to the parish of Farningham, the place is of secondary, hamlet status and the site, at about 490 ft between two 500 ft contour lines, near the brink of the north-east slope of the Maplescombe valley, would suit an upland enclosure, a *hamm* 5. Chimhams would be a suitable place for an upland meadowing hamlet out on the backside of the parish.' The argument from status is valid here, though it cannot, of course, be said in general that *hamm* names should only refer to minor places. It will be evident from examples quoted above that some undoubted *hamm* names refer to great estates (like Eynsham OXF, Farnham SUR) and to places of early administrative importance. But *hamm* continued in use as a place-name-forming term in the south at least till the end of the OE period, whereas **hām** went out of use about AD 650–700, so *hamm* had the greater chance of being used in the naming of settlements of late origin and dependent status.

In my 1960 article I suggested, I now feel mistakenly, that *hamm* was not to be reckoned with in areas of purely Anglian (as opposed to Saxon and Jutish) settlement. Further study of SHR names makes it apparent that my suggested northern limit—a line through Presteigne HRE, Droitwich WOR, Coventry WAR—was too far south; and I now wonder whether there is any need to assume a northern limit at all as regards *hamm* in ancient settlement-names, though the proliferation of minor names using the word in what I take to be its middle/late OE senses certainly does not occur in the northern half of the country. Two districts of Shrewsbury have names in *–hamm*. These are Coleham, outside the English Bridge, and a lost *Romaldesham*, inside the Welsh Bridge; and in Ford, W. of Shrewsbury, there was a place called *Fordeshom* recorded from the 13th to 17th centuries. Coleham and *Romaldesham* could contain *hamm* in the sense 'land in a river-bend'. For Coleham, which lies between the R. Severn and Meole Brook, the spellings have only *–ham*, but it is doubtful if anyone would consider it likely to be a **hām** name. The other two names have *–hom* spellings. These names, and the characteristic use of Ham in SHR field-names (see above), suggest that *hamm* was well known in its riverine senses in the Shrewsbury area; and the fact that Atcham, a little to the S.E. of Shrewsbury, lies in a loop of the Severn cannot be ignored in any assessment of that name, although it has only *–ham* spellings. A classic instance of an 'enclosed by rivers' position occurs further S. in the county at a hamlet called The Home, 5 miles S.W. of Church Stretton.

In EPNS surveys of counties N. of WAR allowance has not generally been made for the possibility of *hamm* occurring in some major settlement-names, though Ekwall 1922 (p. 12) did not rule it out in LNC. There are, however, spellings for Frodsham in CHE (*Frodshum* and *Frotheshamme* in the early 13th century) which suggest that it may be a *hamm* rather than a **hām**, and the site is a perfect example of a 'promontory into marsh'. If the case put forward here, for *hamm* being a topographical term in place-names until c. 800 and retaining its topographical senses after it had acquired in some areas a meaning 'enclosure for agricultural purposes', be accepted, then it would probably be worth examining the –ham place-names of northern England, as those of the midlands and East Anglia were examined in Cox 1973, in order to identify the ones with sites which are particularly suggestive of *hamm*. If, on the other hand, Dr Sandred's opinion that the element is not a topographical one be accepted, then it is no use attempting to locate examples in areas where pre-Conquest spellings are rarely available.

To return to southern England, I do not accept the view taken in Dodgson 1973 that some names in KNT—Beckenham, Bellingham, Cobham, Mottingham, West Wickham—should be classified as containing *hamm* because they occur in charter boundaries with *–mm–* in such phrases as *Beohhahammes* *gemǣru*, *Cobbahammes mearce*, *wic hammes gemǣru*. The boundary of West Wickham CAM is similarly referred to as *wichammes gemǣre*. As the middle element of a triple compound in these phrases, **hām** would probably lose its long vowel and thus be more easily confused with *hamm*. Even without such vowel shortening there probably was some confusion of **hām** and *hamm* in OE, to add to all the other difficulties discussed above.

Since it is doubtful whether, even in southern counties, a complete list of names in *hamm* will ever be available, it is not advisable to draw over-firm conclusions from an analysis of the types of first elements with which *hamm* is compounded. Some points worth noting emerge, however, from an analysis of names mentioned in preceding paragraphs for which there are early spellings which put the *hamm* etymology beyond serious question.

First, there are at least four –*inga*– names—Beddingham SSX, Birlingham WOR, Buckingham BUC and Wellingham SSX—and three of these contain an –*ingas* folk-name based on a personal name. This removes what might have been considered an objection to considering Atcham SHR (? and Birmingham WAR) to be potential *hamm*, rather than definite **hām** names.

The largest category of first elements in compound names with –*hamm* consists of OE masculine personal names, either monothematic, or belonging to the type considered to be shortened forms of longer names. Only one instance has been noted in major names in which the personal name is certainly dithematic: this is Wittersham KNT, which is *Wihtriceshamme* in 1032; but the lost *Romaldesham* in Shrewsbury is a similar formation in a name of lesser status, and in Brixham DEV the personal name may be OE *Beorhtsige*. Short personal names occur with *hamm* in Benham BRK, Bosham SSX, Culham OXF, Cuxham OXF, Dittisham DEV, Feckenham WOR, Fulham GTL, Hankham SSX, Icklesham SSX, Inglesham WLT, Passenham NTP, Pensham WOR, Tidenham GLO, Todenham GLO, Topsham DEV and Wittenham BRK. A preponderance of short masculine personal names occurs also in compounds with **ēg**.

Other categories are small. Barkham BRK, SSX, Farnham SUR, Fernham BRK, Marcham BRK and Witcham CAM refer to vegetation; Burnham SOM, Cheltenham GLO, Chesham BUC and Powderham DEV to a feature of the topography. Northam DEV, HMP and Westham SSX refer to position; Littleham DEV(2) and Parkham DEV to a special characteristic of the *hamm*. Northiam SSX is probably 'high promontory', with North– prefixed for distinction from *Iham*, the site of the new medieval town of Winchelsea, which was called *Suthyhomme* in 1339. *Iham* may be another 'high promontory', but it is sometimes considered to have **ēg** as first element. Kingsholme GLO refers to royal ownership, and Damerham HMP is '*hamm* of the judges'. Only Dyrham GLO contains a reference to an animal; more of these, particularly domestic ones, might have been expected if *hamm* meant primarily 'man-made enclosure'.

Some compound names in *hamm* are obscure or ambiguous. Harrietsham

KNT could be 'Heregeard's *hamm*', but a noun *heregeard*, which would mean 'army enclosure', appears to be the source of Herriard HMP, and could be the first element of Harrietsham. Shrivenham BRK has as first element the past participle of the verb *scrīfan*, modern *shrive*, and it can only be suggested that it was given into ecclesiastical ownership as an act of penance. Eynsham OXF has not yet been satisfactorily explained: a pre-English river-name like that of R. Ehen CMB might be considered. Chippenham WLT is discussed in Gelling 1970. Twickenham GTL may be 'Twicca's *hamm*', but Ekwall 1960 suggests an OE word *twicce* 'river-fork' as an alternative.

hamm is frequently used as a simplex name, liable in the midlands to be corrupted to Holme, as in Holme Lacy HRE. Some simplex examples are disguised by affixes. Hammoon DOR and Hamsey SSX have manorial owners' names added. In Georgeham DEV the affix is the church dedication. Hampreston DOR is a combination of two names, Ham and Preston. Evesham WOR was alternatively *Cronuchomme* ('crane *hamm*') in OE, and may have been a simplex name originally; Eves– is the genitive of a personal name *Ēof*. Hamworthy DOR was a simplex name till the 15th century, when it was felt necessary to distinguish it from Hampreston by the prefixing of *South–* or the addition of **worthig**. Woodham BUC was part of a district called *Ham*, another part of which was called *Fieldham*.

hamm is rarely used as a first element, but it does occur in some instances of Hampton, i.e. Hampton near Bodenham, Hampton Bishop HRE, Hampton GTL, Hampton Lucy WAR. Southampton HMP is a *hammtūn*, to which *South–* was prefixed in the mid 11th century to distinguish it from the other county town called *Hamtun*, Northampton, though that had actually a different origin, from **hāmtūn**. There is an exhaustive discussion of the name Southampton in Rumble 1980.

holmr ON 'island, inland promontory, raised ground in marsh, river-meadow'. This is probably the commonest ON topographical term in England. It was adopted into late OE, and there is some interchange between *holm* and **hamm** in the west and north midlands. As with **ēg**, the characteristic use in settlement-names is for an island of firm ground in a marsh.

It is stated in place-name reference books that Hulm(e), –hulme is from a specifically Danish, as opposed to Norwegian, form of the word, and some names in LNC and CHE (such as Oldham, Cheadle Hulme, Davyhulme, and Hulme and Levenshulme in Manchester) are cited as evidence that some Danish vikings were involved in what was predominantly a Norwegian settlement. Dr Kristian Hald has demonstrated that this argument is not tenable (Hald 1978). The form *hulm* hardly ever occurs in place-name spellings from Denmark, or in those from the English Danelaw, so *hulm* is much more likely to be a form which persisted in Norwegian until the date of the Viking settlements in N.W. England. Dr Hald stresses that many names in the N.W. only have *–holm(e)* spellings because this was the form which the word took when adopted into late OE. Many of the names recorded in ME are likely to have been coined by English-speaking people using this borrowed term.

The fact that *holm* became an English word means that minor names and field-names which contain it are not direct evidence of Scandinavian settlement. Major settlement-names, however, especially those recorded in DB, are likely to date from the 10th century and to result from an expansion of settlement after the Viking invasions.

There are about 50 names containing *holmr* in Ekwall 1960. Most of the places have remained small, and they are often rather isolated; but Oldham LNC and Durham DRH are notable exceptions.

holmr is used in the naming of coastal islands, smaller than those designated by ON **ey**, round Wales and Scotland. In settlement-names the characteristic use is for a patch of slightly raised ground in a marsh. Instances which can be easily identified on the 1″ map as having the last sense include Holme CAM (W. of Ramsey), Holme NTT (N. of Newark on Trent), Holme HNT (S. of Peterborough), Holme Pierrepoint NTT (E. of Nottingham), Holme upon Spalding Moor YOE, Holmes Chapel CHE. 'River-meadow' is often given as the meaning of *holmr*, and many of the sites are in low ground by rivers, but a large-scale map or local knowledge would probably reveal that some of the settlements are on very slightly raised ground. Balkholme YOE, which has OE *balca* 'ridge' as first element, probably occupies a low ridge like that noted in the discussion of Holbeach, under **bæc**.

Sometimes the raised ground is a promontory. Holme YON, W. of Thirsk, is a good example of this, and the sense may also be found in Cheadle Hulme CHE. There are two dramatic 'promontory' sites: Oldham LNC (*Aldhulm* 1227) and Durham DRH (*Dunholm* c. 1000). Neither name is easily explained; both are discussed in Gelling 1970.

Most names containing *holmr* refer to low-lying sites, but there are a few exceptions, in addition to Oldham and Durham. For some of these high sites it would be reasonable to postulate a meaning 'cultivated land on the edge of moors', with the same sense-development as is suggested for **hamm**. There are three settlements in YON with the name Sleightholme, two surviving and one lost. None of these is a 'raised ground in marsh' or 'river-meadow' site. Sleightholme S.W. of Barnard's Castle is in high moorland, admittedly surrounded by bog, but not 'river-meadow' country. Sleightholme Dale in Kirkby Moorside is high up its river-valley, a very different situation from those of N. and S. Holme, a few miles to the south, in which *holmr* has its common meaning 'raised ground in marsh'. The lost Sleighholme was in Barnby, W. of Whitby, where neither marsh nor meadow are likely to have been extensive. A fourth Sleightholme in CMB, E. of Silloth, however, is by an island in low, wet ground, one of several –holme names around the moss called Wedholme Flow. The first element of Sleightholme is explained as ON *slétta* 'level field' in Ekwall 1960, and as a related adjective *aléttr* 'smooth' in Smith 1956, but it is not apparent from the map that there is anything outstandingly level about these sites. Formally Sleight– could be the ME word which means 'wile, cunning device', and a comparison might be made with OE *wīl*, modern *wile*, also used in place-names (Monkton Wyld DOR, Wylam NTB) in some sense which has not yet been explained. Another possibility for Sleightholme is OE *sleget* 'sheep pasture'. Another high site to which a meaning 'enclosure in marginal land' would be suitable is Hulme E. of Stoke on Trent STF, and there are some minor names on the Yorkshire Wolds for which it seems to be the only possible sense. Such a meaning was envisaged for an Orkney name, Holmes in Paplay, in Marwick 1952 (p. 91): 'There is no island in Paplay to give rise to such a name, and it would thus appear to be ON *holmar*, plur. of *holmr*, a small island, but used in the secondary sense of a patch of ground situated like an island in the midst of ground of a different nature.'

Of the names containing *holmr* in Ekwall 1960, about half are simplex, having the modern forms Holm(e) or Hulme. (But Holme or Holme– can have other origins, OE *holegn* 'holly' being probably the commonest. Holme on the Wolds YOE is the dat. pl. of ON *haugr* 'mound', and Nunburnholme YOE is the dat. pl. of **brunnr**. Lealholm YON is the dat. pl. of OE *lǣl* 'twig', and Moorsholm YON contains the dat. pl. of *hūs* 'house'.) Holm(e) and Hulme have not been given affixes as frequently as most recurring simplex names, but Davyhulme LNC has the unexplained *Defe–* prefixed in 1434.

Among compound names, there are four which probably have an ON personal name as first element. These are Broadholme NTT, Gauxholme LNC, Kettleshulme CHE, Torrisholme YON. Alternatively Gauxholme could refer to cuckoos, and the 'kettle' of Kettleshulme could be a topographical feature. Levenshulme LNC contains the OE personal name *Lēofwine*. Vegetation or crops are referred to in Almholme YOW and Haverholme LIN, with ON qualifying terms, and in Bromholm NFK and Hempholm YOE, with OE first elements. Balkholme YOE and Langham Row LIN have OE descriptive terms. Keldholme YON and Sookholme NTT contain references, ON and OE respectively, to topographical features. In the district-name Axholme LIN, *holmr* has been added to an earlier place-name. In Broxholme LIN the Old Danish word *brōk* (used in Danish place-names of a marsh) may have been a district-name. Burtholme CMB contains a river-name. Only Trenholme YON and Tupholme LIN refer to living creatures.

kjarr ON 'brushwood'. The ME derivative *kerr* was used of 'a marsh, especially one overgrown by brushwood', and it is likely that this is the sense of *kjarr* in place-names. The word is used mainly in minor names and field-names in the Danelaw, but it is the second element of a few settlement-names. In Altcar LNC it is added to a British river-name. In Broadcarr NFK and Holker LNC it is qualified by OE *brād* 'broad' and *holh* 'hollow'. Redcar YON is another hybrid, with OE *hrēod* 'reed' as first element. Ellerker YOE also refers to vegetation but contains an ON word, *elri* 'alder'.

Bicker LIN and Byker NTB have been explained in several ways. Ekwall

1960 thinks they mean 'village marsh' with bȳ as first element, and this is supported, for Bicker LIN, in Fellows Jensen 1978 (p. 152). Smith 1956 prefers '(place) by the marsh', with OE *bī* 'by' used as in Biddick DRH, Biddulph STF. A third suggestion, of derivation from ME *biker* 'fight, quarrel, dispute', is included in Smith 1956, but seems much less likely.

It is reasonable to assume that at all these settlements the landscape was in an undeveloped state when Norse-speaking people moved in.

mersc, merisc OE 'marsh' occurs in about 60 names in Ekwall 1960, leaving aside those, like Burgh le Marsh LIN and Marsh Baldon OXF, in which it is used as an affix. In over half the instances it is the first element, the compound with **tūn** accounting for 33. As a simplex name it occurs in Marsh SHR, Marsh Gibbon BUC, Marishes YON and Marske YON(2). Smith 1956 explains Marske as containing ON *-sk*, Ekwall 1960 prefers to derive it from the OE dat. pl. *merscum*.

Apart from the compound with **tūn**, *mersc* is seldom used as a first element, but it does occur in Marsham NFK (**hām**) and Marshwood DOR. (Marshwood is the OE equivalent of ON Myerscough.) Combined with **tūn**, *mersc* occurs in Marston BDF, BUC(2), CHE, DRB(2), GLO, HRE(2), HRT, LEI, LIN, NTP(2), OXF, SOM(2), STF(2), WLT(3), WAR(6), YOW; in Merston IOW, KNT, SSX; and in Morston NFK. It is possible (as is here suggested for other recurrent compounds of topographical terms with **tūn**) that these settlements had a specialized function in relation to the exploitation of the marsh.

As a second element in major settlement-names *mersc* is occasionally combined with a personal name, as in Killamarsh DRB, Titchmarsh HMP, and possibly Bickmarsh WAR, though the last name could contain a noun *bica* 'projection'. Burmarsh KNT ('marsh of the city-dwellers') refers to the inhabitants of Canterbury in the same way as Bulverhythe SSX refers to the people of Hastings. Tidmarsh BRK is probably 'marsh of the people', with the same first element as Thetford. Crakemarsh STF, Crowmarsh OXF, and Henmarsh GLO refer to birds, but only one name—Stodmarsh KNT—mentions animals. Vegetation is specified only in Peasmarsh SSX. Descriptive terms are used in Lamarsh ESX and Lamas NFK ('loam'), Michelmersh HMP ('large'), Rawmarsh YON ('red') and Saltmarsh(e) HRE, YOE.

Chelmarsh SHR is considered to have as first element an OE word *cegel* 'pole', and Kelmarsh NTP may be the same name with ON influence causing *Ch-* to be replaced by *K-*. Cheylesmore WAR contains the same word in the genitive. These marshes may have been marked out by posts.

In spite of the occasional compounds with personal names it seems likely that names with *mersc* as second element were coined to describe areas of marshland, and were later transferred to settlements. Warwickshire names in *mersc* are discussed in Maynard 1974, and her conclusion, that *mersc* was used of potentially valuable land, deserves testing in other areas.

mōr OE 'marsh, barren upland'. The sense-development of this word has not been worked out. It is used for low-lying marshes, like Otmoor OXF, the Weald Moors SHR, Sedgemoor and Wedmore SOM, and for the high marshes of the north country, like Stainmore on the YOW/WML border. This is not inconsistent, as both are characterized by extreme wetness. The moors of the South West, Dartmoor and Exmoor, are boggy, at least in parts. But the restriction of the meaning to 'barren, upland' in modern English, and the use of the term in place-names for dry heathland such as Dunsmore WAR and Snelsmore BRK, indicates either that the word underwent a drastic change of meaning, losing an early connotation of wetness, or that the idea of barrenness was always paramount. NED, though without total conviction, cites derivation from a root meaning 'to die', which suggests an original meaning 'barren land', but other authorities suggest a connection between *mōr* and **mere** 'sea, lake', which could be taken to indicate that the 'marsh' sense is earlier.

It seems probable that *mōr* was generally applied to less fertile areas than **mersc**; but some of the low-lying marshes for which it was used, such as Otmoor and the Weald Moors, became of considerable economic value, though the Weald Moors must have been 'waste' when the English first saw the area.

The meaning 'low-lying marshy area' may be the earliest one in place-names. It is the commoner of the two senses, and it is well represented in some areas of very early English settlement, such as the Oxford region. Sometimes a major name which contains *mōr* in this sense has in its vicinity minor names, likely to be of later origin, in which *mōr* is used of barren upland. Poltimore DEV, N.E. of Exeter, is a good example of 'low-lying marsh', but the hamlets of Dunsmore and Moorland, 3 miles to the N., contain the term in the modern sense. The meaning 'low-lying marsh' was probably current till the end of the 9th century as it occurs in areas of late English settlement, such as DEV and LNC; but some names in which *mōr* refers to dry heathland, like Dunsmoor WAR and Southmoor and Draycott Moor BRK, are also likely to have been current before the end of the 9th century, so it appears necessary to assume that there was a period of overlap in which the two senses did not appear inconsistent. It would be possible to envisage the two senses as being of equal antiquity.

As a simplex name *mōr* has become Moore CHE (E. of Runcorn) and More SHR (N.E. of Bishop's Castle). Northmoor OXF was *Mora* until the late 14th century. Allensmore HRE, first recorded as *Mora Alani* in 1241, was probably a simplex name before the association with Alan de Plokenet in the 13th century.

As a first element *mōr* is the most frequent of the 'fen' words, and is used to qualify a wide range of second elements. It qualifies other topographical terms in Morborne HNT, Morebath DEV, Moreleigh DEV, Morley DRB, DRH, NFK, YOW. The compound which becomes Morden, Moredon or Mordon is discussed under **dūn**. With OE habitative terms *mōr* occurs in Morcott RUT, Murcot OXF and Morwick NTB; and most frequently in the compound with **tūn**.

Moorton occurs in GLO and OXF, Moreton in BUC, BRK, CHE(2), DEV, DOR, ESX, GLO(2), HRE(2), NTP, OXF, SHR(2), STF(3) and WAR, Morton in DRB, DRH(3), IOW, LIN(3), NFK, NTT(2), SHR, WAR, WOR(2), YON(2) and YOW, Murton in DRH(2), NTB, WML, YON(2). Most of these have affixes. Ekwall 1960 gives the blanket translation 'tūn by a fen', but these 45 names are not a homogeneous group, and it would be better to distinguish between those which mean 'tūn by a fen' and those which mean 'tūn by a moor'. Moretonhampstead DEV, for example, is on the edge of Dartmoor, and 'moor' is also the sense in Morton DRB (S.E. of Clay Cross), Morton YOW (N.E. of Keighley) and Murton WML (N.E. of Appleby). Where the sense is 'tūn by a moor' the statement is likely to be a purely geographical one, the settlement being at the limit of cultivated land. Where the name refers to a low-lying marsh the meaning may be more complex. It was suggested in Gelling 1978 (p. 200) that Moreton near Blewbury BRK was so called because of the role it played in the economy of the great estate centred on Blewbury, and this argument may be relevant in other instances.

The juxtaposition of Murcott and Fencott OXF is curious. They are on the edge of Otmoor, to which they obviously both refer, and it is difficult to account for the use of synonymous names for adjacent settlements.

As a second element *mōr* is found in about 30 major settlement-names. In the analysis which follows, which includes some district-names, items which are considered to refer to upland situations have been starred, but the situations have not been examined closely, and local knowledge may reject the classification of some. Personal names occur as first element in *Chackmore BUC, *Cottesmore RUT, *Dunsmore DEV, WAR, Gransmore YOE, *Mentmore BUC, Otmoor OXF and Pedmore WOR. It is likely that the people named in these compounds were responsible for reclamation of land in the vicinity of the settlements. Words describing the marsh or moor occur in *Blackmoor DOR, Blackmore ESX, WLT, WOR, Littlemore OXF, Radmore STF, Silkmore STF, *Stainmore YOW/WML, Swarthmoor LNC, *Whitmore STF and Wildmore LIN (identical with Weald Moors SHR). Vegetation is mentioned in *Barmoor NTB, *Breamore HMP, *Brymore SOM, *Ringmore DEV(2) and Sedgemoor SOM. Wild creatures are referred to only in Podmore STF. *Quernmore LNC refers to quern stones. Wedmore SOM may mean 'hunting marsh'. Frenchmoor HMP apparently means 'French marsh'. Cheylesmore WAR is discussed under **mersc**. Poltimore DEV and Twigmore LIN are of uncertain etymology.

Wigmore HRE is rendered 'Wicga's moor' or Welsh *gwig mawr* 'big wood' in Ekwall 1960. It is in fact a marsh, not a moor, and the compound recurs as a minor name and field-name frequently enough to cast doubt on the derivation from a personal name, if it is English. Some examples are in areas where a minor name or field-name is most unlikely to be Welsh. Another major name is Wigmore N. of Westbury SHR which, though not in Ekwall 1960 and no longer shown on the 1″ map, was a DB manor. Some instances in field-names in BRK are listed in EPNS survey p. 916, there is a well-recorded example in the EPNS CHE survey 4 (p. 55), and some could certainly be found in other counties, though it should be noted that modern Wigmore is sometimes a corruption of ME *Widemore* or *Widemere*, so it is desirable to have early spellings with *Wig(g)–* before associating such a name with Wigmore HRE and SHR. OE *wicga* means 'beetle', and there is always the possibility that place-names in which it occurs could refer to insects rather than to men named *Wicga*. In a compound with *mōr* 'marsh', *wicga* might be used metaphorically of quaking ground. Wigmore might even be a specialized term for an unstable marsh in which beetle-shaped mounds appear and disappear.

The corresponding ON word, **mór**, cannot be distinguished in place-names from OE *mōr*. The ON word is probably the first element of Moreby YOE, Morland WML, Moorby LIN and Moorsholm YON, and may be the second element of Carlesmore and Kexmoor YOW, which contain ON personal names.

mēos OE, **mos** OE, **mosi** ON 'moss'. It is convenient to consider these closely-related words in the same article. *mēos* is only recorded with reference to the plant. *mos* is only recorded once in OE, in a charter boundary where it is considered to mean 'bog' (see below), but it was presumably in general use for the plant, since it is the ancestor of the modern word *moss*. (*mēos* became *mese*, which survived in dialect till the 19th century.) ON *mosi* is said in Smith 1956 to have the same meaning as OE *mos* ('moss, lichen', also 'bog, swamp'). The sense-development of the three words in place-names has not been fully worked out. In N.W. England *moss* became, and remains, a term for a bog. In place-names this use spreads as far south as SHR and STF, and there may be an isolated instance in Moze ESX.

For *mēos* Smith 1956 gives the meaning 'a moss, a marsh, a bog'; but Ekwall 1960 only says 'moss', presumably meaning the plant. The word was used uncompounded in Coldmeece and Millmeece N. of Eccleshall STF, and in two river-names, R. Mease LEI/DRB/STF and R. Meese Brook STF/SHR. Used in this way *mēos* could mean 'mossy place' or 'mossy river', but there does not appear to be much warrant for a translation 'bog'. The only major settlement-name in which *mēos* seems likely to be the first element is Meesden HRT, where it is compounded with **dūn**. Meesden occupies the summit of a small hill on which several streams rise. There could well have been mossy places, but since the village is situated there it is not likely that the summit was boggy.

mos is only recorded once in OE, as a place-name element in the charter boundaries of Madeley STF. These date from AD 975, and inlcude the boundary-marks *hedenan mos* and *micle mos*. By 975 the word could have been borrowed from ON, or at any rate influenced in its meaning by the corresponding ON term. But there are reasons to believe that OE *mos* meant 'bog' before the Viking invasions. It occurs as the first element of a number of names likely to have been in use before the Norse settlements. These include Moston near Middlewich CHE, Moston S.E. of Wem SHR, Moston near Manchester LNC, and Moseley YOW. The last place is in the township of Moss, and here the meaning must be 'bog'. Mostyn in Whitford FLI is another *mos-tūn*. Further south there are two simplex names apparently derived from *mos*: Mose near Quatford SHR, and Moze ESX, in the marshes opposite the Naze. There are some compound names in southern England which may contain *mos*— Muswell Hill GTL is perhaps the likeliest—but none has been noted in which a meaning 'marsh' (as opposed to 'moss') seems clearly indicated.

If *mos* in the sense 'bog' is an OE usage, it might be worth considering whether its continuous use in the area N. from STF and SHR is due to geological factors. There were a number of words available for marshes besides this one, and the addition of *mos* to the words in use in the N.W. midlands may indicate that the marshes there had different vegetation from the marshes further south. Mose near Quatford SHR is a special geological area and the factors which have led to the place being mentioned in geological textbooks may have had some influence on the vegetation in Anglo-Saxon times.

As a final element *mos* or ON *mosi* occurs in the names of bogs in LNC, such as Chat Moss and Rathmoss. As a first element it occurs with ON terms in Mosedale CMB, Mosser CMB, Mozergh WML.

mýrr ON 'swamp' is the source of ME and modern *mire*. It occurs mainly in minor names, most of them probably of ME origin. It is the first element of Myerscough LNC, and there was another instance of this compound in IOM, where it was the ON name for the marsh now called The Curraghs. *mýrr* is used as an affix in Ainderby Mires YON.

slæp OE 'slippery place' occurs in some minor names, such as Sleap in Myddle and Sleap in Crudgington SHR; and *Slepe* was the former name of St Ives HNT. As a first element it occurs in Slapton BUC, DEV, NTP, and as a final element in Hanslope BUC, Islip NTP, OXF. In spite of their identical modern forms the last two have different river-names, *Ise* and *Ight*, as first elements. Smith 1956 and Ekwall 1960 give *slæp* as the second element of Postlip GLO and Ruislip GTL; but another, equally likely, explanation is that they contain *hlēp*, *hlīepe* 'leaping place'.

The nature of the *slæp* at each of the settlements listed could probably be discovered by local investigation. At Slapton NTP the church and manor house occupy a knoll, with the village lying between the knoll and the R. Tove. A spring rises near the church, and the water from this must have made the tracks up the hill from the village very treacherous. *slæp* is not certain to have been used of marshes.

slōh OE 'slough'. This word is fairly well evidenced in minor names and field-names in counties as far north as BDF and CAM. It is the source of Slough BUC, and occurs uncompounded also in minor names in BDF, ESX, SSX and SUR. Smith 1956 cites a number of names in which it is the second element, but only one of these, Polsloe DEV, achieved sufficient status to be listed in Ekwall 1960. The growth of a major settlement at Slough BUC was presumably due to economic factors which overrode the unpromising nature of the site.

Slaughter GLO is generally agreed to derive from an unrecorded OE word **slōhtre**, which is related to *slōh*. The term occurs also in some minor names in SSX and SUR (*Slaughters* in Billingshurst, Slaughter Bridge in Slinfold, Slaughterford Fm in Itchingfield, Slaughterbridge Fm in Shipley SSX, and Slaughterwicks Barn in Charlwood SUR). Ekwall 1960 proposes 'muddy place' for the GLO name, but the EPNS survey (1, p. 207) is not altogether happy with this. Löfvenberg 1942 (pp. 190–1) suggests such senses as 'ravine', '(deep) river-valley', 'watercourse running in a (deep) hollow', 'ditch', on the grounds that these would accord with the use of related words in other Germanic languages.

Slaughterford WLT has spellings which suggest derivation from OE *slāh-thorn* 'sloe-thorn', but Smith 1956 (2, p. 128) is probably mistaken in suggesting that *slāh-trēow*, another term for the blackthorn, would suit the SSX names.

soc OE 'suck' is considered to be used as a term for a marsh in Sock Dennis and Old Sock SOM. Sockbridge WML, in which *–bridge* is a late substitution for *–bred*, probably means 'marsh board', referring to a footbridge or causeway over marshy land. Most instances of Soke, Soken, Socon in place-names derive, however, from OE *sōcn*, ME *soke* 'district over which special rights of jurisdiction were exercised'.

sol OE 'muddy place, wallowing place for animals' occurs uncompounded in Soles KNT, and there was a lost hamlet of *Solum* near Solway Moss CMB which derived its name from the dat. pl. Bradsole KNT and Grazeley BRK have the word as second element. *sol* is not limited to the south of England, but it is most common in minor names in KNT. Professor A Everitt informs me that in KNT the element occurs mainly in the Downland, with a few instances on the Chart. It is absent from the Weald, the Gault and Blean Forest. He suggests that *sol* sometimes refers to a pool constructed for watering stock.

strōd OE, generally rendered 'marshy land overgrown with brushwood', is only recorded in charter-boundaries and OE place-name spellings, and the sense is inferred from that of Germanic cognates. It occurs fairly frequently in the south of England as a simplex name. Strood KNT and Stroud GLO have become major settlements, but most instances are farms or hamlets. Stroud Green occurs in several southern counties. Strode is another modern form.

In Bulstrode (near Gerrards Cross) BUC *strōd* is compounded with **burh**, referring to the large hill-fort E. of Bulstrode Park. It is doubtful whether 'marsh' is applicable here, and it is certainly inappropriate to the hamlet of Bulstrode (first element 'bull') in King's Langley HRT. Possibly *strōd* designates a type of vegetation not always associated with marsh.

In counties to the north and west of CAM/HNT *strōd* is very rare, possibly absent, but it occurs in two names, identical in meaning, in the north country—Langstroth YOW and Long Strath (near Keswick) CMB. In the early spellings for Langstroth there is interchange between *strōd* and *strōther*, which is a derivative. *strōther* is found occasionally in minor names in the north (e.g. Haughstrother E. of Haltwhistle NTB).

The cognate ON word, **storth**, which occurs in some names in the east midlands and the north (e.g. Dalestorth in Mansfield NTT, Storth N.E. of Arnside CMB, Storrs E. of Carnforth LNC) is rendered 'brushwood', and is not considered to have any connotation of marsh. Storiths N.E. of Skipton YOW is translated 'the plantations' in EPNS survey 5 (p. 74).

wæsse OE? 'land by a meandering river which floods and drains quickly'. This is not the accepted definition of *wæsse*: previous reference books give 'swamp'. The word is only known from place-names. The translation suggested here is based on the situation of the seven west midland names which certainly contain *wæsse*, and a chance observation of the nature of the flooding at Buildwas SHR in a recent wet December. The west midland names are Alrewas STF, Bolas SHR, Broadwas WOR, Buildwas SHR, Hopwas STF, Rotherwas (immediately E. of Hereford) HRE, and Sugwas HRE. It is not always possible to distinguish with certainty between *wæsse* and some other words. OE *gewæsc* 'washing, flood' occurs in The Wash LIN/NFK and probably in Strangeways LNC and R. Wash RUT/LEI/LIN. OE *wæsce* 'place for washing (of sheep or clothes)' is the likeliest first element of Washbourne DEV, Washbrook SFK, Washfield and Washford DEV. For the seven west midland names listed above, however, the early spellings indicate OE *wæsse* as second element, and since these comprise the bulk of the material the nature of the sites should be considered for its bearing on the meaning of the term.

Alrewas STF is on the R. Trent, near where the Tame and the Mease flow into it, and Hopwas STF is on the R. Tame. Buildwas SHR is on the Severn. Bolas SHR is at the junction of the R. Meese with the R. Tern. Broadwas WOR is on the R. Teme, and Sugwas and Rotherwas HRE are on the R. Wye. The first point to be noted is that in these three counties major names in *–wæsse* occur only on major rivers or on their larger tributaries. Alrewas, Broadwas, Buildwas, Rotherwas and Sugwas are by meandering stretches of river. Hopwas is by a right-angle bend in the R. Tame.

Buildwas SHR overlooks a flat area through which the R. Severn meanders, and at midday one Saturday in December 1976 this area was a broad lake, but by Sunday afternoon the river had returned to its bed and cattle were grazing on the recently flooded meadows. It was as if a plug had been pulled out. Possibly a temporary ponding back had been caused by the constriction of the river in the Ironbridge Gorge, a few miles downstream. Broadwas and Sugwas are also upstream from relatively confined stretches of river-valley, though these are much less dramatic features than the Ironbridge Gorge.

Alrewas STF and Bolas SHR occupy similar situations to each other. Both are at major river-junctions, and it is possible that in times of flood the main rivers (Trent and Tern respectively) were temporarily unable to accommodate the contributions of the tributaries. Hopwas STF is a few miles down the Tame from Alrewas, and might also be affected by the flooding of the Trent. I am told that at Alrewas floods appear and disappear very quickly, as at Buildwas.

Outside these three counties *wæsse* is very rare in major place-names. The only certain instances noted are Allerwash NTB and Alderwasley DRB, which repeat the compound with 'alder' found in Alrewas STF. The situation of Allerwash, on the R. Tyne W. of Hexham, is very like that of Buildwas SHR. Alderwasley doubtless refers to a *wæsse* on the R. Derwent. In Wasperton WAR, which lies in a meander of the R. Avon, *wæsse* has been prefixed to a name meaning 'pear orchard'.

There are a few minor names. A lost *Arnewas* HNT was in Sibson cum Stibbington parish, where the R. Nene makes a great loop. Washbourne GLO is *Wassanburna* in charters, and may have the genitive of *wæsse* as first element. The **burna** is a small meandering stream which joins the Carrant Brook at Beckford. If this is a *wæsse*, it is a miniature version of the phenomenon, and another such may be *pirewasse* on Pur Brook STF, a boundary mark in a charter of AD 951 relating to Marchington. Yet another *wæsse* by a small stream is referred to in the first element of Westley in Condover SHR.

Ekwall 1960 gives *wæsse* as the source of Wass, W. of Ampleforth, YON, but this name, which is first recorded in 1541, is considered by Smith (1956 2, p. 230) to be probably the plural of **vath** 'ford'. Washingley HNT, also considered in Ekwall 1960 to contain *wæsse*, is perhaps more likely to contain a personal name *Wassa*. In the EPNS survey of BRK (3, p. 117) I suggested that *wassan hamme* in the bounds of Waltham BRK meant 'meadow of the *wæsse*', but now that the material has been assembled it appears that *wæsse* is an Anglian term, so not likely to occur in BRK; the personal name *Wassa* would suit this boundary-mark also.

wagen OE 'quaking bog' was conjectured in Ekwall 1928 as the source of Wawne YOE, and the first element of the river-name Waveney SFK/NFK. A related word is considered to be compounded with **fenn** in Warne DEV (*Wagefen* 1194).

wemm OE 'filth' is the source of Wem SHR. Ekwall 1960 says 'The meaning would be marshy ground'; but Smith 1956 says 'There is no evidence for the meaning "marshy place" sometimes proposed.' Ekwall's opinion is the more convincing. Much of the very large parish of Wem is marshy. The Wems occurs as a farm-name near Adderley SHR, about 12 miles N.E. of Wem, also in wet ground; this has not yet been traced back further than the 1st edition 1″ map and the Tithe Award of 1840, but it is likely to be an ancient name. There is a single instance of Wem in CHE as a 19th-century field-name in Great Warford.

The minor name Whempstead, N.E. of Watton-at-Stone HRT, appears to be the only other settlement-name besides Wem SHR which is likely to contain *wemm*. A meaning 'marsh' is not suitable in this instance.

Adel YOW derives from OE *adela*, which also means 'filth'.

3

River-crossings and Landing-places,
Roads and Tracks

The preceding chapters have shown that water and marsh are frequently mentioned as the dominant factors in settlement-sites; and it is natural that settlement-names should also make many references to the fords, bridges and causeways by which such places were linked to their neighbours. Major settlement-names in –ford do not appear to have been counted previously; they are more frequent than I had realized, and the word may be presumed to have had a quasi-habitative sense in place-names. This ubiquitous term must have been applied to many types of river-crossing. There is less variety here than is usual in topographical place-names, and this may be why descriptive terms are by far the largest category of first elements in compound names in –ford. It is possible that **ford** ousted a number of other terms which conveyed more precise information about the nature of the crossing. The rare words **fær** and **gelād** were probably specialized, but it is very difficult to discern their meaning from the evidence now available. Readers with local knowledge may be able to add to the discussions of these terms. Another rare word for a ford, **gewæd**, may be a very early term.

In the discussion of the Celtic term **ritu–** it is a pleasure to be able to bring before a wider public Richard Coates's clever solution of the name Leatherhead. Only a few surviving names contain the Primitive Welsh word for a ford, but many of the crossings denoted by the English word must have been well established in prehistoric times. Those used by Roman roads are commemorated in the Startforth/Stratford/Strefford/Stretford/Trafford names.

In addition to being obstacles for crossing, rivers were highways and trade routes, and considerable interest attaches to place-names which refer to landing-places. The assembling of major names containing **hȳth** was a rewarding exercise, bringing out the two main concentrations, on the R. Thames, and in the Fens, where Aldreth, Swavesey, Earith, Clayhithe, Lakenheath and Methwold Hythe lie at the junction of marsh with firm ground. Such names are rare enough to suggest that a **hȳth** was a noteworthy feature, perhaps an inland port, and this is of some significance for regional history. Names in which ON **stoth** can be positively identified and distinguished from OE **stæth** may indicate new or increased trading activity after the Viking settlements.

It has seemed convenient to consider settlement-names which refer to roads together with those referring to river-crossings and landing-places. Here again there is scope for further investigation by people with local knowledge. It is not at all clear why Broadway WOR should have its distinctive name, or why Morpeth NTB, which is now a notable river-crossing place, should be named from one of the roads which converge there. A reasonable assumption about Morpeth would be that the development of the region was relatively late and that the name, which sounds like that of an isolated hamlet, was conferred when conditions were still wild.

A new proposal is made in this chapter concerning the significance of the place-name Anstey/Ansty/Anstie.

ānstiga or **ānstīg** OE is a compound of *ān* 'one' and *stīg* 'path'. It is the source of seven major settlement-names and at least three minor names, and is the name of a wapentake meeting-place. Smith 1956 (1, p. 12) and Ekwall 1960 (p. 10) interpret *ānstiga* as 'single-file path' and regard it as a term for a narrow footpath up a steep hill. Study of the situations of all the places listed by both authorities, however, reveals that 'single-file path up a hill' is only really suitable for one example, and is not admissible at all for some others; so a different interpretation is offered here. The word only occurs once in literary OE, in a gloss which equates it, obscurely, with *fæsten* 'fortress' and with the Greek name Thermopylae.

The major names from *ānstiga* are Anstey DEV, HMP, HRT, LEI, and Ansty DOR, WAR, WLT. The minor names are Anstie Grange S. of Dorking SUR, Ayngstree Fm in Clifton upon Teme WOR and Ansty S.W. of Cuckfield SSX. Ansley WAR may be a compound of *lēah*.

E. and W. Anstey DEV are adjoining parishes near the SOM border. The parishes are separated by a small stream, and the villages lie below the summits of two separate hills. It is difficult to say which road the name refers to. There are N./S. roads through both villages, and as both roads have a similar character it is possible that both were called *ānstiga*. On the other hand, the O.S. map shows traces of an E./W. route, in part a footpath, which crosses the stream and connects the villages. All these routes make steep ascents, and this is the site best suited to the accepted definition of *ānstiga*.

Anstey HMP adjoins Alton in the E. of the county. Anstey Manor lies on rising ground in the valley of the R. Wey, and there is downland behind it, but the slopes are gentle, and a number of parallel tracks run up them from the river. The application of the name to this settlement is very difficult to explain.

Anstey HRT (S.E. of Royston) is on a road just over half-a-mile long which runs between two low hills. The road forks at the N. and S. ends of the village.

Anstey LEI lies in the valley of Rothley Brook, N.W. of Leicester. There is no question of a steep ascent. The main street is a quarter of a mile long, forking at the E. and W. ends.

Higher and Lower Ansty DOR lie on either side of a road junction called Ansty Cross. Here (1″ map 178, G.R. 770036) a short length of road runs E./W. across a col, forking at either end.

At Ansty WAR, N.E. of Coventry, the Hall is on the tip of a low hill-spur. There is a single road across the spur, forking at either end.

Ansty WLT, N. of Cranborne Chase, lies at the head of a small valley. The access road from the N. ascends the valley, but it is neither steep nor narrow. It does, however, like the last four roads described, fork into divergent routes at either end of the village.

On the evidence of the sites of at least 5 places examined above, it can be suggested that in place-names an *ānstiga* is a short stretch of road used by at least four roads which converge on it at either end. The use of **stīg** rather than one of the other OE terms for a road in this compound appellative suggests that some climbing is involved, or at least that the convergence of routes into a short stretch of single track is due to some obstacle; but the topography of the sites does not support the view that the road had to be a narrow one or that traffic had to go in single file, and some of the ascents which have to be made are gentle ones.

Smith lists two minor names, Anstie Grange S. of Dorking SUR and Ayngstree Fm in Clifton upon Teme WOR. His discussion of Anstie Grange implies that this is a 'stronghold' name, connected with the nearby hill-fort called Anstiebury Camp. About a quarter of a mile S. of Anstie Grange, however, there is an excellent example of the type of short road forking at both ends which is described above. Ayngstree Fm in Clifton upon Teme stands on a stretch of ridgeway upon which a number of tracks converge from S. and N., but the distance between the road junctions is greater than it is in the other roads instanced. Another minor name, not listed by Smith, is Ansty S.W. of Cuckfield SSX, and this is a perfect specimen. The hamlet lies on a quarter-mile stretch of road which forks into two roads at the S. end and three at the N. end.

The final example which requires discussion is Ainsty Cliff in Bilbrough YOW, which was the meeting-place of Ainsty Wapentake. This is probably a Scandinavianized form of OE *ānstiga*. EPNS survey 4 (p. 235) says that the road referred to was 'a small narrow lane leading from Steeton Fm over Ainsty Cliff (1″ O.S. 97 – 528460) on into Bilbrough'; but in spite of the name Ainsty Cliff the region is low-lying, with 50′ and 100′ contours widely spaced, and it is not apparent why a road or path here should have been a single-file one. Easy access is a usual feature in hundred and wapentake meeting-places, and there may have been a network of ancient tracks here which joined for a short stretch.

There are a few instances of *ānstiga* in charter boundaries; these have not been studied.

brycg OE 'bridge' occurs in about 60 major place-names. No instances occur among names recorded by c. 730 (Cox 1976), and probably most of the bridges were built to supplement the fords which were of major importance in the early years of the Anglo-Saxon kingdoms. In one instance a change of name from

–ford to –bridge is documented: for Redbridge HMP, Ekwall 1960 gives the following forms: *Hreutford* c. 730, *Hreodford* c. 890, *Hreodbrycg* c. 956. Brigg LIN was earlier Glanford Brigg, and the river-crossing at Stourbridge WOR was earlier called *Swinford*.

brycg was occasionally considered adequate as a simplex name, as in Bridge KNT, and in the earliest forms of Bridgenorth SHR, Bridgerule DEV, Bridge Sollers HRE, Bridgewater SOM (the last three of which had a personal name or surname added in the medieval period). Handbridge CHE and Swimbridge DEV were simplex names in DB, but had prefixes added later. In Swimbridge the prefixed personal name (*Sǣwine*) is that of the pre-Conquest tenant of the manor. Handbridge has as prefix ME *hōne* 'rock', alluding to the outcrop of sandstone on which the hamlet stands.

brycg occurs as the first element of some compound names, as Breighton YOE, Bridgford NTT, STF, Bridgehampton SOM, Brighouse YOW, Brigsley LIN, Brigstock NTP, Bristol GLO, Brushford DEV, SOM. Brig– in some of these is due to ON influence. Bridgham NFK and Brigham CMB, YOE must refer to early bridges, as **hām** was probably not used to form place-names later than AD 800. It might be more satisfactory to consider these names as referring to Roman bridges. Bridgham is on the R. Thet, between two Roman roads, and not too far from the crossing of the Peddar's Way to have been named from a bridge there. Brigham (near Cockermouth) CMB is not far from the supposed Roman road running from Papcastle to Egremont. Brigham YOE is on the R. Hull, in a region where only short stretches of Roman road have been identified, and the pattern cannot be reconstructed. The existence of a bridge, whether Roman or Anglo-Saxon, at these places sufficiently early for the bridge to be considered the distinguishing feature of a **hām** deserves note by the local historian.

The first elements of compound names in *–brycg* show a fairly even spread over a number of categories. The largest is that which refers to the material or the method of construction. Here belong Elbridge KNT, Rumbridge HMP, Stalbridge DOR, Stambridge ESX, Stanbridge BDF, HMP, Trowbridge WLT, and possibly Budbridge IOW and Woodbridge SFK. Additions can be made to this list from minor names, e.g. Bow Bridge IOW(2), Drockbridge HMP, Trobridge DEV, Trussel Bridge CNW, Turn Bridge YOW. There are several names in which ON *fjǫl* 'board, plank' is combined with OE *brycg*; these include Felbrigg NFK, Fell Beck Bridge (earlier *Felebrigbec*) YOW, Fell Briggs YON.

Personal names are the first elements of Abridge ESX, Attlebridge NFK, Curbridge OXF, Dudbridge GLO, Edenbridge KNT, and possibly Harbridge HMP. The river-name is used in Axbridge SOM, Cambridge CAM, Doveridge DRB and Weybridge SUR, and the name of a Roman fort in Corbridge NTB. Vegetation is referred to in Brambridge HMP, Ivybridge DEV, Piercebridge DRH, Redbridge HMP and Sawbridge WAR. Domestic animals are mentioned in Bulbridge WLT, Cowbridge ESX and WLT, and the SSX hundred-name Rotherbridge (from which the R. Rother is a back formation). Gad Bridge in Bray BRK means 'goats' bridge'. The only reference noted to wild creatures is Beobridge SHR. A feature of the topography or the soil is mentioned in Fambridge ESX, Felbridge SUR, Heronbridge (S. of Chester) CHE, Hubbridge ESX, Slimbridge GLO, Wombridge SHR. Categories of people are referred to in Groombridge KNT, Isombridge SHR, Kingsbridge DEV, Knightsbridge GTL, Uxbridge GTL; and Fordingbridge HMP has as first element an –**ingas** formation from an earlier place-name *Ford*.

Eastbridge KNT means what it says. Horrabridge DEV and Harrowbridge CNW are 'boundary bridge'. Bembridge IOW means '(place) within the bridge'; it occupies a peninsula which formerly could only be reached by boat or across a bridge. Highbridge SOM and Heybridge (near Maldon) ESX contain 'high', which may be used here, as in High Street, to mean 'most important'. The first elements of Pembridge HRE and Tonbridge KNT are uncertain.

There are a few names in which *brycg* means 'causeway'. Slimbridge GLO may be one of these, and it is certainly the sense in Bridgend LIN, which is at the end of a causeway across the Fens. There was probably a compound appellative *hrīsbrycg*, 'brushwood causeway', which occurs in minor names in ESX (Risebridge in Romford Rural, Rice Bridge in Little Clacton), SSX (Rice Bridge in Bolney), SUR (Ridgebridge Hill in Wonersh, Ricebridge Fm in Reigate), DRH (Risebridge near Durham), YOW (Risebrigg Hill in Martons Both), NTT (Roy's Bridge Lane in Rufford), and in field-names in various counties. Risingbridge in Geddington NTP contains an adjective *hrīsen* 'made of brushwood'.

Smith 1956 (I, p. 54) cites Bracebridge LIN as an example of the sense 'causeway', but as Bracebridge is the point where the Foss Way crosses the R. Witham before turning north into Lincoln it seems more likely that the name refers to a bridge over the river. Smith was possibly influenced by the suggestion in Ekwall 1960 that the first element is an OE word which lies behind modern dialect *brash* 'small branches, twigs'. The type of causeway envisaged is not, however, appropriate to the Foss Way. The first element of Bracebridge should be regarded as obscure for the time being.

The cognate ON **bryggja** means 'jetty, quay', not 'bridge'. This occurs in Brig Stones near Braystones CMB and Filey Brigg YOE.

fær OE 'passage' (probably 'difficult passage') occurs in Denver NFK, Laver ESX, and the minor name Walter Hall in Boreham ESX. The word probably went out of use as a place-name-forming term at a very early date, and it is unlikely to be found in areas of late English settlement. It has been supposed to occur in Hollinfare in Warrington LNC, but see the discussion under **ferja** for an alternative suggestion. For the same reason it is not likely to occur in Farway DEV (discussed under **weg**).

Denver NFK is on the E. bank of the R. Ouse, near the southern limit of the great fen which lies to the W. of the river. There is a Roman road from Peterborough which runs past Denver and on towards the E. coast. The first element of Denver must refer to traffic from Denmark much earlier than the Viking invasions.

Laver (High, Little and Magdalen) ESX is from OE *lagu-fær* 'water passage'. The places are situated by the Roman road from London to Great Dunmow, at a point where its course has disappeared for about two miles, perhaps because the ground was marshy. Another village in the gap is called Moreton. Denver and Laver may contain *fær* used in somewhat the same way as the Norman French *malpas* in Malpas CHE and a number of minor names in England and Wales.

Walter Hall in Boreham ESX is *Walhfare* in its earliest reference. The Roman road from Chelmsford to Colchester must have been known in this stretch as 'Welsh passage'. It crosses a small stream within the district to which the name applied.

ferja ON, **ferrye** ME, 'ferry' occurs in Ferriby LIN, YOE, Ferrybridge YOW, and Kinnard's Ferry LIN. It is occasionally used as an affix, as in Ferry Fryston YOW, Stoke Ferry NFK. Hollinfare in Warrington LNC is *Le Fery del Holyns* 1352, *Holynfeyr'* 1504, *Helingfare* 1550, *Hollynfayre* 1556. In this name there has probably been confusion of *ferry* with *fare* 'excursion for which a price is paid'. It is not likely that OE **fær** survived long enough as a place-name-forming term to be used in LNC.

ford OE 'ford'. This is probably the most frequently used topographical term in English place-names, apart from **lēah**. It enters into about 550 names in Ekwall 1960. There are 9 examples among names recorded by AD 730 (Cox 1976); 5 of these refer to settlements, 2 refer only to river-crossings, and the remaining 2 are ambiguous in this respect.

Some places with *–ford* names have become towns or cities, such as Bedford, Bradford, Chelmsford, Dartford, Guildford, Hereford, Hertford, Knutsford, Oxford, Stafford, Stratford-upon-Avon, Watford; but these are only a small proportion of the whole corpus, and this should be borne in mind when their meaning and historical significance is discussed. No attempt has been made at a geographical study of all settlement-names in *ford*, but even without this it is clear that the majority of them must have referred to river-crossings of local, rather than national, importance. Where they cluster thickly, as for instance in the Thames Valley west of Oxford, some of the crossings, like Oxford, Frilford, Garford, Wallingford, are on long-distance medieval routes, but most, like Duxford, Shellingford, Stanford, Hatford, Appleford, south of the Thames, and Shifford and Yelford north of the river, can only reflect routes by which villagers communicated with their neighbours. It is likely that most *–ford* names arose in the latter context, and that the patterns of travel and transport which caused some of the places to become military, trading and administrative centres emerged later than the coining of the names, and their application to the settlements near the fords. This consideration may affect the interpretation of some names, particularly Oxford.

Ford occurs by itself as a major name in DOR, HRE, NTB, SHR, SOM, SSX, and other instances occur as minor names. As a first element *ford* is found in Forcett YON, Fordham CAM, ESX, NFK, Fordley SFK, Fordwich KNT, Forton HMP, LNC, SHR, STF, Furtho NTP; but the characteristic use is as the second element of a compound.

Analysis of the first elements in the compound names in –*ford* in Ekwall 1960 reveals a marked bias towards certain categories of qualifying terms. Much the largest category consists of words which describe the ford. There are about 150 names in this class. The two classes which are next in order of size are that containing personal names, and that containing references to topographical features. There are about 70 names which mean 'x's ford'; and if references to roads are counted with references to topographical features such as hills, valleys, stream-junctions and springs, this yields another category with about 70 examples. The total of this last category would be reduced by about 20 if the 'road' names were separately classified. These three categories will be discussed first, as they contain over half of the material.

The compounds in which the first element is an adjective or noun describing the ford are too numerous for all to be listed. The following first elements recur:

'broad' Bradford CHE, DEV, DOR(3), LNC, NTB(2), SOM, WLT, YOW(2); Bradiford DEV; Broadward HRE, SHR, Brafferton YON.
'hidden' (OE *derne*) Darnford SFK, Dornford OXF, Durnford WLT
'deep' Defford WOR, Deptford GTL, WLT, Diptford DEV
'foul' Fulford DEV, SOM, STF, YOE (there is one Fairford, in GLO)
'long' Langford BDF, DEV, ESX, NFK, OXF, SOM(2), WLT; Longford DRB, GLO, HRE, MDX, SHR, WLT
'red' Radford DEV, NTT(2), WAR(2), WOR(2); Retford NTT (there are two Blackfords in SOM, a Blackfordby in LEI, a Greenford in GTL, and a Whitford in DEV)
'rough' Rufford LNC, NTT; Rufforth YOW
'shallow' Scalford LEI, Shadforth DRH
'bright' (OE *scīr*) Shereford NFK, Sherford DEV(2), SOM
'double' Twyford BUC, BRK, DRB, HMP, LEI, LIN, MDX, NFK

The nature of the ground is referred to in Girtford BDF, Greatford LIN ('gravel'), Mudford SOM ('mud'), Sampford DEV(3), ESX, SOM(2), Sandford BRK, DEV, DOR, OXF(2), SHR, WML ('sand'), Stafford DOR, Stainforth YOW(2), Stamford LIN, NTB, YOE, Stamfordham NFK, Stanford (12 examples), Stoford SOM(2), WLT, Stowford DEV(3), OXF, WLT ('stone'). Chillesford SFK also refers to gravel, and Chingford ESX to shingle. There may be an oblique reference to the nature of the ground in Hungerford BRK and the identical minor name in Munslow SHR.

The meaning of Longford/Langford probably varies, and local investigation would be needed to determine the appropriate sense in each instance. Some may refer to an oblique river-crossing, but the name would also be an appropriate description of a crossing which required a causeway for an approach. Longford N. of Gloucester looks like a causeway over land traversed by several streams. Twyford usually refers to a place where the road has to cross two streams in rapid succession.

Some –*ford* names refer to the use of planks or posts to improve or mark the crossing. Bretford WAR and Bretforton WOR refer to the use of planks, and Bamford DRB, LNC to the use of a tree-trunk. Flawforth NTT had flag-stones. At Stapleford CAM, CHE, ESX, HRT, LEI, LIN, NTT, WLT, posts were used, either for marking, or in some feature of construction. Stocking-ford WAR and Treyford SSX may belong in this class.

Another type of descriptive first element is that which implies comparison with other fords. Here belong Aldford CHE, Offord HNT, Orford LNC and Somerford CHE, GLO, WLT.

As regards the second large category, consisting of about 70 names which mean 'x's ford', it may be noted that this includes Bedford and a few other towns, such as Chelmsford ESX, but most of the examples refer to places of local rather than regional importance. Frilford BRK, however, is noteworthy as a name of this type applied to a settlement which had been of special importance in the Romano-British period. In Knutsford CHE and Snarford LIN *ford* is compounded with ON personal names.

The remaining compounds of *ford* with OE personal names are too numerous for all to be listed. Analysis of the personal names reveals that only 2 are feminine (*Ēadburh* in Aberford YOW and *Ealdgȳth* in Alford SOM). There are 12 dithematic names (e.g. *Ealhmund* in Ansford SOM, *Cēolmǣr* in Chelmsford ESX, *Wihtlāc* in Wixford WAR, *Cynemǣr* in Quemerford WLT). The remainder are mostly monothematic (e.g. *Bēda* or *Bīeda* in Bedford BDF, LNC, *Ceolla* in Chelford CHE, *Dodda* in Dodford NTP, WOR, *Mūl* in Moulsford BRK, *Otta*, in Otford KNT, *Sibba* in Sibford OXF), with a fair proportion of hypocoristic formations (e.g. *Duduc* in Duxford BRK, *Fitela* in Fiddleford DOR, *Haneca* in Hankford DEV, *Wittel* in Whittlesford CAM). A few, such as *Ǣgen* in Eynsford KNT and *Hroppa* in Rofford OXF, may be short forms of dithematic names.

Since individuals cannot have owned fords without owning the estates on which they were situated, the relatively large number of compounds with personal names probably indicates that *ford* had a quasi-habitative sense and was understood to mean 'settlement near a ford'.

Topographical features used to define a ford include cliffs (Clifford GLO, HRE, YOW), hills (Backford CHE, Peckforton CHE), valleys or hollows

(Halford DEV, WAR), stream-junctions (Meaford STF, Midford SOM, Mitford NTB) and woods (Ashford KNT, Barrasford NTB, Barrowford LNC, Woodford CHE(2), CNW, ESX, NTP(2), WLT). References to springs are fairly common, as in Walford HRE, (near Leintwardine), SHR, Welford-on-Avon GLO, Welford NTP, and Wansford NTP. Dishforth YON, Ditchford NTP, WAR refer to ditches. Hatford BRK is 'ford by a headland' referring to a river-terrace. Garford BRK and Garforth YOW contain *gāra* 'gore', perhaps used of a wedge of dry ground. Ludford SHR refers to a rapid in the R. Teme. Wonford DEV is 'meadow ford'. Byford HRE is included in this category because the outline of the parish boundary appears to be following an old, very sharply curving, course of the R. Wye; Ekwall 1960 rejects derivation from *byge* 'bend' on the grounds that it does not suit the present river-course.

The fords which are named from the roads on which they occur are Harpford DEV, SOM, Startforth YON, Stratford (12 examples), Strefford SHR, Stretford HRE, LNC, Trafford LNC, Stifford ESX, Styford NTB and Wayford SOM.

After these three categories, the next largest consists of words for vegetation. There are 45 names in which *ford* is qualified by such terms. Plants and trees which are mentioned more than once are 'alder' (Alderford NFK, Allerford SOM(2), Alresford HMP), 'apple' (Appleford BRK, IOW), 'ash' (Ashford DEV(2), DRB, SHR, Axford WLT, Ayshford DEV), 'burdock' (Clatford HMP, WLT, Cloford SOM), 'oak' (Oakford DEV, Okeford DOR), 'willow' (Salford BDF, LNC, Welford BRK, Widford ESX, HRT, OXF, Wilford NTT, SFK, Wytheford SHR), and 'wych-elm' (Wichenford WOR, Wishford WLT, Witchford CAM). Slaughterford WLT contains OE *slǣhthorn* 'blackthorn'. Guildford SUR is stated in previous reference books to refer to golden flowers, but F G Mellersh in EPNS *Journal* 2 (p. 38) locates the ford to the S. of the present bridge and says there is rich golden sand there, so Guildford belongs in the first category of *ford* compounds.

A fairly large category of *–ford* names refers to types of people. There are 8 *–inga–* compounds: Billingford (near E. Dereham) NFK, Hemingford HNT, Horringford IOW, Kingsford (N.W. of Kidderminster) WOR, Manningford WLT, Shellingford BRK, Sleningford YOW, Wallingford BRK; and Marlingford NFK may be another. Two names refer to brides (Birdforth YON, Bridford DEV) and one to maidens (Maidford NTP). Two names refer to kings (Conisford NFK, using the ON word, and Kingsford WAR), and one to thegns (Thenford NTP). Coppingford HNT refers to traders, Huntingford DOR, GLO to huntsmen, Halford SHR to hawkers. Lattiford SOM refers to beggars, Poundisford SOM to a pinder, Thursford NFK apparently to a giant. Racial origin is mentioned in Orford LIN (Irishmen), Scotforth LNC, Walford near Ross HRE, Walshford YOW and Comberford STF. Whichford WAR was near the boundary of the *Hwicce*. Salterford NTT and Salterforth YOW refer to salters. Thetford CAM, NFK and Tetford LIN are 'people' ford (OE *thēod*), perhaps a way of indicating their special importance. Harford (N.

of Ivybridge) DEV, Hartford HNT, Hereford HRE(2), and the first part of Harvington near Evesham WOR mean 'army ford'. It has sometimes been assumed that this is a shortened version of *herepæth-ford* (the source of Harpford DEV, SOM), but Hartford HNT is outside the area in which *herepæth* is used of main roads. Possibly an 'army ford' was one wide enough for an army to cross in broad ranks, a consideration of some strategic importance.

Animals, birds and fish are mentioned less frequently than might have been expected in the compound names in *-ford* in Ekwall 1960. Wild creatures are referred to in about 25 examples, and domestic animals or birds in about 21. Wild creatures occur in Beaford DEV, Beeford YOE, Blandford DOR, Boresford HRE, Buntingford HRT, Carnforth LNC, Cornforth DRH, Cranford MDX, NTP, Cransford SFK, Catford GTL, Catforth LNC, Durford SSX, Enford WLT, Harford GLO, Hartford CHE, NTB, Hartforth YON, Hertford HRT, Lostford SHR, Stinsford DOR, Taddiford HMP. There are a few others of which the etymologies are less certain. Most of these creatures must have been mentioned because they were frequently seen in the vicinity of the ford.

Domesticated creatures are mentioned in Gateford NTT, Gateforth YOW, Gosford DEV, OXF, WAR, Gosforth CMB, NTB, Horsford NFK, Horsforth YOW, Oxford OXF, Rochford ESX, WOR, Shefford BDF, BRK, Shifford OXF, Swinford BRK, LEI, STF, WOR, Tickford BUC, Warnford HMP; and Handforth CHE and Hanford STF may contain *hana* 'cock', but other etymologies are possible. The birds and animals in this list (goats, geese, horses, oxen, hunting dogs, sheep, swine, kids and stallions) are creatures likely to be herded or led from one place to another, so there is at least a possibility that they regularly crossed the ford, unlike the wild creatures referred to in the last paragraph. Oxford should perhaps be seen as a member of this group of names, rather than accorded special significance as denoting a river-crossing on a major travel route used by oxen-drawn carts (Davis 1973; Professor Davis's location of the ford, near Folly Bridge, is however, wholly convincing). On the other hand one of the noteworthy points brought out by this analysis is that domestic creatures are not often used as the defining characteristic of fords, and the category is probably too small to enable safe conclusions to be drawn as to the likeliest significance of any one example. There are a few comparable names to Oxford among minor names in other counties: these are another Oxenford in Witley (near Godalming) SUR, a lost *Rutherford* in North Huish DEV, Stafford in Ifield SSX and Sturford in Corsley WLT (both containing *stēor* 'steer').

The remaining categories of first elements are all small. Some names refer to goods carried over the ford. Here belong some examples of Barford (probably those in BDF, NFK, NTP, OXF, WLT) and Barforth YON; this means 'barley ford', and Heyford NTP, OXF means 'hay ford'. Salford OXF, WAR, and Saltford SOM are of similar significance to Salterford and Salterforth, already mentioned. Coleford GLO, SOM(3) probably refers to the transport of charcoal. Chalford GLO, OXF(2) is 'chalk ford', probably referring to lime-stone. Only two names have been noted which refer to wheeled traffic, these being Yoxford SFK and Wangford near Thetford SFK (Wangford near Southwold SFK has different early spellings and is thought to contain OE *wang* 'open ground', but the compound with *wægn* 'waggon' occurs again in a minor name, Wainforth Wood near Markington YOW).

Buildings are mentioned in Bottesford LEI, LIN, Castleford YOW, Leeford DEV, Melford SFK, Melverley SHR, Milford DRB, HMP, WLT, YOW(2), Milverton SOM, WAR, Weeford STF, Wyfordby LEI. Burford OXF, SHR means 'ford by a fort'. Wickford ESX and Wigford LIN contain wīc, perhaps with reference to Romano-British settlements. Bridgford NTT, STF and Brushford DEV, SOM are probably 'ford by a foot-bridge'.

A few fords are named from activities which presumably took place in the vicinity. Here belong Glandford NFK, Glanford Brigg LIN, Mutford SFK, Plaitford HMP, Playford SFK, and Watford HRT, NTP. Trafford NTP ('trap ford') can be loosely included in this group. Christian Malford WLT is 'ford near a crucifix', first element OE *cristel-mǣl*.

It is very rare for a ford to be named from a nearby settlement, perhaps because *ford* had a quasi-habitative function in place-names, and was felt to include a reference to the village. Earlier place-names are the first elements in Lintzford DRH, Ludford LIN and Washford SOM. Lintzford means 'ford by Lintz', but the other two are 'ford on the road to Louth/Watchet'. Slaughter-ford GLO, though recorded earlier than Slaughter, probably means 'ford near Slaughter'.

A surprising feature to emerge from this analysis is that there are only about 20 major names in *–ford* in which the first element is the name of the river to be crossed. Certain examples are Blithford STF, Blyford SFK, Brentford GTL, Camelford CNW, Crayford KNT, Dartford KNT, Exford SOM, Har-bourneford DEV, Helford CNW, Ilford SOM, Ilford GTL, Kentford SFK, Lydford DEV, Pontesford SHR, Sidford DEV, Sleaford LIN, Tideford CNW, Warenford NTB. There are a few other possible instances. The rarity of this type of name reinforces the impression, mentioned at the beginning of this discussion, that most settlement-names in *ford* arose in the context of local, rather than regional or national, communications. In such a context travellers would not feel it necessary to comment on the identity of the river or stream they were crossing.

Tempsford BDF, 'Thames ford', presents a difficult problem. Ekwall 1960 suggests 'ford on the road to the Thames (i.e. to London)', but this does not fit the pattern of the mass of *–ford* names. The earlier suggestion, that this part of the Ouse was called Thames in Anglo-Saxon times, is not wholly convincing, either.

There are a number of names, e.g. Dibberford DOR, Duxford CAM, in which modern –ford is a replacement of original **–worth**. In Batsford GLO and Boxford BRK –ford has replaced **–ōra**.

gata ON 'road, street' occurs mainly in street-names in towns in the Danelaw and the north country. It has, however, been used in names of two places which have become major settlements: Galgate LNC and Harrogate YOW, and it is probably the final element of Huggate YOE. Galgate is considered by Ekwall (1922, 1960) to mean 'Galloway road' and to refer to Scottish drovers. Two roads in WML (EPNS survey 1, p. 21) have this meaning. The LNC place is late-recorded, however, (*Gawgett* 1605), and is not certain to have the same derivation as the WML roads. For Harrogate, Smith's EPNS survey (using earlier material than was available to Ekwall) gives the etymology 'road to the cairn'. Holgate, 'road in a hollow', occurs several times as a minor name in YOW.

gelād OE ' ?difficult river-crossing'. *gelād* and **lād** are treated as variants of the same term in Smith 1956 (2, p. 8) and Ekwall 1960 (p. 284); but Ekwall perceived a distinction of sense, *gelād* usually meaning 'passage over a river' and **lād** 'water-course', and this distinction has been followed here, **lād** being discussed with other terms for watercourses in Chapter 1. The small group of major settlement-names which certainly or probably contain *gelād* has seemed more appropriate to this chapter.

The word *gelād* occurs twice in OE poem *Beowulf*: *fen gelad* is listed as one of the desolate places inhabited by the monsters, and *uncuth* ('unknown') *gelad* as one of the grim places traversed by Beowulf on his way to Grendel's mere.

Cricklade, Evenlode, Framilode and Linslade are the only major place-names with early spellings which show unequivocally that *gelād* is the final element. Lechlade and Portslade are probably examples. Shiplate has a site very similar to that of Cricklade, and the OE spelling does not rule out derivation from *gelād*. Two GLO minor names, Abloads Court and Wainlode, probably also belong here.

Aqualate STF is probably not to be included in this group, despite Ekwall 1960 and Smith 1956. The topography is atypical, Ekwall's etymology 'oak-stream' does not fit well with the meanings of the other examples, and the spellings (*Aguilade* 1227, *Akilot* 1275, *Akilote* 1282, *Aquilot* 1327, *Aquilade*, *Aquilone* 14th cent.) show a development to *–lot(e)* which is not found in the other names. Duignan 1902 suggested that Aqualate was a transferred Continental name, like Cause SHR and Montgomery MTG.

For Cricklade WLT there are a number of OE references in which the second element is most frequently spelt *–gelad*. The first element shows a bewildering variety in these pre-Conquest spellings (*Crecca–*, *Creocc–*, *Creac–*, *Creca–*, *Cric–*, *Crac–*, *Croc–*, *Crec–*) and no certain conclusion can be reached about the etymology of this part of the name. There is little doubt that *gelād* here refers to a crossing place on the R. Thames. Cricklade is mentioned in the Anglo-Saxon Chronicle as the place where a Danish army crossed the river in AD 902. It had been fortified shortly before this as part of King Alfred's system of *burhs* for the defence of Wessex. T R Thomson (1978) has suggested that the Rivers Thames and Churn were diverted at the time of the fortification, destroying the original line of Ermine Street, and causing all traffic to make a detour through the *burh* to cross the river at the spot which the *burh* controlled, and to continue via a causeway to Weaver's Bridge where it joined Ermine Street again. The point to notice for the present purpose is that this is a crossing place on a major river in very wet country, where a causeway, more than one bridge, and perhaps (T R Thomson's suggestion) an emergency ferry would need to be established and maintained. There is no way of knowing whether the name Cricklade originally referred to a crossing by Ermine Street on its direct course and was transferred to King Alfred's *burh*, or whether the name was a new one at the date of the fortification.

Evenlode WOR was originally the name of the village, the river being called *Bladene* in OE and ME (Bladon OXF preserves this name, and it is the first element of Bledington GLO). Early spellings make it certain that Evenlode has *gelād* as second element. The road from Addlestrop to Broadwell crosses the R. Evenlode S. of Evenlode village, making a considerable detour to do so, which perhaps indicates that the upper course of the river was not easy to negotiate. It flows in a shallow valley, and the settlements of Evenlode and Addlestrop are clearly sited so as to be above the flood-plain.

Framilode GLO lies beside the Severn estuary, where the R. Frome flows into it, and the first element of the name is Frome. The river-crossing referred to is not necessarily a ferry across the Severn. It may be a crossing which enabled the north-south road to negotiate the outfall of the Frome and continue along the east bank of the estuary. The area is low-lying, and there may have been a number of channels to be crossed.

Lechlade GLO has no OE spellings and is not certain to contain *gelād* as opposed to **lād**. The village is situated at a crossroads, the north-south road of which crosses the R. Leach and the R. Thames. The settlement is much nearer to the Thames, but the first element is the name of the R. Leach. This is a very wet area, and if the meaning is 'river-crossing near the Leach' the name could have referred to a causeway running for some distance on either side of the river. Lechlade is 8 miles N.E. of Cricklade.

Linslade BUC appears in two Anglo-Saxon charters with the spellings *Lhincgelade* (966) and *Hlincgeladæ* (c. 970). The bounds attached to the first charter begin at *Lincgelade* and then go 'along the river to Tiddingford'. The *gelād* is thus shown to have been a precise point on the R. Ouzel on the N. boundary of the parish (the present town of Linslade is of 19th-cent. origin, the old settlement being marked by the church and manor house near this point in the OE boundary). The Ouzel is a meandering river in a shallow valley, and may have been difficult to cross. The first element of Linslade is **hlinc**, which may refer to a steep river-bank.

For Portslade SSX the early spellings do not unequivocally demonstrate *gelād* as second element, but it seems unlikely that this major settlement would be named from either a **lād** or a **slæd**, so it probably belongs in this category.

The first element, *portes*, gen. of *port*, may refer to Romano-British harbour installations. The early topography of this coastline is impossible to estimate for a person with no local knowledge. The road along the old coastline may have required causeways, and there may have been inlets of the sea to cross.

Shiplate SOM is beside the R. Axe, S.E. of Weston super Mare. The earliest reference is in the OE bounds of Bleadon, which run to *Scypeladœs pyll* (or *wyll*) shortly before they reach the Axe. The use of the name Shiplate as first part of a compound could have caused simplification so that the middle element was not written *gelad*. The place does not appear in records again till 1203. The road S. from Shiplate Ho makes what must in early times have been a very difficult crossing of the Axe.

Abloads Court in Sandhurst GLO and Wainlode Ford and Hill in Norton GLO are considered in EPNS survey to refer to crossings of the R. Severn. Abloads (for which the spellings include *Abbilade* 1210, *Abylode* 1267) certainly contains *gelād*. Wainlode has only late spellings (*Weynlodebrugg'* 1378, *Waynelodus Brugge* 1424), so its inclusion in this discussion depends on inference from the topography. The two names could be interpreted as referring to two areas on the E. bank of the Severn where roads leading N. out of Gloucester have to cross very wet areas. This goes better with the meaning of Wainlode ('waggon crossing') than the idea of a ferry across the Severn.

Smith's interpretation in EPNS survey of Framilode, Abloads and Wainlode as referring to ferries over the Severn involves a projection back into OE of the meaning 'ferry' which belongs to the word *lode* along this river in the counties of GLO, WOR and SHR in early Modern English.

The clearest evidence noted for *lode* 'ferry' occurs in some records relating to property at Apley in Stockton SHR. The property included a weir and a ferry. The ferry is mentioned in Latin in an inquisition of 1272–3, and a boat called the *feriboot* is mentioned in 1436. In 1480 the property is described as the weir of Apley and *the loode* with a house and close, and in 1494 the ferry is 'the fery other whyles called the loode of Apley with the were to the same fery or lode belongyng.' Further down the Severn, Hampton and Hampton Loade occur on either side of the river at a point where there is a ferry, and Hampton Loade is first recorded as *Hemptons Lood* in 1594.

Smith 1956 (2, p. 9) suggested that the meaning 'ferry' arose because there were coincidentally ferries at several points on the river where there were names containing *gelād* or **lād**, but in the EPNS survey of GLO he takes the different view that all names by the Severn containing these terms referred originally to river-crossings effected by boat. GLO names by the Severn not already discussed include Lower and Upper Lode S.W. of Tewkesbury (*passagium de Wulmareslode* 1248, *passage de Overlode* 1300), the parish of St Mary de Lode in Gloucester, and a field-name Stanley, earlier *Stanilade*, in Minsterworth. WOR names by the Severn considered to contain **lād** are Clevelode in Powick and Saxon's Lode in Ripple. Both are recorded early, Clevelode in c. 1086 and Saxon's Lode in the 12th cent. Clevelode probably contains **lād**, but the spellings do not rule out *gelād*. Saxon's Lode may be a corruption of a name which originally contained **slæd** 'small valley'. Some of the spellings (*Cestaneslede* 1202, *Cestaneslade* 1298, *Sextaneslade* 1299, *Cesterneslade* 1303) are consistent with this, and the 50′ contour makes an appropriate little valley at precisely this point on the river bank. If this be correct, the name has been remodelled because –*lode* was felt to be appropriate to a name by the Severn.

It could, perhaps, be argued that a meaning 'difficult river-crossing', appropriate to OE *gelād*, was remembered in GLO, WOR and SHR until a date when regular ferry services were maintained, and that this memory combined with the presence of some place-names in –*lode* on the river-banks produced a local dialect sense 'ferry'.

It remains to consider briefly the occurrences of *gelād* in OE charter boundaries, which are conveniently assembled in Forsberg 1950. An agreement for a lease at Worcester defines some meadow by a reference to a *gelad* by the Severn. Two boundary-marks in BRK charters (*dyrnan gelade* and *eanflæde gelade*) are by the Thames near Appleford and near Wytham. There is no certainty that any of these refers to a crossing-place over the river, though obviously that is possible. They could be tracks negotiating streams and wet ground on the river-banks. The fourth boundary-mark, *hafocgelad* in Haseley OXF, is odd man out, being not on a major river, but on the small stream called Haseley Brook. There is certainly no question of a ferry here, but the boundary-mark occurs in a flat area which could have been marshy. The next boundary-mark in the survey is Rofford, where the stream is confined in a shallow valley, by contrast to its course at the 'hawk crossing'.

hȳth OE 'landing-place on a river, inland port'. Ekwall 1960 says 'fairly common', but there are fewer than 30 major names which contain it, and it is rare in minor names except in CAM. Among minor names in other counties, Hithe Bridge in Oxford is an ancient name, and so is Hythe in Egham SUR, but in Bablock Hythe OXF the term may be a late addition to the earlier stream-name Bablock (the full name is recorded in 1580). Queenhithe in London is a medieval name, first recorded in 1151–2, for a landing-place which was called *Ætheredes hyd*, 'Æthelræd's landing-place', in a charter of King Alfred dated 898–9.

Of the 27 examples noted in major names, seven are situated on the lower Thames: these are Putney, Chelsea, Lambeth, Rotherhithe, Stepney and Erith GTL, and Greenhithe KNT. Another two—Maidenhead BRK and Bolney (S. of Henley) OXF—are on the middle Thames, and the minor name Hythe in Egham SUR is also on the river, roughly half-way between Maidenhead and Putney. Two examples—Hythe KNT and Bulverhythe (W. of Hastings) SSX—are by the coast, but the landing-places may have been a short distance inland, on nearby rivers. There is a notable group in the Fens: Aldreth and Swavesey CAM and Earith HNT lie fairly close together on branches of the R. Ouse, and Clayhithe (near Waterbeach) CAM is on the R. Cam in the same region. These are at the junction of fen with slightly raised ground, and Lakenheath SFK and Methwold Hythe NFK (earlier *Oteringhithe*) are similarly sited near the E. edge of the Fens. Two examples are on the lower Trent: Knaith (S. of Gainsborough) LIN and Stockwith LIN/NTT (E. and W. Stockwith lie on either side of the river, N. of Gainsborough). Riverhead KNT is on the upper course of the R. Darent. Hidden BRK ('valley of the hithe') refers to a landing-place on the N. bank of the R. Kennet opposite Kintbury. Creeksea ESX is on the estuary of the R. Crouch, and Setchey NFK is on the R. Nar, S. of King's Lynn; the latter could be seen as a member of the Fenland group described above. Bleadney SOM, N.W. of Glastonbury, commands a narrow gap where the R. Axe flows through a chain of hills running from Wedmore to Wells and separating two areas of Moor. Bleadney was granted to Glastonbury Abbey by a charter of AD 712 which speaks of it as *portam de Bledenithe*.

The above names are easily understood as referring to installations of commercial importance, but a few other examples are more difficult to explain on the evidence of the modern landscape. In Huyton LNC and Hyton (near Bootle) CMB, *hȳth* is used as a qualifier for *tūn*. Huyton LNC seems to imply that either the R. Alt or Ditton Brook was suitable for navigation, and only local knowledge can say whether this is reasonable. Old Hyton CMB stands on Annaside Beck, a mile from the sea, and the river may in early times have been navigable to this point. Hive YOE is not on a river, but the EPNS survey (p. 247) says 'there may have been a navigable drain connecting it with the R. Foulness (a mile away).' Rackheath NFK is two miles from the R. Bure, but the 1″ map shows a tributary of the Bure flowing past the church, and there may have been enough water here in early times to form a small harbour away from the marshes which border the main river. The first element of Rackheath might be *hraca* 'throat', used of the narrow gully in which this tributary rises.

Analysis of the first elements in names in –*hȳth* shows that topographical terms and words describing the immediate surroundings predominate. Earith HNT and Erith GTL are identical names, apparently referring to the gravelly soil at the landing-places or to a gravel bed in the river. Greenhithe KNT, which means what it says, may imply that grass was normally trampled and discoloured at such sites, so that the surviving greenery was noteworthy at this one. Aldreth CAM is the only other compound referring to vegetation. Creeksea ESX and Knaith LIN refer to nearby topographical features (Knaith contains *cnēo* 'knee' used of a river-bend), and so does Rackheath if the etymology suggested above be accepted. Lakenheath SFK was the landing-place of a group of people called *Lacingas*, who may have acquired their tribal name from the frequency in their region of streams to which the term lacu was appropriate. In the minor name Clayhithe CAM, hithe is a 13th-century addition to an earlier place-name *Cleie*, 'clayey place'.

Stockwith LIN refers to the construction of the *hȳth*, and this may be the case with Stepney GTL, if the first element can be interpreted as a weak form, *stybba*, of the noun *stybb* 'stump'. Bolney OXF, Lambeth GTL, Rotherhithe GTL and Riverhead KNT refer to domestic animals, presumably either as cargo or as creatures to be seen in the vicinity. One of the CAM minor names in –*hȳth*, Horseway in Chatteris, probably refers to horses. Maidenhead BRK and Bulverhythe SSX refer to categories of people. Bleadney SOM contains a personal name. *Oteringhithe* NFK and Putney GTL contain words meaning 'otter' and 'hawk', which may be personal names, as may *Swæf* 'Swabian' in Swavesey CAM.

Chelsea GTL is probably 'landing-place for chalk', though some of the early spellings, such as *Cælichyth* 801, tell against this. At any rate, the first element was sometimes considered to be 'chalk'. Cole 1988 suggests that chalk cargoes were shipped along the Thames for spreading on clayey fields round London. The first element of Setchey NFK is uncertain.

lane, lone, lanu OE 'lane' is common in the names of the less important streets in towns, but rare in other place-names. In Laneham NTT, which means 'at the lanes', it may have had a specialized sense. The village is one of a number in the marshy land by the R. Trent, and it is no more clearly at a road-junction than are its neighbours. The LNC R. Douglas is called Asland in its lower course. Early spellings are *Asklone*, *Askelone* c. 1200, and Ekwall 1928 considers the second element to be *lane* in the Scottish dialect sense 'hollow course of a large rivulet in meadow-land; a brook whose movement is scarcely perceptible; the smooth, slowly moving part of a river'. This might suit Laneham NTT, and Lenwade NFK, of which *lone* is a possible first element.

pæth OE 'path' is more frequent in minor names and field-names than in major settlement-names, but it occurs as the final element of at least 6 major names, and is the probable first element in several others. It is a fairly frequent term in charter boundaries (in addition to occurrences of the compound *herepæth*, discussed below). Pave Lane, S. of Newport SHR, preserves the second element of *diowuces pæth* in the OE bounds of Church Aston, and Pathe S.W. of Othery SOM may preserve the *pæth* element of *Wilbrittis pathe* in the bounds of Zoy.

Major names with *pæth* as final element are Alspath in Meriden WAR (a DB manor, and probably the name of the parish until replaced by Meriden), Brancepeth DRH (the spellings for which do not support Ekwall's suggestion that the first element is the gen. of a reduced form of the nearby Brandon), Gappah N. of Newton Abbot DEV (a DB manor), Horspath OXF, Morpeth NTB, and Urpeth N.W. of Chester-le-Street DRH. The situation of most of these would support a hypothesis that *pæth* was felt to be specially appropriate to a road over moorland or heath. The first elements of Gappah, Horspath and Urpeth refer to goats, horses and wild cattle. Morpeth contains *morth* 'murder', suggesting that one of the roads which converge on the river-crossing there had an evil reputation.

Some minor names listed in Smith 1956 have similar first elements: Bagpath GLO refers to badgers, Doepath NTB to does, Dupath CNW to thieves. Some minor names and field-names in *–pæth* have descriptive words as first element: Sticklepath ('steep') occurs twice in DEV, and a compound with *smæl* 'narrow' is well evidenced in field-names. Smythapark in Loxhore DEV is 'smooth path'. Roppa N. of Helmsley YON (a dramatic moorland site) has ON *rauthr* 'red' as qualifier.

By contrast with these first elements, Alspath WAR and Brancepeth DRH have personal names, and there are a number of charter-boundary names in this category, besides the two mentioned in the first paragraph.

There are a few names in which *pæth* is the first element. These include Pateley Bridge YOW (probably gen. pl.) and possibly Patton WML. Pathlow N.W. of Stratford upon Avon WAR was a hundred meeting-place; it stands on a road which, a good deal further north, on the outskirts of Birmingham, is called Monkspath Street.

There are traces in an OE charter boundary of an alternative form *pathu*, a fem. noun, which would have a gen. pl. *pathena*. This would be a suitable first element for Painley YOW, N.E. of Gisburn (*Pathenhale* c. 1200) and for Panborough SOM (*Patheneberga* 971). Ekwall 1960 suggests the gen. pl. of a weak noun *patha* meaning 'wayfarer' for these names, but 'hill of the tracks' would suit Panborough SOM which is on a narrow ridge between two areas of the Somerset Levels, and which could have a name referring to the ancient log causeways recovered by archaeologists from the moors. Theale, adjacent to Panborough means 'planks', and this may be another reference to the prehistoric causeways.

It is clear from charter boundaries that in a large area of S.W. England *herepæth* 'army-path' was the regular OE term for a main road. Harepath occurs three times as a minor name in DEV, and the compound appellative is the first element of Harpford DEV, SOM, and of two instances of Harford (in Crediton and Landkey) DEV.

ritu– British 'ford' is the ancestor of Welsh *rhyd* and is cognate with Latin *portus* and English *ford*. It is well evidenced among the place-names recorded from Roman Britain, e.g. *Anderitum* (Pevensey SSX), *Camboritum* (Lackford SFK), and *Durolitum* (Chigwell ESX). Rivet and Smith 1979 (p. 251) discuss its use in Continental names. Rhydd WOR (2 examples) is listed there and in Smith 1956 (2, p. 82) as a relevant name, but this is more likely to be a fanciful modern spelling for an English name meaning 'clearing' (Smith 1956 2, p. 89, rejects this on the grounds that *rȳd, rīed* 'clearing' is only found in the S.E., but a substantive use of the adjective *gerydd* 'cleared' which he discusses on p. 90 would suit the WOR names).

British *ritu–* occurs in Leatherhead SUR and Penrith CMB, and possibly in Ridware STF. The etymology of Leatherhead was satisfactorily elucidated for the first time in Coates 1980; it is a British name meaning 'grey ford', an important addition to the corpus of names which indicate substantial British survival S.W. of London. Penrith means 'hill ford' or 'chief ford'. The crossing referred to was probably about a mile S.E. of the modern town, where the Roman road from Brougham to Carlisle crossed the R. Eamont; the high ground E. of Penrith might be felt to overlook this ford.

Ridware (Hamstall, Pipe and Mavesyn) STF has OE–*ware* 'dwellers' as second element, and if the first element is the Primitive Welsh descendant of *ritu*– the word would appear to have been functioning as a simplex place-name when English-speaking people settled in the area. Or it may have been in frequent use as an appellative by Welsh speakers and mistakenly apprehended as a proper name by the English. In either case the feature must have been an important one. The 'ford' was perhaps a road through wet ground between the Rivers Blithe and Trent.

Tretire HRE (*Rythir* 1212) is a Welsh name meaning 'long ford', probably, in view of the order of elements, a post-Roman coinage.

stæth OE 'landing-place' occurs as a simplex name in Stathe (E. of Athelney) SOM. Statham (near Lymm) CHE is from the dative plural. This word is the first element of Stafford STF, and the second element of Bickerstaffe LNC, Birstwith YOW, Brimstage CHE and Croxteth (near Liverpool) LNC.

The cognate ON **stǫth** is considered to occur in Toxteth (in Liverpool) LNC, because the first element is the ON personal name *Tóki*. The plural of *stǫth*, which is *stǫthvar*, occurs in Burton Stather and Flixborough Stather on the R. Trent in LIN. Other places in eastern England have such names associated with them, e.g. Brancaster Staithe and Overy Staithe on the Norfolk coast, but there is no way of knowing whether the element is OE or ON when it is singular. Staithes YON was *Setonstathes*, from Seaton Hall, when it was first recorded in 1451.

Smith 1956 gives more of these names under *stǫth*, and considers that OE *stæth* only acquired the sense 'landing-place' when it was influenced by the ON word. The only meaning recorded for *stæth* in OE is 'river-bank, shore', which is very well evidenced. Stafford STF, however, seems likely to be an early OE name, and 'ford by a landing-place' makes more sense than 'ford by a river-bank', so it seems best to assume, as in Ekwall 1960, that *stæth* had the sense 'landing-place' before the period of the Norse settlements. It is possible that this was an earlier meaning than 'bank' in OE, and that it became obsolete and was revived by the influence of ON.

The nature of the 'landing-place' requires careful consideration in some instances. Bickerstaffe LNC is not on a river. The village occupies a slight ridge in what may, in early times, have been very wet ground. Possibly there was here a marsh settlement, of a type known to archaeologists, whose inhabitants depended on dug-out boats for their communications. A similar explanation might suit Brimstage in the Wirral. Dodgson (EPNS CHE survey 4, p. 235) says 'the meaning of *stæth* "a landing-place" is improbable here for the smallness of the water at Brimstage', but by the same token the use of a word meaning 'river-bank' seems pointless. Croxteth Hall LNC, however, is lower down the R. Alt than Huyton, so seems more appropriate to a landing-place than Huyton, which is considered to contain **hȳth**. The early topography of Toxteth could only be evaluated with the help of expert local knowledge.

Birstwith YOW is included here, in spite of the rejection by Smith (EPNS survey 5, p. 131) of Ekwall's derivation from OE *byrg-stæth* 'landing-place of the fort'. Smith says that this is 'an improbable explanation topographically', but it looks appropriate on the 1″ map. Birstwith stands on a hill overlooking the R. Nidd.

stæth and *stǫth* are rare elements in minor names and field-names, but a few instances have been noted in CAM, DRB, GLO, NTT, YOE and YOW.

stīg OE, **stígr** ON, 'path, narrow road' were probably felt to be specially appropriate to an ascending path, since they are related to the OE verb *stīgan* 'to climb'. The OE word or (in appropriate areas) the ON one is the second element of Bransty CMB, Bringsty HRE, Corpusty NFK, Gresty CHE and Wolsty CMB, and a possible first element in Styal CHE, Stifford ESX and Styford NTB. It is impossible to distinguish early spellings of *stīg* 'path' from those of *stigu* 'sty', but *stīg* seems preferable for Stifford and Styford because there is a group of names in –ford in which the first element is a term for a road; and it is perhaps a more likely second element in other names even when the nature of the first element does not absolutely rule out 'sty'. Compounds with *hogg* and *swīn*, however, are usually translated 'pig-sty'.

Bransty CMB, now a minor name in Whitehaven, means 'steep path' and refers to the old road to Cockermouth which ran along the present Bransty Road, and which is steep. Bringsty HRE, the name of a common E. of Bromyard, means 'brink path'; the road here follows the curving edge of a hill-spur. Corpusty NFK is explained in Ekwall 1960 and Smith 1956 as 'Corp's path' from an Anglo-Scandinavian personal name, but it may be an ON name from *stígr* and ON *korpr* 'raven' (rather than a byname derived from it). Ravensty, perhaps another path from which ravens were seen, occurs as a minor name in Colton LNC. Gresty CHE is translated 'badger-run' in EPNS survey, and Wolsty CMB is 'wolf path'.

Smith 1956 cites some minor names in addition to the examples given above. He says of the group Corpusty NFK, Hardisty YOW, Ravensty LNC, Spruisty YOW, Thorfinsty LNC and *Wolmersty* LIN 'all with pers. n.'; but this is not necessarily true of Corpusty and Ravensty and in EPNS survey 5 (p. 100) a different origin (from *sprota* 'sprout, shoot') is put forward for Spruisty. Personal names do, however, occur in Hardisty, Thorfinsty and probably *Wolmersty*, and in this, as in the use of animal names, the compounds with *stīg*, *stígr* are comparable to those with **pæth**.

stīg is fairly common in some counties as an element in field-names and minor names, though there are other counties (e.g. BRK) where it does not occur at all. SSX has a number of examples, and so have GLO, WAR, NTT. It is fairly common in field-names in DRB and (perhaps in the ON form) in field and minor names in WML and YOW, and in street-names in Lincoln. A full study would have to take account of more material than is provided by major settlement-names.

strǣt OE 'Roman road' is a West Germanic loan from the second component of the Latin term *via strata* 'paved road'. It occurs as a simplex name in Streat SSX, Street HRE, KNT, SOM(2), Strete DEV(2) and Stroat (in Tidenham) GLO, but is most commonly used as the qualifying element of a compound name. The words most frequently qualified by *strǣt* are **ford, hām, lēah** and **tūn** (Stretford, Stratford, Streatham, Streatley, Streetley, Stratton, Stretton). Places called Stratton, Stretton may have performed a special function in relation to traffic on the road.

The translation 'Roman road' is sound when the word occurs in major settlement-names (*v.* Gelling 1978, p. 153); but it does not always hold good for boundary-marks in Anglo-Saxon charters, and cannot be automatically applied to field-names. In the charter boundaries 'main road' is sometimes an acceptable rendering; but cf. Hooke 1981 p. 302, '*Strǣt* features do seem to be most in evidence near centres of known Roman development.' In field-names and minor settlement-names it is necessary to allow for the modern dialect sense 'straggling village'.

The modern sense 'urban road' is found in late OE, and in this sense *strǣt* is the commonest term in the names of more important streets in towns.

vath ON 'ford' occurs as a simplex name in Wath YON(2), YOW, and Waithe LIN. It is the first element of Wassand YOE, and the final element in about 15 major settlement-names. As an element in minor names and field-names it is present in some of the counties where there was Norse settlement, but not in all of them. It is probably commonest in CMB. It is the second element of Solway in Solway Firth CMB.

Modern forms often have –with or –worth, due to confusion with ON **vithr** and OE **worth**.

The small corpus of compound names in –*vath* resembles the much larger corpus in –**ford** in that the commonest type of first element is a word which describes the ford. Here belong Brawith YON, Helwith YON, Langwathby CMB, Langwith DRB, NTT, YOE, Langworth LIN(2), Sandwith CMB, Stenwith LIN. Personal names probably occur in Mulwith YOW, Ravensworth YON, Snilesworth YON (though these may be references to mules, ravens and snails) and there is certainly a personal name in Winderwath WML. For Flawith YON and Rainworth NTT alternative etymologies are available. Flawith may contain ON *flatha* 'flat meadow' or OE *fleathe* 'water-lily'; and Rainworth may be 'clean ford' or 'boundary ford'. Ekwall 1960 has a third suggestion for Flawith.

gewæd OE 'ford' is cognate with ON **vath**. Most of the settlement-names in which it certainly occurs are situated in BDF, IOW, KNT, NFK and SFK, and it is likely that in most of England *gewæd* went out of use at an early date, being superseded by the ubiquitous **ford**. Langwathby CMB is sometimes cited under this heading, but it seems more satisfactory to interpret it as containing ON **vath**, with some interchange of *–th* and *–d* in the early spellings. Wadebridge CNW, however, which is *Wade* 1382, cannot be an ON name, and it seems necessary to assume that *gewæd* remained in occasional use in the south west till a relatively late date. There was also a lost *Ayleswade* in Harnham near Salisbury WLT, *Aylyswade* or *Aylesford* Bridge being an early name of Harnham Bridge. The word occurs in some ME field-names in Langton Matravers DOR in a manner which leads David Mills (EPNS survey 1, p. 42) to suggest that it had acquired a more general sense, perhaps 'sheep walk'. The CNW and WLT names, however, refer to river-crossings. Apart from the DOR occurrences *gewæd* is very rare indeed in field-names; 2 instances have been noted in ESX.

The settlement-names in the south and east which certainly contain *gewæd* in the sense 'ford' are Biggleswade BDF, Cattawade SFK, Iwade KNT, Lenwade NFK, *Wathe* (now St Lawrence) IOW and Wade in N. Cove SFK. Biggleswade has a personal name as first element, Cattawade refers to cats, and Iwade to yew-trees. Lenwade is discussed under **lane**. There is a KNT parish called St Nicholas at Wade, and here Wade may have been the name of the settlement before the church was built, though this does not emerge so clearly from the early references as the comparable process does for St Lawrence IOW.

Landwade CAM may contain *gewæd*, but the early spellings show an unusual degree of variety.

weg OE 'way' is the general OE term for a road, and is the commonest one in charter boundaries. All the other words for roads, streets and paths discussed in this chapter probably had specialized senses. Major settlement-names containing *weg* only number about 25, but the term is very frequent in minor names and field-names.

As a first element *weg* occurs in Wayford SOM, Whaley CHE and (according to Gelling 1973) in Weyhill HMP; but a stream-name seems more likely in Weybread SFK. As a second element it is most frequently compounded with a word which describes the road. Bradway DRB and Broadway SOM and WOR refer to width, Holloway GTL and Holway SOM to the hollow in which the road runs, Stantway GLO, Stanway ESX, GLO, HRE and SHR, and Stowey SOM, to a stony surface. Three major names, Garmondsway DRH, Hanwell OXF (earlier *Haneweie*) and Thoresway LIN, have personal names as first element. Halsway SOM and Roundway WLT refer to the nature of the surroundings, Highway WLT to material transported, Barkway HRT to vegetation. The meaning of Farway DEV is not clear; the same compound (*ferweg, færweg*) occurs occasionally in charter boundaries. Radway WAR and Rodway SOM are probably 'way fit for ~~riding on~~'. Flotterton and Hartington NTB are *Flotweyton* c. 1160 and *Hertweitun* 1171, showing that **tūn** has been added to compounds in *–weg*. Hartington refers to the presence of stags, but Flotterton is an unsolved mystery. Ekwall 1960 says 'an OE *flot-weg* designating some kind of road, perhaps one made partly on floats'; but it does not seem likely that this area W. of Rothbury was ever marshy.

4

Valleys and Remote Places

The subtlety of the Anglo-Saxon topographical vocabulary excels itself in the matter of words for valleys and hollows. Only an exhaustive geographical study will make it possible to say what extent the differences in size and shape of such features are faithfully and consistently reflected in the words chosen for them by the coiners of place-names. Some broad distinctions are noted here, but it is not a subject which can be investigated adequately without large-scale maps and field-work.

An indication of the exciting results which may be expected from more detailed studies is provided in a recent article by Mrs Ann Cole (Cole 1982). Here, the precise use made by the Anglo-Saxons of the two commonest 'valley' words, **cumb** and **denu**, is explained most convincingly. It is a relief to find that my earlier impressions about the meaning of these elements were roughly correct, though in need of refinement.

I hope there will be detailed geographical studies of names containing some other words discussed in this chapter. The most difficult term to evaluate is **halh**. The difficulty arises partly from the variety of meanings, but also from its use for features which (albeit probably of great importance to the people who lived in them) are not sufficiently dramatic to show clearly on maps. Every **halh** which cannot be explained in terms of administrative geography or relationship to rivers and marsh needs to be inspected on the ground. Even by this last method some of the names may defy interpretation, as a change of settlement-site, such as would not obscure the relationship of a village to a **dūn** or a **denu**, may destroy the evidence when one of these slight depressions is in question.

OE **denu** and ON **dalr** are the words which regularly denote main valleys, and there are some names in which **dalr** replaces **denu**, suggesting that OE and ON speakers recognized them as equivalents. There are a number of terms, in addition to **cumb** and **hop**, which could be used for side valleys and for slighter or less extensive features, and these may not have been used according to an absolutely rigid system. It would be a very dogged theorist who claimed always to be able to distinguish a **halh** from a **cumb**, or a **dell** from a **slæd**. There may have been regional and chronological fashions for some words, though no clear dialect distinctions have been noted in this study.

The use of **hop** for valleys is here clearly shown to be a regional phenomenon, but it does not appear possible to ascribe it to dialect, to date of coinage, or in all cases to the physical characteristics of the valleys. Valleys called **hop** exhibit considerable variety, and many of them could, to the modern eye, have been described by **cumb** or **halh**. Perhaps the concept of remoteness, so well illustrated by the single literary occurrence of **hop**, enters into the choice of this word for valleys in north HRE, south SHR, the Pennines and the mountainous areas of NTB and southern Scotland. Perhaps **hop** could be considered to some extent a specialized term for a mountain valley.

It seems likely that **halh**, on the other hand, though occasionally used for valleys of moderate size, was a specialized term for the slightest hollow which could afford shelter to a settlement. These two words **hop** and **halh**, are not exclusively used for valleys, though this meaning may be the basic one for **halh**, since the word is related to *holh* 'hollow'. Whether 'valley' is considered an original sense for **hop** depends on what view is taken of the origin of that word. Here (as with **mōr**) it is surprising that the standard dictionaries offer so little guidance. Both **halh** and **hop** have 'watery' senses, and both occur in some contexts where 'valley' is an impossible translation. This causes them to overlap with some words discussed in other chapters. If the 'valley' sense had not been so pronounced in some areas, **hop** could have been included with the terms studied in Chapter 7, under the heading Ploughland and Pasture, or perhaps, because of its occasional use for marshland sites, among the terms discussed in Chapter 2. The use of **halh** for riverside sites in the north might have brought that word also within the scope of Chapter 2. 'Land in a river-bend' and 'dry ground in marsh' (if the last be accepted) are less prominent meanings of **halh** than they are of **hamm**, but there is a considerable area of overlap between the two terms. The dialect use of *haugh*, which probably arises from the 'river-bend' sense of **halh**, is the nearest modern equivalent to the OE term **wæsse**, which is also discussed in Chapter 2.

botm, bothm OE, **botn** ON 'bottom'. In the moorland E. and N. of Manchester this term was used in names of settlements situated in relatively wide parts of river-valleys, and it is probable that 'broad river-valley' is its ancient topographical sense in all areas. This is different from the modern use of Bottom to designate a particular part of a valley, which causes the word to appear frequently on modern maps. It is possible that in some ancient names the reference is to the flat bed of a silted-up lake.

Ramsbottom LNC is by the R. Irwell, and other names in –bottom are to be found along this river and beside the Bradshaw Brook to the west. Broadbottom CHE is in a relatively wide part of the valley of the R. Etherow. Longbottom in the township of Luddenden Foot YOW is said in the EPNS survey to refer to 'a long stretch of fairly level ground along the R. Calder.' The same usage is found elsewhere in YOW, as in Starbotton (from the ON word) in the broad valley of the R. Wharfe, and the minor name Bottom Boat, which lies in a very wide stretch of the Calder Valley N.E. of Wakefield.

Wythburn CMB has early spellings in which forms from *botm* interchange with forms from ON *botn*. The settlement is now marooned on a tiny promontory at the foot of the precipitous S.E. shore of Thirlmere, but all this end of Thirlmere is shown as dry land on the 1st edition 1″ map, and Wythburn occupies a wide 'bottom' at the mouth of its stream, the Wyth Burn.

Further south, *botm* and *bothm* are rarely used in ancient settlement-names, though frequent in minor names in the modern sense mentioned above. There is one major name in NTT, Bothamsall (second element **scelf**), where the village stands on the highest point of a broad shelf overlooking the parallel courses of the Rivers Meden and Maun, which are separated by half a mile of level ground. 'Shelf by a broad river-valley' is an appropriate etymology. The term is rare in the south and south west. The single instance in DEV, Brithem Bottom S. of Halberton, is in a broad stream-valley. Bothenhampton DOR stands above a small tributary of the R. Brid, and the *bothm* is perhaps the open land at the junction with this river.

Bothampstead or Bottomstead in Hampstead Norris BRK presents topographical difficulties despite the attempt in EPNS survey (p. 250) to locate a 'bottom', and the personal name *Bōta* might be considered as a more probable first element for this place-name.

The related OE term **bytme, bytne, bythme** is considered (Smith 1956 1, p. 74) to mean 'the head of a valley', but it seems possible that in fact it had much the same sense as *botm*. Castle and Little Bytham LIN are by no means at the head of their valley. Bitteswell LEI overlooks a broad stream-valley N. of Lutterworth. (Bitteswell is only an instance if there was an unrecorded neuter noun *bytme*, as well as the recorded feminine.) The Bittoms in Kingston upon Thames GTL is said in the EPNS survey of SUR to have been 'low-lying ground in an angle between the Thames and the Hogs Mill River.'

clof, clofa OE 'something cut'. Only the weak form *clofa* is on record, meaning 'a cut-off section of a chirograph', but it is believed that both forms existed and that the strong form, *clof*, had a topographical meaning similar to that of the related ON word *klofi* 'crevice'.

If the place called *Clofesho*, where the rulers of Mercia held synods during the period 716–825, is correctly identified with Brixworth NTP (Davis 1962), the *clof* will be the valley of the stream which rises S. of the church and bisects the western edge of the spur on which the settlement stands. Professor Davis points to the topographical appropriateness of the name as one of the factors in favour of the identification. The gen. sg. of *clof* is also considered to be the first element of Closworth SOM, S. of Yeovil. Closworth is on a hill-spur with narrow stream-valleys on either side. The other ancient settlement-name considered to contain *clof* is Clovelly DEV. Ekwall 1960 suggests that Velly ('wheel-rim') was the name of the hill between Velly and Clovelly, the latter name having *clof* as prefix. The term would seem appropriate to the v-shaped cliff-indentation in which the village lies.

clof is related to *clēofan* 'to split', modern *cleave*. The past participle *geclofen* is the first element of Clannaborough, N.W. of Crediton, DEV ('cloven hill'), and a derivative, *clēofung*, is thought to be the source of Cleaving near Londesborough YOE, referring to a steep valley in the Wolds.

clōh OE, **clough** ME, 'ravine'. Only used in the north and the north midlands. Duignan 1902 says: 'Clough. A common name in the N. Staffordshire moorlands, but unknown S. of Stone . . . It means a ravine or narrow valley, with steep sides, usually forming the bed of a stream.' This suits ME *clough*, which is common in names of topographical features, sometimes becoming –*cleugh*. But the situation of the two ancient settlement-names in which the element is considered to occur, Clotton CHE and Cloughton YON, suggests that the OE word, which is not on independent record, was used of much less dramatic valleys. Clotton N.W. of Tarporley has a low-lying site enclosed by the 150' contour. Dodgson EPNS survey 3 (p. 272) translates Clotton 'farm at a dell'. Cloughton N. of Scarborough occupies a small stream-valley in undramatic country. OE *clōh* may have been an Anglian term used occasionally for a slight valley, which developed the specialized sense 'ravine' in ME. It seems likely that Haltcliff CMB (S.E. of Hesket Newmarket), which was *Halteclo*, *Hautecloch* in the 13th century, is a ME name in which *clough* 'ravine' is qualified by French *haut* 'high'.

Apart from the two instances with –*tūn*, *clōh* occurs occasionally as a first element, as in Cloffocks near Workington CMB and Clougha, a hill S.E. of Lancaster, both with –*hōh*; but it is more frequently the second element, as in Deadwin Clough LNC, Wilboarclough CHE, or used as a simplex name.

corf OE 'pass, valley'. This is a derivative of *ceorfan* 'to cut', modern *carve*. In SHR it was the name of the long valley between Wenlock Edge and the Clee Hills. The name was transferred to the R. Corve, and the valley then became known as Corve Dale. Corfham and Corfton SHR are in this valley. In the south west, *corf* acquired the specialized sense 'pass'. In Corfe Castle DOR it is used of the pass which divides the ridge of the Purbeck Hills. A less dramatic gap between hills is referred to in Corfe Mullen DOR, but Corfe S. of Taunton SOM refers to a pass in a steep ridge, as does Corton Denham N. of Sherborne. Coryates and Corton DOR refer to a pass through an escarpment E. of Abbotsbury. Corscombe DOR and Croscombe SOM are from OE *corfweges cumb* 'coomb of the pass way'. The only recorded instance of *corf* in OE is the boundary mark *micla corf* in a survey of Corscombe DOR. Corscombe DEV is a different name.

cumb OE 'coomb'. This is generally regarded as an OE adaptation of the Primitive Welsh word which became Modern Welsh *cwm*. NED points out, however, that OE had another word *cumb* 'vessel, cup, a small measure', association with which may have encouraged the Anglo-Saxons to adopt the

Welsh word for a valley. In fact it could be argued that this OE word is the true source of the topographical term, and that the resemblance to the Welsh word helped *cumb* to emerge as by far the most frequently used of a number of OE words of similar meaning which were sometimes employed in a topographical sense. Other such words are:

byden 'tub', which is the source of Bidden HMP, Beedon BRK, Bidna CNW, DEV;

cetel 'kettle', which is the source of Chettel DOR and occurs in several names in DEV;

canne 'can', which is used in Cann DOR and Canna DEV;

trog 'trough', found in Trough LNC, YON, YOW, and in Trow WLT.

cumb and **denu** are 'valley' words which can profitably be studied together. Both are often found in the same region, and it is clear that they were used for different types of valley. The distinction was adumbrated in the EPNS survey of BRK (p. 925) and has now been clearly defined in Cole 1982. Ann Cole's conclusion about *cumb* is that it is 'mostly used of shorter, broader valleys than *denu*, and these valleys are usually bowl- or trough-shaped with three fairly steeply rising sides'.

cumb enters into about 180 names in Ekwall 1960, and is frequent in minor names in some areas. A regional survey of the major names will illustrate the manner in which the term is used.

cumb is rare in KNT, but the single major name, Ulcombe S.E. of Maidstone, provides an excellent example of one type of valley to which the term is regularly applied: a short, wide valley in a fairly steep escarpment. There are some examples in minor names in the county, several near Wye.

SSX contains a considerable number of minor names in *cumb* in addition to the major names which are the basis of the present study. There are a few examples in major names in W. SSX. Compton near the HMP border is in a broad, short side-valley opening out from a long, narrow, curving valley. The minor name Malecombe refers to a comparable though narrower feature opening off the long, curving valley which gives name to E. and W. Dean, and Molecombe N.E. of Chichester is in a similar valley on the S. side of the same ridge. The main concentration of *cumb* names in SSX is, however, in the east of the county, in the hinterland of Brighton. Saddlescombe and Pyecomb overlook short, broad valleys in the steep escarpment N.W. of Brighton. Telscombe, E. of Brighton, nestles at the bottom of a bowl-shaped hollow, with the ground rising abruptly on three sides. Moulsecoomb is in a small side-valley opening off the long, curving feature which gives name to Upper and Lower Bevendean. Ranscombe Fm S.E. of Lewes is on a platform of dry land poised over the Ouse marshes, at the joint mouth of three short coombs. Pyecombe, Saddlescombe, Moulsecoomb, Ranscombe and Telscombe are discussed and mapped in Cole 1982. One major name in the extreme east of the county, Sedlescombe, is in a small valley N.W. of Hastings.

In HMP *cumb* appears to have been found especially appropriate to side-valleys. Compton S.W. of King's Sombourn overlooks a broad, short valley opening off the valley of the R. Test, and Chilcomb and Compton near Winchester are in similar features opening off the valley of the R. Itchen. Coombe S.W. of East Meon is in a broad hollow at the head of a long valley. Faccombe near the BRK border overlooks a short side-valley. By contrast to its rarity in HMP, *cumb* is very common in IOW, where it enters into 8 major names: Appuldurcombe, Bowcombe, Compton, Gatcombe, Luccombe, Nettlecombe, Shalcombe and Whitcombe. Most of the valleys are very short. Bowcombe occupies a longer one, but is near the mouth of a short side-valley, to which the name perhaps refers.

BRK and SUR are the two remaining counties S. of the Thames in the area where fairly extensive English settlement is known to have taken place in the 5th century. In BRK, *cumb* enters into 3 major names (Compton, Compton Beauchamp, Letcombe) and more than a dozen minor names, and is fairly frequent in field-names and OE charter boundaries. It was in this county that the consistent use of *cumb* for short, shallow, broad valleys was first noted. In SUR *cumb* enters into the major names Compton, Farncombe and Hascombe, and Coombe in Kingston upon Thames GTL belongs to the ancient county. The last is a very good instance of the use of *cumb* for a broad, shallow valley. Compton is described in the EPNS survey as lying 'in a slight depression below the Hogs Back'. Farncombe (in Godalming) is in a broad valley opening out from the R. Wey, and Hascombe to the S.E. and another Compton to the N.W. are in broad, short valleys.

KNT, SSX, HMP, IOW, BRK and SUR have been considered first because it is probably in these areas that the Anglo-Saxons first encountered valleys for which their topographical vocabulary did not contain an appropriate word, and may have been motivated to adopt the Celtic term. The word cannot have been borrowed in the south west and then spread eastwards into the place-name-forming vocabulary of the south-eastern areas, since this would indicate an unacceptably late date for the coining of the south-eastern names. *cumb* is absent from the elements noted in place-names recorded before AD 730, which might be taken to indicate a late origin for place-names which contain it; but this must be seen in the context of the general scarcity of 'valley' terms in the list in Cox 1976 (pp. 47–51). Such terms are represented there only by one instance of **denu** and one of **halh**, and the use of **clof** as a first element in *Clofeshoh*.

Counties W. of BRK show an increasing frequency of major names containing *cumb*. In WLT, where there are 14 instances in major names, it is clear that the specialized senses outlined above still predominate. In SOM, DOR and DEV, *cumb* is so frequent that it must have been the standard OE term for a valley. The EPNS survey of DEV says (p. 676) '**cumb** is, except for **tūn**, the commonest of all elements found in Devon.' There are 42 major names containing *cumb* in SOM, 36 in DEV and 26 in DOR, so these three counties have more than half of the instances included in Ekwall 1960. On the other hand, no names containing *cumb* in CNW are included in Ekwall 1960, and this suggests that new settlement-names containing the element were less likely to be formed after the middle of the 9th century. Smith 1956 (1, p. 119) lists some minor names in CNW, however.

North of the R. Thames, *cumb* is just sufficiently represented in eastern counties to suggest that it was available in the place-name-forming vocabulary, though used sparingly because the topography did not often demand it. ESX has a few simplex minor names, e.g. Combe Wood in Thundersley, where there are references t. John to *Norhcombe* and *Estcumbe*. There are a few minor names in BDF and HRT, but *cumb* does not become a noteworthy element until the Chilterns are reached. In the Chilterns in OXF and BUC the contrasting use of *cumb* and **denu** is particularly apparent, as demonstrated by Ann Cole's map (Fig. 2). The BUC use of the term is not confined to the Chilterns; Liscombe is in a broad valley W. of Linslade. It should be noted that High Wycombe does not contain *cumb*.

In GLO, *cumb* is frequent mainly because it is appropriate to the valleys of the Cotswold escarpments. Winchcombe, 'coomb with a bend', perhaps emphasizes that a *cumb* is normally straight. This settlement is a rare instance of a place with a *cumb* name which was of outstanding administrative importance. The use of *cumb* for Cotswold valleys extends into S. WAR, where there is a concentration of settlements called Compton, 6 of them situated near the northern end of the range. WAR has a few other *cumb* names. Coombe Abbey near Coventry is enclosed by a bend in the 250′ contour, and Luscombe Fm in Snitterfield is similarly situated. Welcombe in Stratford has a classic *cumb* site, the settlement (now a hotel) nestling in the bowl-shaped end of the valley.

The east midlands do not offer a great deal of scope for names containing *cumb*. Chacombe NTP is in a broad side-valley opening on to the R. Cherwell near Banbury, and this and Westcombe and Snorscombe are in the Northampton Heights which are an extension of the Cotswold escarpment. No major names containing *cumb* have been noted in East Anglia, LEI or NTT. LIN, however, has Oxcombe, in a tiny round-ended valley S. of Louth. In DRB there are a few minor names. All but one are in the High Peak area, and these are clear evidence for the precise, specialized use of the term. At Coombes in Charlesworth the settlements bearing the name are on the rim of a broad, round-ended valley, a feature which is shown clearly on the 1st ed. 1″ map. Coombs Fm in Bakewell is in a short side-valley off the valley of the R. Wye, and Combs in Chapel-en-le-Frith is at the junction of several short stream-valleys, which are different features from the surrounding valleys with names in –dale.

In STF the major names containing *cumb* are Compton and Congreave. Compton, now part of Wolverhampton, is said in Duignan 1902 to lie in a hollow. Congreave lies in a very small indentation of the 300′ contour beside the R. Penk. The sense 'small side-valley' is clearly instanced in the minor name Combridge, S.W. of Rocester.

In the counties of the Welsh Marches *cumb* is a very rare place-name element, another fact which supports the hypothesis that if it is a Celtic loan the word was borrowed in the 5th century from British people in southern and south-eastern England, not acquired at a later date from contact with the Welsh of Wales and Cornwall. The only major name in HRE is Pencombe, where the village lies in a side-valley opening off the valley of the R. Lodon. For Combe near Presteigne it would be desirable to know where the ancient settlement was. In SHR it is doubtful whether the term occurs at all in ancient names. In CHE there is one major name, Seacombe and a few minor names. Seacombe, in Wallasey, is in a broad recess in the 50′ contour. *cumb* has not been noted in English names in Wales.

In north-west England N. of CHE, the only major name containing *cumb* is Holcombe LNC, W. of Ramsbottom, where the settlement overlooks a small side-valley off the R. Irwell. Ekwall 1960 includes Cowm in Rochdale parish; this is an ancient name with spellings from the 13th century, but it only appears on the 1″ map as the name of a reservoir, and it is not clear that it was ever a settlement-name.

In Yorkshire, *cumb* is rare but clearly retains its specialized meanings. YON has two striking examples, Darncombe in Brompton and Horcum in Lockton. Darncombe, a hamlet N. of Trouts Dale, is in a short side-valley which is a distinctive feature contrasting with the surrounding Dales. High and Low Horcum, N.E. of Pickering, are in a broad opening at the end of a narrow valley. This is called The Hole of Horcum, and is sufficiently striking to be featured on picture postcards. The name probably means 'hollow coomb', in spite of the inconclusive early spellings. In YOE *cumb* is only noted in a few field-names. In YOW there is one major name, Compton in Collingham, which is in a tiny, round-ended valley.

OE *cumb* probably does not occur as an ancient place-name element N. of Yorkshire. In CMB the British word *cumbo–* was used in British names of post-Roman origin, such as Cumcatch, Cumcrook, Cumrew, Cumwhinton, Cumdivock, and it is used as an affix to an OE name in Cumwhitton.

It will be clear from the foregoing discussion that *cumb* is commonly used as a simplex name, and that it occurs frequently as a first element, especially in Compton. As a second element, *cumb* is probably most frequently combined with a personal name. Here may be classed Babbacombe DEV, Batcombe DOR, SOM(2), Bettiscombe DOR, Bittiscombe SOM, Branscombe DEV, Burlescombe DEV, Butcombe SOM, Catcombe WLT, Chacombe NTP, Chaffcombe, DEV, SOM, Elcombe WLT, Faccombe HMP, Iccombe GLO, Ilfracombe DEV, Luccombe IOW, SOM, Malecombe SSX, Moulsecoomb SSX, Odcombe SOM, Snorscombe NTP, Sutcombe DEV, Telscombe SSX and Winscombe SOM, although alternative etymologies could be urged for some of these, and the double appearance of *Ceaffa* and *Lufa*, and the treble appearance of *Bata*, are obviously suspicious. The next largest category is probably that in which vegetation is specified: here belong Appuldurcombe IOW, Ashcombe DEV, Boscombe WLT, Farncombe SUR, Kingcombe DOR, Lyscombe DOR, Nettlecombe DOR, IOW, SOM, Thorncombe DOR(2), Widdecombe, Widdicombe DEV, Witcombe SOM, Withcombe DEV, SOM (the last 5 names referring to willows).

Another fairly large category contains a reference to a topographical feature. Here belong Awliscombe DEV, Chettiscombe DEV, Chilcomb HMP, Corscombe DOR, Croscombe SOM, Rendcombe GLO, Saddlescombe SSX, Seacombe CHE, Watercombe DOR, Welcombe DEV, WAR, Woolacombe DEV, Woolcombe DOR, Yarcombe DEV; 5 of these refer to springs, and 2 contain ancient river-names. The minor name Combwell S. of Goudhurst KNT may also be noted. A crop or product is mentioned in Bincombe DOR, Melcombe DOR(2), Pitchcombe GLO, Salcombe DEV(2), Timberscombe SOM, Watcombe DEV, Wexcombe WLT and Whatcombe DOR. Wild creatures are named in Creacombe DEV, Crowcombe SOM, Molecombe SSX, Pyecombe SSX, Stinchcombe GLO, Stitchcombe WLT, Ulcombe KNT and Yarnscombe DEV, but domestic animals only certainly in Challacombe DEV (in Combe Martin) and Oxcombe LIN. The goats of Gatcombe IOW and the swine of Swyncombe OXF were probably domestic, and Liscombe SOM and Loscombe DOR contain *hlōse* 'pig-sty'.

There is a comparative rarity of descriptive words as first element, perhaps because *cumb* was so highly specialized a term that descriptions of size and shape were seldom felt to be necessary. Challacombe near Lynton DEV was 'cold'. Drascombe DEV was characterized by dirt (OE *drosn*). Darncombe YON is 'hidden'. Holcombe DEV(3), DOR, GLO, LNC, OXF and SOM, and probably Horcum YON, are 'hollow', and this compound recurs as a minor name. Shalcombe IOW is 'shallow'. A number of coombs are 'wide' or 'spacious': these include Whitcombe DOR, Witcombe GLO, Witcomb in Hilmarton WLT and Widcombe in Farway DEV. Two instances of Widcombe in SOM may be 'wide' but are equally likely to contain *wīthig* 'willow'. Whitcombe IOW is probably 'white'. Winchcombe GLO has already been noted as a rare reference to irregular shape; Winchcombe Fm in Crundale KNT is another instance of this name.

Some coombs had distinctive owners or occupiers. Charlcombe SOM is 'coomb of the free peasants', Huntercombe OXF 'coomb of the huntsmen', Parracombe DEV, 'coomb of the pedlars'. Hascombe SUR and Hescombe SOM refer to witches, and Hestercombe SOM contains *hægstald*, a word which reference books translate 'bachelor, warrior'.

There are occasional references to structures. Haccombe DEV refers to a fence and Hippenscombe WLT to stepping-stones. Sedlescombe SSX contains the only reference noted in this corpus to a dwelling-place, and Motcombe DOR the only reference to an activity.

A few names in –*cumb* have first elements which are obscure or ambiguous, so are not included in the above analysis. The list of all SSX names in *cumb* in

Dodgson 1978 (p. 69) suggests that an analysis which included more minor names would yield similar results.

dæl OE 'pit, hollow'. This word is here treated separately from ME *dale* 'valley' on the hypothesis that the English word was only used in place-names with the meaning 'valley' after it had been influenced by the cognate ON **dalr**. This hypothesis is tentative, and the occurrence of *dæl* in Doverdale WOR and Dalham SFK may be seen as evidence against it. These names are discussed in the next article. In literary OE the meanings 'pit, gulf' are as well evidenced for *dæl* as the meaning 'valley'.

Two ancient settlement-names in KNT probably contain *dæl*. Dalham near High Halstow is on a low hill overlooking a broad recess called Buck Hole. The early topography of the other example, Deal, is difficult to evaluate, but there might have been a similar feature there. A well-recorded minor name, Wormdale W. of Sittingbourne, appears from the 1″ map to be in a hollow. There are a few minor names in *–dale*, probably of late origin, in SSX, but there appears to be no use of *dæl* in major names S. of the Thames between KNT and DEV. The single instance in DEV, Dalwood, is first recorded in 1195, and may be of ME origin. In Stavordale SOM it is apparent from the early spellings that *dale* replaced **denu** in the mid-13th century.

North of the Thames, the only ancient settlement-name in the S.E. midlands which may contain *dæl* is Dawley GTL. The EPNS survey of MDX objects to derivation from *dæl* on the grounds that the area is flat; but the word may have been used of a pit or hollow. There are no settlement-names containing *dæl* in BUC, OXF or GLO, or in the counties immediately north of these, with the single exception of Doverdale WOR, which is discussed below.

Probably, although *dæl* existed in the language, it was not felt to be a useful place-name element until the introduction of ON **dalr** influenced its meaning, after which it replaced **denu** in some areas. Some north-country names in *–dale* might, if their sites were closely examined, appear more likely to contain *dæl* 'pit' than late OE *dale* 'valley'. Givendale S.E. of Ripon YOW is a possible instance.

dalr ON, **dæl** late OE, **dale** ME, 'valley'. If the suggestion put forward in the preceding article be accepted, ON names containing *dalr* may be earlier coinages than names in which OE *dæl*, ME *dale* are used in the sense 'valley'. In the north of England it is impossible to separate the ON and the OE words, but the conventional treatment is to consider *dalr* to be the term involved in compound names where the other element is certainly ON.

Dalby occurs in LEI(2), LIN, YON(2), and there is an instance in IOM. As the final element of a compound, *dalr* occurs in, e.g., Allerdale, Borrowdale, Bowderdale, Crossdale, Ennerdale, Grinsdale, Mungrisdale, Scawdale Fell, Uldale and Wasdale CMB, Birkdale, Bleasdale and Grizedale(2) LNC, Bannisdale, Borrowdale, Grisedale, Ravenstonedale and Wasdale WML, Thixendale YOE, Baysdale, Cundall and Rosedale YON. These are not all settlement-names; some are district-names, like Allerdale, or mountain-names, like Scawdale Fell. There is no obvious bias towards any category of qualifying element, but references to vegetation are rare, Birkdale being the only instance in the names cited.

ME *dale* (or OE *dæl* in the sense 'valley') is only common north of a line from the Mersey to the Humber, excluding NTB and DRH. The comparative rarity in NTB and DRH is significant, suggesting, as pointed out by Smith (1956 1, p. 125), that the crucial factor in the use of the word is the degree of ON influence in an area. Dalton is only found in northern counties, occurrences being in DRH(2), LNC(2), NTB(2), WML, YOE(2), YON(3), YOW(2). Apart from this compound, Ekwall 1960 lists 3 names in CMB containing *dæl*, 10 in LNC, 9 in WML, 2 in YOE, 13 in YON and 5 in YOW. Most of these are named in the analysis of first elements *infra*.

South of LNC and Yorkshire, the county with most major names in *dæl* is DRB, where Cowdale, Edale, Longdendale and Kingsterndale are in the N.W. of the county, and Dale Abbey (earlier *Depedale*) is E. of Derby, and Ravensdale N.W. of Derby. For *Depedale*, a refashioning of an earlier OE *deopandene* may be suspected, as in Debdale NTP (*infra*). In Longdendale, *dæl* has been added to a name in –**denu**. The other DRB names may be relatively late formations. In NTT *dæl* is the commonest word for a valley, but only one example, Saxondale, is a major settlement-name, and in this it is clear that *dæl* replaced **denu**: the name is *Saxeden* in DB, *Saxenden* 1316; the –*dala*, –*dale* spellings start c. 1130. LIN has Cadwell (earlier *Cattedale*) and Ravendale. LEI has one major name, Ragdale.

In the N.W. midlands, STF has Apedale Hall and Dimsdale, both N.W. of Newcastle. Apedale, first recorded in 1277, is probably not an early OE name, and Dimsdale is *Dulmesdene* in DB. In SHR, *dale* is used in district-names, such as Ape Dale, Hope Dale and Corve Dale, but these are of ME origin. In CHE, *dæl* is common in minor names and field-names, but is not evidenced in ancient settlement-names.

Further south than SHR, STF and LEI, the small corpus of major place-names in which *dæl* means 'valley' comprises Doverdale WOR and a few names in SFK. Doverdale, N.W. of Droitwich, is recorded in OE charter boundaries as the name, not of a village, but of Elmley Brook, by which the village stands. The stream-valley is an unusually narrow one for this area, and might well have been deemed worthy of a special term, but the use of *dæl* here is not necessarily fatal to the suggestion that it did not mean 'valley' till after the Danish wars, as the boundaries in question date from the 10th to 11th centuries, and *dæl* may be a late affix to the pre-English river-name Dover.

In SFK, Botesdale and Withersdale occur near the NFK border, and Dalham SFK is near the CAM border. Dalham is the piece of evidence most likely to contradict the theory that *dæl* did not mean 'valley' in place-names till c. 900, as names in **hām** were not being formed at that date. It is possible, however, that in all three SFK names *dæl* is a substitution for **denu**. Denham

E. of Dalham is *denu-hām*, and there might have been a desire to differentiate between the two settlements if they both had this name originally. Certainly **denu** is the normal term for a sinuous valley in north SFK, and the three settlements with Dal–, –dale are in this type of valley.

Substitution of *dæl* for **denu** can be demonstrated in NTP, where Debdale Lodge in Rothwell is named from a valley which is called *deopandene* in the OE bounds of Kettering. NTP is the most southerly of the counties in which *dæl* is well represented, but none of the instances is a major settlement-name.

Late OE *dæl*, ME *dale*, is not often used as a simplex name, and is rare as a first element except in Dalton. As the final element of a compound it occurs about 8 times with a personal name (Ainsdale LNC, Bilsdale YON, Botesdale SFK, Bransdale YON, Ladhill YON, Martindale WML, Patterdale WML, and probably Cuerdale LNC). Another 10 compounds refer to vegetation or crops. Here belong Farndale YON, Garsdale YOW, Grassendale LNC, Grindale YOE, Lindal and Lindale LNC, Matterdale CMB, Rydal WML, Smardale WML, Yewdale LNC. Domestic animals occur in Cowdale DRB, Kiddal YOW, Withersdale SFK; wild creatures in Cadwell LIN, Ravendale LIN, Ravensdale DRB, Woodale YON, Wooldale YOW. River-names are compounded with *dæl* in Givendale YOE, Glaisdale YON, Kendal WML, Lonsdale LNC, and probably Clapdale YOW. A topographical feature is mentioned in Edale DRB, Knaresdale NTB, Mardale WML, Mosedale CMB, Sleddale WML(2), and in Wheldale YOW, if 'wheel' refers to a bend in the R. Aire. Kingsterndale and Earlsterndale DRB are on either side of a rocky ridge which was probably called *Stæner* 'stony place'. Words describing the valley are rare, but occur in Deepdale LNC, YON, Silverdale LNC and possibly Ragdale LEI, Kildale YON. The only reference noted to a building is in Kirkdale LNC, YON; such references are commoner with ON *dalr*, and Kirkdale may be an ON, rather than a late OE, name. A class of owner or occupier is mentioned in Bishopdale YON, Bretherdale WML, Colsterdale YON and Cummersdale CMB. Position has only been noted in Westerdale YON. Ramsdale YON could refer to wild garlic or to rams.

dell OE 'dell'. This word is related to **dæl**. It has a limited provenance in place-names in southern England, and is mostly used in minor names and field-names; but it deserves mention here because two names in which it occurs, Arundel SSX and Ramsdell HMP, have become those of major settlements. Ramsdell HMP, N.W. of Basingstoke, is first recorded as *Ramesdela* in 1170; a fuller collection of spellings is needed for a certain etymology, but the tiny valley with a stream rising in it to the S.W. of the village may be a good example of the sort of natural feature likely to be designated a *dell*. At Arundel SSX a similar 'dell' runs along the west boundary of the town. The only instance in SUR, Farthingdale in Lingfield, overlooks a tiny stream-valley. It seems probable from occurrences in field-names and charter boundaries that *dell* was also used of artificial hollows. It is commonest in HRT.

denu OE 'valley'. This was the standard OE term for a main valley. It occurs in about 185 major settlement-names, and the distribution is widespread; in counties where there are no examples in major names there are usually a few in minor names. There was probably no region in which it was not part of the place-name-forming vocabulary, though in northern counties it was to some extent replaced by **dæl** in the late OE period.

The incidence of *denu* is heavily disguised on modern maps by confusion with **dūn** and **tūn**. It is also necessary to bear in mind that in S.E. England many names now ending in –den are from **denn**, not *denu*.

The type of valley to which *denu* was applied can be seen on Ann Cole's map of part of the Chilterns (Fig. 2). Good examples elsewhere include Croydon GTL, Helmdon NTP, Sheldon DEV and Turkdean GLO. Most valleys designated *denu* in place-names are long and sinuous. Such features can be found in isolation (as at Croydon), or in series along the dip-slopes of escarpments. Sometimes where there is a fine series of such valleys there are no *denu* place-names, because the settlements are named from the rivers which flow in the valleys. This can be seen in DOR, where the villages called Tarrant, Winterborne, Milborne, Dewlish, Cerne, and those named from the R. Piddle, might have had *denu* names. Ann Cole's definition (Cole 1982) is: '*denu* is mostly used of long, narrow valleys with two moderately steep sides and a gentle gradient along most of their length.'

No attempt has been made to check the topography of all the ancient settlements with *denu* names, but it is probable that the great majority conform to the pattern outlined. The only striking anomaly noted is Howden near Goole YOE.

Howden is recorded as *Heafuddene* in a charter of AD 959, when it was the centre of a large, composite estate. Smith (EPNS survey p. 251) argues for a meaning 'valley by the spit of land', saying that the *denu* is the old course of the R. Derwent, and the *hēafod* ('headland') the stretch of land between the Ouse and the old Derwent. This is very forced, however, and it seems wiser to concede that nothing in the topography of the area is ever likely to have deserved the term *denu* in the sense in which it is evidenced elsewhere. It is worth noting that Onions 1966 says under *dean* (the modern form of *denu*) that the word is related to *den* 'animal's lair etc.', and under *den* he says 'the basic meaning may be "open or flat place" '. This sense (though difficult to reconcile with the later meanings of both words) is apparent in some of the Indo-European cogantes cited under OE *denn* in Holthausen 1934. There were Germanic mercenaries at York and at Sancton in the last century of Roman Britain, and it may be suggested, very tentatively, that in Howden we have an ancient Germanic name for the Vale of York. An alternative translation to Smith's 'valley by the spit of land' would be 'chief valley', and this would be very appropriate if 'plain' could be substituted for 'valley'.

denu is used as a simplex name in Dean BDF, CMB, DEV, GLO, HMP(2), OXF, SSX(2) and WLT, Deane HMP, LNC, Deene NTP and Denes NFK.

Deanham NTB and Denholm YOW are from the dative plural. As a first element *denu* occurs in Dendron LNC, Denford BRK and NTP, Denham (near Uxbridge) BUC, SFK(2), Denwick NTB, and, most commonly, with **tūn**. Denton occurs in CMB, DRH, HNT, KNT(2), LIN, LNC(2), NFK, NTB, OXF, SSX and YOW.

As a second element, *denu* (like **cumb**) is compounded most frequently with a personal name. Here belong Addlestone SUR, Agden HNT, Balsdean SSX, Bevendean SSX, Buckden HNT, Calmsden GLO, Chaddesden DRB, Chidden HMP, Croxden STF, Duddoe NTB, Dunsden OXF, Egdean SSX, Essendine RUT, Figheldean WLT, Framsden SFK, Gaddesden HRT, Gransden CAM, HNT, Helmdon NTP, Hoddlesden LNC, Hughenden BUC, Hundon SFK, Kelvedon ESX, Lavendon BUC, Lexden ESX, Lyveden NTP, Minsden HRT, Ovenden YOW, Paddington SUR, Polesden SUR, Riddlesden YOW, Togstone NTB, Walsden LNC, Wantisden SFK, Wilsden YOW. Only Buckden and Kelvedon have feminine names, and only Kelvedon and Calmsden dithematic ones. In Scammonden YOW an ON personal name has probably been prefixed to a simplex OE name from *denu*.

The next largest category is (in contrast to **cumb**) that which has a descriptive word as first element. There are recurrent compounds with 'black' (Blackden CHE, Blagdon NTB), 'deep' (Debden ESX, Depden SFK, Dibden HMP, Dipton DRH, NTB), 'hollow' (Holden YOW, Howden NTB, YOW), 'long' (Longdale WML, Longdendale CHE/DRB), 'shallow' (Salden BUC, Shalden HMP) and 'stone' (Standen BRK, LNC, WLT). Ballidon DRB has OE *belig* 'bag' (modern *belly*), an allusion to the rounded embrasure in which the village lies. Cheesden LNC is 'gravelly'. Hambleden BUC is 'maimed', probably a reference to the broken sides, which are apparent on Fig. 2. Horden DRH is 'dirty', Nevendon ESX is 'level', and Trowden LNC is 'trough-shaped'. The only aesthetic comment is that in Meriden WAR, which may be of ME origin. Baxenden LNC is 'bakestone valley' and Flaunden HRT is 'flagstone valley', both names perhaps referring to appearances.

There are at least 15 names which refer to vegetation: Agden YOW, Aspenden HRT, Berkesdon HRT, Bramdean HMP, Croydon GTL, Haslingden LNC, Hatherden HMP, Hebden YOW(2), Hesleden DRH, Rushden HRT, NTP, Sabden LNC, Sawdon YON and Wilden BDF. Grendon HRE can be placed here or in the preceding category. Ramsden ESX, OXF may refer to wild garlic. Crops are only mentioned in Barden YOW, Heydon CAM, Whaddon (near Salisbury) WLT, Wheddon SOM, and possibly Barden YON. Wild creatures are mentioned in Amberden ESX, Cogdean DOR, Elveden SFK, Harden YOW, Ousden SFK, Ravensden BDF, Rodden SOM, and possibly Frostenden SFK. Domestic animals occur only in Assendon OXF, Shipden NFK, Swinden YOW and Wetherden SFK, and the paucity of such references makes 'wild-garlic' seem more likely for Ramsden than 'ram', especially as the plant is prolific in the appropriate area of OXF.

River-names and other topographical terms are relatively rare, but occur in

Brogden YOW, Campden GLO, Droylesden LNC, Frithsden HRT, Ipsden OXF, Pegsdon BDF, Ripponden YOW, Sheldon DEV, Turkdean GLO and Waterden NFK. Man-made constructions are referred to in Biddlesden BUC, Biddlestone NTB, Burdon DRH, Hidden BRK, Sarsden OXF, Thedden HMP and Worden LNC. Stagsden BDF and Stavordale SOM were apparently marked by posts. Hampden BUC may contain **hamm** in the sense 'enclosure in marginal land'; it can be seen from Fig. 2 that the settlement is unusually high. Plowden SHR seems to be the only name which refers to an activity (whether human or animal), and references to position are also very rare, the only certain instance being Marden WLT, though Marsden LNC, YOW, and Todmorden YON, may have a similar significance.

As regards the inhabitants, or the people in whose territory the valley lies, there are a number of names in which *denu* is added to the genitive of an –**ingas** name. These are Bagendon GLO, Essendon HRT, Monewden SFK, Ovingdean SSX, Rottingdean SSX, Whissendine RUT, Yattendon BRK, and possibly Manuden ESX and Pangdean SSX. (Dodgson 1978, p. 71 takes a different view of Pangdean, Ovingdean, Rottingdean.) Ethnic groups are referred to in Saxondale NTT and Walden ESX, HRT, YON. Lothersdale YOW (earlier *Lodersden*) is apparently 'beggar's valley', but as this type of first element is so rare with *denu*, a personal name is perhaps to be preferred.

Rather a large number of names in –*denu* are too obscure or ambiguous to be classified. These include Harpenden HRT and Harpsden OXF, and Scackleton YON, in which the identity of the first element is clear but the nature of the reference is mysterious.

gil ON 'ravine, deep narrow valley with a stream'. This term was used by Norwegian settlers in the north west. It is commonest in minor names, but occurs in a few settlement-names, including Gaisgill (near Tebay) WML, Gazegill and Howgill (near Barnoldswick) YOW, Ivegill (near Dalston) CMB, Reagill, Rosgill and Sleagill WML. In Gillcamban (near Greystoke) CMB, *gil* is used as the generic in a compound made in the Gaelic manner, with the qualifying element (an ON personal name of Irish origin) placed last.

glennos British 'valley'. This is the likeliest origin of Glen LEI, which is the name of two villages, Great Glen and Glen Parva, 5 miles apart on the R. Sence, S. of Leicester. Ekwall 1960 considers that it was the pre-English name of the river; but *Glenne* is a settlement-name, not a river-name, in its only pre-Conquest appearance, and it is possible that it was a district-name, which was adopted by the Anglo-Saxons from the Britons, and was given to two settlements which lay in the district, only coincidentally by the river. (The river-name Glen in LIN and NTB has a different British origin.)

Gaelic **gleann**, from the same root, is a common place-name element in Scotland and the Isle of Man, where Glen– names are very frequent. Welsh **glyn** and Cornish **glin**, which are the direct descendants of British *glennos*, are much less frequent in Welsh and Cornish names than *gleann* is in Scotland.

There are a few names in the most northerly English counties, such as Glencoyne CMB/WML, Glendue NTB, Glenridding WML, which are considered to contain the British word. Smith 1956 postulates an OE word *glenn*, but the evidence for this appears to be very slight indeed. The modern English word is a borrowing from Gaelic.

halh OE (Kentish and W. Saxon **healh**) 'nook'. It is difficult to give a single satisfactory translation of this word. It is related to *holh* 'hollow' and the idea of a sunken place is sufficiently prominent to bring *halh* clearly into the scope of this chapter, but it does not always mean 'valley' or 'recess'. NED gives pertinent OE and ME quotations under the modern forms *haugh* and *hale*, and the general impression conveyed by these is probably more illuminating than any translation. The 'nook' is sometimes formed not by contours but by water: *halh* is used in some areas for land between rivers or in a river-bend, and perhaps for slightly raised ground isolated by marsh. This last sense, which seems to me the only possible one for some names in LIN and East Anglia, is not considered in previous reference books. There is also a clearly evidenced 'administrative' sense: *halh* sometimes means 'piece of land projecting from, or detached from, the main area of its administrative unit'.

The dative of *halh* is *hale*, and the nominative plural is *halas*, dative *halum*. Modern northern dialect *haugh* ('flat alluvial land') is from the nominative singular, and the obsolete word *hale* ('nook') is from the dative. As the final element in a compound the word is usually in the dative singular, and it appears in modern forms as *-hal*, *-hall*, *-al*, *-all*, *-hale*, *-ale*. Care must be taken not to confuse it with *hall* 'hall', a word which is common enough in place-names of ME and modern origin, but very rare in those of OE origin. This is a well-known snare for unwary users of place-name evidence. Care is also needed in distinguishing names containing *halh* from those containing **hōh**.

halh is one of the commoner English place-name elements, occurring in about 260 names in Ekwall 1960, and commonly in minor names and field-names. Different senses predominate in different areas, and a regional survey will show up both the various meanings and the varying frequency.

In KNT *halh* is very rare; Wadden Hall is the only instance in Ekwall 1960, though there are a few instances of Hale as a farm-name. Wadden Hall is on a broad, flat hill; the *halh* may be one of the small valleys round the hill, but it seems more likely that this is the administrative use of the term, as Wadden Hall is the eastern projection of the parish of Waltham. Among minor names in KNT, Hale N.E. of Chiddingstone is an excellent example of one of the commonest senses of *halh*: the 100' contour makes a shallow, smooth curve to the E. of the tiny settlement. Hale Fm between Lamberhurst and Horsmonden, however, has a more conventional 'valley' situation. Hale Place in E. Peckham illustrates another use of *halh*, for a tongue of land between streams.

In SSX, as in KNT, there is only one major name containing *halh*, this being Lurgashall, which is discussed below. There are a number of minor names, and no attempt has been made to study the topography of all of these, but it may be noted that Fitzhall S.W. of Midhurst lies in a tiny hollow made by a curve of the 100′ contour. Several examples, however, are on the peninsula S. of Chichester, where 'hollow' is not likely to be the meaning, and these may be instances of the postulated sense 'dry ground in marsh'.

The only major name in HMP is Hale N.E. of Fordingbridge, possibly an 'administrative' name, as it lies in an angle of the N. HMP boundary. The IOW has Wroxall, discussed below, and Hale (a DB estate) in S. Arreton. Kökeritz 1940 (p. 12) says of Hale: 'the farm itself lies in a small valley . . . on the sloping eastern bank of the Yar, and this is evidently the topographical feature expressed by OE *h(e)alh* in this particular case.' It is in fact a minute valley, a nick in the 50′ contour.

DOR and DEV, like most of the counties touching the S. coast, have only one name apiece containing *healh* which is of sufficient status to be included in Ekwall 1960. The DOR name is Wraxall, discussed below. The DEV name is Halford, N.W. of Newton Abbot; this lies at the junction of two streams. As an element in minor names, however, *healh* is particularly common in DEV, mostly as a simplex name. Among names for which there are early spellings there are 7 instances of Heal(e), 19 of Hele, and one of Hale. No attempt has been made to examine the topography of these. SOM has 3 major names, Hele, Holton, and another Wraxall. Hele SOM may be an 'administrative' name, as it occupies a projecting corner of the parish of Bradford, N.E. of Wellington. Holton S.W. of Wincanton, however, occupies a well-marked recess in the 300′ contour, probably not steep enough to be a **cumb**.

In WLT, *healh* occurs in 6 names which are in Ekwall 1960. These include Ludgershall and 2 examples of Wraxall, which are discussed below. The others are Midgehall, Mildenhall and Rushall. Mildenhall is probably to be understood as a 'valley' name: recesses in escarpments in this area are regularly termed **cumb**, but the series of indentations in Mildenhall Hill by which the village stands differs in shape from the coombs. Rushall S.E. of Devizes is by a small valley which was perhaps not deep enough to be a **cumb**. Midgehall N. of Wootton Bassett is a marsh settlement, and here the sense of *healh* may be 'island of dry ground'.

In BRK, the commonest use of *healh* in settlement names is 'land in a projection of an administrative unit'. This is the sense in Bracknell and Broomhall, the only BRK examples which appear in Ekwall 1960, and it is clearly evidenced in some minor names, such as Hale Fm in the projecting N. tip of Kingston Lisle parish. SUR names in Ekwall 1960 are only Dippenhall and Hale, both in Farnham. These are probably 'valley' names, but the administrative sense is also clearly evidenced in SUR in minor names like Portnall in Egham and Michen Hall in Godalming.

North of the Thames, *halh* is particularly common in the east of the country. Ekwall 1960 gives 7 names in ESX (where *halh* is frequent in minor names), 15 in SFK and 17 in NFK. In ESX the usual sense is probably 'small valley', though the settlements are sometimes so dispersed that the original application of the name may be in doubt. The component parts in Chignall St James are tucked into shallow recesses in the 150' contour, N.W. of Chelmsford, and Coggeshall has a similar relationship to the 150' contour. Rivenhall is probably named from the tiny side-valley which runs between the church and the manor house. At Willingale (for which the DB spelling indicates dative plural *–halum*) the reference may be to the two small valleys on either side of the village. Chrishall and Strethall, on the CAM border, overlook more impressive valleys running down to the R. Cam, but these were perhaps too open and shallow to qualify for the term **denu**.

As regards the large numbers of *halh* names in NFK and SFK, no attempt has been made at a systematic topographical study, but it is clear from a casual look at the 1″ maps that in many instances the word is used for shallow recesses in the 50', 100' or 150' contours. Spexhall (the manor), Westhall and Uggeshall (N. of Halesworth) SFK are good examples. A few, like Tittleshall NFK, are in larger valleys, but in general it is the low relief of these counties which is likely to have made *halh* a useful place-name-forming term. A different meaning from that of 'valley' or 'hollow' must, however, be sought for Wiggenhall NFK, the name of a number of settlements S. of King's Lynn. These lie in deep fenland, and presumably owe their existence to the presence of patches of slightly raised ground. Some 'islands' in this area are the sites of villages with names in ēg, such as Tilney All Saints, adjoining the Wiggenhalls. It may be that *halh* was used for the lowest eminence on which building was possible. Otherwise it can only be suggested that *halh* was felt appropriate to the isolated situation of the Wiggenhalls. Mildenhall SFK is another East Anglian name which cannot be explained as referring to a valley or hollow.

In CAM, although Mepal is the only name to appear in Ekwall 1960, *halh* is frequent in minor names and field-names, and the EPNS survey notes that 'the examples come from fenland parishes, particularly from the Isle of Ely.' Mepal has an island site in fenland W. of Ely, lower than some, at least, of the neighbouring islands which have names containing ēg. 'Dry ground in marsh' may be the usual sense of *halh* in CAM.

In the counties to the west of ESX and CAM, *halh* is fairly common, though in some (e.g. NTP and OXF) a large proportion of the examples are minor names. The meaning of *halh* in the S.E. midlands is usually 'small valley' (though 'dry ground in marsh' would suit Northolt and Southall GTL). The EPNS survey of BUC (p. 94) draws attention to the group Dagnall, Northall, Ringshall and a lost *Hudnall*, all in the parish of Edlesborough, and says: 'They all . . . lie in nooks on the slopes of the Chilterns.' This applies also to Halton BUC. Worminghall BUC and Meppershall BDF offer difficulties which only local knowledge could hope to resolve. Ludgershall BUC is discussed below, and some other S.E. midland names are listed in the analysis of first elements.

In the N.E. midlands, LEI has only one major name containing *halh*, this being Hallaton, overlooking a long, curving stream-valley, which might equally well, to judge by the 1″ map, have been called **denu**.

NTT is one of the few counties where *halh* is more prominent in major than in minor names. It occurs in a series of names to the W. and N. of Nottingham, comprising Cossall, Nuthall, Hucknall, Arnold, and (further north) Halam and Halloughton. Hallam DRB can be included with this group. Other major names in NTT are Kneesall and Kersall, N.E. of Southwell, and Ordsall, S. of E. Retford. The frequency of *halh* in this county may be due to the occurrence of valleys which are too short to deserve the term **denu** and too open for **cumb** or **hop**.

In LIN, 7 names in *halh* are included in Ekwall 1960, these being Bucknall, Hale, Halton(3), Rippingale and Tattershall. Hale S.E. of Sleaford is a very clear instance of the names for which 'dry ground in marsh' seems the most satisfactory rendering. The villages of Great and Little Hale occupy distinct islands of gravel in the predominant boulder clay, as shown by one of the maps in Cameron 1965, reproduced in Gelling 1978 (p. 218). The same meaning is probable in Bucknall, Tattershall and East Halton. West Halton, however, further inland on the Humber estuary from East Halton, is in a tiny indentation of the 100′ contour and other 'valley' sites in LIN are Rippingale, in a shallow valley in the low escarpment on the W. edge of the fens, and Halton Holegate by a tiny valley in the rising ground on the N. edge of the fens.

On the west side of the country, north of the Thames, GLO has at least 25 names containing *halh*, but most of them refer to minor settlements. Only Abenhall, Cromhall and Luggershall appear in Ekwall 1960, though Oxenhall might have been included as it is a parish and DB manor. Luggers Hall is discussed below. Cromhall, N.W. of Wickwar, overlooks a narrow valley, and it is presumably the narrowness which prevents the site from being a **cumb**, like nearby Stinchcombe, which overlooks a much wider feature. Smith's statement (EPNS survey 3, p. 4) that *halh* means 'land in a river-bend' in Cromhall is not convincing, as this would make the compound tautologous. Cromhall probably means 'valley with a stream-bend', the first element being OE *crumbe*. Abenhall, S.E. of Mitcheldean, overlooks a narrow side-valley, shorter and straighter than the long, curving feature which gives name to Mitcheldean. Oxenhall N.W. of Newent may contain *halh* in the sense 'tongue of land between streams'.

In WOR *halh* is commoner than in GLO, but again mainly in minor names. Halesowen, Hallow, Hawne, Rednal and Wribbenhall are in Ekwall 1960. Halesowen and Hawne are both from the plural of *halh*, Hales– from the nominative and Hawne from the dative. Probably this was a district-name, suitable for the broken country W. of Birmingham, and the variant grammatical forms became attached to different settlements in the same great manor. Rednal refers to a small valley in the Lickey Hills, and Wribbenhall to a small valley across the R. Severn from Bewdley. Hallow near Worcester, however, is not a 'valley' name, but a striking example of the use of *halh* for a tongue of land between two rivers. The Laughern Brook flows nearly parallel with the R. Severn for several miles and Hallow is at the narrower, northern, end of the tongue thus formed. Hallow is a compound name with *halh* as first element and the dative plural of *haga* 'enclosure' as second.

In HRE, Winnall, S.W. of Hereford, is an isolated *halh* name which may have an administrative significance, as the area is a S.W. projection of the parish of Allensmore. (Dewsall, adjoining, is 'St David's spring' from the W. Midland form of **well**.) Lyonshall S.E. of Kington is at the head of a long, broad valley, and at Leinthall S.W. of Ludlow, also, the valley is big enough to seem deserving of another term.

The SHR names containing *halh* are not evenly distributed; there is a cluster round Shifnal and Albrighton, and most of the rest are spread over the northern part of the county. There are not many instances S. of the R. Severn, in the region where **hop** is prominent, but there are Halton (Lady, Hill and Prior's) W. of Ludlow, and a line of names running up to the Severn at Ironbridge. As regards the Haltons, it is difficult to say for which of the settlements the name was coined, but there are appropriate valleys at both Hill and Prior's Halton. Ruthall, W. of Ditton Priors, is in a recess formed by two of the headsprings of the Rea Brook, a situation perhaps too open to be thought of as a **hop**. Haughton, N. of Morville, the next in this line of names, overlooks a straight, narrow valley, and Benthall overlooks a dramatic example of this type of valley, a narrow cutting running in from Ironbridge Gorge. Nearby Posenhall, on the other hand, overlooks a curving stream-valley which was appropriately called **denu**, as witnessed by The Dean lower down its course, so perhaps there is a feature here which does not show on the 1″ map. In the area S. of Much Wenlock, *halh* is used of broad, shallow depressions in a number of minor names such as Monk Hall W. of Monkhopton, Sidnall W. of Chetton and The Hales S.W. of Burwarton.

Shifnal SHR is an excellent example of a settlement in a slightly sunken position which is experienced rather than seen. It is notorious as a place where fog forms first and disperses last. Haughton, N.W. of Shifnal, is in an adjoining hollow, and Sheriffhales to the N., and Boningale and Kilsall near Albrighton are probably similar. The series of names in which *halh* refers to a slight hollow probably continues into STF, with Codsall and Tettenhall, though these are not easy to evaluate on the modern map. Wappenshall on the edge of the Weald Moors, however, may contain *halh* in the sense 'dry ground in marsh', and this sense is clearly apparent further north, in the wet lands on the SHR/CHE border. There was a district called Hales in the N.E. corner of SHR. Market Drayton was formerly *Drayton in Hales* and the affix survives in Norton in Hales. Other names in the north of SHR in which this sense is apparent include Whixall N. of Wem, which has a raised site in a very wet area. The sense 'valley' is also apparent in the northern part of SHR, however, as Broughall E. of Whitchurch is enclosed by an indentation of the 350′ contour, and Haughton and Rednal, S. of Ellesmere, are in slight recesses in the higher ground on the edge of the marshes which border the R. Perry. Lyneal, S.E. of Ellesmere, probably refers to a slight hollow, and Hadnall, N. of Shrewsbury, is at the mouth of a small valley which is not much more than a nick in the 250′ contour. Another sense is found in Rossall, N.W. of Shrewsbury, which is in a bend of the R. Severn.

By contrast with the topographical senses described above, Haughton N.E. of Shrewsbury contains *halh* in its administrative meaning. The parish boundaries of Upton Magna reach Haughton by a narrow corridor, then enclose it in a tight knob. The administrative sense may also be the relevant one in Wrentnall, S.W. of Shrewsbury. It seems clear that in SHR *halh* was used with nearly the whole range of its toponymical meanings. The picture is even more complete if some Welsh names are included. Haughton MTG, on the SHR border W. of Melverley, for which no early spellings are available, is in the junction of the R. Severn and the Afon Vyrnwy, and the sense 'land between rivers' is appropriate also to Halghton FLI, N.E. of Ellesmere.

Major names in *halh* are very frequent in STF, and most of the sites fall into the categories of 'small valley' or of 'dry ground in marsh'. 'Small valley' or 'hollow' seems the likely meaning of the *halh* names round Wolverhampton, such as Ettingshall, Gornal, Pelsall, Walsall, Rushall, Stonnal, Willenhall and (as already noted) Tettenhall and Codsall. This is the appropriate sense also in Bednall, and in some names in other parts of the county such as Gnosall (which nestles into a little valley), Tixall S.E. of Stafford, Moddershall N.E. of Stone, Yoxall N. of Lichfield, and Bucknall N.E. of Stoke on Trent. The hypothesis of a meaning 'dry ground in marsh' suits some of the *halh* names round Stafford. It seems highly appropriate to Badenhall, N.E. of Eccleshall, and to Haughton. Coppenhall may be a promontory into marsh, and Ellenhall could be a tongue of land between streams. Edingale N.E. of Lichfield could be held to contain *halh* in the sense 'land in a river-bend' with reference to the winding of the R. Mease; but 'promontory into marsh' is also suitable. Eccleshall occupies a shallow curve in the contours of the gently rising ground S. of the R. Sow, and the meaning of *halh* could be 'recess', but there is a possibility of this being an area with a special administrative status at a very early date, and this is discussed below.

WAR, CHE and DRB are the remaining midland counties to be considered. In WAR, *halh* is used of very small valleys. Balsall is said in the EPNS survey to be an 'administrative' *halh*, as it was until 1863 a chapelry of Hampton in Arden, and formed the S.E. angle of that parish. It may nevertheless be a topographical name, but location of the site of the early settlement would be necessary before this possibility could be assessed. Wroxall (discussed further below) and Beausale are adjacent settlements in the open country between Knowle and Warwick which is characterized by broad, shallow gullies. Halford, S.E. of Stratford on Avon, is in a recess in the 200′ contour, Ullenhall, E. of Redditch, lies in a slight hollow, and Willenhall appears from the 1st edition 1″ map to be overlooking a tiny gully on the W. of a road into Coventry. Stivichall is difficult to interpret. It stands on a hill-spur S. of Coventry, but the reference may be to one of the valleys on either side. The two Exhalls are discussed below.

In CHE, the senses 'small valley' and 'dry ground in marsh' are both appropriate to names containing *halh*. The two types of site can be seen in proximity in Darnhall and Wettenhall, N.W. of Crewe. Wettenhall is in a belt of flat ground traversed by small streams, while Darnhall occupies a little valley in the raised ground which borders the area to the N. The use of 'wet' and 'hidden' as qualifiers may show awareness that the word is used in contrasting senses. Coppenhall N. of Crewe is in the same belt of marshy ground, and Blakenhall and Broomhall are similarly situated N.E. of Audlem. At Hassall, N.E. of Crewe, Hassall Hall stands on an island made by the 250′ contour, overlooking Hassall Moss. In other parts of the county, 'valley' sites include Taxal S. of Whaley Bridge, Bramhall S. of Stockport, Hale in Altringham, and Pownall and Styal N. of Wilmslow. Grappenhall S.E. of Warrington occupies a recess in the 100′ contour. Kelsall E. of Chester is a very good example of a 'small valley' site, and at Iddinshall, W. of Tarporley, the Hall lies in a nick in the 150′ contour. Tattenhall S.W. of Iddinshall and Haughton S.E. of Tattenhall refer to similar, slightly larger, valleys. Saughall N.W. of Chester stands on the flat ledge which overlooks the Dee marshes; the *halh* may be the valley in the 100′ contour, E. of Great Saughall. Saughall Massie in the Wirral, on the other hand, is more likely to refer to a dry patch in marsh.

This leaves, for CHE, the difficult problem of the name Wirral. Wirral is apparently a compound of *halh* with a plant-name, OE *wīr* 'bog-myrtle'. Some pre-Conquest spellings indicate derivation from the dative plural (*Wirhalum*), others are from the dative singular (*Wirhale*). Dodgson (EPNS survey 1, p. 8) suggests that the singular form refers to the whole peninsula. This could be seen as an extension of the sense 'land between rivers' already noted, and a parallel can be found in Rossall LNC, considered by Ekwall (1922, p. 158) to be the name of the Feetwood peninsula. There is a doublet of the name Wirral in YOW, Worrall N.W. of Sheffield, and a third *Wirhal* has been noted as a 13th-century field-name in Wadworth YOW. Worrall is situated on a tongue of land between the R. Don and the R. Yoxley, and this position seems the likeliest meaning of *halh* in the name, but the 'bog-myrtle' presents some difficulty, as the land between the rivers is a high, dry ridge. Possibly some other explanation should be sought for *Wir–* in Wirrall and Worrall.

In DRB, *halh* is mainly, perhaps exclusively, used of valleys or recesses in hills. Bonsall, S.W. of Matlock, is in a narrow, steep little valley, and Chunal, S. of Glossop, overlooks a similar feature called Long Clough. Monsal Dale, N.W. of Bakewell, is a very steep stretch of the valley of the R. Wye. Somersal, N.E. of Uttoxeter, however, is more like some of the CHE sites discussed above, in a broad, short valley in relatively low-lying country, and

Sedsall to the N.W. is in a hollow in the low escarpment which overlooks the flood plain of the R. Dove. Ticknall, S.W. of Melbourne, is another 'recess', enclosed by the 350′ contour. Calow, E. of Chesterfield, is a compound of *calu* 'bare' and *halh*. The church is on the edge of a small, sub-circular hill, overlooking a very slight valley. It is possible that the adjective *calu* is here used as a substantive and is the name of the hill. Breadsall, N.E. of Derby, refers to a widening of the valley of the R. Derwent.

In the counties N. of the Mersey and Humber, *halh* is a common element, except in DRH and WML. In LNC there are some 'valley' sites. These include Crumpsall, N.W. of Manchester and Langho, N.E. of Burnley (Old Langho is in a broad, shallow valley). Hothersall W. of Ribchester is an excellent example of a 'little valley' site. Ellel, S. of Lancaster, is in a broad valley in low-lying country, and Halton, N.E. of Lancaster, is in a broadening of the valley of the R. Lune. In spite of these examples, the 'watery' senses of *halh* probably predominate in LNC. There is a series of names running from near Liverpool to near Garstang for most of which 'dry ground in marsh' seems the likeliest sense. Hale, S.E. of Liverpool, was originally plural (*Halas* 1094), and the name may refer to those parts of the promontory which are above the 50′ contour. Halewood is 'wood belonging to Hale'. Maghull, N. of Liverpool, presumably occupies a slightly raised site, and this applies also to Midge Hall near Leyland. Halsall, N.W. of Ormskirk, overlooks a low valley in the 50′ contour on the edge of a broad area of moss; *halh* in this name could be 'promontory into marsh', or it could refer to the breaks in the contour on either side of the settlement. Houghton N. of Warrington is on an 'island' made by the 50′ contour. Catterall S.E. of Garstang looks like a 'promontory into marsh' site. LNC also provides evidence for the occasional use of *halh* in the sense 'land in a river-bend': Haughton E. of Manchester is in a great bend of the R. Tame, and Kersal N.W. of Manchester is in a bend of the R. Irwell. Haulgh in Bolton is said in Ekwall 1922 (p. 45) to be between two rivers.

halh is particularly common in YOW and Smith (EPNS survey) was confident that 'land in a river-bend' was well attested in this county. He considered this to be the meaning in Beal, Hensall, Gowdall and the minor name Smeathalls, which occur beside the R. Aire E. of Knottingley. The compound found in Beal, however, which is from OE *bēag* 'ring' and *halh*, suggests (as does Cromhall GLO) that *halh* did not convey the sense 'river-bend' so unequivocally that another word for the bend was otiose. A sense 'dry ground in marsh' would also suit these names. Other YOW names in which *halh* could mean 'river-bend' include Kirk Sandall by the R. Don and Cattall, N.E. of Wetherby, on the R. Nidd. This could be the sense also in Halton West, S.W. of Hellifield, though 'dry ground in marsh' may be more appropriate. The latter sense is suitable for Wighill S.E. of Wetherby. Burnsall S.E. of Grassington is in a shallow curve of the R. Wharfe, but also in the valley of a tiny tributary. 'Little valley' is an appropriate sense of *halh* in Loversall near Doncaster, Darnall near Sheffield, Gomersal near Bradford and Wilsill E. of

Pateley Bridge. Killinghall N.W. of Harrogate overlooks a little valley. Other YOW names containing *halh* belong to settlements in broad, shallow valleys in low-lying country; these include Sicklinghall W. of Wetherby, Campsall near Doncaster and Pannal S. of Harrogate. Great Houghton near Doncaster is in a shallow valley. Frizinghall N.W. of Bradford is probably another 'valley' name, and Hallam (dat. pl.) refers to the dramatically broken country W. of Sheffield. Elmsall is difficult to classify as it is not immediately obvious where the earliest settlement lay. The most seriously intractable of the YOW names which have been investigated is Halton East, N.W. of Ilkley, which has an unequivocal hill-top position. Eccleshall is discussed below.

YON has 10 major names containing *halh*. Here, as in YOW, the sense 'land in a river-bend' is likely in some examples. It seems most probable for High and Low Worsall, S.W. of Middlesbrough, which stand on either side of the base of a sharp loop in the R. Tees. At first sight it seems equally compelling for Over Dinsdale in the even sharper bend of the Tees to the W., but Dinsdale is considered to be from OE *Dīctūneshalh* 'nook belonging to Deighton', and if it was indeed an outlying property of Deighton (N. of Northallerton) the administrative sense of *halh* may be the relevant one. Low Dinsdale is immediately across the river in DRH. Crakehill S. of Dalton and Pickhill W. of Thirsk could refer to bends in the R. Swale, and Bossall N. of Stamford Bridge could refer to a loop in the R. Derwent. The 'valley' or 'recess' senses of *halh* are represented in YON by Bedale and Crakehall which adjoin, and Finghall, a short distance to the W. Brignall S.E. of Barnard Castle is also in a tiny valley.

YOE has only 3 major names containing *halh*: Birdsall S.E. of Malton is in a little valley, Riccall is by a great curve of the R. Ouse, and Arnold, E. of Beverley, looks like a very clear instance of 'dry ground in marsh'.

North of Yorkshire, the use of *halh* for land in a river-bend becomes much more pronounced, and has led to the dialect sense of *haugh* noted above. This is the obvious meaning of the three major names in DRH: Houghall and Finchale refer to loops of the R. Wear, and Haughton le Skerne near Darlington lies in a loop of the R. Skerne. In NTB, where *halh* is very common, most of the names fall into the category of 'river-bend' or 'small stream-valley'. In the first category are Etal E. of Coldstream, Humshaugh N. of Hexham, and Hepple W. of Rothbury. In the second are Bothal, E. of Morpeth, in the valley of a tiny tributary of the R. Wansbeck, and Broomhaugh, S.E. of Corbridge, by a small tributary of the R. Tyne. Similarly, Greenhaugh N.W. of Bellingham and Henshaw E. of Haltwhistle refer to the valleys of small tributaries of Tarset Burn and R. South Tyne. Kirkhaugh and Barhaugh N. of Alston are in small stream-valleys, and so is Seghill, N.W. of Whitley Bay, though the last is in much lower country. Howtel S.E. of Coldstream is at the head of a small stream-valley. Beadnell and Tughall, S. of Seahouses, may contain *halh* in the sense 'hollow'.

halh is rare in WML and less common in CMB than in NTB. Edenhall

CMB is by a loop in the Eden, but this explanation of *halh* cannot apply to Wetheral, higher up the river. 'Raised ground in marsh' would be appropriate to Wetheral. Isel Hall CMB, N.E. of Cockermouth, is in a tongue of land where a small tributary joins the R. Derwent. Haile CMB, S.E. of Egremont, is in a little stream-valley.

Some compound names containing *halh* occur so frequently that they must be regarded as appellatives rather than as *ad hoc* place-name coinages, and these may conveniently be discussed before a general analysis of first elements is offered. Doublets, or even triplets, of compounds with plant-names and animal-names need not be more than coincidence (this may apply to Wirrall/Worrall discussed above), and it is unremarkable in this quantity of material to find the same personal names occurring two or three times as first element. But there are some compounds whose recurrence cannot easily be ascribed to chance, and these certainly include Eccleshall/Exhall; Ludgershall/Lurgashall/Luggershall; Strensall; and Wraxall/Wroxall.

Eccleshall STF, YOW, and Exhall WAR(2) were discussed in Gelling 1978 (p. 97), and it was tentatively suggested that they might contain an early administrative use of *halh*, not in the precise later meaning 'land in a projecting part of an administrative area', but in a sense 'land not included in the general administrative arrangements of a region'. This suggestion accords quite well with the latest discussion of *eccles* in place-names, Thomas 1980 (pp. 262–5). Professor Thomas argues that *eccles* may have meant 'Christian community' rather than 'church building'. The statement in Gelling 1978 that the WAR Exhall sites are not appropriate to *halh* in the sense 'hollow' requires emendation, however, as it has been pointed out to me that at Exhall near Coventry the church is in just such a hollow.

The 5 place-names which derive from OE *lūtegareshalh* were also discussed in Gelling 1978 (p. 171), and Professor Tengstrand's solution 'hollow of the trapping-spear' was cited as the most satisfactory etymology. The only observation to be added in the light of the present study is that *halh* in these names now seems more likely to refer to a small natural valley than to a hollow in a hill-side or to a cave or an animal's lair, as suggested by Tengstrand. Lurgashall SSX is in a little stream-valley, and Ludgershall BUC is in an indentation of the 250' contour. At Ludgershall WLT the modern village adjoins the castle on a flat-topped hill, but the name may originally have referred to one of the valleys which run into the hill. Luggers Hall Fm in Owlpen GLO is not on the 1" map, but a valley sense is likely as this is broken country. The fifth example, a lost name near Saffron Walden in ESX, has been located by Mr S Bassett, and is in a little valley.

Strensall YON is the surviving example of a group of names which are also discussed in Gelling 1978 (p. 189), though no conclusion is reached there about the meaning of the compound. The problem has been reviewed more recently by R Coates (1981), who puts forward the entertaining suggestion that OE *strēoneshalh* means 'begetting corner', and may be translated 'secluded spot used by lovers'. Coates comments on the irony of the fact that one of the four places with this name was the site of St Hilda's abbey.

Wraxall DOR, SOM, WLT(2), and Wroxall WAR, IOW, mean 'buzzard's nook', and there are additional instances in minor names. The EPNS survey of WAR (p. 229) points out that places with this name lie in valleys. It is likely that a secluded valley harboured prey which attracted buzzards, and that these are places over which the birds regularly hovered and circled. The frequency of the name suggests that *wrocceshealh* was an appellative for such a valley.

Analysis of first elements in compound names containing *halh* reveals that by far the largest category consists of personal names. There are between 80 and 90 such compounds in the corpus examined, and this could be considered to show that *halh* had the sort of quasi-habitative significance suggested for some other elements, such as **ēg, dūn** and **ford**: that is, it was often used for a situation obviously suited to a settlement, not just for a natural feature as such. The personal names are rarely dithematic, though this type is found in Bossall YON, Gomersal and Loversall YOW, Kersall and Kneesall NTT, Modders-hall STF, Monsal DRB, Tattershall LIN and Wappenshall SHR. Dunken-halgh LNC contains an Irish name, and Ilketshall SFK a Scandinavian one, but the majority of the personal names which occur with this element are mono-thematic, masculine, and OE. No feminine names have been noted.

There are at least 8 place-names in which *halh* is apparently added to the genitive of a group-name in –ingas. These are Arminghall NFK, Edingale STF, Killinghall YOW, Ricklinghall SFK, Rippingale LIN, Sicklinghall YOW, Stanninghall NFK, and Willingale ESX. Finghall YON, Iddinshall CHE and Kenninghall NFK may belong in this category, but may contain connective –ing–, as, probably, does Boningale SHR. The comparative fre-quency of –inga– compounds could be held to suggest that *halh* was fashion-able in the 7th to 8th centuries.

After personal names, references to vegetation form the next largest group of first elements compounded with *halh*. There are about 30 of these in the corpus examined. References which are repeated include that to 'broom' (Bramhall and Broomhall CHE, Broomhall BRK, Broomhaugh NTB, Brun-dall NFK), 'peas' (Peasenhall SFK, Posenhall SHR) and 'willow' (Saughall CHE(2), Willenhall WAR, Winnal HRE and Wyddial HRT). Crops are only referred to in Benhall SFK, Ryhall RUT and possibly Ellenhall STF.

There are 15 compounds in which the first element is a descriptive term: Blakenhall CHE, Chisnall LNC, Darnall YOW and Darnhall CHE, Dip-penhall SUR, Greenhaugh NTB, Gressenhall NFK (which, like Chisnall, refers to gravel), Langhale NFK and Langho LNC, Pannal YOW, Rivenhall ESX, Sandal YOW(2), Stonnal STF, and Wettenhall CHE. Topographical terms are rare, but occur in Beal YOW, Calow DRB, Cromhall GLO, Houghall DRH, Howtel NTB, Strethall ESX, and possibly in Pickhill YON and Styal CHE. Earlier place-names or river-names are very rare, the first being noted only in Dinsdale YON and Lyonshall HRE, and river-names only in Edenhall CMB, Leinthall HRE and possibly Bethnal Green GTL and Seghill NTB. There are only four references to position: Mildenhall SFK, Westhall SFK, and Northolt and Southall GTL, the last two being named in relation to each other.

Wild creatures are mentioned in Arnold NTT, YOE, Cattall YOW, Crakehall and Crakehill YON, Finchale DRH, Midge Hall LNC and Midgehall WLT, and possibly Knettishall SFK, Renhold BDF, Spexhall SFK and Worminghall BUC. The two 'eagle nooks' should be compared with the 'buzzard' names discussed above. Domestic animals are named in Oxenhall GLO, Rossall LNC, SHR, Shephall HRT, Ticknall DRB, Tixall STF and Wetheral CMB.

There are very few references to buildings. Gornal STF is probably 'mill nook', Kirkhaugh NTB had, or belonged to, a church. Wighill YOW might contain **wīc** in its earliest sense 'Romano-British settlement'. Grappenhall CHE refers to a drain. Chrishall ESX is 'Christ's nook'. Brignall YON, Campsall YOW, Catterall LNC, Etal NTB, Ettingshall STF, Gnosall STF, Rednal WOR and Yoxall STF have not been classified as the nature of the first elements is not sufficiently clear.

hop OE 'remote enclosed place'. This word has other meanings besides 'valley', but that is the most prolific of its senses in place-names. Neither the significance nor the origin of the word can be regarded as established. The only certain occurrence in literary OE is in *Beowulf*, where the monsters' lairs are called *fenhopu* and *morhopu*, 'marsh retreats', but there may be another instance, with similar meaning, in a gloss. Onions 1966 says 'ultimate origin disputed', but Holthausen 1934 relates *hop* to Latin *cubare* 'to lie', *cubitus* 'elbow', to a Greek word one of the meanings of which is 'hollow near the hip', and to an Old Indian word meaning 'hollow, pit'. He regards OE *hype* 'hip', *hēap* 'heap' and *onhupian* 'to recoil' as related words.

NED, under the modern form *hope*, lists the following three meanings, expressing a doubt as to whether they all belonged originally to one word:

1   A piece of enclosed land, e.g. in the midst of fens or marshes or of waste land generally. This sense is evidenced in a charter boundary of AD 995 in KNT, and in later sources till 1607.
2   A small enclosed valley . . . a blind valley . This sense is not evidenced in literary sources till the late 14th century, but it is demonstrated below that it must have been current in OE.
3   An inlet, small bay, haven. English (as opposed to Scottish) occurrences are noted from 1587–1887. With this sense NED compares ON *hóp* 'a small land-locked bay or inlet, salt at flood tide and fresh at ebb.' The earliest references given in NED for the sense 'bay' are to Scottish place-names.

The first and third senses given in NED may be considered first, as they require less discussion than the 'valley' meaning. It is doubtful whether the third sense is to be reckoned with in names of OE origin. It is seen in a few coastal names in southern England, including Stanford le Hope ESX and Hope (by Bolt Head) DEV, but no evidence has been noted for it earlier than the 13th century, and it may be a ME development due to association with the ON word mentioned above. ON *hóp* is not certainly instanced in names in England. It may occur in a few coastal names in PEM, and is certainly found in the names of harbour villages in Orkney.

In the sense 'piece of enclosed land in a fen', *hop* is clearly evidenced in KNT (as in Hope All Saints in Romney Marsh) and in ESX, where the EPNS survey notes that it is common in field-names in the coastal marshes. There are a few minor names in both these counties for which 'enclosure in waste' is more appropriate than 'enclosure in fen'; these include Hope House in Little Bursted ESX and Hope Fm in Hawkinge KNT. It is possible that (like **hamm** and **holmr**) *hop* developed a meaning 'promontory jutting into marsh'. This would be appropriate in Hopton on the N. boundary of SFK, and seems possible for Hopton N. of Lowestoft SFK. Hope Fm in Beckley SSX is on a promontory jutting into the Rother Levels, and Hope Fm in Rudgwick SSX is on a promontory by the R. Arun.

The senses 'enclosure in marsh or moor' are found in north-eastern and north-western England. Hope Green S. of Stockport CHE looks like 'enclosure in marsh', and Mythop LNC, E. of Blackpool, and Meathop WML, N.E. of Grange over Sands, are very good instances of this meaning. The north-eastern instances are less certain, but Ryhope DRH (on the coast at the mouth of a very tiny valley) and Cassop S.E. of Durham may refer to enclosures in moor. Hoppen NTB, S. of Bamburgh, seems much more likely to mean 'at the enclosures' than 'at the valleys'. A notable instance of 'enclosure in marsh' is Skellingthorpe W. of Lincoln, earlier *Scheldinghop*.

In the sense 'valley', *hop* is characteristic of a limited area of the Welsh Marches, of the E. and W. edges of the Pennine Chain, and of the mountainous areas of DRH and NTB and southern Scotland.

South of the R. Thames, the meaning 'valley' has only been noted in one name, though more thorough search might reveal a few others. The single major settlement-name is Wallop HMP. Nether, Over and Middle Wallop are in the upper part of the valley of Wallop Brook. The northernmost village, Over Wallop, is at the head of the valley, where a brook rises, and if the first element is **well** the name refers to this river-source. But the normal form of **well** in HMP is Well– not Wall–. The name Wallop is anomolous, both as regards the apparent use of the west-midland form of **well** and as regards the choice of the word *hop* for a valley in this area. It may be necessary to postulate the presence of people from the west midlands to account for it. It may be relevant that the valley is narrow, making the settlement-site unusually constricted. There is another Wallop in SHR, W. of Pontesbury, and Wallhope Fm in Tidenham GLO has the same origin.

There is a DOR dialect word *ope* 'an opening in the cliffs down to the water's edge', which is probably the same as *ope* used in street-names in CNW for a narrow close. It is not certain that these are related to the place-name element *hop*; they may be, but they would not constitute evidence that *hop* was regularly used in southern England for an inland valley, like that at Wallop HMP. In BRK and WLT *hop* does not occur in this or any other sense.

North of the R. Thames, in the S.W. midlands, there is a belt of country stretching from the Forest of Dean in GLO to the R. Severn in SHR in which *hop* is used mainly for valleys. The western limit of this area is a little to the W. of Offa's Dyke, and its eastern limit is the HRE/WOR border. WAR has no names containing *hop*, and apart from some names on the HRE border WOR has only Hopwood in Alvechurch, where the meaning cannot be 'valley'. Within the area just defined there are many ancient settlement-names in which *hop* means 'valley', and as this is well outside the sphere of ON influence, no credence should be given to Smith's statement (1956, 1, p. 260) that the meaning ' "small enclosed valley . . ." is not evidenced before ME and may originate in fact in ON *hóp* "a small inlet or bay".'

There are a few minor names in GLO—Cannop Brook, Hope Fm in Falfield and Wallhope Fm in Tidenham—in which *hop* means 'valley', but the use of the term in this sense in major names starts on the GLO/HRE border, where Longhope GLO and Hope Mansel are to be found, and the first concentration of such names lies a few miles to the north, where Sollers Hope, Fownhope, Littlehope and Woolhope are associated with the feature known to geographers as the Woolhope Dome. There is another concentration N.W. of Hereford, where Hope under Dinmore, Gattertop, Westhope, Lawton's Hope and Burghope surround another massif. Brinsop and Yarsop are in valleys in a massif to the S.W. of this, and there are relatively isolated examples N.W. and N.E. of Hereford, such as Cusop on the W. boundary of the county, Hopton near Stoke Lacy, and Hopleys Green near Almeley (*Hope* in DB). In the northern tip of HRE *hop* is less common, but Covenhope and Brinshope Fm occur in the hilly land near Wigmore, and Miles Hope is N.E. of Leominster.

The densest concentration of names in which *hop* means 'valley' is probably in SHR, S. of the R. Severn. One of the most striking features of the toponymy here is the series of *hop* names between the parallel ridges of Wenlock Edge and the Aymestrey Limestone escarpment. Part of the valley between them is known as Hope Dale. The settlements are called Presthope, Easthope, Wilderhope, Millichope, Middlehope, Westhope and Dinchope. All but the first lie in funnel-shaped valleys, and the openings run through the Aymestrey Limestone to the R. Corve, except for that at Dinchope which faces W. through Wenlock Edge. Presthope, at the N. end of the series, is not in a valley now, but overlooks the broad end of an identical feature.

In the hilly country to the E. and W. of this double escarpment *hop* is used for valleys of more varied shape and size. Hopton Cangeford (sometimes called Hopton in the Hole) and The Hope are at the southern end of the Clee Hills,

Hopton Wafers is in a deep valley W. of Cleobury Mortimer, and Monkhopton and Woolshope (an excellent example) are in escarpment valleys S. of Much Wenlock. To the W. of Wenlock Edge are Hope Bowdler, Hopton Castle and Hopesay, the last two in valleys in the hills which continue the line of the Long Mynd. Ratlinghope occupies a very secluded site in a deep valley on the western side of the Long Mynd. Edenhope is in the mountains S.E. of Montgomery. There are other *hop* names (including Wallop near Westbury) in the hills which run up to the Severn on the SHR/MTG border, and the MTG names discussed below belong to this, mainly SHR, group.

Names in which *hop* certainly means 'valley' are confined in SHR to the area S. of the R. Severn. North SHR has a few names in *hop*, the best recorded being Hopton S.W. of Hodnet and Hopton N. of Nesscliffe. Hopton near Hodnet is associated with Hopley and Hope Wood. The hamlets are on the S. and E. side of a narrow hill. There is a broad belt of heathland round these sides, and while the names could refer to small recesses in the hill, the meaning 'enclosure in waste' is also possible for *hop* in these instances. Hopton near Nesscliffe lies at the foot of Nesscliffe Hill, in a very slight recess, not at all like the valleys of the *hop* names S. of the Severn.

The most puzzling *hop* name in SHR is Cantlop E. of Condover. This is S. of the R. Severn, but the site is totally unlike that of the other *hop* names in the south of the county. The village is on a flat shelf on the side of a broad, low hill overlooking the Cound Brook, to which the first element of the name possibly refers. The meaning 'valley' seems impossible here. While some uncertainty attaches to the meaning of *hop* in Cantlop and in names in the northern part of SHR, it is clear that the R. Severn is the northern limit of an area where *hop* is used of deep valleys in mountainous country.

In CHE, *hop* is rare in settlement-names, though better represented in field-names. The sense 'valley' is probably not the commonest one, though it does occur in a number of instances of Harrop, the same name as Harehope NTB, which is discussed below.

Welsh names containing *hop* occur in a narrow belt close to the W. boundaries of HRE, SHR and CHE. The line starts with Burlingjobb RAD, S.E. of New Radnor. To the N. of this are Evenjobb, Cascob and Heyop, all in RAD. There is then a gap, after which the line is taken up in MTG by Hopton S. of Montgomery, and continued by Hope E. of Welshpool. There is then a long gap until the line is completed by two FLI names, Hope N. of Wrexham, and finally Northop S. of Flint. In the two FLI names the meaning could be 'enclosure' rather than 'valley'; but the examples just across the border from SHR are in mountain valleys. Two of these latter, Burlingjobb and Evenjobb, have attracted the attention of historians as having a possible bearing on the historical context of Offa's Dyke. The problems raised by these two names are discussed below, after the regional survey.

In LNC, Mythop E. of Blackpool is a noteworthy instance of *hop* in the sense 'enclosure in marsh', but names in which *hop* means 'valley' are concentrated in the area N. of Manchester. Here are Bacup, Cowpe, Hope in Eccles, Hopwood, and a number of minor names. These can be considered as part of a Pennine group.

In the Pennines, *hop* is used in the names of settlements at the ends of long, narrow valleys. The southern end of the series is to be found in DRB and STF, in an E./W. line to the north of Ashbourne. Here are Bradnop, Hope and Stanshope STF, and Alsop and Hopton (S.W. of Wirksworth) DRB. Other DRB examples occur at the heads of the deep valley which runs into the Pennines from Matlock: Hassop is N. of Bakewell, and Hope and Ashop are at the tip of the eastern branch of the valley, further N. than Hassop. Glossop DRB is near the tip of a narrow valley running in from the western edge of the Pennines, N.E. of Stockport. Midhope YOW, S.W. of Penistone, is another member of this group of names. The series continues northwards along the mountain range, but before looking at the *hop* names of the Lake District and Yorkshire it will be useful to note the occasional occurrences of the word, sometimes in contrasting senses, in the non-mountainous areas of the east midlands.

In the S.E. midlands, and in East Anglia, *hop* is very rare. MDX (GTL) has Hope House in Edmonton and a few field-names. BUC, OXF, HRT, BDF, HNT and CAM have apparently no occurrences at all. In ESX *hop* occurs in the sense 'enclosure in marsh', as noted above. There is as yet no detailed survey of NFK or SFK, but the only major names containing *hop* in these counties which are noted in Ekwall 1960 are the two SFK Hoptons discussed above. No names containing *hop* in LEI or RUT, are noted in Ekwall 1960, but LIN has one major name, Swinhope, S.W. of Grimsby. Swinhope occupies an embayment in a very long, curving, stream-valley. There are two major names in NTT, Worksop and Warsop. Specialized local knowledge would be required for the location of the sites of the early settlements, and for the evaluation of the topographical setting. There should be some special factor involved, as *hop* is not otherwise noted in NTT, though it occurs S.W. of Nottingham in the DRB name Hopwell, where it refers to a small valley.

It remains to consider the use of *hop* in CMB, WML, NTB, DRH and Yorkshire. An instance on the W. side of the Pennine Chain is Middop YOW, which lies in hilly country on the edge of high moorland S.W. of Barnoldswick. In CMB and WML, *hop* is used occasionally for valleys, as in Hartsop S. of Ullswater and Wythop on the W. shore of Bassenthwaite. Kershope CMB refers to the long, narrow valley of Kershope Burn on the Scottish Border, and N. of this, in southern Scotland, *hop* becomes more frequent.

On the E. side of the Pennine Chain, Bramhope and Eccup YOW are 'valley' names to the N. of Leeds, but there is then a gap till the DRH border. Hope YON, S.W. of Barnard Castle, is the southernmost member of the next group. Staindrop DRH, the next *hop* name to the north, is uncharacteristically situated in a broad, shallow valley, but probably to be reckoned in the series, as it is on the E. edge of the Pennines.

Although *hop* is not well represented in Yorkshire, there is one example in the separate massif of the Yorkshire Moors; Fryup YON, near the head of a valley running off Esk Dale.

In DRH, Weardale is the centre of a major concentration of names in *hop*. Most of the tributary streams of the Wear, which rise in moorland to the N. and S. of the main valley, flow through narrow blind valleys with –hope names. Some of these valleys have given names to settlements, including Stanhope and Rookhope. Settlements on the S. side of the R. Wear are named from the streams, rather than from the valleys, so have –burn added, e.g. Swinhopeburn, Westernhopeburn. Ekwall 1928 (p. 200) gives examples of other tributary streams in CMB, DRH, NTB and southern Scotland with names formed by adding **burna** to a valley-name in *–hop*.

In NTB, the main concentration of *hop* names is on the Scottish border, round Otterburn. Broomhope, Sweethope and Chesterhope are S. of Otterburn, and many other examples occur to the W. and N., including Emblehope and Ramshope. Harehope NTB is a tiny settlement in a very small valley N.W. of Eglingham. Dodgson in the EPNS survey of CHE (1, p. 138) draws attention to the occurrence of the same name, in the form Harrop, several times in CHE and YOW. Alternative etymologies to 'hares' valley' are possible, such as derivation from *hær* 'rock'; but a term meaning 'hares' retreat' is convincing for small valleys in moorland. An addendum to Dodgson's discussion quotes Professor K Jackson as saying that Harehope is a common name for valleys in S.E. Scotland in hilly country where hares abound.

This concludes the topographical survey. Two subjects remain to be considered: the nature of the compounds which were formed with *hop*, and the interesting problems raised by the *–inghop* names of the Welsh Marches.

hop is frequent as a simplex name, though the incidence is somewhat disguised by affixes, as in Longhope GLO, Brinsop, Fownhope and Woolhope HRE. As a first element, *hop* occurs at least 13 times with **tūn**, 6 of the Hoptons being in SHR. These are not a homogeneous group: some are in deep valleys, others more likely to be enclosures in marsh or waste. In the sense 'enclosure' *hop* is the first element of Hopwas STF and Hopwood WOR.

As a second element, *hop* is combined with personal names in Alsop DRB, Eccup YOW, Edenhope SHR, Glossop DRB, Wilderhope SHR (a fem. name), Worksop NTT, Yarsop HRE, and possibly in Covenhope HRE, Hassop DRB, Stanshope STF and Warsop NTT. The group of names in the Welsh Marches in which *hop* is combined with personal names and either –ing– or –inga– is discussed below.

The first element refers to vegetation in Ashop DRB, Bramhope YOW, Broomhope NTB, Kershope CMB, Wythop CMB and probably Ramshope NTB. A descriptive term is used as qualifier in Bradnop STF, Heyop RAD, Ryhope, Staindrop and Stanhope DRH, Sweethope NTB; and a topographical term in Bacup LNC and Wallhope GLO, Wallop HMP, SHR. A river-name (or a derivative of it) is the first element of Cantlop SHR and Cusop HRE. Wild creatures are mentioned in Emblehope NTB, Harehope NTB, Hartsop WML, Rookhope and possibly Cassop DRH; domestic animals in Cowpe LNC and Swinhope LIN. Burghope HRE and Chesterhope NTB refer to ancient remains, Presthope SHR to ecclesiastical ownership. Lurkenhope SHR, a hamlet N. of Knighton, was probably inhabited by a wise woman, as the first element appears to be an OE compound *lār-cwene*, which would have that meaning.

A distinctive group of *hop* names has as first element a reference to relative position. No 'south' *hop* has been noted, but Northop occurs in FLI, Easthope and Westhope in SHR. Middlehope in SHR is certainly 'middle valley', but it is doubtful whether the same meaning can be given for Meathop WML, Middop and Midhope YOW, and Mythop LNC. In these the first element is apparently OE *mid*, influenced or replaced in two of them by ON *mithr*. Ekwall 1960 (p. 324) translates *mid* as 'middle', but OE *mid* is not an adjective, and these place-names, together with Midridge DRH, SOM, Midhurst SSX and Midsyke YON, present a grammatical problem. Smith 1956 (2, p. 40) gives for the first element '**mid** OE prep., adv., "among, amidst", probably used also in an elliptical fashion, as of the land between two ridges or valleys.' This shows awareness of the problem, but is not a conclusive solution, as other ways of expressing such thoughts are much better evidenced in place-names. For 'among, amidst' the normal place-name practice would be to put the generic in the dative plural, as in Hoppen NTB, and for 'between' the identical word, OE *betwēonan*, is well evidenced. Elliptical names meaning 'place surrounded by wooded hills' (Midhurst) or 'place between ridges' are convincing enough, but it is not clear why this construction should be especially appropriate to *hop*. The four apparent *mid-hop* compounds are not topographically homogeneous. Meathop WML and Mythop LNC are notable 'enclosure in marsh' names, while Middop and Midhope YOW are in, or overlooking, deep valleys. A question mark is the best that can be offered. Midhope WLO (Macdonald 1941, p. 17) has early spellings with *Med–*, so is 'meadow valley'.

An intriguing problem is posed by some of the *hop* names in the Welsh Marches which have *–ing–* or *–inge–* in their early spellings. Names already listed which belong to this category are Burlingjobb and Evenjobb RAD and Dinchope, Millichope and Ratlinghope SHR. To these should be added Bullingham S. of Hereford, which, despite its modern spelling, had the ending *–hope* till at least 1396. There is no doubt that Bullingham is a *–hop*, though the topography would be highly appropriate to a **hamm**. The village occupies the tip of a low promontory between two streams which unite to flow into the R. Wye. Each of the streams has a little valley, but these are quite different from the valleys of the nearby Hope names round the Woolhope Dome, and it seems preferable to regard Bullingham as containing *hop* in the sense 'enclosure in marsh', or perhaps 'promontory jutting out into marsh', as a large part of the parish consists of flat ground across the river from Hereford. It is an open question whether, here and elsewhere, the two main senses belonged to *hop* at the same time, or whether Bullingham (and e.g. Meathop WML, Mythop LNC) are names of earlier coinage than those in which *hop* refers to deep valleys in hill or mountain-massifs. Uses which appear contrasting to us may have seemed consistent to the Anglo-Saxons because the underlying semantic connection was apparent to them. A seventh –*inghope* name, which marks the eastern edge of the group, is Easinghope Fm in Doddenham parish near the WOR/HRE border. This overlooks a small valley.

Burlingjobb and Evenjobb RAD (for which characteristic ME spellings are *Bertlinghope* and *Eminghope*) have been noted by historians as possible evidence for English settlement to the W. of Offa's Dyke before the Dyke was built in the late 8th century. Stenton 1943 (pp. 212–13 and n. 1) says: 'Villages bearing names which are very unlikely to have arisen after the eighth century occur in this quarter far to the west of the dyke. The name Burlingjobb, borne by a hamlet within the Radnorshire border, is as ancient in type as any place-name in the western midlands. It appears in Domesday Book in the form *Berchelincope*. A name of this type is very unlikely to have arisen as late as the ninth century.' Stenton should not have said 'far to the west of the dyke'. Burlingjobb is only two miles W. of the earthwork, and Evenjobb is almost touched by it. The most recent study of Offa's Dyke (Noble 1983) postulates that the Dyke was sited some distance back from the true frontier, and was a patrol line rather than the actual boundary; and on this assumption all the *hop* names in RAD and MTG could lie in territory which was not, in fact, ceded to the Welsh by King Offa. Our present concern is, however, with the line of reasoning which led Stenton to assert that the name Burlingjobb must have been coined before AD 800.

By referring to Burlingjobb as 'a name of this type' Stenton avoided a definite statement as to what he considered the type to be, but there can be little doubt that he believed it to contain –**inga**–, the genitive of the plural suffix –**ingas**, and that he would have translated it 'valley of the followers of Berhtel'. This is not, however, the only interpretation which can be put upon it, and Burlingjobb and Evenjobb must be considered as items in the group of –*inghop* names which were listed in the last paragraph but one.

Place-name studies offer three possible explanations for these names. They could (as Stenton assumed for Burlingjobb) be formed by the addition of *hop* to the genitive of group-names meaning 'the followers of x'. The spellings for Ratlinghope are (in terms which would have been familiar to Stenton) particularly appropriate to this hypothesis because the earliest available ones (*Rotelingehope* 1086, *Rodelingehope* 1208–9) have the –*e*– which can be considered to repreent the –*a*– of –**inga**–. This type of spelling is also well represented in the material available for Bullingham HRE.

Alternatively, some of these names could contain –*ing*–, a connective particle believed (at least by most EPNS editors) to be used in the formation of names like Buttington and Hyssington MTG, which can be translated 'estate connected with Butta or Husa'. Some of the evidence for the existence of this connective particle *-ing-* is given in Gelling 1978 (pp. 177–8), and more could be adduced. It is firmly documented in the south east in the 9th century, though Professor Ekwall never accepted the EPNS view of its widespread appearance in place-names. EPNS editors generally consider names to contain this connective particle if their ME spellings have *-ing-* much more frequently than *-inge-*. Professor Ekwall, on the other hand, considered *-ing-* spellings to result from the shortening of *-inga-*. In the ME spellings for the names under consideration here, there is no sign of *-inge-* in those available for Burlingjobb and Easinghope. For Evenjobb there is a single late *Emyngehope* (1426), and for Dinchope and Millichope there are several *-inge-* spellings, but only for Ratlinghope and Bullingham could the available spellings be held clearly to suggest an original **-inga-**.

The third explanation to be found in the works of place-name experts is one put forward by J McN Dodgson (1967–8). This lays stress on the linguistic phenomena known as palatalization and assibilation, one or both of which is manifested in the middle element of six of our seven names, either by early spellings or by modern pronunciation, or by both. Easinghope WOR does not display such a development, but in the other names palatalization is shown by the development of ME *-ing-* to *-indge-*, and assibilation is shown in some by the further development to *-inch-*. In Dinchope (where these developments have transformed the name, which was *Dod(d)inghope* or *Dodynghope* in the 13th and 14th centuries) the modern form first appears as *Dynchop* in 1503, but it is probable that this pronunciation was current much earlier, and that *Dodynghope* etc. were traditional spellings not necessarily representing the spoken name. In Millichope the assibilated form appears much earlier, in the spelling *Myllincheope* c. 1175, though *Millinghope* remains the commonest form throughout the 13th century. The assibilated, and abbreviated, form of Ratlinghope also appears early in the spelling *Rotchop* 1255, and the pronunciation *Ratchop*, derived from this, survived into living memory though the longer form represented by the traditional spelling Ratlinghope has become the present-day one. Domesday Book spellings for two of the names—*Boniniope* for Bullingham and *Berchelincope* for Burlingjobb—may be attempts to represent palatalized and/or assibilated pronunciations, and it is possible that *-inge-* spellings noted above in some of these names may be scribal representations of an *-indge-* pronunciation rather than indications of derivation from an OE name containing **-inga-**.

For our present purpose it is necessary to consider John Dodgson's explanation of such names as Dinchope. Palatalization of *-ing* is commonest in such names as Wantage, Lockinge BRK, Giddinge, Hawkinge KNT, Pillinge BDF, in which *-ing* is a place-name-forming suffix, not a device for linking two elements together. The most convincing explanation for the palatalized **-ing** in these names is that it is caused by an ancient locative ending *-i*, and this is very satisfactory, but it is far from certain that the same explanation can be adduced for three-element names like the *-inghope* ones under discussion. Dodgson, however, believes that it can, and his solution is that the final element in names like Dinchope must have been added to an earlier place-name which had already become established in this locative form. He believes that there were place-names such as *Rōtelingi* and *Doddingi*, in which *–ingi*, the locative form of the place-name-forming suffix *–ing*, had been added to a personal name to give a meaning 'place associated with Rōtel or Dodda', and that these had become established with the palatalization caused by the locative *–i* before the word *hop* was added. This is a very forced argument, and it is open to objection on chronological grounds. The *–ing* suffix found in numerous names in eastern and southern England seems likely (despite its absence from Cox 1976) to be among the earliest place-name elements used by the Anglo-Saxons. It is doubtful whether it was still in use when the English names of the Welsh Marches were being coined, but if it had been in common use then it should have survived in some names to which final elements like *hop* and **hām** or **hamm** had not been added (Dodgson's argument embraces names like Altrincham CHE, Atcham SHR, as well as the SHR and HRE –inghope names).

Dodgson's suggested explanation of the development of *–ing–* to *–indge–* or *–inch–*, which is summarized in the last paragraph, is in direct contradiction to that given by E Ekwall, whose belief that *–ing–* is usually to be considered as a shortened version of OE **–inga–** has already been noted. Ekwall was, of course, aware that palatalization and assibilation in these names had to be accounted for, and in Ekwall 1962 (pp. 172–3) he offers the following explanation. OE folk-names could be formed by other suffixes besides **–ingas**, and some of the suffixes used, *–hǣme*, *–sǣte*, *–ware*, belonged to a class of nouns called i-stems, which would, in the earliest OE period, have had *–ia* in the genitive plural. Ekwall suggested that although the correct genitive of **–ingas** is *–inga*, group-names (like *Rōtelingas* and *Doddingas*, which he assumed to lie behind Ratlinghope and Dinchope) were sometimes given a grammatically incorrect genitive *–ingia* to make them conform with group-names from *–hǣme*, *–sǣte* and *–ware*. If this were so, the *–ia* of *–ingia* could cause palatalization of *–g–*. He says (p. 170) that palatalization must also have taken place in some names containing *–ingatūn*, but that when this was shortened (as he believed happened) to ME *–ington*, the *–g–* would revert to being a hard sound because it was then influenced by the immediately-following *–t–*. In this way he seeks to account for the fact that tangible evidence of *–indge–* or *–inch–* pronunciations is only to be found in names where *–ing–* is followed by *h*, *w*, or a vowel. (In the Welsh Marches all the examples seem to be followed by *hop*, **hām** or **hamm**, but elsewhere there are some, like Bengeworth SUR, where this development has happened before *w*, and a few, like Ballinger BUC, where it has occurred before a final element beginning with a vowel.)

Ekwall's explanation is scarcely less forced than Dodgson's and is open to similar chronological objections. It is not likely that the formation of group-names with **–ingas** was sufficiently common at the time of the settlement of SHR and HRE to give rise to all the –ington, –ingham –inghope names of the area. Nor is it likely that an archaic genitive plural ending *–ia*, proper to some folk-names, was sufficiently well remembered in the late 7th century to cause an analogous, grammatically incorrect, treatment of *–inga–*. The normal manner of forming folk-names in the Welsh Marches appears to have been by adding *–sǣte* to a place-name, and the normal genitive of *–sǣte* as seen in the place-names of the region was *–sǣtna*, not the archaic *–sǣtia*, which Ekwall's argument requires.

The only explanation which appears to me tenable, on chronological grounds for the *–inghope* and *–ington* names of the Welsh Marches is that they contain the connective *–ing–* which (despite Ekwall's scepticism) I believe to have been widespread in OE place-names. This connective *–ing–* was probably characteristic of the period AD 750 to 850, and it is possible that many of the English names of the Welsh Marches came into existence during the earlier part of that period. English rule was probably established at least a century earlier, but the displacement of Welsh speech and Welsh place-names may have been a gradual process.

It is a reasonable hypothesis that a fashion for such place-name formations as *Hussingtūn* (modern Hyssington MTG) and (probably) *Bolinghalh* (modern Boningale SHR), in which the connection between a place and a landowner or tenant is expressed by using the particle *–ing–* rather than by putting the personal name in the genitive, coincided with a fashion for using the word *hop* in the naming of settlements in enclosed valleys. This would explain the presence of seven *–inghop* names between the WOR/HRE border and the western limit of early English settlement in RAD. I suggest that Bullingham, Burlingjobb, Dinchope, Easinghope, Evenjobb and Ratlinghope are 'enclosed settlement associated with Bulla / Berhtel / Dodda / Ēsi / Emma / Rōtel'. There is no personal name on record which offers a suitable base for Millichope, but that place-name is likely to have been a similar formation.

As regards palatalization and assibilition in names like Dinchope, and in many names with other final elements beginning with *h–* or *w–*, it may be worth considering whether this is actually caused by the proximity of these consonants, rather than merely being preserved by them after it had been caused by some ancient grammatical inflexion of the plural suffix *–ingas* (as considered by Ekwall) or the place-name-forming suffix *–ing* (as considered by Dodgson).

nant, nans Cornish, **nant** Welsh, 'valley'. Pool 1973 (p. 24) says that this word is commonly found as *nance* in W. Cornwall and as *nant* (the earlier form) in E. Cornwall, and that in Cornish names it is often corrupted to *lan* or *lam*, leading to frequent confusion with *lan* 'sacred enclosure'. Trenance, Trenant mean 'valley farm', Pennance, Pennant mean 'end of the valley'. Hodnet SHR is considered in Ekwall 1960 to be a Welsh name meaning 'pleasant valley' with *nant* as second element. Oliver Padel (1981) draws attention to the occurrence of two names, Nanplough in Cury CNW and Lamplugh CMB, which derive from an original Welsh *Nant bluch* 'bare valley'. This was put forward in 1955 by Paul Quentel, but was not noted in Ekwall 1960 or in Smith 1957.

slæd OE 'valley'. This word is much commoner in OE charter-boundaries and in field-names than it is in settlement-names. It is possible that in names of OE origin it was used for a short valley which lacked the bowl-shaped end which might have suggested the terms **cumb** or **hop**, but it developed other meanings which are found in field-names of later origin. The distribution is widespread.

   Names containing *slæd* which are included in Ekwall 1960 are Bagslate LNC (W. of Rochdale, in no sense a 'major' name), Castlett Fm GLO (S. of Temple Guiting, a DB manor), Weetslade NTB (a well-recorded name belonging to two small settlements N. of Newcastle), Sleddale WML(2), and Sledmere YOE.

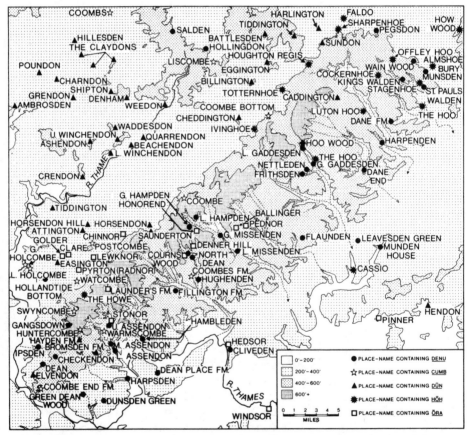

2   Chiltern country: 'hill' and 'valley' names. (From a map drawn by Ann Cole.)

The 1″ map shows nothing to account for the GLO name, but High Weetslade NTB overlooks what may be a good example of the sort of valley to which *slæd* was felt to be appropriate, and there are a number of short, deep valleys near Sledmere YOE. Wet Sleddale and Longsleddale WML, which are fairly close together S.W. of Shap, may be dales which have a number of small side-valleys; the name also occurs twice in YON. Walderslade KNT, S. of Chatham, however, is at the head of a long valley.

The nature of a *slæd* in any region is a matter for local investigation, taking account of field-names and, in some areas, of charter-boundaries. Foxall 1980 (p. 18) says: 'The field-name *Slade* is also common in Shropshire . . . it can mean a damp valley . . . However, the name *Slade* in Shropshire usually means a patch of ground in a ploughed field too wet for grain and left as greensward.' The EPNS survey of CAM (p. 343) suggests some specialized meanings in the Fens, but a few of the field-names quoted there may contain **lād** rather than *slæd*. Waterslade is a common field-name in some counties.

slakki ON 'shallow valley' is fairly common in minor names and field-names in some areas of Scandinavian settlement, and occurs in a few settlement-names, including Hazelslack and Witherslack WML. It is perhaps a more likely second element of Elslack YOW than OE **lacu**, which is preferred by previous reference books. Smith (EPNS survey 6, p. 45) rejects the possibility of *slakki* as inconsistent with two early spellings, *Ailselaik* 1219 and *Elselak* 1240, but the evidence of these is by no means conclusive and is outweighed by that of numerous other early forms. The watercourse at Elslack is a small mountain stream, and this would be an atypical use of **lacu**, which is otherwise only recorded once in YOW, in Fishlake, where it is used of a side-channel of the R. Don.

5

Hills, Slopes and Ridges

This is the longest chapter of the book, and it would be even longer if it contained an exhaustive list of words used to denote hills or rising ground in English place-names. Various omissions have been deemed advisable in order to keep the chapter in reasonable proportion. Summary treatment has been accorded to OE **hlāw**, on the grounds that it probably refers more frequently to burial mounds than to natural hills, and ON *haugr* has been omitted because, although occasionally used in names of hills and mountains in north-west England, it probably refers to tumuli when it occurs in settlement-names in any of the areas of Norse colonization. Both these words were discussed in Gelling 1978 (pp. 134–8, 154–7). Other 'hillock', 'rock' or 'ridge' terms have been omitted because they seldom occur in major settlement-names. There are a number of English and Welsh words beginning with *c –* in this category, such as OE *canc*, *clacc*, *clūd*, *cnæpp*, and Welsh *cefn*, *cnwc*, *cnycyn*. Omitted also are some 'one-off' names like Cogges OXF, Kilve SOM, Swell GLO, which are descriptive of a hill near the settlement. A few anatomical terms are included—OE **bæc** and **hēafod** and Welsh **pen**—but there are others which are not discussed because the chapter is already too long without them. These include OE *bile* 'beak', *brægen* 'top of the head', *brū* 'brow', *ears* 'buttock', *hals* and *swēora* 'neck', *horn* 'horn', *tunge* 'tongue' and *wrōt* 'snout'.

One of the factors which expands the corpus of terms to be discussed is the adoption by the Anglo-Saxons of many British hill-names. PrW terms included are **barr**, **blain**, **breȝ**, **brig**, **brinn**, **crūg**, **mönith** and **penn**—a larger number than appears in any other chapter. There are proportionately rather few ON terms for hills in major settlement-names.

Among the OE terms discussed, there is probably none which does not have at least a degree of specialization, though there are substantial areas of overlap. It is evident that the configuration of the hill was a more important factor in the choice of a word than absolute or comparative height. Some broad distinctions of shape are noted between various items, such as **dūn**, **hyll**, **hōh** and **bæc**. The 1″ map is a coarse instrument for this study, however, and hills (like some other categories of settlement-site) probably need to be viewed on the ground, or better still experienced as dwelling-places, before the vocabulary of their naming can be truly understood. There will be nuances of slope and overhang, perhaps crucial for a choice between such terms as **scelf** and **ofer**, which only people with local knowledge can hope to appreciate.

A great many of the names discussed here do not strictly refer to hills. Some indeed, like Holderness YOW and Ower DOR, refer to very low ground. But in all instances the name refers to the position of the settlement or area in relation to something lower; Holderness and Amounderness jut out into the sea, the 'river-bank' **clif** and **scelf** names refer to dry ground above the river or its marshes, linear features called **ric** or **ræc** are (at least as interpreted here) raised above the surrounding ground-level. Some of the terms, like **bæc** and even **dūn**, are occasionally applied to islands in marshes, but all are most characteristically used of hills or ridges, and in no case is there serious doubt about this being the appropriate chapter for any of the words discussed here.

Perhaps the extensive nature of this category of topographical place-name elements indicates that a low hill is the commonest of all types of settlement-site. There are many varieties of hills, slopes and ridges, and this study of the topography of such sites has led to suggestions for revised definitions of OE **copp**, **hēafod**, **hlinc**, **ofer**, **ric/ræc** and **scelf**.

bæc OE 'back'. This anatomical term is used in place-names of a ridge, varying in type from a low ridge in marshy ground to a steep escarpment. In OE charter-boundaries in BRK it is used several times for the bank of linear earthworks and once for a strip linchet. In major place-names *bæc* is best evidenced in the northern half of the country, but it occurs also in the south west, and it is suggested here for the first time that it occurs in East Anglia. It is not common, and is not evidenced in all counties.

Bashall YOW (earlier *Bacschelf*) refers to a very narrow tongue of land between two brooks extending for half a mile from Backridge (also named from it) to Bashall Town. The elevation is less than 100'. Backford CHE lies on a low hill which is the southern end of a broad ridge. Beckhampton WLT is probably named from the long narrow ridge west of the village, which is a higher feature than those at Bashall and Backford. High ridges are also referred to in Bacup LNC and Backwell SOM.

It is important to note the topography of names which contain *bæc* as a first element, because when the word occurs as a final element it is difficult to distinguish from **bæce**, **bece** 'stream-valley', and the topography may be the deciding factor. As a first element *bæc* gives *Bac–* in early spellings, but as a final element the dative inflexion (in *bæce*) could cause palatalization of *–c–*, resulting in ME spellings like *–bache* and modern forms like *–bache*, *–bage*. There may also have been a locative form (*bæci*) in which the vowel was raised, giving OE *bece*. ME and modern spellings from this last form would be indistinguishable from those derived from **bæce**, **bece** 'stream-valley'.

There are three instances of the name Burbage, in LEI, WLT and DRB. These consist of **burh** compounded with either *bæc* or **bæce**, **bece**. The etymology 'fort ridge' seems particularly appropriate to Burbage LEI, which occupies a low ridge. Burbage WLT lies on a broad, flat shelf, and an OE charter boundary mentions an *eorthburh* in the vicinity. Burbage DRB (near Buxton) is beside a very narrow watershed called Burbage Edge. A word meaning 'ridge' is suitable for these three names, and would fit the situation of some other names ending in –bage, –badge; but if there is a ridge there are usually streams running out of it or flowing on either side, so it is seldom possible to exclude **bæce, bece** as an alternative second element. Debach SFK, N.E. of Ipswich, is perhaps more likely to contain *bæc*. This assumption would give an etymology 'ridge overlooking the R. Deben' (whose OE name was probably *Dēope* 'deep one').

A group of names in the fens of CAM, HNT and LIN which have previously been considered to contain **bæce, bece** 'stream-valley' require reconsideration. These are Landbeach, Waterbeach, Long Beach Fm and Wisbech in CAM, Ashbeach Fm and Chalderbeach Fm HNT, and Pinchbeck and Holbeach LIN.

The two settlements called Waterbeach and Landbeach N. of Cambridge are named from the same feature, whether it be a stream (as stated in previous reference books) or a low ridge in the fens. They occupy slightly raised ground on the edge of North Fen, the height rising from 3' in the fen to 20' in Waterbeach village. Wisbech occupies a slighter elevation in deep fenland, and Long Beach is near Wisbech. Holbeach LIN has a raised site from which many small streams flow away. Ekwall 1960 translates Holbeach 'hollow, i.e. deep, brook', but a slightly concave ridge seems a more likely topographical feature. If *hol* is a noun, not an adjective, the meaning might be 'ridge in a hollow place'. Pinchbeck LIN, which may contain the same second element as Holbeach modified by Scandinavian pronunciation, occupies a similar situaton. Ashbeach and Chalderbeach, N.W. of Ramsey HNT, lie in deep fenland.

There are watercourses and drainage channels everywhere in these fenland regions, so it cannot be said that the –beach, –bech of these names cannot derive from a word meaning 'stream'. But **bæce, bece** is not evidenced in settlement-names in CAM or HNT outside the fenland, and it seems curious that a word which in some other counties is consistently used of small streams in well-marked valleys should here be reserved for streams in areas where valleys are impossible. Some information is available about medieval field-names in CAM, and this confirms the fenland distribution; the main concentration of names in –*beche* is in Upwell, with other occurrences in Sutton and Chippenham. I suggest that the element involved is an ancient locative case of *bæc* 'ridge' used of slight elevations in the deepest part of the fens. Several of the fenland names are those of major settlements, and a ridge rather than a stream would determine the choice of settlement-site in such areas. ModE *beach* 'shore' might have been a possible alternative to *bæc* 'ridge' in fenland names, but the late appearance of the word in literary sources tells against this.

It is not noted till c. 1535, and then in the specialized sense 'shingle' rather than the general sense 'seashore'.

There are three instances in S.W. CAM of a minor name *Holebec*, *Holbeke*, *Holebecke*, and these may be parallels to Holbeach LIN. Two of them have become Hoback Fm on the modern map, perhaps showing influence from the modern word *back*. These farms are in the adjacent parishes of Whaddon and Wimpole, and lie on either side of the R. Cam. The third is a lost medieval name in Little Gransden, a few miles to the north. All three could be stream-names, but the streams which run near the Hoback Fms cannot be described as running in hollows and are not likely to be deep. It seems probable that the farms occupy slightly raised ground in the flood-plain of the Cam.

barr PrW 'top', **barrǭg** PrW 'hilly'. *barr* occurs in Barr STF and (with the addition of ON **ey** 'island') in Barrow in Furness LNC. Berkshire is named from a wood called *Bearruc*, which is the OE form of a Welsh name derived from *barrǭg*, and this term occurs also in Barrock Fell CMB. Gaelic and Welsh words from this root occur in Scottish names such as Barra and Barrhead, and in Welsh names such as Barry.

beorg OE (Anglian **berg**) 'hill, mound'. This is a fairly common place-name element, but because of its resemblance to some other words, particularly **bearu** 'grove' and **burh** 'fort', it is sometimes difficult to identify with certainty. It is commoner in minor names and nature names than in names of major settlements, and there is no reason to suspect that it had the quasi-habitative sense suggested here for **dūn**.

In the southern half of England, roughly south of Birmingham, *beorg* is frequently used of tumuli, and this probably accounts for its high frequency in charter boundaries. It survived in this sense in the dialect of Wessex and the south west, and because that area attracted much early archaeological attention *barrow* (the modern form from *berwe*, dat. sg. of *beorg*) became the usual archaeological term for a prehistoric burial mound. There is a discussion of this aspect of the word in Gelling 1978 (pp. 132–4).

As a simplex name *beorg*, *berg* has become Barrow RUT, SOM, Barugh YON, Berrow SOM, WOR, Burrow SOM, Burgh NFK, SUR. It should be noted, however, that the name Barrow more frequently derives from **bearu** 'grove', and that Burgh is usually from **burh** 'fort'. In north-country names *berg* sometimes becomes Barf. In areas of Norse settlement the Anglian form *berg* cannot be distinguished from the corresponding ON word *berg*; Berrier CMB, e.g. could contain either.

As a first element, *beorg*, *berg* occurs in Barham CAM, HNT, SFK, Barpham SSX and Barholm LIN (all with **hām**), Barrowden RUT, Barway CAM, Bearstead KNT, Bergholt ESX, SFK, Broughton HMP, LIN, and Burghfield BRK. (With regard to Broughton and Burghfield, it should be noted that Broughton more frequently contains **brōc** or **burh**, and that all names in Burgh– are more likely to contain **burh**.) The list of early-recorded names in Cox 1976 contains three instances of *beorg*, and this, together with the proportionately high incidence of compounds with **hām** suggests that the word was part of the earliest place-name-forming vocabulary of the Anglo-Saxons.

No attempt has been made at a thorough analysis of first elements in compound names which have *beorg*, *berg* as second element, since the major settlement-names in which it occurs are a fairly small proportion of the material. In a comprehensive study it would be advisable to discriminate as far as possible between names in which the word is used of a natural hill and those in which it refers to a burial mound. Analysis of about 55 major settlement-names and a few minor names and hill-names yields the following results.

The commonest type of qualifier is a word which describes the hill. Here belong Blackberry Hill LEI, Blackborough DEV, NFK, Brokenborough WLT, Caldbergh YON, Chiselborough SOM, Clannaborough DEV, Emborough SOM, Flawborough NTT, Grandborough BUC, WAR, Holborough KNT, Roborough DEV, Rowberrow SOM, Rowborough IOW(2), Singleborough BUC, Stoberry SOM, Stoborough DOR, Wanborough WLT. Next in size to this is the category in which the first element refers to vegetation. This includes Brackenborough LIN, Bromsberrow GLO, Farnborough BRK, HMP, KNT, WAR, Mappleborough WAR, Risborough BUC, Thornborough BUC, Thornbrough YON(2), Wadborough WOR, Woodbarrow SOM and Woodborough WLT. Personal names are well represented, as in Attleborough WAR, Baltonsborough SOM, Edlesborough BUC, Handborough OXF, Inkberrow WOR, Oldberrow WAR, Rodborough GLO, Symondsbury DOR, Wanborough SUR and Wigborough ESX.

A smaller category refers to wild creatures: Crowborough SSX, Durborough SOM, Finborough SFK, Todber YOW and Wolborough DEV. Domestic animals have only been noted in Harborough WAR ('hill of the herds') and the minor name Hensborough Hill WAR. Pulborough SSX, and Welbury YON, Wisborough Green SSX and possibly Panborough SOM define the hill by reference to a topographical feature. Numerals occur in Seaborough DOR, and Thrybergh YOW. Warborough OXF is 'watch hill'. Shuckburgh WAR was haunted. Litchborough NTP may be 'hill with an enclosure'. One –inga– compound has been noted: Lenborough BUC, near Buckingham. Harborough LEI is ambiguous. Malborough DEV and Marlborough WLT have the same first element, which is variously interpreted as a plant-name or as a personal name.

blain PrW, PrCumb, **blaen** Welsh 'point, end, top' occurs in names of post-Roman origin in CMB: Blencarn, Blencogo, Blencow, Blencathra, Blennerhasset, Blindcrake. Ekwall 1960 considers that it occurs also in Plenmeller NTB.

bre3 PrW, PrCorn, PrCumb (Brit **brigā**) 'hill'. This word, which is cognate with OE **beorg**, is the commonest of several British words meaning 'hill' which survive in English place-names. In Mellor DRB, LNC, Mulfra CNW, the second part of Plenmeller NTB, and the first part of Mallerstang WML, *breʒ* is qualified by PrW, PrCorn, PrCumb *mēl* 'bald', and Mellor Knoll in Bowland Forest YOW may be another instance, though Smith (EPNS survey 2, p. 214) prefers to derive it from the surname Mellor. Moelfre is a common hill-name in Wales. *breʒ* is the final element of Clumber NTT and Kinver STF. As a simplex name it survives in High Bray DEV (but not in Bray BRK). It is the first element of the hybrid Welsh/English names Bredon WOR, Breedon LEI, Brewood STF and Brill BUC. Bredon, Breedon and Brill are tautological hybrids, and may have arisen through a mistaken belief by English speakers that Welsh speakers were using the name of the **dūn** or **hyll** when they were actually referring to it by a common noun. A similar process has caused modern English speakers to add 'on the Hill' to Breedon LEI.

There is a discussion of the solitary recorded instance from Roman Britain, and of the use of this term in Continental names, in Rivet and Smith 1979 (pp. 277–8).

brekka ON 'slope' is fairly common in LNC and of very occasional appearance in some other northern counties. No instances have been noted in CMB. Ekwall 1960 includes Haverbrack WML, and Norbreck, Scarisbrick, Warbreck LNC.

brig PrW (Brit **brīco–**) 'top'. Brickhill BUC and Brickhill near Bedford are believed to be tautological hybrids from this word and **hyll**.

brinn PrW, **bryn** Welsh 'hill' occurs in Brynn LNC, and in several instances of Bryn in SHR, and of Brin, Bryn, Brynn in CHE. It is the final element of Malvern WOR. It is common in Welsh names.

camb OE 'comb, crest'. The topographical use of this word is rare, but there is little doubt that it is found in Cambo NTB, Cam YOW, Camshead YON and Combs SFK. In Cambo, *camb* qualifies **hōh**, perhaps because the raised knob on which the settlement stands has a distinctive outline. Cam YOW, by the Pennine Way, is on a long, straight escarpment. Combs S. of Stowmarket SFK (*Cambas* in DB) may have been a district-name, referring to the series of low ridges which run up to the R. Gipping.

There are probably a few other instances in minor names and field-names. Combe Hill, E. of Colne LNC, is a likely example. Cams Head and Cold Cam YOW, near Byland Abbey, are usually derived from *camb*, but as they are on either side of a conspicuously crooked escarpment it may be legitimate to suspect a British name from PrW, PrCumb *camm* (Brit *cambo–*) 'crooked'. Ekwall 1960 includes Combs DRB with Combs SFK, but no name in DRB is recognized in the EPNS survey as containing *camb*. There are a number of lost names in Little Wilbraham CAM (Reaney, EPNS survey, 21) which may contain *camb*, but these require further study.

There seems no reason to ascribe any of the above names to ON *kambr*, though the distribution renders this possible.

clif OE 'cliff'. It has been generally recognized that this word is used in place-names both for an escarpment or hill-slope and for a river-bank, but the contrast between the senses at their extremes has been insufficiently stressed. Smith 1956 says *clif* can be used 'of the steep bank of a river'. Ekwall 1960 says, more accurately: 'The meaning varies. The most common one seems to be "a slope" (not necessarily a steep one) or "the bank of a river".' The exercise of locating on the 1″ map all the names containing *clif* which are listed in Ekwall 1960 brings out the apparent dichotomy between the senses 'escarpment' and 'river-bank' very clearly.

In literary use, the meaning 'river-bank' is not apparent, and though a few occurrences could be taken to refer to the sea-shore, the usual meaning is roughly that of the modern word. NED gives 'land adjacent to a sea or lake; shore, coast, strand' as an obsolete sense, first noted in *Beowulf*, and says this is an extension of the meaning 'sea-cliff'. Onions 1966 says the word is of unknown origin. Holthausen 1934 connects it with *clīfan* 'to adhere' (modern *cleave*).

There are about 90 place-names in Ekwall 1960 which are derived from *clif*, or which have the word as first or second element. In the topographical analysis which follows, most of these, together with some additional minor names, will be listed under three headings: steep escarpments, low river-banks, small hills or bluffs. They have not been further sub-divided into those in which a stretch of river or sea is or is not a dominant topographical factor, but notes on this are included in the discussion of individual examples. Readers with local knowledge will doubtless wish to move some examples from one category to another, but there is no doubt that the first two categories exist, at least in terms of the modern landscape, and are distinct from each other. Whether the third category could be distributed among the other two may be left to the reader's judgment.

The sense 'steep escarpment' is represented in most parts of England where it is topographically possible, but it is probably commonest in the west midlands and YOW. In KNT there are two examples in major names: Trottiscliffe, S.W. of Rochester, at the foot of the escarpment followed by the Pilgrim's Way, and West Cliffe, N.E. of Dover, where the cliff is coastal. Trottiscliffe is recorded in AD 788, and this together with some GLO evidence discussed below establishes a relatively early date for the use of *clif* for an inland escarpment which has no significant relationship to a major river. In minor names in SSX and IOW *clif* is evidenced both for inland escarpments (e.g. Cliffe Hill near Lewes, Gatcliff near Godshill) and for coastal cliffs. No minor-name material is conveniently available for HMP, or as yet, for DOR.

In DOR the only clear-cut 'escarpment' name noted is Whitecliff Fm (a DB manor) N. of Swanage, named either from the sea-cliff or from the steep slope of Ballard Down. In DEV, where *clif* is rare in major names but very common in minor names, there is a dramatic 'inland escarpment' at Clifford, on the S. bank of the R. Teign. In SOM, Cleeve S.E. of Clevedon refers to an inland escarpment, in this case not overlooking a river. Clevedon ('hill of the cliffs') is at the junction of two narrow, steep-sided ridges. Old Cleeve, S.W. of Watchet, is difficult to classify from the map; it belongs either in this category or in the third one. WLT has good 'inland escarpment' examples: Clevancy and Clyffe Pypard, which are on the same bank S.W. of Swindon, and Swallowcliffe, which is discussed below. In BRK, the best 'escarpment' name is Winslow (earlier *Wendelescliva*). This name only survives as an affix in Kingstone Winslow, but it is recorded from the 12th century as a separate estate, and is presumed to be named from the escarpment of the Downs near Ashbury.

N. of the Thames, in the eastern half of the country, the use of *clif* in the sense 'escarpment' is rare, but this may be due as much to topographical as to linguistic causes. Cliveden BUC is dramatically sited above the R. Thames, and Swalcliffe OXF may belong in the escarpment category, though it is not a good specimen. Scarcliffe DRB, S.E. of Bolsover, is in hilly country, but probably only qualifies for inclusion in the third category, that of small hills or bluffs. Priestcliffe E. of Buxton DRB is on a fairly steep slope, but there are steeper slopes all round it.

The west midlands is a much better hunting-ground for names in which *clif* means 'escarpment'. GLO has two examples: Clifton in Bristol, overlooking the Avon Gorge, and Bishop's Cleeve. The latter is important for dating the usage. In a charter of c. 780 the monastery here is said to be *æt Clife*, and the estate granted to it is described as 'under the rock of the hill which is in the old vocabulary called *Wendlesclif* on the north side of the stream called *Tyrl*.' This seems to indicate that *Wendlesclif* (discussed further below) was the OE name of what is now Cleeve Cloud, a rocky outcrop on the edge of Cleeve Hill. In HRE, Clifford N.E. of Hay probably belongs in this category, as it stands on a steepish bank overlooking the R. Wye. WOR has 'escarpment' sites at Cleeve Prior (named from Cleeve Hill, which has Marlcliff WAR at its N. end) and at Cookley. Austcliff is near Cookley, and refers to the same bank, which overlooks the R. Stour. Guy's Cliffe in Warwick may perhaps be put in this category since, although the bank of the Avon is not steep, there are rocks. In SHR, as in WAR, the sense 'escarpment' is poorly represented, but it is applicable to Clive, at the W. end of Grinshill Hill, which has a fairly steep bank along its S. side. No 'escarpment' names have been noted in STF.

In the north-west midlands, the use of *clif* for escarpments is best evidenced in LNC. Here are Baycliff in Furness, Briercliffe N.E. of Burnley, Clifton N.W. of Pendlebury and Cliviger S.E. of Burnley. At Cliviger there is a dramatic escarpment overlooking the R. Calder. CHE has only Clifton, S.E.

of Runcorn, which is on a moderate escarpment overlooking the R. Weaver.

In northern England, convincing 'escarpment' sites have been noted only in Yorkshire. N. and S. Cliffe YOE are excellent examples, on the S.W. outer edge of the Wolds, where a long bank rises from 30' to 150'. The two villages stand at its foot, overlooking a wide area with names in **holmr, mōr, kjarr** and **fen.** YON has Arncliffe, preserved as an affix in Ingleby Arncliffe. The 'eagle cliff' of this name is a dramatic escarpment on the W. edge of the Cleveland Hills, and the Cleveland Hills themselves are named from the 'cliffs' which surround them. In YOW there are several good examples: another Arncliffe in Littondale, Felliscliffe (in hilly country S. of the R. Nidd, with minor names Swincliffe and Swarcliffe nearby, Langcliffe N. Settle, and Wharncliffe Chase N.W. of Sheffield. In some of these the references may be to rock outcrops.

The second sense of *clif*, 'low river-bank', is found in two major names in KNT: Cliffe-at-Hoo and Swalecliffe. Cliffe-at-Hoo straddles the 50' contour overlooking the Thames marshes, N. of Rochester. This name can be regarded as established by the 9th century, as the people living there are called *Clifwara* in some OE bounds which probably date from then. Swalecliffe is on the N. coast of KNT, in very low ground, where a small stream runs into the sea. Nearby spot heights are 14' and 17'. No instances of this sense have been noted in SSX or IOW. There may be some among the large numbers of minor names in DEV which contain *clif*: these have not been systematically checked. In fact, apart from the two KNT names, no certain instances have been noted south of the R. Thames. In Clewer BRK *clif* may refer to the low Thames bank, but it is not impossible that the reference is to the rising ground S. of the settlement.

N. of the Thames, in the eastern half of the country, 'low river-bank' seems the only possible sense for Ratcliffe in Stepney GTL and Cliff Fm in Mistley ESX (a DB manor). N. and S. Clifton by the R. Trent in the northern tip of NTT should possibly be included in this category. In the western half of the midlands the score is slightly higher. It may include Clive S.E. of Winsford CHE and Clifford Chambers GLO. It must include two LNC names, Clifton beside the Ribble estuary, and Out and Upper Rawcliffe on the N. bank of the lower course of the R. Wyre. Upper Rawcliffe is so called because it is higher up the river. In a valiant attempt to find a 'cliff' Ekwall 1922 (p. 160) says: 'Out Rawcliffe stands between two patches of higher land, reaching an elevation of 50ft.' These patches of land above 50' might have been adduced to explain a name in **holmr** or **ēg**, but they do not seem relevant to a name in *clif*. The evidence of the two villages called Rawcliffe suggests that 3 to 4 miles of flat land on the N. bank of the Wyre was called 'red cliff'.

In the Northumbrian counties the sense 'low river-bank' is evidenced in Rockcliffe CMB, on the estuary of the R. Eden, Clifford YOW (S.E. of Wetherby), Rawcliffe YOW (S.W. of Goole), Cliffe YOE (near Hemingbrough), Rawcliffe YON (N. of York), and Topcliffe YON (N. of Boroughbridge). Rawcliffe near Goole is the lowest *clif* site noted in this study, with nearby spot heights of 11′ and 17′. For Topcliffe, Smith (EPNS survey, p. 186) says: ' "The highest part of the cliff" from OE *topp* . . . on the upper edge of a very steep and lofty bank, overlooking the Swale R.' This seems unusually wide of the mark.

A west-midland name which deserves special mention because it may explain the 'low river-bank' usage is Cleeve HRE, S.W. of Ross. Cleeve is not on modern maps, but the 1st ed. 1″ shows it standing on a low bank overlooking the flood-plain of the R. Wye. There are cliffs in the modern sense round Chase Wood, a mile away, but the *clif* of this name is clearly the single contour which marks the rise from the river. It may be that close acquaintance with some of the sites placed in this category would reveal low banks which do not show on the 1″ maps, and it may be that silting in historic times has concealed some features like that observed at Cleeve HRE. Whatever allowances are made for these factors, however, it is clear that *clif* was used both of low river-banks and of great escarpments. Regional distribution of the two senses is probably due to topography rather than dialect, and neither sense is clearly a late development. Here, as with some other terms (e.g. **hop, mōr**) there was probably an underlying semantic connection which was more apparent to the Anglo-Saxon peasant than it is to the modern student.

The third category of names in *clif* discerned in this analysis consists of those in which the reference appears to be to slight or moderate slopes. Nearly all of them overlook rivers. Few examples have been noted in southern England, but here may be placed three DOR names: Catsley Fm (a DB manor, S.E. of Corscombe), Clifton Maybank (S.E. of Yeovil), and Clyffe (a DB manor, E. of Dorchester). This category is well represented in the east midlands, however, and it may be that the low land-relief in parts of this area caused what are here classified as 'slight slopes' to seem deserving of a word which meant 'escarpment'. Clifton BDF is on the 150′ contour, and these are places called Hoo on the gently-rising ground to the S.W. In all other directions there is flat land with small streams draining to the R. Hiz, which is a mile away. Hockliffe BDF is on Watling Street, where it crosses Clipstone Brook. The slope down to the brook on the village side looks gentle, but there is a sharp rise on the other side, where Hockliffe Grange stands on what would pass here for a headland. Similar sites occur in BUC. Clifton Reynes is on the 200′ contour beside the R. Ouse. Radclive, W. of Buckingham, is on what would pass for a headland jutting into a sharp bend of the Ouse—a site where **hamm** would have seemed appropriate. At Clifton Hampden OXF the church stands on a small cliff over the R. Thames. King's Cliffe NTP is on a headland overlooking Willow Brook, a large tributary of the R. Nene; Fineshade (**hēafod**) adjoins. Ratcliffe on Soar NTT is on the 100′ contour. At Clifton NTT, S.W. of Nottingham, Clifton Hall is on a low headland overlooking the R. Trent, at the end of a little escarpment running to the S.W. At Radcliffe on Trent NTT a little escarpment is called The Cliffs. Clifton in Deddington OXF is on a gentle slope overlooking the R. Cherwell. In LEI, Ratcliffe Culey,

N.E. of Atherstone, is on the 250' contour overlooking the R. Sence, and Ratcliffe on the Wreake is on a low bluff above its river. Hatcliffe LIN, S.W. of Grimsby, can perhaps be put in this category; the village straddles a beck with rising ground on either side.

West-midland names which refer to a slope too modest to be called an escarpment include Clifton WOR (at 50', overlooking a large area of flood-plain on the R. Severn), Whitcliff GLO (S.W. of Berkeley, near the N. end of a long narrow hill overlooking the flat bank of the Severn estuary), and Clifton Campville STF (N.E. of Tamworth, on the 250' contour overlooking the R. Mease). Clifton upon Dunsmore WAR is at the end of a low ridge overlook-ing the R. Avon. There are at least 6 relevant names in LNC. These are Aldcliffe (S. of Lancaster, overlooking land probably reclaimed from the R. Lune), Oxcliffe (across the Lune from Aldcliffe), Cleveley (township of Cockerham, on a low hill by the R. Wyre), Stanycliffe (in Middleton, on a low bluff over a tiny stream), Rockliffe (in Bacup, on a steepish bank over a little stream), and Radcliffe (N.W. of Manchester, by the R. Roch, which has a little escarpment on its S. bank).

In the northern counties, also, there are a fair number of names which seem to fall between the two extremes of meaning possible for *clif*. WML has Cliburn, on a modest hill by the little R. Leith, and Clifton, on a slightly higher hill overlooking the R. Lowther. Smith EPNS survey 2, p. 136) says there are scars along the hill-side at Cliburn, so this might go into the first category on similar grounds to Guy's Cliffe WAR. Clifton CMB is on a hill overlooking the R. Eamont. In Yorkshire, the North and West Ridings each have three names which can be put in this category. These are Clifton near York, Clifton upon Ure, and Wycliffe, YON, Attercliffe in Sheffield, Clifton E. of Brighouse, and Roecliffe, YOW. Cliffe YON can be taken with Conis-cliffe DRH, as they are on either bank of the R. Tees. Shincliffe DRH is on a steepish hill overlooking the Tees, and Horncliffe NTB is on a low bluff made by the 100' contour overlooking the R. Tweed. A rare instance of a *clif* name which refers to a modest hill not overlooking a river is Clifton YOW, N.W. of Otley. The slope may be steep enough to put this name in the first category. Cleadon DRH, N. of Sunderland, is the same name as Clevedon SOM, but the relief is low, and the 'cliffs' are not to be identified on the 1" map. A hamlet on the 150' contour, half a mile E. of Cleadon church, is called Undercliff.

clif resembles **hōh** in being used as a simplex name or a first element in over half the examples studied. There are at least 17 major settlement-names derived from *clif*: Cliff WAR, YOE, Cliffe KNT(2), NTP, WLT, YON, YOW, and Clyffe DOR are from the nominative, Cleeve GLO, SOM(2), WOR, Clevancy WLT, Cleve HRE, Clive CHE, SHR are from the dat. sing. (*clife*) or the nom. pl. (*clifu*). There are many minor names which could be added to this total, especially in DEV, where the EPNS survey lists 22 instances of Cleave and 3 of Cle(e)ve. As a first element *clif* (again like **hōh**) occurs most frequently with **tūn**; there are 23 Cliftons in the material studied here. There are 12 major names in which *clif* qualifies a generic other than tūn: these are Cleadon DRH, Clevedon SOM, Cleveland YON, Cleveley LNC, Clewer BRK, Cliburn WML, Clifford DEV, GLO, HRE, YOW, Cliveden BUC, Cliviger LNC.

This leaves a rather small corpus of names in which *clif* is qualified by a first element. The discussion in Smith 1956 gives the impression that animal or bird names are particularly frequent, but in fact such compounds are heavily outnumbered by those in which the qualifier is a word describing the 'cliff', and in this group much the commonest type is that in which the descriptive word is a colour adjective, 'red' being the commonest colour. There are 14 names in the material studied here which mean 'red cliff', and others could be found among minor names, field-names, and boundary-marks in Anglo-Saxon charters. The 14 names are: Radcliffe LNC, NTT, Radclive BUC, Ratcliff GTL, Ratcliffe LEI(2), NTT, Rawcliffe LNC, YON(2), YOW, Redcliff (in Bristol) GLO, Rockcliffe CMB, Roecliffe YOW. The CMB name and all the Yorkshire ones have ON *rauthr* 'red'. This could indicate that they are ON coinages, but there seems little reason to suspect that names were formed in England from ON *klifr*, and it is more likely that the ON adjective was substituted for an original OE *rēad*. This substitution suggests that the names were understood and felt to be topographically appropriate by Norse settlers. All the 14 names listed refer to river-banks. They are almost equally divided between the second and third categories postulated above, those where the bank can fairly be described as 'flat' and those where there is a modest hill. Rawcliffe LNC and YOW have been noted as particularly low lying. The reference can only be to red soil, and the point of the name may be that a flat river-bank by a settlement is particularly liable to erosion by traffic, so that the soil-colour is always apparent. Examples could, of course, be found in which Redcliff refers to sandstone escarpments.

Whitcliff GLO, Whitecliff DOR, and probably Wycliffe YON, mean 'white cliff'. This name is not restricted to river-banks. Whitcliff near Berkeley GLO is on a hill, and another GLO example, Whitecliff near Coleford, could be placed in the 'escarpment' category. Whitecliff DOR refers either to the chalk sea-cliffs or to an escarpment at right angles to the coast. Wycliffe YON is on a hill-side above the R. Tees. The reference may not be to geology in all these names; vegetation and relationship to daylight are possible factors. Other colours may occur in minor names. Swarcliffe YOW is 'black cliff'. Other descriptive terms occur in Langcliffe YOW, Scaitcliffe LNC(2), and Scarcliffe DRB.

The discussion of compounds with *–clif* in Smith 1956 says 'rarely with a pers. n.', but this category contains at least 10 of the names studied here. Aldcliffe LNC is probably 'Alda's cliff'. Attercliffe YOW is said by Smith (EPNS survey 1, pp. 208–9) to contain a shortened form of *Æthelrēd* or *Ēadrēd*, a conclusion reached after very careful discussion. Austcliff WOR, Baycliff WLT, Cookley WOR, Felliscliffe YOW, Guy's Cliffe WAR, Hatcliffe

LIN, Marlcliff WAR, Topcliffe YON, Trottiscliffe KNT and Winslow BRK cannot be explained satisfactorily on any other grounds. In Winslow, however, the name may not be that of an Anglo-Saxon landowner. The early spellings show Winslow to be identical with *Wendlesclife* GLO (discussed above), and the double occurrence of *Wendel* with *clif* is surprising. *Wendel* is to be understood as an 'ordinary' personal name in some place-names, e.g. Wandsworth GTL, Wansley NTT, but there are some others, e.g. Wendlebury OXF, Vandlebury CAM, in which *Wendel* may be suspected of being a mythological character, and the two instances of *Wendlesclif* should perhaps be classed with these.

References to wild creatures are less common than might be expected. Rockliffe in Rochdale LNC is probably 'roe cliff'. Eagles occur in Arncliffe YON, YOW, and there are a few other instances of this name in Yorkshire. Cats are referred to in Catsley DOR, and there is a Catcliff in Bakewell DRB. Ravens are mentioned in some minor names, such as Ravenscliff in Fenny Bentley DRB. There are two, possibly three, names referring to swallows. The certain examples are Swallowcliffe WLT and Swalcliffe OXF. The third is Swalecliffe KNT. Ekwall 1960 suggests that the KNT name refers to the R. Swale, but the mouth of that river is 4 miles W. of Swalecliffe, so the proximity is probably coincidental. (The river-name, which occurs also in BRK and YON, is related to the bird-name.) There is no reason why swallows should not be associated with the river-bank at Swalecliffe as well as with the long escarpment at Swallowcliffe and the hill at Swalcliffe. Ekwall 1960 gives 'cliff where swallows nested' for Swalcliffe OXF and cross-references this under Swallowcliffe WLT, but the image (which is presumably that of a cliff with sand-martins' nest-holes) is not applicable.

Domestic creatures only occur in two major names, Gatley CHE and Oxcliffe LNC, but there is another Gatcliff in IOW, and Swincliffe occurs as a minor name in YOW. Briercliffe LNC is the only reference noted to vegetation, and Horncliffe NTB the only one to a nearby topographical feature. Wharncliffe YOW refers to quern stones. Coniscliffe DRH is 'king's cliff', Priestcliffe DRB is 'priests' cliff', and Shincliffe DRH is 'demon cliff'. Egglescliffe DRH contains *ecles* 'Christian community', probably a pre-existing place-name. Hockliffe BDF is not classified.

cnoll OE 'knoll'. The northern English form of *knoll* is *know(e)*. Of the definitions given for *knoll* in NED, sense 2 'a small hill or eminence of more or less rounded form' is the relevant one in place-names. Sense 1 'the summit or rounded top of a mountain or hill' is the most clearly evidenced in literary OE, but this is not likely to be represented in settlement-names. Brent Knoll SOM is a good example of the type of hill designated *cnoll*. The word is commoner in minor names than in those included in Ekwall 1960.

The simplex name Knole occurs as a major name in KNT and SOM. In the form Knowle it occurs in DOR and WAR, and four times in SOM. Knowlton

DOR, S.W. of Wimborne St Giles, is probably named from the nearby Knowle Hill. Church Knowle DOR, on the Isle of Purbeck, was a simplex name till the 14th century; close by are Bucknowle and Cocknowle, and the three names probably refer to three individual knobs projecting from the lower slopes of the Purbeck Hills. Chetnole DOR, S.E. of Yetminster, is probably named from the hill to the S.E. of the village. Chipnall SHR, S.E. of Market Drayton, stands on the edge of a small, sub-circular hill.

Knill HRE, S.W. of Presteigne, is considered to derive from a related term *cnyll(e)*. The settlement is on a small bluff overlooking a stream.

cōc or **cōce** OE 'hill'. This word is not on record, but may reasonably be inferred from Swedish and Norwegian parallels. In the EPNS survey of DOR (1, p. 229), Professor M Löfvenberg is quoted as suggesting that such a word may be the first element of Cookham BRK. Another name for which it would provide an excellent solution is Cook Hill in Inkberrow WOR.

There was also an OE **cocc** 'hillock', which survives in the word *haycock*. This is fairly common in minor names (e.g. Weycock Hill in Waltham St Lawrence BRK) and field-names, and occurs occasionally in major names. It is the final element of Withcote LEI (earlier *Withcoc*), and the probable first element of Cockhampstead HRT and Coughton HRE, WAR. Cookham and Cook Hill cannot be derived from *cocc*, as only a word with –ō– could have given the early spellings of Cookham and the modern forms of both names. Other place-names beginning with Cock– are likely to contain OE *cocc* 'cock' (the bird) or a personal name *Cocca*.

copp OE 'summit'. This is a rare term in place-names, and the available material is probably insufficient for a firm definition, but a case could be made for a specialized use denoting a hill or ridge with a narrow summit. Mow Cop CHE is a long, narrow hill. At Copp LNC, S.W. of Great Eccleston, there is a low ridge made by the 50' contour, and this may have a narrow crest, as the village stands at 84'. Orcop HRE is below the tip of a narrow ridge, and Pickup Bank LNC, E. of Darwen, is on the side of a similar feature. At Warcop WML the village occupies a level space with a range of hills to the S.W. and mountains to the N.E. The nearest hill to the village is an isolated, very narrow one, running to the N.W.

Two names are unexplained. Coppull LNC, S.W. of Chorley, is said to mean 'peaked hill', but the village appears from the map to have a low, flat site. Sidcup GTL (*Cetecoppe* 1254, *Setecoppe* 1301) has parallels in ME field-names in CAM, ESX, HRT and NTT, and this suggests that there was compound appellative, the sense of which has not been recovered; 'seat-shaped hill' has been suggested.

crūg PrW, PrCorn, PrCumb 'hill, mound, tumulus'. The British ancestor of this word is found in a few of the place-names recorded from Roman

Britain. The most notable example is *Pennocrucium*, modern Penkridge STF, which means 'headland tumulus', and is now known to refer to a tumulus at Rowley Hill Farm in the parish of Stretton, 1200 yards N. of Watling Street, at GR 90251180 on 1″ map no. 119. The tumulus has been virtually ploughed out, but there is a description of it from 1797, and it was 3′ high in 1907. The site is a typical one for a barrow, the brow of a shoulder of land from which the ground falls abruptly to the R. Penk. Recent commentators on the Romano-British place-name, notably Gelling 1978 and Rivet and Smith 1979, failed to note the records of this tumulus, and a good deal of ingenuity was wasted on the search for a topographical explanation without it. We have been appraised of the evidence by Mr J Gould, a local scholar; and the story is an object lesson in the extent to which even the most ancient topographical place-names can be related to obviously appropriate features in the modern landscape.

It is clear from the use of the British word in *Pennocrucium* that PrW *crūg* could mean 'tumulus', and this use occurs in several minor place-names, such as Crookbarrow Hill WOR and Crooksbury Hill (in Farnham) SUR; but it is probably only one of the senses. The evidence of other names suggests that *crūg* was used by Welsh speakers for a small abrupt hill, or for a larger hill with a small, distinctively-shaped, summit. The word is relatively common, especially in minor names, and this suggests that it may have been borrowed into OE as an appellative to be used in place-name formation, rather than being in every instance the pre-English name of a particular hill.

crūg is the source of Creech DOR, SOM, Crich DRB, Cricket SOM, Crook DEV, DOR, Crutch WOR, Crouch OXF. It is the second element of Evercreech SOM and Gilcrux CMB, and the first element of Christon SOM, Churchdown GLO, Cruckton and Crickheath SHR, Crewkerne SOM, Cruchfield BRK. Minor names containing *crūg* include Croichlow Fold LNC (S.W. of Holcombe Brook) and Cumcrook CMB (W. of Bewcastle). The identification of the hill or tumulus referred to in these names could best be attempted by students with local knowledge.

It will be noted from the above list that there is considerable variety in the forms which develop from this word. Crook, Crouch and Crutch are from an OE *crūc*, and these are assumed to have been adopted from Welsh speakers before the vowel in the Welsh word had been rounded to *ü*. If the word (or a hill-name derived from it) was borrowed from the Welsh at a later date, when the Welsh language had *ü* but the Old English language had not yet developed a similar sound, English speakers substituted *ī* for the vowel of *crūg*, and this substitution gave the form found in Penkridge. When OE developed its own rounded *u*, spelt *y*, in the 7th and early 8th centuries, English speakers were able to represent the vowel of *crūg*, more exactly, and this must have resulted in an OE form *crȳc*. This is evidenced in Creech SOM, where the feature from which Creech St Michael is named is spelt *Crycbeorh* in a charter of 682. Without OE spellings there is no way of knowing whether other names, such as Creech DOR, Crich DRB, were borrowed with *ȳ* or *ī*. OE *ȳ* did not correspond exactly to PrW *ǖ*, and the appearance of the form Crook in DEV and DOR may indicate that Anglo-Saxons sometimes continued to substitute *ū* for the Welsh sound after their language had developed *ȳ*.

Crichel DOR is a compound of *crüg* with OE **hyll**. The name is believed to refer to Crichel Down, a low hill with a small, oval-shaped summit. Crook Hill N.E. of Edale DRB is a well-recorded minor name from this compound, and Crickley Hill GLO may also contain it. The compound with **hyll** has, however, more frequently become Churchill, a documented instance being Church Hill near Wells SOM, which is *crichhulle* in OE bounds. Where there are no pre-Conquest spellings it is usually impossible, on formal grounds, to distinguish instances of Churchill which contain OE *cirice* 'church' from those which contain PrW *crüg*, but study of the site will often suggest an answer. In WOR, there is no doubt that Churchill E. of Worcester means 'hill with a church', but this etymology is less obviously appropriate to Churchill E. of Kidderminster. At Churchill OXF the church stands on the slope of a long ridge, and the tip of the ridge is crowned by a tumulus, so the name could be either 'church hill' or 'tumulus hill'. There are a number of instances (some cited in Gelling 1978, p. 139) of Church Hill applied to isolated hills with no settlement in the vicinity, and such names almost certainly contain *crüg*. Church Hill Wood near Pontesbury SHR crowns a hill of sharper outline than the surrounding eminences, and in this name *crüg* is obviously a comment on the distinctive shape.

There are three settlements in DEV called Churchill. These are:

1 Churchill near Loxbeare, which lies in a valley overlooked by a hill with a peak of over 900', and which has no church.
2 Churchill in East Down. This is in an area S.E. of Ilfracombe where most settlements could be said to be beside hills, so a meaningful etymology is difficult to arrive at; but the village does not seem likely to have had an ancient church.
3 Churchill Fm in Broad Clyst, near which the 150' contour makes a small, round promontory, which is the sort of feature which might well have been called *crüg*.

In Crigglestone YOW, **tūn** has been added to the genitive of a name derived from the compound of *crüg* with **hyll**.

No attempt has been made here to assemble a full list of names containing *crüg*. The element is difficult to identify with certainty, and would repay further study. It should be noted that Smith 1956 (1, p. 115) should not have listed Pentridge DOR (on which see EPNS survey 2, p. 235), and Ekwall 1960 (p. 134) probably should not have listed Cricklewood GTL. In assessing the likely incidence in minor names and field-names it should be remembered that Crouch most frequently derives from ME *crouche* 'cross', and Crook from ME *crōk* 'bend'.

Welsh names containing *crüg* include Criccieth CRN and Crickhowell and Crucadarn BRE. The Cornish form occurs in Trencreek.

dūn OE 'hill' (modern *down*). This word enters into a much greater number of major place-names than any other term of similar meaning, the total being at least 350; but owing to a high degree of confusion with other words, particularly **denu** and **tūn**, it is not possible to assess its incidence without painstaking use of reference books.

Cox 1976 establishes *dūn* as an element in the earliest English names. There are six examples in the 224 place-names recorded by c. 730, and four of these are likely to be names of settlements. My own study convinces me that *dūn* ranks with **ēg** and **ford** in a category of topographical words which could have a quasi-habitative significance in the coining of place-names during the earliest years of English speech in this country.

dūn is generally regarded as a Germanic borrowing from Celtic speech, and British *dūno–*, the form of the Celtic word which was current in the Romano-British period, was an important element in the place-names of Roman Britain. The latest discussion of *dūno–* is in Rivet and Smith 1979 (pp. 274–5) and this may usefully be quoted here, though mainly to emphasize the fact that it has no bearing on the use of *dūn* in English names:

Dūnum is one of the most important elements in Celto-Latin toponymy. Sixteen names in Britain, perhaps more, are formed of it or with it, and scores on the Continent. It appears uncompounded (British *Dunum*[1], *Dunum*[2], *Dunum Sinus*; there was a *Dunum* in Ireland, Ptolemy II, 2, 9; Vincent 209a has ten examples from Gaul), more commonly compounded and then always in second place. Its geographical range was immense: common throughout Britain and Gaul, it extended into north Italy, eastward as far as Belgrade (*Singidunum*), *Carrodunum* on the Oder (modern Krappitz) and *Noviodunum* now Isaccea near the mouth of the Danube; it is also known, though not commonly, in Iberia . . .

The Celtic word was apparently **dūnŏs–*, a neuter with *–s* stem; as *dūnon* it was regularly represented in Latin as *dūnum*, neuter. In sense it seems to have developed from 'hill' (it is glossed 'montem' in the Vienna Glossary) to 'fort', perhaps strictly 'ville close' . . . Cognates include Germanic *tūna–*, whence Anglo-Saxon *tūn* and English *town* (*–ton* in place-names), German *Zaun* 'fence'. Evidently *dunum* had an independent existence in Vulgar Latin as a borrowing from Celtic. While some uncompounded names were originally—if recorded in ancient sources—the creation of Celtic speakers, others not so recorded are probably of early medieval date and were created by Latin speakers, as shown by, for example, Thun (Berne, Switzerland), and in France Dun-le-Poelier (Indre), Châteaudun (Eure-et-Loire), Dun-sur-Meuse (Meuse) and Dun-sur-Auron (Cher). The word was taken into Latin as a common noun and survives in dialects of Cantal and Haute-Loire: *dun* 'colline', *dunet* 'petite colline' (Vincent). The free way in which the element was used by Latin speakers is shown by such creations as *Caesarodunum* (now Tours, Indre-et-Loire, France) and *Augusto-dunum*>Autun (Seine-et-Loire, France); these were not latinisations of older Celtic names. The present name *Branodunum* shows the same free use of the element, since it applies to a third-century construction and means 'fort (of any kind)', there being no hill on the site.

There is no way that the material bearing on OE *dūn* can be brought into direct relationship with the developments so usefully outlined in that extract. The OE word does not mean 'fort' or 'ville close' in the written language or in place-names. The senses demonstrated for British *dūno*– and for the Welsh and Gaelic derivatives (Welsh *dinas*, Irish *dun*) are much more akin to those of OE **burh, byrig**. OE *dūn* means 'hill'. On the basis of the abundant place-name evidence a tentative extension of meaning might be suggested, such as 'hill suitable for a settlement-site'; but there is certainly no connotation of defence, and the word is not used to describe great prehistoric hill-forts, such as Maiden Castle DOR, Badbury Rings DOR and Old Sarum WLT. Nor is there any likelihood that English names in which it occurs are hybrids or refashionings of pre-English names in *dūno*–.

Perhaps the derivation from the Celtic word is not to be relied upon. M Förster, in an article (Förster 1921) which is still considered to contain the authoritative list and discussion of Celtic loan-words in Old English, includes *dūn* 'Hügel, Berg' as a possible specimen, commenting that the correspondence between it and equivalent Continental Germanic words shows that the borrowing did not take place in England. Smith 1956 (1, p. 139) says: 'This el. . . . is thought by some to be a WGerm loan from an old Celtic *dūno*–.' NED, under the word *down*, says 'supposed to be of Celtic origin'. Jackson 1953 (p. 320) mentions OE *dūn* as likely to have influenced some names of British origin, specifically Dunchideock DEV and Dommett SOM, causing them to have *Dun*– where *Din*– would have been the regular form, but he does not discuss the possibility of the British and OE words having a common origin.

If the Celtic and Germanic words are connected it seems necessary to assume that Germanic speakers on the Continent made this borrowing either before the sense 'fort' had developed, or in circumstances which caused that to be a less prominent meaning than it was in Roman Britain. Whatever its origin, the Anglo-Saxons must be assumed to have come to England with the word *dūn* established in their vocabulary, and with no consciousness of it having a relationship to such Romano-British place-names as *Margidunum* and *Camolodunum*.

dūn was probably in use for the formation of settlement-names in the earliest years of the English settlements, but it may not have been much employed after AD 800. The earlier date is supported by the occurrence of six examples in English names recorded by AD 730 (though in view of the total number of *dūn* names this is not very striking). The upper limit of c. 800 is suggested by its being fairly common in the west of DEV but hardly used in CNW; and its virtual absence from the KNT and SSX Weald agrees with this. It remained in use as a term for field-name and minor name formation, and for features of the landscape, however, till modern times.

The detailed distribution of names in *dūn* is governed more by geography than by the date of the English settlement. From a study of the sites of all major names in *dūn* I have no doubt that the commonest meaning is 'hill with a summit which is suitable for a settlement-site'. Earlier commentators give the impression that a name in *dūn* will usually have been coined to describe a hill, and the nature-name thus created will later have been transferred to a nearby farm or village. This process certainly happened. Among instances in which the name clearly refers to the hill, and only secondarily to the village, may be cited Bredon WOR, Breedon LEI, Pilsdon and Blackdown DOR, Bleadon SOM, Raddon DEV, Churchdown, Oxenton and Dixton GLO, Brandon NFK, Puleston SHR, Quorndon and Bardon LEI, Baildon YOW, Billington LNC. But these are outnumbered by examples in which the village is on top of the hill, not beside it, and in which it seems more likely than not that the village was there when the English arrived. In many instances I believe the *dūn* name to be an English place-name given to a pre-English settlement in recognition of its characteristic situation.

dūn is most common as the final element of village-names in regions where the geography offers a series of flat-topped hills suitable for village-sites. The most noteworthy area is a fairly compact one in the south midlands, comprising east OXF, BUC north of the Icknield Way, and MDX. Smaller areas where this use is clearly evidenced include north-east WLT, and it is well represented in WAR, and in NTB and DRH. Most of the examples noted are named in the county-by-county survey below. The rarity of settlement-names in *dūn* in SSX, HMP and BRK I take to be the result of absence of water-supply on top of chalk hills. The extreme rarity in the north west, however, as opposed to the frequency in NTB and DRH, may be due to the comparatively late establishment of english speech in that region.

dūn is often used of ridges, as well as of sub-circular hills of the type referred to in the last paragraph, and it sometimes denotes a flat shelf, often on the side of a high hill. For examples of the last use, see what is said below about Shenington OXF and Edgton SHR. By contrast, there is a small but clearly identifiable group of names in which the use of *dūn* overlaps with that of ēg as a term appropriate to a rise of 50' or even less in marshy ground. The lowest *dūn* in the country is probably Hedon YOE, and the choice of the word in this instance is perhaps due to the absence of ēg from the place-name-forming vocabulary of the area. Some of the south ESX *dūn* names come into this category (see the discussion of Mundon). Reydon SFK stands on a cluster of islands made by the 50' contour. The category might be widened to include some instances where the settlement lies at between 50' and 100', as, for example, Farndon and Huntington CHE, and Cowden YOE. Other villages with *dūn* names are at the junction of marsh and rising ground, as Willingdon SSX, Faringdon HMP, Kingsdon and Wembdon SOM, Blaisdon and Boulsdon GLO.

As previous commentators have stressed, there is a great range in the height of features referred to by the term *dūn*. At one end of the scale is Hedon YOE, at a height of about 25', at the other is Chelmorton DRB, at about 1200' in a recess in a hill which rises to 1450'. But the majority of places so designated are on hills of 200'–500', and it is only in north STF and north DRB that the term is well evidenced in really high country.

The use of *dūn* for some very low hills led to the suggestion in Stenton 1913 (p. 3 n.1) that it sometimes meant an expanse of open land without reference to height. Stenton adduced Farndon NTT as proof of this, and the statement was repeated in the EPNS survey (pp. 213–14), and echoed in Smith 1956 (1, p. 138), with the additional example of Brimsdown in Enfield GTL. I believe the suggestion to be unfounded. Farndon NTT is discussed below. Brims-down (whatever the explanation of this enigmatic name may be) should not be considered together with ancient settlement-names, as it is first recorded in 1420. There may be a few other names which are difficult to explain, but the vast majority of instances certainly do refer to height, and I suggest that the characteristic use is for a hill where the elevation is a crucial factor in the choice of settlement site. The word does not seem to me to have received the attention it deserves as a potential clue to settlement history, and I am therefore including a county-by-county survey in this discussion. First, however, it will be useful to consider the types of first element with which *dūn* is compounded.

dūn is rare as a simplex name, but it occurs in East and West Down, Down St Mary DEV, and in Downe GTL. The dative plural, *dūnum*, becomes Downham LNC, NTB, Downholme YON. As a first element *dūn* is found with **hām** in Downham CAM, ESX, NFK, Dunham CHE(2), NFK, NTT; and with **tūn** in Downton HRE, SHR, WLT, Dunton ESX, LEI, NFK, WAR. There are a few other names in which *dūn* is used to define an adjacent feature (e.g. Downwood HRE, Dunwood STF, Duntish DOR), but Dun– usually has other origins, and the use of *dūn* as first element is very slight compared to the large number of names in which it is the final element.

Much the largest class of compound names is that in which the first element describes the appearance or the geological nature of the *dūn*. The colour is referred to in Blackdown DOR, Blagdon DEV, DOR, SOM(2), Bleadon SOM, Fallodon NTB, Fawdon NTB(2), Grendon BUC, NTP, WAR, Grin-don DRH(2), NTB(3), STF, Kelvedon Hatch ESX, Meldon DEV, WML, Raddon DEV and Rawdon, Rawden and Rowden YOW. The shape is defined in Baildon YOW, Ballingdon SFK, Billington LNC, Boldon DRH, Bowden DRB, Bowdon CHE, Cleadon DRH, Clevedon SOM, Hambledon (var. cos.), Hambleton RUT, Horndon on the Hill ESX, Horrington SOM, Langdon and Longdon (var. cos.), Longden SHR, Neasden GTL, Sheldon WAR, Shildon DRH and possibly Sholden KNT. Bowden 'curved hill' is a common minor name in DEV; Hambledon (sometimes Hameldon, Humbledon, Humbleton) 'maimed/crooked/scarred hill' is widespread, but particularly common in the north east. In Billington, Horndon and Horrington, *dūn* has probably been added to an earlier hill-name, *Billing* 'sword-shaped' and *Horning* 'horn-shaped'. Geology is referred to in Claydon BUC(2), OXF, SFK, Sandon BRK, ESX, HRT, STF, Sandown SUR, Saunderton BUC, Standen IOW, Standon BRK, HRT, STF, Staunton on Wye HRE, Stondon BDF, ESX. Other hills are 'clean' (Clandon SUR, Glendon NTP) or 'rough' (Rowden HRE). The only reference noted to comparative elevation is that in Hendon GTL.

It is difficult (as always) to be precise about the number of instances in which the first element is an OE personal name, but there is no doubt that the category is a large one, comprising about 50 certain examples, and another 12 possible. Frequent combination with a personal name is a characteristic of the topographical elements for which I postulate a 'quasi-habitative' use.

Another category of *dūn* names, also comprising at least 50 examples, has as first element a word referring to something which grows on the hill. Some compounds (those with *brōm* 'broom', *fearn* 'fern', **hǣth** 'heath', for example) occur several times. A sub-division of this class consists of names which refer not to trees or natural ground-covering plants, but to crops. Bandon Hill SUR is 'bean hill'. Hay is referred to in Clayhidon DEV, Haydon DOR, SOM, WLT, Heydon NFK, according to the most commonly adduced etymologies (though one would like a local opinion as to the likelihood of these hills producing hay crops for early farmers). A similar significance attaches to Garsdon WLT, Garsington OXF, Butterton STF and Meddon DEV. Rye is mentioned in Raydon and Reydon SFK, Roydon ESX, NFK(2), SFK, wheat in Whaddon BUC, CAM, GLO, WLT (a second Whaddon in WLT is 'wheat valley'). Waddon DOR and SUR have 'woad' as first element.

The category in which the first element refers to animals or birds is surprisingly small, comprising less than 30 names, about half of them mentioning domesticated rather than wild creatures. Callerton NTB(3), Cauldon STF, and Chaldon DOR, SUR refer to calves, Coundon DRH to cows, Oxenton GLO to oxen, Shipton Lee BUC to sheep, Swindon GLO, STF, WLT, YOW to pigs. Horsenden BUC and Horsendon MDX refer either to use by horses or to ownership by a man named *Horsa*; Stottesdon SHR is probably 'hill of the stud', and Beachendon BUC is 'hill of the bitch'. Wild animals are referred to in Dordon WAR, Hartington DRB, Harton DRH, Wooden NTB, and the *eofor* of Everdon NTP, Eversden CAM is likely to have been a wild boar. Birds (rather than men with names like *Heafoca*) are probably referred to in Croydon Hill SOM, Foulden NFK, Hawkedon SFK, Pudleston HRE and Yagdon SHR.

Another small category is that in which *dūn* is combined with a word for a man-made structure. For Harrowden and Weedon see Gelling 1978 (pp. 158–61). Burradon NTB(2), Great Burdon DRH, Burdon, Burden YOW contain **burh** 'fort', Berrington NTB contains **byrig**, dat. of **burh**.

Wigton YOW is interpreted in EPNS survey (4, p. 187) as 'hill belonging to Wike', with reference to an adjacent township. Malden SUR, Maldon ESX, Maulden BDF and Meldon NTB are considered to mean 'hill with a crucifix', and Trimdon DRH is probably a similar compound with *trēow-mǣl* 'tree crucifix'. Staden DRB is 'stave hill'. A few names allude to the use of the hill for an industrial process: Quarlton LNC, Quarndon DRB, Quarrendon BUC, Quarrington DRH and Quorndon LEI have 'quern' as defining element, referring to the quarrying of quern-stones or mill-stones. Cowden YOE is 'charcoal hill', and Spondon DRB contains *spōn* 'roofing shingle'. Several instances of Warden mean 'watch hill'.

When a village stands on a hill-top a water-supply must be available, and perhaps because this is taken for granted it is seldom mentioned in a *dūn* name. Aldon SHR, Willesden GTL and Weldon NTP are the only instances noted. Nackington KNT and Watton YOE mean 'hill at the wet place'. Morden CAM, DOR, SUR, Mordon DRH and Moredon WLT mean 'marsh hill', referring to the low ground surrounding the *dūn* rather than to the state of the hill itself. Marden SSX, 'boundary hill', is a rare instance of a *dūn* distinguished by its position in relation to an administrative boundary. Aesthetic judgments are also rare, but Merrington SHR means 'pleasant hill', and Shenington OXF 'beautiful hill'. Although personal names are common there are very few references to classes or groups of owners or users. Repton DRB contains a tribe-name. Huntsmen are referred to in Huntingdon HNT, Huntington CHE, STF, YON, and possibly Wembdon SHR. Bishopton WAR is 'bishop's hill', and royal ownership gives Kingsdon SOM, Kingsdown KNT(3). Hindon WLT is 'hill of the religious community'. There are very few –inga– names, but here belong Annington SSX, Harlington, Shillington and Toddington BDF, and Tillingdown SUR.

There are surprisingly few instances in which *dūn* has been added to an earlier place-name. Bredon WOR, Breedon LEI, Churchdown GLO, and possibly Brickendon HRT, Charndon BUC consist of a pre-English hill-name combined with *dūn*. Billington LNC, Brendon Hills SOM, Horndon ESX, Horrington SOM, Lansdown SOM, Longsdon STF and Longstone DRB may have English hill-names as first element. Laindon ESX and Brandon LIN may contain river-names.

There are only about a dozen major settlement-names in *dūn* which cannot be classified in the categories discussed above. It remains to study the distribution county by county.

In KNT, where *dūn* is not a very frequent element in major place-names, the topographical features referred to vary in height from 50' to 600'. The lowest *dūn* is probably that referred to in Sholden, near Deal, where a low spur made by the 50' contour runs out into marshland. Nearby are Kingsdown in Ringwould, at the end of a spur which rises to over 250', and East and West Langdon, on either side of a narrow spur which rises to 300'. Another area where a *dūn* could be a low eminence is the east coast of Sheppey; here,

Leysdown has a very small hill and Warden a rather more impressive one, both overlooking the extensive marshes of the south part of Sheppey. Harbledown is on a low, flat-topped hill W. of Canterbury. Some examples are on broad shelves: Kingsdown S. of Sittingbourne is on a shelf between the 250′ and 300′ contours, and Nackington S. of Canterbury lies at 250′ on a broad shelf. Luddesdown S.S.E. of Gravesend lies at the foot of a hill of 300′. Two higher *dūn*s are Kingsdown N.W. of Wrotham, near the top of a flattish shelf of 550′–600′, and Downe (GTL), S.W. of Orpington, which lies on a wide shelf made by the 500′ contour, a relatively flat area in broken country.

In SUR *dūn* is a more important element in major names than it is in KNT, but the range of meaning is similar, varying from quite low eminences in marshy land to flat-topped hills of 500′. The latter use is illustrated by Chaldon, Coulsdon, Waddington in Coulsdon, and Selsdon in Sanderstead. These lie close together S.W. of Croydon (which is a **denu** name). Chaldon and Coulsdon adjoin a large hill made by the 500′ contour, part of which is occupied by Coulsdon Common, and Waddington adjoins a smaller hill of similar height. Malden, Morden, Wimbledon and Chessington, on the other hand, occupy much more modest hills in well-watered land near the Thames. Another low eminence is referred to in Worplesdon, which lies in a marshy area N.W. of Guildford. East and West Clandon are on the lowest slopes of the Downs which stretch from Guildford to Dorking. For Hambledon, S. of Godalming, see above.

A noteworthy feature in the overall distribution of major names in *dūn* is their rarity in SSX, HMP and BRK. The SSX examples include East, North, Up and West Marden, in high ground near the SSX/HMP border. This name, which means 'boundary hill', was probably that of an extensive district before it became restricted to the settlements. Slindon is a large village on the lowest slopes of the rising ground which overlooks the broad coastal plain inland from Bognor Regis. Many villages to east and west have similar situations, and it is surprising that only this one has a name in *dūn*. Findon and Annington, approximately 10 and 13 miles E. of Slindon, also contain *dūn*, but they are in a different setting, among higher hills which here come closer to the coast. Much further east again is Willingdon, near Eastbourne, at the junction between high ground and marsh. Ecclesden Manor near Angmering probably preserves the OE name of Highdown Hill, a small, abrupt hill in the coastal lowlands. It is noteworthy that apart from the district-name Marden these few examples are in the extreme south of the county, which suggests that *dūn* was not in use as a settlement term when the Weald was colonized.

There is as yet no published place-name survey for HMP, but it is clear from Ekwall 1960 that the county contains very few major names which had *dūn* as a final element. There are Bullington, N. of Winchester (beside a river, but surrounded by low hills), Faringdon, S. of Alton (at a junction of high ground with low, well-watered land), and another Hambledon.

BRK may be ranked with HMP as a county in which *dūn* is little used in settlement-names. Faringdon in the north west of the county (the site resembles those of the WLT examples clustered round Swindon 10 miles to the S.W.) is the only good example. Standon and Lollingdon are 'major' names in the sense of being recorded in DB. Standon refers to a flat-topped hill S.W. of Hungerford, Lollingdon to a small abrupt hill S.W. of Cholsey. *Æscesdūn*, the OE name of the Berkshire Downs, was a district-name, not descriptive of the site of any one settlement, and it is my opinion that Abingdon resembles it in that it was originally the name of the whole Boar's Hill massif to the north of the town. The monks of Abingdon Abbey, however, believed that the Abbey was originally founded at a spot called *Æbbandūn* on the eastern tip of Boar's Hill, and that the name was transferred to the low ground by the Thames when the Abbey was moved there in the late 7th century, and modern commentators other than myself accept this story as having a factual basis.

dūn is not an important element in settlement-names in DOR, probably because few of the county's hills are possible village-sites. Exceptions are Morden, N. of Wareham, where the village lies on a low shelf overlooking a stream, and Haydon, E. of Sherborne, which is comfortably situated on a hill of 384'. Chaldon, the name of several villages E. of Weymouth, refers to the high ground called Chaldon Down which lies between them and the coast. The long ridge called Bindon Hill to the E. of this was named from Bindon Abbey, and the Abbey (later transferred to Wool) was named from its position 'within the down'. Some of the dramatic hills N.E. and N.W. of Bridport have given name to settlements which lie beside them. Pilsdon is overlooked by the highest hill in DOR, Pilsdon Pen, and Blackdown by Blackdown Hill which is the northern part of the same narrow ridge. Eggardon Hill is a high ridge E. of Bridport.

There is no place-name survey for SOM, but it is apparent from Ekwall 1960 that *dūn* enters into a larger number of ancient settlement-names in this county than in DOR. The names are widely spread, not showing the tendency to cluster which is observed in other regions. Lansdown N.W. of Bath has a classic site, lying at over 700' on the flat top of a wide ridge. Kilmersdon, S.W. of Radstock, is on the lower slope of a large hill. There are two examples of Blagdon, one on the N. edge of the Mendips, the other S. of Taunton. Both villages are built up and down the steep north slope of their hills, and this situation may have made them comparatively dark and led to the name 'black hill' (though the long ridge at the E. end of which Blagdon near Taunton is situated is called Black Down, so this may be an instance in which the hill-name was transferred to the settlement). Several SOM names refer to long ridges or escarpments. Clevedon is at the junction of two long ridges, and Bleadon is under Bleadon Hill, a narrow ridge overlooking the R. Axe. The Polden Hills and the Brendon Hills are long ridges with names in *dūn* which have not been transferred to settlements. Other *dūn* names in SOM refer to gently rising ground on the edge of marsh: Kingsdon, N. of Ilchester, over-looks the marshy Yeo valley, and Wembdon near Bridgwater lies where the ground begins to rise from the valley of the R. Parrett. Downhead and Dunnett are discussed below.

dūn is very well represented in DEV, occurring in 17 names of the type classified as 'major' and in a similar number of 'minor' names. The distinction has little meaning in DEV; some names of farms and hamlets are classified as 'major' because they are mentioned in the Domesday Survey and other early medieval records, but others, like Kismeldon in West Pudford or Whiteoxen in Rattery (*Whittekesdon* 1242) are certainly of OE origin, though appearing later or more sparsely in records. There are several parishes with *dūn* names, including East and West Down, which lie 5 miles apart, inland from Ilfracombe. East Down is high, near the summit of its hill, but West Down village is in a stream-valley, surrounded by flat-topped hills, and is perhaps not in its original position. Also in N.W. DEV is Meddon in Hartland parish, on a spur of the 650' contour, one of a number of farm and hamlet names in this high moorland which end in –don, many of them probably from *dūn*, though not so well documented as Meddon which is in DB. Another group of *dūn* names occurs near Plymouth: Manadon, N. of Plymouth, occupies a small spur made by the 250' contour, Hemerdon, N.E. of Plympton, lies under a small round hill called Hemerdon Ball, Staddon in Plymstock is at one end of a large, flat-topped hill, and Down Thomas in Wembury is on the summit of a less extensive hill immediately to the S. of Staddon. Two examples occur in S.W. DEV: Marldon (a parish, N.W. of Paignton), where the village is on a small hill-spur, and Ingsdon Hill, N.W. of Newton Abbot, a steep peak of 600' where there appears to be no settlement now though the name is well documented from DB onwards. Examples near Exeter are Farringdon (the village lies by a small stream so Farringdon House, on a flat shelf just below the top of a low hill, may be the earlier settlement), and Hillersdon House in Cullompton. Raddon Hills, N. of Exeter, which is a steep ridge not suitable for settlement, has given name to Raddon and West Raddon, near its foot. Two comparatively isolated examples are Cheldon, E. of Chulmleigh, in a slight recess on the edge of a large hill, and Rousdon, on the S. coast between Seaton and Lyme Regis. Rousdon (which is *Dona* in DB, the prefix, Ralph, being an owner's name added in the 12th century) is situated on the 500' contour, at the edge of a large hill. Clayhidon is on the SOM boundary, on a flat-topped spur of the Black Down Hills. For the common minor name Bowden, see above.

dūn must have been an active element in the formation of settlement-names for the whole period of the English penetration into DEV, though it does not appear to have been used as a final element in major place-names in CNW.

Some of the WLT names in *dūn* occur in clusters, the main concentration being in the N.E. of the county. The parish of Hannington extends to the Thames, but the village lies on top of a well-marked hill. The next well-marked hill to the S.W. has Blunsdon on its slopes, and at a short distance to the S. of that is the hill on which the old town of Swindon is situated. Between Blunsdon and Swindon there is a narrow hill between two streams, and Haydon and

Moredon lie on this. South of Swindon lies flat land traversed by small streams, then a fairly steep escarpment as the land rises towards Marlborough Downs. Wroughton, the OE name of which was *Ellendun*, lies on the lower slopes of this escarpment. Mannington and Chaddington, two very small settlements with *dūn* names situated W. and SW. of Swindon, are adjacent to small, abrupt hills in the belt of low ground. Further S. in WLT, the parish of Clarendon Park E. of Salisbury comprises an area of undulating high ground; Whaddon in Alderbury, to the S., lies in the same hilly country overlooking the R. Avon, and Gomeldon, to the N., is similarly placed overlooking the R. Bourne. More isolated examples include Baydon on the BRK/WLT boundary—which has a very high site—and Edington S.W. of Devizes, on the lower slopes of a steep escarpment. Hindon, in the S.W. of WLT, lies in a belt of high country.

Donhead St Mary and St Andrew, E.N.E. of Salisbury, share a name which means 'head of the down'. The earlier settlement is presumably Donhead St Mary, the situation of which agrees with the etymology. The village occupies a projecting wedge which might well be thought of as the 'head' of the steep hill which rises to 750′ N.W. of the settlement. (The name occurs again in Downhead SOM, W. of Frome, where the reference also seems to be to a jutting shelf below a hill-summit. Another SOM example is Dunnett Fm in Compton Bishop, at one sharp tip of a curving hill. Yet another instance, *Dunheved*, was the old name of Launceston CNW.)

North of the Thames, in GLO, *dūn* occurs in 9 names of places which are parishes, or mentioned in DB, or both. Churchdown, S.W. of Cheltenham, was obviously the name of the hill before it was transferred to the settlement at its foot. Probably so were Oxenton, N. of Cheltenham, and Dixton, which refers to a knob on the S.E. of the same hill. Swindon, nearer to Cheltenham, however, looks like a name coined for the settlement that occupies very gently rising ground between two small streams which unite with others to drain into the Severn at Tewkesbury. The use of *dūn* for such a site (though easily paralleled in other counties) contrasts so markedly with the use of the word for the hills at Oxenton, Dixton and Churchdown, that it seems necessary to conclude that the names arose at a different date, Swindon perhaps being earlier than the others. Whaddon, S. of Gloucester, occupies a piece of ground between two streamlets which is a small-scale version of the site of Swindon. Matson, N. of Whaddon, lies on a shelf at the bottom of Robins Hill Wood. Rissington, the name of three settlements on the OXF border, was clearly a district-name, referring to the long down which runs north from the R. Windrush. Withington, S.E. of Cheltenham, is situated on a spur running out from a long ridge, and here it seems likely that the name was coined for the settlement. Blaisdon, N.E. of Cinderford, like a number of other names in *dūn*, is at the junction of low, well-watered land with sharply rising ground, and Boulsdon in Newent, to the N. of Blaisdon, is similarly placed.

In OXF there are 13 major settlement-names in *dūn*, all but two lying in a band which runs from N.E. to S.E. of Oxford, from Godington, Bletchingdon and Ambrosden to Easington. Headington near Oxford is one of the examples; the others are Oddington, Cuddesdon, Attington, Tiddington, Garsington and Baldon. The two outliers are Shenington in the N. W. of the county and Claydon in the nothern tip.

Shenington is the only OXF *dūn* which is really high; the village stands at over 500', and the hill behind it rises to a wide plateau over 600', with two small peaks of 743'. The typical *dūn* of the other OXF names is a flat-topped eminence of between 300' and 350', its highest part being at least a mile long and half-a-mile broad. Bletchingdon, N. of Oxford, is a very good example. The village is on top of the *dūn*, and Emery 1974 (p. 113) comments on its good water-supply from springs and wells. Garsington and Cuddesdon occupy the S.W. and S.E. ends of a horseshoe-shaped *dūn*, with Denton ('valley farm') lying in the cleft made by the small stream which runs between the two ends. The Baldons (Toot –, Marsh – and Little –) are on the E. edge of the N. end of a narrow *dūn*, 3½ miles long. Emery 1974 (p. 75) describes some of these sites: 'Toot Baldon . . . stands on a low hill. It is one of several in this countryside, in plain sight of Garsington, Cuddesdon and the Miltons, a constellation of Old English settlements perched on the outer edges of slopes where the sands and limestone above give way to the clays below.'

Two of the OXF *dūns* are less notable features. Ambrosden occupies slightly raised ground between headstreams of the R. Ray, and Oddington has a modest eminence which perhaps seemed noteworthy because it overlooked Ot Moor.

The belt of major settlement-names in *dūn* noted in OXF continues in a north-easterly direction across BUC, keeping mostly to the N. of the Icknield Way. The main concentration is S. of Buckingham. Here (from N. to S.) are Hillesden, the Claydons, Poundon, Charndon, Grendon, Shipton Lee and Denham (earlier *Dundon*) in Quainton, Weedon, Waddesdon, Winchendon, Beachendon in Winchendon, Quarrendon, Ashendon and Crendon. East of this concentration are three much more widely spaced examples: Cheddington, Wavendon and Whaddon. The southern outliers on the slopes of the Chilterns are Horsenden, Saunderton and a lost village in West Wycombe called *Haveringedune* in 1222. (Some names in *dūn* occur in the more easterly part of the Chilterns, as can be seen from Fig. 2, and there are minor names in *dūn* in the OXF portion of the Chilterns.) The typical *dūn* of these BUC names is of similar elevation to that of the OXF names, but with a smaller area of flat top. Ashendon is higher than most, with a summit of 517', and the village is rather cramped on the shelf below this summit. At Grendon Underwood the Hall occupies what looks like the typical site on top of the *dūn*, and the village straggles along the road below it. A position on top of the *dūn* is the norm in this area, despite a few exceptions. This is the predominant type of parish-name in the area between Hillesden and Long Crendon. Weedon is geographically a typical member of the group.

The pattern which has been observed in east OXF and in BUC dissolves in

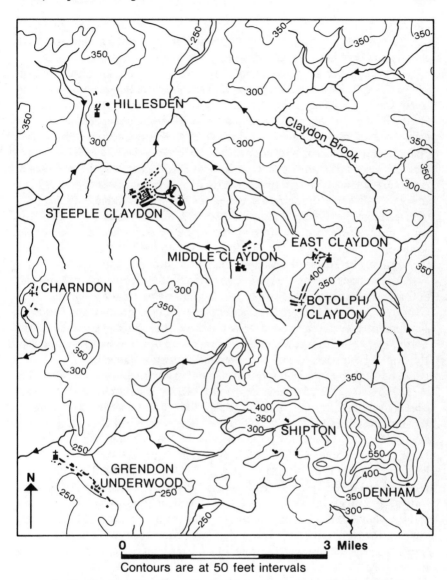

Contours are at 50 feet intervals

3 Buckinghamshire *dūn* country. (From a map drawn by Ann Cole.)

BDF. Billington is a *dūn* like the BUC ones which it adjoins, but east of this the hills are of different shapes, Toddington and Sundon being on rather steep hills with not much flat area. Other *dūn* names—Shillington and Stondon for instance, which adjoin each other—are on small islands made by the 200′ contour, and some—e.g. Battlesden and Harrowden—are on the end or on a spur of a low ridge. Maulden is part of a ridge, rather than a discrete hill.

Caddington near Luton, on the S. boundary of the county, fits the BUC pattern quite well, lying on a flat-topped spur of over 550', but the BDF countryside does not offer a series of such sites.

HRT has 7 parish-names in *dūn*. Apart from Bovingdon (which means 'above the hill' and is a different type of formation from the other names), they are in the east of the county. Brickendon and Hoddesdon adjoin, S.E. of Hertford. Brickendon is no longer a settlement, and Hoddesdon has become part of continuous settlement along the A10, so the topography is difficult to evaluate, but there is raised ground here in the bend of the R. Lea. Hunsdon to the N.E. lies on a flat shelf overlooking the R. Stort. Standon, to the N. again, is certainly not on a *dūn*; it is beside the R. Rib, so either this is not the original site of the village, or the name was that of the highest ground to the E. and was transferred to the settlement. Sandon, near the N.E. boundary of the county, has a more convincing *dūn* site, which can be regarded as a member of the cluster in the adjoining part of CAM. Meesden, to the E. of Sandon, occupies the summit of a small hill made by the 450' contour.

dūn is well represented in the ancient county of MDX (which includes part of GTL). Hillingdon occupies a broad, low hill rising from the marshes E. of Uxbridge. At Hendon there is a large expanse of raised ground, and the use of *dūn* for this may be contrasted with the use of **hrycg** for the site of nearby Totteridge. Neasden and Willesden adjoin, occupying the two hills to the S. of Hendon. The topography of Islington is difficult to evaluate.

In ESX, also, *dūn* is an important element in settlement-names. Some sites in the north (e.g. Ashdon) and centre (e.g. Kelvedon Hatch) are flat-topped *dūn*s of over 300'. But the characteristic ESX use is in the south and south east, above the marshes of the Rivers Thames, Blackwater and Crouch. Here the *dūn*s of the place-names are mostly made by the 100' contour, some by the 50'. Longdon Hills ('long' perhaps referring to the ridge as seen from the Thames) has a summit, where the village stands, of 389', and the suffix 'Hills', first recorded in 1485, may have been added in recognition of the contrast between this site and its neighbours. Ockendon and Horndon, respectively just below and just above 100', are typical of this area. Mundon, S.E. of Maldon, is a very low *dūn*: the Hall stands at 36', and Mundon Hill reaches 50'. If the etymology 'protection hill' be correct, the protection is presumably from the floods of the Blackwater.

In NFK and SFK there are about 20 settlement-names in *dūn*, not clustered, but dotted about in the vast expanse of territory covered by the two counties. The word is not an important element in any part of the area. In a number of instances the reference is to an extensive, relatively level area of ground above the 150' contour. Here belong Raydon SFK, S.E. of Hadleigh, Thorndon SFK, S. of Diss, Flordon NFK, S.E. of Wymondham, and Heydon NFK, S. of Saxthorpe. Roydon NFK, W. of Diss, occupies a small island of 150', rising from a flat shelf made by the 100' contour, which overlooks the marshes by the R. Waveney. A few instances have more constricted sites:

Hawkedon, N.E. of Clare, is on a spur between two brooks. Some are very low, as Reydon SFK, N.W. of Southwold, which occupies a cluster of 'islands' made by the 50' contour. In two instances, at least, *dūn* is used not of a hill suitable for settlement, but of a 'down' which provides a hinterland for the village. Here belong Brandon on the NFK/SFK border, the village lying by the Little Ouse River, but the name referring to the large raised heath to the south, which can never have been suitable for settlement-sites. Foulden NFK is in a similar situation. Downham Market NFK, by contrast, is on the edge of the largest patch of raised ground in a wide region of fenland, and there are a number of other settlements on the same higher area; *Down* may have been the name of this district. Great and Little Dunham NFK, N.E. of Swaffham, occupy a splendid flat-topped *dūn*, most of the area being between 250' and 300'.

dūn is not an important element in settlement-names in CAM, the characteristic word for a raised site in marshland being ēg. Little Downham, N.W. of Ely, occupies a small island which may have been called *dūn* rather than ēg because it is slightly higher than most of the fenland islands. Linden End in Haddenham may preserve the OE name of the long hill on which Haddenham and Wilburton are situated. There are three *dūn* names in the S.W. of the county. Guilden and Steeple Morden are at the end of a low ridge overlooking the R. Cam, and Whaddon, a few miles E. of the Mordens, also has a slightly raised site overlooking the river. A few miles N. of Whaddon are Great and Little Eversden, on the N.W. edge of a spacious hill between the R. Cam and Bourn Brook. The villages of Haslingfield, Halton and Orwell also stand on the edges of this hill.

HNT contains only two settlement-names in *dūn*, Haddon, on a long narrow ridge in the N. of the county, and Huntingdon, on a low hill overlooking the wide bed of the R. Ouse.

By contrast with its comparative rarity in a great belt of territory to the east, *dūn* is a common element in major names in NTP. There are a few sites which resemble those of the OXF *dūn*s, e.g. Eydon, not far from the northern tip of OXF, situated on a shelf on the E. side of a hill which rises to 586', and Boddington, which refers to the next *dūn* to the N.E. of Claydon OXF. Weedon Lois, a few miles S.E. of Eydon, has a similar site, but West Farndon and Chipping Warden, the two *dūn*s to the W. of Eydon, are not quite comparable. West Farndon lies just off the tip of a narrow ridge, and this use of *dūn* for a ridge, rather than a flat-topped sub-circular hill, is seen in a number of names in other parts of NTP, e.g. Glendon and Grendon. Warden means 'look-out *dūn*', and it has been considered that the name applies not to the large raised area occupied by Chipping Warden village but to the peak called Warden Hill which is a mile to the N.E.; but perhaps 'down on one part of which there is a peak suitable for a look-out place' is a fair rendering of the name. Haddon, in East and West Haddon, which are 3 miles apart in the hilly, broken country N. of Daventry and Northampton, may have been a district name.

dūn enters into more than 10 major settlement-names in WAR. Elmdon and Sheldon, S.E. of Birmingham, are on adjoining broad spurs, contrasting with the narrow ridge of Bickenhill, which adjoins Elmdon. Longdon in nearby Solihull is on the edge of a flat-topped spur. Another small cluster occurs in the N. tip of the county, where Grendon refers to a flat-topped hill made by the 200′ contour and Dordon stands on higher ground across the R. Anker. Seckington, N. of these, is just below the 300′ contour which forms a narrow ridge rising from a broad, flat shelf. Near the centre of the county, on the R. Avon, is Brandon, at the edge of a broad, low hill (highest point 315′) overlooking the R. Avon. Claverdon, N. of Stratford-upon-Avon, has a classic site, the village occupying the top of a hill which rises to just over 400′. The name Bishopton, on the outskirts of Stratford, is not likely to refer to the settlement; it is more appropriate to Bishopton Hill, a spur of higher ground to the N.W. Ettington, S.E. of Stratford, is on the watershed between the catchment areas of the Rivers Stour and Avon. Characteristically there are few names in *dūn* on the much higher ground of the Cotswolds, but Ilmington is on one of the lower spurs, and Longdon in Tredington (WOR) adjoins Ilmington.

In WOR and HRE *dūn* is poorly represented in settlement-names. In Bredon WOR its use resembles that in *Æscesdun* BRK. At Warndon, E. of Worcester, the church is at the end of a narrow, low ridge, and Longdon N.W. of Tewkesbury is on a low ridge in wet country. Stildon Manor in Rock WOR has a high site, occupying a spur of the massif called Clows Top. In HRE there is one settlement-name in *dūn* with a site resembling the typical ones in counties further east; this is Staunton on Wye, where the village is spread along the top of a long, narrow hill with a summit of 354′. At Shobdon, W.N.W. of Leominster, the village lies on raised ground overlooking marsh, and the name is as likely to refer to this as to the great massif of Shobdon Hill to the N. Rowden Abbey in Edvin Ralph is in a cleft between two flat-topped hills.

dūn is more important in SHR than in WOR or HRE, being the final element in 11 major names. The height of the hills varies from 200′ or 250′ at Sugdon and Edgmond (formerly *Egmendon*) in the marshy land round the Weald Moors, to 700′ or 800′ at Aldon, Bouldon and Edgton in the hilly country S. of Wenlock Edge and the Long Mynd. Edgmond and Aldon are on the summit of their hills, and Edgton lies on a shelf between the 750′ and 800′ contours. Bouldon, on the other hand, is by the Clee Brook in a cleft between hills occupied by the settlements of Heath and Cold Weston. Merrington, N.W. of Shrewsbury, lies on a small *dūn* made by the 350′ contour. Stottes-don, N. of Cleobury Mortimer, occupies the top of a hill-spur at 571′, and Eudon George and Eudon Burnell, S.W. of Bridgnorth occupy flat shelves on either side of the Borle Brook. Puleston, N.W. of Newport, lies at the foot of an abrupt pear-shaped hill. There are two 'long downs'. Longden near Pontes-bury is on the end of a narrow ridge, and when approached from Shrewsbury this presents a smooth whale-back profile. Longdon upon Tern, N.W. of Wellington on the western edge of the Weald Moors, is raised above the marsh by a ridge and two islands made by the 175' contour; perhaps the use of *dūn* in this name and the adjacent Sugdon indicates that the surrounding ground was less wet than in the Weald Moors, where some settlements have names in **ēg**. The absence of *dūn* names in the northern part of SHR accords with the rarity of the element in CHE.

Most of the sparse examples in CHE refer to very low hills. Dunham on the Hill, N.E. of Chester, occupies a small island made by the 100' contour. Farndon and Huntington, S. of Chester, lie beside the R. Dee at elevations of between 50' and 100'. Bowdon, W. of Altrincham, refers to a hill of little more than 200', and Bosden, S.E. of Stockport, is not much higher. Only in the name Siddington ('place south of the down') is *dūn* used of a high massif, a hill S.W. of Macclesfield which rises to 500'.

STF has about the same number of major names in *dūn* as SHR, and there is somewhat the same range of variation in the heights of the features. In the S. and centre of the county the hills referred to are 250'–350' (e.g. Hixon N.E. of Stafford and Longdon N.W. of Lichfield), but they are much higher in the N., where Grindon, N.W. of Ilam, lies at 954', and Cauldon, N.E. of Cheadle, at about 830'. Intermediate examples include Sandon, S.E. of Stone, where the hill is 400'–500', and Great and Little Saredon, S.W. of Cannock, on either side of a hill which rises to 505'. Standon, W. of Stone, occupies the top of a hill reaching 472'. Slindon, S.E. of Standon, is between two somewhat lower hills.

The majority of the *dūn* names in DRB are in the mountainous N.W. of the county. Chelmorton, S.E. of Buxton, lies in a recess in a massif rising to 1438'. The *dūn* referred to in Hanson Grange, N. of Ashbourne, rises to 1136'. Hartington lies under a hill of over 1000'; and Staden in Kingsterndale is at 1200'. Over and Nether Haddon, S. of Bakewell, lie along a high ridge. In the southern part of the county, however, *dūn* is used as in the neighbouring counties for low hills and ridges. Spondon, E. of Derby, is a typical lowland *dūn* of 200'–300', and Ilkeston and Bupton, N.E., and W. of Derby, are similar. Repton occupies quite low ground, under 200', but rising up from the R. Trent.

In NTT *dūn* is the final element of only two major place-names. One of these is Farndon, which is often cited as evidence that *dūn* must have developed a meaning 'open land' with no reference to elevation. Farndon is S.W. of Newark-on-Trent, and the village lies in low, flat ground immediately beside the river. The name means 'fern hill', and the position is inappropriate to the first, as well as to the second, element of the compound. The next parishes to the S. are Thorpe and East Stoke, and it is legitimate to suggest that the two names indicate a relatively late origin for both units. Thorpe and East Stoke contain islands of raised ground made by the 50' contour, and Farndon may originally have been the name of a wedge of slightly raised ground between the R. Trent and the R. Devon. Headon, S.E. of East Retford, lies on the 150' contour, at the edge of a hill rising to 219'. At Dunham, on the NTT/LIN border, the *dūn* is an island made by the 50' contour beside the R. Trent.

dūn is well represented in LEI and RUT, but there are not many instances in which the name refers to a hill with a settlement on or near the summit. Upper Hambleton RUT, S.E. of Oakham, does stand on the summit of its hill, however, and Barrowden, to the S.E., is at the edge of a long, narrow ridge overlooking the R. Welland. There are several instances of the use of *dūn* for a flat or gently sloping ledge. Sibson, S.W. of Market Bosworth, is on a shelf between the 250′ and 300′ contours; Great Bowden, N.E. of Market Harborough, stands on a wide shelf of similar height overlooking the R. Welland, and Lyndon RUT is on a shelf overlooking the R. Chater. Quorndon N. of Leicester has a very low site by the R. Soar, and the name may refer to the hill S. of the settlement. Bardon S.E. of Coalville lies on a shelf between the 550′ and 600′ contours, overlooked by Bardon Hill, which reaches 912′. Breedon lies under Breedon Hill; the church is on the hill-top, but it seems probable that in Quorndon, Bardon and Breedon the *dūn* names applied primarily to the notable hills and were transferred to, rather than being coined for, the villages at the foot. Billesdon E. of Leicester stands at the source of Billesdon Brook, one of six streams which rise on the slopes of the adjacent hill. Local knowledge would be required in order to judge whether an earlier settlement was likely to have stood on the top of the hill.

dūn is an almost negligible element in major place-names in LIN, but two sites deserve discussion. Brandon N. of Grantham lies at about 70′ in very flat land. There must be a slight rise which determined the site of the village, and the name may refer to that, but it is noteworthy that the parish contains the settlement of Hough-on-the-Hill which is situated just below the broad, flat summit of an extensive hill at 250′–300′. Hough is not, in this instance, a topographical name; it is OE *haga* 'enclosure'. It seems possible that Brandon was originally the name of this large hill. Evedon N.E. of Sleaford stands on the tip of a low ridge made by the 50′ contour, and this use of *dūn* can be paralleled elsewhere.

In the counties which remain to be considered, there is a marked difference in the frequency of *dūn* names as between the east, where they become more common as one goes further north, and the west, where they become very scarce. They are rare in the whole of Yorkshire, but better evidenced in YOE than in YON or YOW.

In YOE *dūn* only once refers to a substantial hill: Fordon near Hunmanby ('place in front of the down') refers to Prior Moor, which has an extensive flat top of over 500′. Other instances (Cowden, Hedon and Watton) refer to slighter features. Watton (*Uetadun* in Bede's *Ecclesiastical History*) is on the lowest slopes of a hill which has an extensive flat top made by the 100′ contour. OE *wǣt* is perhaps used as a substantive here, rather than an adjective, so that Watton means 'hill in the wet places', a name which would correspond to Morden SUR. Smith (EPNS survey, p. 158) says: 'Watton is on the lower slope of a long, gradually rising hill to the west of the marshes, which must then have been more extensive than now.' Cowden Magna and Parva lie on the coast of North Holderness in very flat country. Cowden Magna is at 68′ in an area where the general level is 55′–60′, and Cowden Parva lies at a little over 60′ in an area where the general level is below the 50′ contour. Many other settlements in this region have similar slightly elevated sites, though only Cowden has a *dūn* name; it is possible that some of the other villages had *dūn* names at an early date but these were replaced by habitative names in **tūn** and **wīc**. Hedon E. of Hull must be about the lowest *dūn* in the country, and the use of the word in this instance may be due to the absence of **ēg** from the place-name-forming vocabulary of the people of YOE.

In YON, apart from three instances of Hambleton (discussed above), there are only Downholme ('at the hills', the dat. pl. of *dūn*), which is S.W. of Richmond, surrounded by small peaks in high moorland, Warthermarske near Masham (earlier *Wardonmerske* 'marsh by watch-hill') referring to a small peak, and Wildon Grange in Coxwold parish, again in an area of small peaks. In YOW there are several more instances of Hambledon (and some other hill-names in *dūn*), but *dūn* is not much used in settlement-names. Such instances as do occur are mainly concentrated in an arc N. of Leeds, where Rawdon, Yeadon, Brandon, Burdon Head Fm and Rawden Hill refer to relatively slight peaks in undulating ground. The only impressive detached hill which has a *dūn* name in this area is Baildon, the most westerly of the group, where the village lies under a circular hill rising to 927′. Swindon in Kirkby Overblow, S. of Harrogate, refers to a very low hill, and Rowden in Hampsthwaite to a tiny peak of 506′. Sheldon Hill in Ledston is said in the EPNS survey (4, p. 51) to be 'a small peak'.

In the north-western counties *dūn* is very rare in settlement-names. LNC has 3 instances of Hameldon, but they are hill-names, not transferred to settlements. They are near Burnley on the Yorkshire border. Two settlement-names in this part of LNC are Billington, N.W. of Accrington, huddled between the R. Calder and a long narrow ridge which must be the *Billingdūn* ('sword-shaped hill'), and Downham, which lies under Pendle Hill. There is one LNC name, Smithdown, an ancient manor S. of Liverpool, where the word is used as in CHE of a slight rise in low ground. In WML the only ancient name in *dūn* is the mountain-name Meldon, and in CMB there is no certain instance of the word.

A most noteworthy feature of the distribution is that after virtually dying out in YON, CMB and WML, *dūn* again becomes an important element in settlement-names in DRH. Durham itself is a hybrid of *dūn* with ON **holmr**, and the Durham sheet of the 1″ map shows 11 names which have *dūn* as final element. Brandon occupies the eastern tip of a long ridge S.W. of Durham. Trimdon, Pittington, Quarrington and Hetton lie E. of Durham, Trimdon on a hill of 500′, Pittington beside a similar eminence, Quarrington by a star-fish-shaped hill with peaks of over 600′. Hetton-le-Hole and Hetton-le-Hill lie in broken moorland. Coundon, Eldon and Shildon adjoin each other E. of Bishop Auckland. Coundon occupies a hill rising to 600′, separated by a small stream from the slightly lower hill of Eldon, and Shildon is on the side of the next hill to the S.W. At Mordon, E. of these, the 250' contour marks off habitable land from an area of Carrs, and Mordon village lies just inside the contour. Burdon, N.E. of Darlington, is similarly situated. Grindon, E. of Mordon, is on a low hill between streams. On the DRH portion of the Newcastle upon Tyne 1" map are Boldon, Cleadon and Harton, adjoining each other on ground slightly raised above the wide bank of the Tyne estuary, and another Grindon, on a low hill overlooking Sunderland.

In the adjoining part of NTB the *dūn* names are more widely spaced, none of them referring to an impressive hill, and some only to low shelves of land. Burradon, N. of Longbenton, is on the 200' contour, Earsdon, W. of Whitley Bay, on the 150', and Fawdon, N. of Gosforth, on a slight rise above the 200' line. The other Earsdon, N. of Morpeth, occupies a low hill of 250'–300'. Meldon, S.W. of Morpeth, is on a hill rising to 362'. Higher sites are Black Heddon, N. of Stamfordham, which refers to a hill of 580', and Callerton (High and Black) and Heddon-on-the-Wall, which refer to the same ridge, N.W. of Newcastle, rising to 477'. In the more mountainous ground to the W. names in *dūn* become very rare: Warden-on-Tyne lies at the foot of an abrupt hill of 593' dominating the junction of N. and S. Tyne, and Grindon, overlooking the Wall to the W.N.W., has a high position.

Further north the *dūn* names are again mostly on the lower ground. Dunstan near Craster, not far from the coast, is in undulating country which nowhere reaches 200', Buston, N.W. of Warkworth, is in similar but slightly higher coastal land, and Fallodon, N.W. of Embleton, is in the same sort of country a little further inland. Wooden near Buston is ascribed to **denu** in Ekwall 1960, but the spellings in Mawer 1920 point to *dūn*. Two higher sites are Glanton, N. of Whittingham, on the side of an impressive hill rising to 695', and Cartington, N.W. of Rothbury, which occupies a knoll of 641'. Further north still are Berrington, N. of Lowick, in the same sort of country as Fallodon; Felkington, W. of Berrington, on a small hill of 300'; and Grindon, just inside the 150' contour W. of Felkington. Downham ('at the hills'), S.E. of Coldstream, is in a valley surrounded by peaks.

There is as yet no respectable place-name dictionary for Scotland, so it is not possible to say how much further north *dūn* is to be reckoned with as an English place-name element. No examples are noted in Macdonald 1941, however, so it probably does not occur as far north as Edinburgh.

ecg OE 'edge' is a rather rare place-name element, better represented in minor than in major settlement-names, fairly common only in a few counties, which include CHE, GLO, YOW. It is used of slight slopes (e.g. in Drakenage, a well-recorded minor name in Kingsbury WAR, N.E. of Coleshill), rock scars in fairly low ground (e.g. Edge CHE), long, low ridges (e.g. Edge SHR, Liversedge YOW), and occasionally of dramatic rocky escarpments (e.g. Hathersage DRB). At Harnage SHR, S.E. of Shrewsbury, the village is on the edge of a low hill, but the name seems more appropriate to Harnage Grange, over a mile S., which stands at the foot of a long, fairly steep slope. Heage DRB is in very broken country N.E. of Belper. Edge Hill WAR is an early-recorded example (from c. 1250) of a hill-name which recurs in several counties. In some GLO names, Aston and Weston Subedge and Wotton under Edge, the word is used as part of an affix. The EPNS survey (3, pp. 27–8) prefers an alternative derivation of Liversedge from *secg* 'sedge', but this is less convincing than 'Lēofhere's edge'.

Ecg– is a common first theme in dithematic OE personal names, and this is sometimes the explanation of Edg– in modern place-names, as Edgbaston WAR 'Ecgbald's estate' and Edgerley SHR 'Ecghard's wood/clearing'. Edgeworth GLO, LNC should probably be derived from the monothematic personal name *Ecgi*, which occurs in Edgware GTL. Edgefield NFK, Edgeley CHE, SHR contain *edisc* 'enclosed pasture'.

fjall, fell ON 'mountain' is used in mountain-names in northern England, Scotland and IOM. These names are seldom transferred to settlements, but cf. Whinfell CMB, WML.

hēafod OE 'head'. In the mid 10th century, which is the period when most surviving OE boundary surveys were composed, *hēafod* had a number of topographical senses. These included 'end' or 'source' (e.g. *cumbes heafod*, *holan broces heafod*, *mænan mores heafud* in BRK surveys) and 'headland in a field-system'. The first sense is fairly common in minor place-names, probably mostly of ME or modern origin, and the second survives in field-names, usually in the plural form Hades. In the earliest period of English place-name formation, however, *hēafod* was probably used only for a projecting piece of ground, in which sense it occurs in more than 30 major settlement-names. It is very rare as a first element, Hatford BRK being possibly the only uncontroversial instance. In that name it refers to the very slight elevation which raises the village above the marshy course of Frogmore Brook. Howden YOE poses special problems, which are discussed under **denu**.

As a second element in major place-names, *hēafod* is used of features varying in height from a few feet above fenland to the elevation of considerable hills like those at Hartside NTB (S. of Wooler) and Minehead SOM; but examples predominate in which it refers to hills of less than 500', and no instance has been noted of an ancient name in which *hēafod* is used of the highest hill in an area. It seems unlikely that it ever meant 'peak' or 'summit'. The choice of *hēafod* for projecting pieces of ground in preference to other terms such as **bæc**, **hōh** and **næss**, was probably dictated by the shape of the feature.

Some recurring compounds were probably appellatives. One such is OE *dūn-hēafod*, found in the names Donhead WLT, Downhead and Dunnett SOM and *Dunheved* CNW, which are discussed under **dūn**. Another is OE *swīneshēafod* 'pig's head'. This gives rise to three names (Swineshead BDF, LIN and Swinside in Lorton CMB) of sufficient status to be included in Ekwall 1960, and another 10 instances can be easily assembled in names of lesser status. Surviving examples among these 10 names are:

Swinchurch STF (*Sueneshed* DB, *Swineshead* on 1st ed. 1″ map), S.W. of Newcastle. This lies below the tip of a long, narrow ridge.

Swineshead YOW, in Todmorden, not marked on the 1″ map, but obviously in hilly country.

Swinehead Hundred GLO (most early spelling have –*es*–). The meeting-place of the hundred is not known.

Swinesherd WOR (*Swinesheafde* in OE spellings), on a low hill S.E. of Worcester.

Swinside Hall in Oxnam ROX, Scotland (*Swynyshede* 1390). The Hall is overlooked by three hills, but none of them appears on the 1″ map to have a distinctive shape.

There are two occurrences in OE charter boundaries, for Christian Malford WLT and Calbourne IOW, and three field-names, in Cookham BRK, Nether Peover CHE, and North Mimms HRT. Other instances could probably be found. The topography of the three examples included in Ekwall 1960 supports the evidence of some of the minor names that *swīneshēafod* was an appellative for a projecting 'snout' of land. Swinside in Lorton CMB is overlooked by a hill with a 'snout'. Swineshead BDF (E. of Rushden) lies by a long spur made by the 250′ contour. Swineshead LIN (S.W. of Boston) is in very low-lying ground, and spot-heights of 9′, 10′ and 16′ chart the slight rise that would make settlement possible.

There are at least 5 names derived from *heoroteshēafod* 'hart's head', but the case for regarding this as an appellative describing the shape of the headland seems much less compelling. Hartside NTB refers (as noted above) to a considerable hill, and so does Hartshead LNC (W. of Mossley). Hartshead YOW (W. of Dewsbury) is in broken, hilly country. Hartside Height CMB is a mountain. All these are places where the presence of a hart would make a strong visual impact. *Herteshede* was an alternative name of Bushey HRT in the 13th to 14th centuries, and this also refers to a prominent hill in ancient forest country. Hindhead SUR, which has a similar significance, is not certain to be an ancient name as it is not recorded till 1571. Read LNC is a compound of OE *ræge*, 'female roe-deer', with *hēafod*.

Among the whole corpus of place-names containing *hēafod* the commonest type is that which has the name of a living creature in the genitive singular as first element. Broxted ESX, Farcet HNT, Gateshead DRH, Rampside LNC and Shepshed LEI are major settlement-names in this category, in addition to the 'swine' and 'hart' names listed above. Such compounds have attracted the attention of scholars, and in an article of 1934 Professor Bruce Dickins listed these and other examples from minor names, and developed a suggestion made by Henry Bradley in 1910 that such names arose from the setting up of an animal's head, or a representation of it, on a pole to mark a meeting-place. To this Professor Dickins added the suggestion that such totem poles were set up after sacrificial killing of the creature followed by feasting on the rest of the carcass. The article was published as an Appendix to the EPNS survey of SUR, because such names are especially well represented in that county. Examples among SUR minor names are Eversheds Fm in Ockley, Heronshead Fm in Leigh ('eagle' not 'heron') and Worms Heath (earler *Wermeshevede*) in Chelsham. Minor names in other counties include Cats Head Lodge in Sudborough NTP and Ravenshead Wood N.E. of Newstead NTT. Two instances of 'man's head' were also noted: Manshead Hundred BDF and a lost name *Mannesheved* in Hawton NTT.

The suggestion that these names, or at any rate some of them, had a ceremonial significance rather than a purely topographical one was regarded sceptically by Ekwall 1960 (p. 229) and rejected in Gelling 1961. I still feel it probable that there is a topographical explanation in all instances, and that the reference is to a projecting piece of land which either resembles the head of the bird or animal, or is characterized by the creature's frequent presence there; but I admit to being puzzled at the numerical preponderance of the Gateshead/Swineshead type of compound. Instances in which a topographical explanation can be adduced from the map include (in addition to those mentioned above) Farcet HNT, S.E. of Peterborough, where the 50′ contour makes a long, narrow finger projecting into the fen, and Shepshed LEI, where there is a low headland made by the 250′ contour. The EPNS survey of BDF says (p. 113) that the meeting-place of Manshead Hundred is 'a long and low but well-defined hill'.

Other categories of first element are small, the largest of them consisting of references to vegetation. Here belong Birkenhead CHE, Fearnhead LNC, Hesket Newmarket CMB, Lindeth LNC, WML, Sparket CMB and Thicket YOE. An earlier hill-name is the first element in Camshead YON, Consett DRH, Mamhead DEV, Minehead SOM and Quantoxhead SOM, and in these *hēafod* refers to a projecting spur of the massif. Kinniside CMB may belong in this category. Portishead SOM is 'ridge of the harbour'. There are four compounds with personal names: Arnside, Burneside and Ormside WML, and Fineshade NTP. Conishead LNC refers to royal ownership. Lupset YOW has an obscure first element.

It will be clear from the above lists that in many instances *hēafod* can only be detected by the study of early spellings. It sometimes becomes –et(t) or –ide (giving –set or –side if the first element is genitive) but in many other names these spellings derive from different sources, notably ON *sætr* 'shieling', OE *sǣte* 'house', OE *geset* 'fold'. All instances of Hesket except Hesket Newmarket CMB are from ON *hestaskeith* 'race-course'.

The corresponding ON **hofuth** occurs in Holleth and Preesall LNC and Whitehaven CMB, and sometimes interchanges with *hēafod* in names of OE origin. Ormside WML and Conishead LNC may be ON. Holleth and Preesall refer to low ridges. In IOM *hofuth* is used of the striking headland at Port Erin called Bradda.

Welsh coastal names (Holyhead AGL, Orme's Head CRN, Worms Head GLA) were bestowed by English and Norse seafarers.

helde (Anglian, Kentish), **hielde** (W. Saxon) OE 'slope'. This is a rather rare term in settlement-names, though fairly well evidenced in field-names and minor names in some counties (e.g. CHE, SHR, SUR, YOW). Foxall 1980, Plate 1, has an excellent photograph of a field called The Yelds.

helde may be the first element of Hilton DOR, Helton and Hilton WML. It is certainly the second element of Akeld and Learchild NTB (N.W. of Wooler and S.W. of Alnwick), Redhill SUR, Shooter's Hill GTL, Stockeld (S.E. of Harrogate) YOW and Tylerhill (N.W. of Canterbury) KNT. In Akeld, Learchild, Stockeld, and probably Redhill, the reference is to land on the lowest slopes of hills.

hlāw OE 'tumulus, hill'. This word is discussed in Gelling 1978 (pp. 134–7, 154–7), and details are given there of names in which it certainly refers to a burial mound. This is by far its commonest meaning in the southern half of England. The usual modern spelling in the south and in the midlands is –low, but some names in the south country and the south midlands (e.g. Lewes SSX and Lew OXF) are from an OE form *hlǣw*.

Since *hlāw* is much more frequent in minor names and field-names than in names of major settlements it is an element which cannot be examined adequately in a book based mainly on the latter. As stated in Gelling 1978, the geographical line between its use mainly for tumuli and its use with greater frequency for natural hills has not been worked out. This could be ascertained by careful work on minor names and field-names in the north-midland counties.

hlāw was certainly used in some instances for tumuli in CHE, and this is considered to be the meaning in three of the four major names in which it occurs in that county, these being Buglawton, Churchlawton and Twemlow; but in Stanlow it is taken to refer to the rocky promontory overlooking the Mersey estuary, E. of Ellesmere Port. Many minor names containing *hlāw* are listed in the EPNS CHE survey 5 (Section 1:ii, pp. 225–6).

hlāw is rare in CMB and WML. In LNC, DRH and NTB, however, and in southern Scotland, it is commonly used of natural hills and occasionally of mountains (e.g. Horelaw and Pike Law in LNC). Careful study would probably reveal a specialized use for hills of a certain shape, perhaps those with a smoothly rounded profile.

In NTB, where *hlāw* is one of the commonest terms for a natural hill, it occurs frequently in settlement-names, mostly of minor status. A few examples are:

Barleyhill N.W. of Consett (*Berlawe* 1236);
Brenkley N.E. of Ponteland (*Brinchelawe* 1177);
Highlaws S.W. of Hartburn and N.W. of Morpeth;
Kearsley N.W. of Ingoe (*Kerneslawe* 1245);
Kellah S.W. of Haltwhistle;
Throckley N.W. of Newbury (*Trokelawa* 1177);
White Hall S.W. of Cramlington (*Wytelawe* c. 1250);
Whitlow N.W. of Alston.

Most of these probably refer to natural hills, but investigation might reveal that some of them refer to tumuli. This is surely the case with Dewley N.W. of Newbury (*Deuelawe* 1251), where the 1″ map marks a tumulus, and it seems probable in Hauxley S.E. of Amble (*Hauekeslaw* 1204). Kirkley N. of Ponteland was discussed in Gelling 1978 (p. 140); a recent visit to the area reveals that (contrary to what was said in the earlier discussion there are a number of small, rounded hills, which somewhat resemble tumuli.

In DRH there are some major names containing *hlāw*, including Kelloe and Moorsley.

hlenc OE 'extensive hill-slope'. This word, which is related to **hlinc** but is not recorded in literary OE, is evidenced in the names of a line of villages stretching north from Evesham WOR. These are Lenchwick, Sheriff's Lench, Atch Lench, Church Lench, Abbots Lench and Rous Lench, and they show that Lench must have been the name of a district extending 5 miles from N. to S. The central feature of the area is a band of Lower Lias limestone, and the massif is referred to as *Lencdun* in the OE boundaries of Twyford. There is a place called Lench in LNC, S. of Rawtenstall, but this name is not recorded till 1526 and should perhaps be ascribed to the dialect derivative *lench* 'ledge of rock', rather than seen as evidence for the survival in the pre-Conquest place-name-forming vocabulary of LNC of the OE term as used in WOR. This consideration applies to a few other minor names in northern England.

hlinc OE 'bank, ledge'. NED and Holthausen 1934 suggest a connection with OE *hlinian* 'to lean, to lie down'. Modern derivatives of *hlinc* are dialect *linch* and the alternative form *link*, which is obsolete except as the second component of *golf-links*. The word is fairly frequent in charter-boundaries, and in some instances there it can be shown to refer to the cultivation terraces on hill-sides which are known to modern students of landscape as strip lynchets. *hlinc* occurs in fewer than 20 major settlement-names, but it is better represented in minor names and field-names. In most instances the reference is probably to a detail of the landscape, and the 1″ map is too coarse an instrument to yield the precise meaning, which was probably more specialized than previous reference books allow.

There are a few instances in which the translation 'terrace' is appropriate, perhaps more precisely 'terrace used by a road'. One of these is Linch SSX, between Treyford and Bepton. This was a DB manor, though Linch Fm is now the only settlement. It is one of a long row of settlements at the foot of the N. escarpment of the S. Downs, and there should be a special reason why this place is the only one to use *hlinc* in its name. The answer probably lies in the behaviour of the Roman road from Chichester to Milland. Cf. Margary 1955 (pp. 71–2): 'There is then little trace till the foot of the downs is reached at Linch Farm. A natural spur of the Chalk greatly eases the first part of the ascent here . . . and it continues the climb by a terraceway of the usual type now worn into a hollow way, curving round the slopes of a slight combe in the very steep escarpment.' Another possible example of this sense is Link WOR, at the N. end of the Malvern Hills. On the 1st ed. 1″ map The Link is shown as the name of the road running S.W. from Malvern Link, climbing the lower slopes of the hills. This was perhaps a terrace-way. At Lyng NFK, N.E. of E. Dereham, the road which follows the course of the R. Wantsum is probably on a river terrace, and the same may be true of the road at Lydlinch DOR, W. of Sturminster Newton. Moorlinch SOM lies on the edge of dry ground overlooking Kings Sedge Moor at the foot of the Polden Hills, and the *hlinc* of this name may be the lowest ledge of raised ground, and the road which runs along it from Greinton to Sutton Mallet. Sticklinch SOM, E. of Glastonbury, stands on a road which runs along one of the lower ledges of Pennard Hill.

Linkenholt HMP, near the BRK border, has the gen. pl. (*hlinca*) as first element, and here the 1″ map marks numerous banks on nearby hill-slopes. Swarling Fm in Petham KNT, S.W. of Canterbury, is recorded in charters of AD 805 and 812 as *Sweordhlincas*; this unusual name may refer to pointed ridges or terraces on the slopes of Chatham Downs.

Other names containing *hlinc* occur on hill-slopes or at the foot of hills, where the 1″ map shows nothing except the sloping nature of the ground; but the element is used too sparingly for a general sense 'hill-slope' to seem satisfactory, and local investigation might reveal banks or terraces at some sites. Lintz S.W. of Gateshead DRH is on a steepish slope, and Lynch N.E. of Porlock SOM is at the foot of a very steep slope. Redlynch and Standlynch WLT lie close together in hilly country on the E. bank of the R. Avon, S. of Salisbury. Charlinch SOM, W. of Bridgewater, is on the tip of an oval-shaped hill.

In some instances *hlinc* appears to refer to a special characteristic of a river-bank. Linslade BUC is the only major name noted in this category, but there are minor names in GLO, such as Lynch House in Longney by the R. Severn, and one example in HRT, The Lynch in Hoddesdon, which is in flat ground by the R. Lea.

Two examples which are difficult to characterize are Lingwood NFK, E. of Norwich, which is on very gently sloping ground, and Shanklin IOW, where the town has probably obscured relevant topographical features except for the Chine, which is referred to in the first element, OE *scenc* 'cup'.

As an element in minor names, *hlinc* is particularly well represented in

GLO and DEV. It does not occur in all counties: no examples have been noted in CMB or WML, in the E. midland counties of DRB and NTT, or in Yorkshire. A full study would have to take account of occurrences in minor names, field-names and charter boundaries.

hlith OE 'slope'. This is a rare place-name element, and it is doubtful whether the material is sufficient to provide a firm basis for a statement about its precise topographical significance. The distribution does not suggest that it was an archaic term, and yet the topography of the sites to which it refers does not suggest that it was reserved for highly distinctive features, so it is not clear why it enters into so few place-names. It is very rare in southern counties, but there are instances in minor names in SSX and SUR. Some minor names are taken into account in the following discussion.

The most dramatic natural feature noted in the small corpus of examples is Lyth Hill SHR, S. of Shrewsbury, from which are named the settlements of Great and Little Lyth, Lythbank and Lythwood. Lyth Hill is a striking escarpment-like slope, curving gently round a hill. Another slope of this kind is to be found at Leith Hill SUR, S.W. of Dorking, curving round the hill in a semicircle; and Lythe Hill SUR, E. of Haslemere, is a mini-version of the same phenomenon. Upleatham YON, S.E. of Redcar, stands on a steep slope curving round one side of a hill, and this is one of a series of similar slopes which probably caused the district to be named *Hlithum*. Kirkleatham, 2½ miles N.W., also preserves the district-name. Howler's Heath on the WOR/GLO border is at the southern end of the Malvern Hills. The only instance noted in which *hlith* refers to a long, straight escarpment is that of Lower and Upper Underley, S.E. of Tenbury HRE.

For some other instances the most that can be deduced from the 1″ map is that they are in hilly country. Adgarley S.E. of Dalton in Furness LNC (earlier *Adgareslith*) has no obviously distinctive features, but mining and quarrying may have affected the relief. Bowler's (or Bowl Head) Green S.W. of Godalming SUR (earlier *Bovelith* 'above the slope') stands on what looks like an ordinary hill, Coreley N.E. of Tenbury SHR is on the lower slopes of Clee Hill, and Evelith S. of Shifnal SHR stands on very gently sloping ground. Leathley N.E. of Otley YOW may have as first element *hleotha*, the form which the gen. pl. of *hlith* would take in the Anglian dialect; the settlement is on the southern edge of an expanse of hill country.

hlith is considered to be the base of the –**ingas** name which occurs in Lenborough, S. of Buckingham ('hill of the slope-people'). Early spellings for Lenborough include *Ledingberge* DB, *Lithingeberg* c. 1200. The suggested folk-name, *Hlithingas*, seems convincing, as a term for the inhabitants of the hilly country between Buckingham and Bicester. Some instances are not in hilly country, however. There was a place called *Lythe* near Normanton on Trent NTT, where the slope must have been very slight. Lytham LNC presumably refers to sand-dunes.

Ekwall 1960 and Smith 1956 adduce a side-form *hlid* to account for Lydd KNT (*ad Hlidum* 744) and two SHR names Lydham (*Lidum* DB) and Lydbury. Both authorities acknowledge that this could not be distinguished on grounds of spellings from OE *hlid* 'cover, gate' (modern *lid*), which is also believed to occur in a few place-names. The three names for which an unrecorded *hlid* 'slope' is conjectured could contain the recorded word *hlid*, perhaps in the sense 'gate', referring to ways of access to common pasture land.

hlíth ON 'slope'. Scandinavian speakers probably used this word a little more frequently in place-name formation in the north of England than the OE equivalent discussed above was used by the Anglo-Saxons. It is fairly well represented in the counties of LNC, WML and YON, and occurs occasionally in CMB, YOW and YOE. It is uncertain whether it occurs S. of the R. Humber, but it could be the source of *Lithe* NTT, discussed under OE **hlith**. There is usually no distinction in early spellings between the OE and ON elements, but the ON word is assumed to be involved in compound names when the other element is ON, and it is on general grounds more likely than the OE word in the counties listed above. Litherskew YON and two instances of Litherland in LNC contain the ON gen. sg. *hlíthar*, and Ekwall 1960 gives this or the gen. pl. as the first element of Little Beck S. of Whitby YON (earlier *Lithebec, Lythebec*).

In LNC, besides Litherland, there are Ireleth (by a long, steep hill-slope N.W. of Dalton-in-Furness) and Nether and Over Kellet (on either side of a moderate hill, S.E. of Carnforth). Examples in YON are Lythe, overlooking a long, steep hill-side N.W. of Whitby, and Ivelet and Eskeleth, which are both, like Litherskew, on dramatic mountain slopes in the Yorkshire Dales. Pickering Lythe Wapentake lay mainly to the N.E. of Pickering where there are many similar slopes.

WML has two major names: Kelleth, which refers to the steep bank of the R. Lune, and Lyth, E. of Windermere, which appears from the map to have been a district-name, rather than a settlement-name. There are a few minor names, including Lytheside in Ravenstonedale, which is on a fairly steep slope above a tarn, and Whitley Crag in Asby. There are also a few occurrences in field-names. Hilton E. of Appleby was *Helton under Lyth, Helton under the Lith* in the 13th to 14th centuries, and in this affix *hlíth* refers to the dramatic slope of Roman Fell.

.For YOW, the EPNS survey (7, p. 205) lists 9 names which contain either *hlíth* or OE **hlith**. One of these is Leathley, which is discussed under **hlith**. Another is Litton, which is not a certain instance of either word. Most of the others are late-recorded. The only major name is Hanlith S.W. of Grassington, which has an ON personal name as first element; *hlíth* here refers to the steep bank of the R. Aire. In CMB, *hlíth* occurs as a district-name in Leath Ward, said in the EPNS survey (1, p. 167) to refer to the westerly slope of the Pennine range, beneath which most of the villages in the ward are situated, and in the settlement-name Ainstable, where it refers more precisely to a particular hill-slope. In YOE, *hlīth* occurs in two district names, Grindalythe and *Hertfordlythe*, the former being used as an affix in the name Kirby Grindalythe and in early forms for the names of adjacent villages, the latter occurring as an affix to names of settlements on the southern side of the upper Derwent valley.

hōh OE 'heel'. This anatomical term is used in place-names for a sharply projecting piece of ground. Some excellent examples in the Chilterns are shown on Fig. 2. The elevation varies according to region. Some SFK examples (e.g. Dallinghoo, Hoo) refer to projections of the 150' contour, whereas some DRH and NTB instances (e.g. Cornsay, Ingoe, Shaftoe) refer to hills of over 800'. A good example in the middle height-range is Belsay NTB, S.W. of Morpeth, where the village stands at 380', and the 350' contour makes a narrow projection to the E. There is a cluster of *hōh* names in this part of NTB, and the uneven distribution of the element in the country as a whole is clearly due to topographical causes. The term was probably current in place-name formation at all periods, since there are two instances in Cox 1976 (Hoo KNT and *Cloveshoh*), and it was still in occasional use when English names were being coined in Wales. The early-recorded KNT example is Hoo N.E. of Rochester; here the term describes the promontory jutting out between the Thames and Medway estuaries. It is very unlikely that *hōh* was ever used of tumuli (see Gelling 1978, p. 138).

hōh occurs in about 145 names in Ekwall 1960. In over half of these it is used as a simplex name or as the first element in a compound. There are 11 simplex names: Hoo KNT, SFK, Hooe DEV, SSX, Hose LEI, Hough CHE(2), DRB, Heugh DRH, NTB, and Howbury KNT (which is *Hou* in DB). In Hose LEI the word is in the plural, referring to a series of projections made by the 150' contour.

As a first element, *hōh* occurs surprisingly frequently with **tūn**. There are 58 instances in Ekwall 1960, these being Haughton NTT, Hoghton LNC, Holton LIN(3), Houghton BDF(2), CMB, DRB, DRH(2), HMP, HNT, LEI, LIN, LNC, NFK(3), NTB(2), NTP(2), SSX and YOW, Hooton CHE, YOW(3), Hoton LEI, Hutton CMB(3) DRH, ESX, LNC(4), SOM, WML(2), YOE, YON(14), YOW. There are 8 instances with **land**: Holland ESX, LIN, LNC(2), Hoyland YOW(3), and Hulland DRB. Other second elements used with *hōh* are **halh** in Houghall DRH, **grāf** in Howgrave YON, **brycg** in Hubbridge ESX, and ON **thveit** in Huthwaite NTT, YOW. The bias towards **tūn**, and to a lesser extent towards **land**, may indicate that English colonization of areas likely to be characterized by appropriate spurs of land took place at a period when these generics were fashionable in settlement-naming. Such areas were perhaps not the first to be selected for arable farming. Everitt 1979 (p. 107) says that in the HRT Chilterns *hōh* seems to denote an outlying pasture farm. This can never have been the meaning of the word, but there may have been a tendency for areas with the sort of relief which led to the use of *hōh* in place-names to be more appropriate to pasture than to arable use at an early period.

As the final element of a compound name, *hōh* is most frequently qualified by personal names. Here belong Aynho NTP, Belsay NTB, Bletsoe BDF, Cogenhoe NTP, Duddo NTB, Fitz SHR, Kersoe WOR, Limpenhoe NFK, Moulsoe BUC, Petsoe BUC, Prudhoe NTB, Silsoe BDF, Tattenhoe BUC, Tudhoe DRH, Wadenhoe NTP, Watnall NTT, Wivenhoe ESX and Wixoe SFK.

The next largest category is that which has as first element a noun or adjective describing the *hōh*. Here belong Cambo NTB, Carrow NFK, Langenhoe ESX, Sandhoe NTB, Shaftoe NTB, Sharpenhoe BDF, Silpho YON, Stanhoe NFK, Staploe BDF and Trentishoe DEV. An interesting group which probably belongs with these comprises Cainhoe BDF, Cashio HRT, Keysoe BDF and Kew GTL. The first three are said in previous reference books to contain personal names *Cǣga* and *Cǣg* or *Cǣgi*, while Kew is said in Ekwall 1960 to contain *cǣg* 'key' in some such sense as 'projecting piece of land'. The personal names *Cǣga*, *Cǣg*, *Cǣgi* (inferred from place-names, but not independently recorded) would be derivatives of the word *cǣg* 'key', and the high incidence of such names with *hōh* arouses suspicion. It is possible that at all four places the hill-spur was felt to be key-shaped. If *Cǣg* or *Cǣge* was an earlier name of the spur it could, when *hōh* was added, have been treated (correctly) as a weak feminine noun with *–an* in the genitive, which would give the modern form Cainhoe, or it could have been given an *–s* genitive (as place-names often were, irrespective of their grammatical gender), and this would result in such forms as Cashio and Keysoe. In the EPNS survey of BDF and HNT (p. 57) it is suggested that the minor name Duloe in Eaton Socon has an unrecorded OE noun *dyfel* 'peg' as first element. In Morthoe and Pinhoe and probably Croyde Hoe DEV the first element is an earlier name of the promontory or hill.

Names in which the first element refers to a nearby topographical feature (as opposed to using its earlier place-name) are Furtho and Halse NTP and Wellow LIN. Totternhoe BDF refers to an ancient fort on the ridge.

Vegetation is referred to in Ashow WAR and Pishiobury HRT. Wild creatures occur in Cornsay DRH, Cranoe LEI, Rainow CHE and Stagenhoe HRT; and domestic creatures in Kyo DRH and Swinhoe NTB. In Midloe HNT, Sharow YOW and Southoe HNT the first element refers to the position of the *hōh*. The only reference noted to an activity is Spellow LNC, which was presumably a meeting-place; Spelhoe occurs as a hundred-name in NTP. References to buildings are very rare, but Millow S.E. of Biggleswade BDF is *Melnho* in 1062, which is considered to mean 'mill-spur', though the precise application of this to a site in the area has not been elucidated.

There are two names containing *hōh* which are considered to refer to pagan Anglo-Saxon religious centres. These are Tysoe WAR and Wysall NTT. More surprising is the apparent occurrence of 7 names which contain *–inga–*. These are Bengeo HRT, Dallinghoo SFK, Fingringhoe ESX, Ivinghoe BUC, Martinhoe DEV and Piddinghoe SSX. Farthinghoe NTP may be a seventh. This seems a rather high number, in view of the nature of the element and the relatively modest number of major settlement-names in which it occurs; and it is possible that some of these contain the connective particle *–ing–*, and have undergone the development which is postulated under **hop** for the *–inghop* names of the Welsh Marches.

Culpho SFK, Flecknoe WAR and Ingoe NTB have not been classified as regards the nature of the first element.

hrycg OE, **hryggr** ON 'ridge'. These are among the less subtle items in the OE and ON place-name vocabulary. Anything which a modern observer would call a ridge was probably eligible for the corresponding word in pre-Conquest and medieval times. It has not, therefore, been deemed necessary to attempt a comprehensive collection of material.

Simplex names from *hrycg* include Ridge HRT and Rudge GLO, SHR. As a first element *hrycg* is found in Ridgeacre WOR, Ridgwardine SHR, Rudgwick SSX and Rugeley STF. It is much more frequent as the second element of a compound: examples among ancient settlement-names include Bageridge DOR, STF, Baggridge SOM, Coldridge DEV, Cotheridge WOR, Curdridge HMP, Curridge BRK, Druridge NTB, Elmbridge WOR, Foulridge LNC, Hawkridge BRK, SOM, Henstridge SOM, Iridge SSX, Lindridge KNT(2), WOR, Lupridge DEV, Marrick YON, Sandridge DEV, HRT, Tandridge SUR, Waldridge BUC, Waldridge DRH.

ON *hryggr* is the first element of Ribby LNC and Rigsby LIN, and has been substituted for *hrycg* in Rigton YOW(2). As a second element it occurs in a few major settlement-names, including Bigrigg CMB, Crossrigg, Grayrigg and Lambrigg WML. In major names ending in *–rigg* in the north of England it is often impossible to distinguish between the ON and the OE words. Some of these names will be of ME origin, in which case the distinction is irrelevant.

hváll, hóll ON 'round hill' is found in Falsgrave YON (on the outskirts of Scarborough), Staffield CMB (N.E. of Penrith), Ward Hall CMB (N.E. of Cockermouth) and Whale WML (S. of Penrith). Near these settlements there are small hills similar to those described by OE **cnoll**.

hyll OE 'hill'. This word is regularly used in place-names for natural eminences of a more spiky outline than those to which **dūn** is applied. With about 185 examples in Ekwall 1960, *hyll* is less common in major settlement-names than **dūn**, but it is probably much commoner in minor names and field-names. It is not represented among names recorded by AD 730, but the wide distribution suggests that it was part of the place-name-forming vocabulary for the whole of the OE period, in addition to remaining in use till the present day.

hyll probably does not have the extreme flexibility with regard to absolute height of some other words discussed in this chapter. No instances have been noted in which a settlement with a *hyll* name is very low-lying or is situated above 1000', but no attempt has been made to check the whole corpus. A systematic comparison of names containing **dūn** with those containing *hyll* in the counties of SHR and STF bears out the hypothesis that **dūn** is more likely to be applied to hills with a large area of relatively level summit; but the distinction between the two terms is not observed with absolute consistency. In the south-midland area N.W. of the Chilterns, where **dūn** is the dominant generic in settlement-names, Brill BUC illustrates the choice of *hyll* for an eminence of unusually broken outline. Credenhill HRE is another good example.

The simplex name Hill occurs frequently as a minor name, but only seven instances (in CNW, GLO, HMP, SOM, WLT, WOR(2)) are included in Ekwall 1960. Hull SOM is also there, and Hillmorton WAR, in which a simplex name Hill has been amalgamated with that of another settlement called Morton. Hillam YOW is the dative plural.

hyll is rare as a first element. There are four instances of Hilton (DRB, HNT, STF, YON), two of Hulton (LNC, STF) and one of Hylton (DRH) in Ekwall 1960. Otherwise there appears to be only Hilfield DOR and Hillhampton WOR among major settlement-names.

This leaves more than 160 major names in which *hyll* is the second element of a compound. Analysis of the qualifying elements shows a fairly even spread among several categories.

Personal names form one of the largest category of first elements used with *hyll*, with at least 25 examples. Here belong Barnhill YOE, Barnsdale RUT (*Bernardeshull* 1202), Bubbenhall WAR, Bubnell DRB, Buersill LNC, Chaxhill GLO, Credenhill HRE, Deuxhill SHR, Hartshill WAR, Hempshill NTT, Hockenhull CHE, Hodnell WAR, Lilleshall SHR, Patshull STF, Pattishall NTP, Pulloxhill BDF, Quixhill STF, Ragnall NTT, Rainhill LNC, Snarehill NFK, Tatenhill STF, Tottenhill NFK, Tutnall WOR, Ughill YOW, Winshill STF and Wolvershill WAR. Three of the personal names (in Barnsdale, Hartshill and Wolvershill) are dithematic, and that in Ragnall is ON. Other possible examples include Coleshill BRK, BUC, Marnhull DOR, Sedgehill WLT, Tintinhull SOM.

The use of descriptive terms to qualify *hyll* is about as frequent as that of personal names. References to shape occur in Burshill YOE, Coppull LNC, Cropwell NTT (*Crophille* DB), Hockerill HRT, Shelfield WAR, Shottle DRB, Smithills LNC, Stapenhill STF, Whitehill OXF, and possibly Bickenhill WAR and Poughill CNW, DEV. Colour is referred to in Grindle SHR, Harnhill GLO, Hernhill KNT, Whitehill DRH, Whittle LNC(2), NTB(2). The hill is characterized by its soil in Chishall ESX and Mansell HRE, and indirectly in Solihull WAR. Calehill KNT is 'bare' and Clennell NTB 'clean'. Snodhill HRE and Snowshill GLO were noted for snow, and Windhill YOW and Windle LNC were exceptionally windy.

Vegetation is the characteristic feature in about 20 names. Here belong Ashill SOM, Aspul LNC, Birchill DRB, Birchills STF, Broomhill KNT, Broomhill SSX, Buckenhill HRE, Dodderhill WOR, Doddershall BUC, Farnhill YOW, Hethel NFK, Lushill WLT, Pishill OXF, Thornhill DOR(2), DRB, WLT, YOW, and Withnell LNC. Blymhill STF may be 'plum-tree hill' from OE *plȳme*, though all the spellings have *B*– not *P*–. The first element is a word for a crop in Bearl NTB, Benhilton SUR (*Benhull* 1392), Cornhill GTL, Haverhill SFK, Odell BDF, Ryal NTB, Ryhill YOE, YOW, Ryle NTB, Smerrill DRB, Wheathill SHR, SOM.

Living creatures form a smaller category of first elements, wild ones in Ampthill BDF, Beal NTB, Catteshall SUR, Catshill WOR, Harthill CHE, DRB, YOW, Hawkhill NTB, Henhull CHE, Roxhill BDF, Sugnall STF and Wormhill DRB; domestic ones in Coole CHE, Cowhill GLO, Keele STF, Goathill DOR, and possibly in Bonehill STF, Bucknell OXF, SHR, Hinxhill KNT and Tickhill YOW. There is the usual uncertainty as to whether such words as *bula*, *bucca* and *ticca* refer to animals or are used as men's names.

The presence of ancient remains on the hill gives rise to compounds with **burh** (Burghill HRE, Burlton HRE, SHR, Burrill YON), and in Burn Hill BUC and perhaps Brindle LNC to a compound with *byrgen* 'burial'. Hordle HMP refers to the finding of treasure. The compound with PrW **crüg** found in some instances of Churchill is discussed under that word. References to contemporary Anglo-Saxon structures are extremely rare. Earle NTB had an enclosure (*geard*) and Throphill NTB had a small settlement (*throp*). Wreighill NTB probably had a gallows. Use for meetings and look-out sites is indicated by Thinghill HRE, Tothill LIN, MDX, Wardle CHE, LNC, Warthill YON. Soothill YOW is thought to refer to soot from the burning of coal.

The only remaining sizeable category is that in which the first element is an earlier place-name. Brickhill and Brill BUC, Pendle LNC, the first part of Pendlebury LNC and Penhill YOW are tautological compounds in which *hyll* has been added to a British word meaning 'hill'. (Pendle LNC is an exception to the statement made above, that *hyll* is not used of features over 1000' high, but the addition of the word to an existing hill-name is not quite the same as its use in a wholly OE coinage.) Penkhull STF has as first part the British place-name which has become Penge GTL, Penketh LNC, Pencoyd HRE. Hill-names of OE origin are the first elements of Cook Hill WOR, Pexall CHE, and possibly Caughall and Cogshall CHE. A river-name is the first element of Coleshill WAR and Earnshill SOM, and possibly of Ightenhill (N.W. of Burnley) LNC. In Redmarshall DRH *hyll* is added to the gen. of a compound OE place-name.

The nature of the first element is uncertain in some names. These include Dosthill WAR, Gopsall LEI, Greenhill WOR, Grinshill SHR, Inkersall DRB, Kelshall HRT, Pamphill DOR, Prawle DEV, Queenhill WOR, Wixhill SHR and Wuerdle LNC.

mönith PrW, PrCorn, PrCumb, **mynydd** Welsh, **meneth** Corn 'mountain, hill'. These Celtic words are cognate with Latin *mons*. The Welsh word is used in Mynde HRE and Long Mynd SHR for large areas of high ground. Myndtown and Minton SHR are by the Long Mynd. In CHE, parts of a ridge of moorland on the boundaries of Sutton, Wincle, Gawsworth and Bosley townships are called Bosley Minn and Wincle Minn.

Mindrum NTB is explained in Ekwall 1960 as a compound of *mönith* and the ancestor of Welsh *trum* 'ridge', with which he compares Mynydd Drymmau GLA.

In the Forest of Dean, GLO, there is evidence that Welsh *mynydd* was borrowed into ME as *munede* and used in a new sense which Smith (EPNS survey 3, p. 218) renders 'a piece of waste or open ground in the forest, a forest-glade'. This has become Meend in a number of modern names in the area.

Ekwall 1960 derives E. and W. Myne and Minehead SOM from *mönith*, although the early spellings for Myne do not have the –*d* which should be present. He suggests that the hill was called *Mynydd*, and the English adopted this, adding **dūn** to give *Myned-dūn*, which became *Mynedūn*, and was then misunderstood, yielding a hill-name *Myne*. The form *Menedun* is recorded in 1255, and this could fairly be taken to support the conjectural development. It is possible, however, that the hill had a pre-English name similar to that of Meon Hill GLO, and that *Mene*, the DB form for Myne, is to be taken as a genuine form, not as arising from a misunderstanding by the English of a compound with **dūn**.

Ekwall 1960 also ascribes Mendip Hills SOM to *mönith*, suggesting that the second part of the name is OE **hop**. This last suggestion is unacceptable in view of the evidence bearing on the distribution and meanings of **hop** presented in Chapter 4, and Mendip should be regarded as an unsolved name.

næss OE 'ness'. The Kentish and Mercian form was **ness**. The word is related to OE *nosu*, modern *nose*. It is not common in any category of place-names, but the distribution suggests that it was available in the place-name-forming vocabulary of all areas throughout the Anglo-Saxon period.

The use of *næss* for flat, marshy coastal promontories is illustrated by Foulness ESX, Sheerness KNT, Bowness on Solway CMB and Widnes LNC. Skinburness CMB, on the other side of Moricambe Bay from Bowness, was perhaps originally the name of the area between Silloth Bay and the estuary of the R. Waver.

In The Naze and Wrabness ESX, *næss* is used for promontories of greater height. Sharpness and Nass GLO are opposite each other on the banks of the Severn estuary, but at both places the configuration of the shore is obscured by harbour works. Cotness YOE and Reedness YOW, which lie opposite each other on the R. Ouse, E. of Goole, are difficult to explain in terms of the modern map; the topography may have been affected by early medieval silting and modern canalization of the river. Bowness on Windermere WML probably refers to a promontory jutting into the lake.

Promontories of dry ground jutting into fen are designated by the word *næss* in E. and W. Ness YON (at the end of a large ridge beside the R. Rye), Levens WML (between the flood plains of the rivers Gilpin and Kent), Claines WOR (between the rivers Salwarpe and Severn), and possibly Neswick in Bainton YOE (by a low bluff in a region of small streams). The most striking instance of this use, however, is the hundred-name Nassaborough in NTP. The district is said in an OE document of c. AD 970 to comprise 'the two hundreds out on the ness on which *Medeshamstede* stands.' *Medeshamstede* is now Peterborough, and the double hundred which lay between the rivers Welland and Nene was the 'ness' which was administered from the 'borough' of Peterborough.

In contrast to these two senses, *næss* is occasionally used for striking inland hills. Here belong Ness SHR and Totnes DEV. Nazeing ESX is on a fairly prominent hill overlooking the marshes of the R. Lea, and Ashness CMB (an Anglicized ON name) is on a steep little headland by Derwent Water. Ewdness SHR, N. of Bridgnorth, might be 'yew-wood ness', referring to the ridge called Apley Terrace. Ness and Neston CHE, on the W. coast of the Wirral, may refer to the ridge of raised ground which runs parallel with the coast.

Hackness N.W. of Scarborough YON is *Hacanos* in Bede's Ecclesiastical History, and is considered to contain OE *nōs* 'headland, promontory', a very rare word in place-names, which had been replaced by its commoner relative *næss* before 1086. The 'hook-promontory' is the distinctively-shaped ridge which runs N.W. from the village. Another related word, *nēs*, is found in Neasden GTL and Neasham DRH. There is a nose-shaped bend of the R. Tees at Neasham.

nes ON 'ness'. Like OE **næss**, this word was used for large areas of projecting land, larger areas than were denoted by the OE word, to judge by Amounderness Hundred LNC, which is an enormous region between the R. Ribble and the R. Cocker, and Furness LNC, which is a very big promontory. Also like the OE word, *nes* was considered appropriate to very low-lying promontories, such as Holderness YOE. It could, however, be used of much smaller topographical features, as in Hornsea YOE (ON *horn-nes-sǽr*), the first part of which denotes the horn-like peninsula which projects into the lake near Hornsea village, Ashness CMB, and Skegness LIN, which possibly refers to the hook-shaped promontory S. of the town. In IOM, *nes* is used of a rocky coastal promontory in Langness, and of an inland promontory in Agneash; and Cregneash, now a village-name, may have been applied originally to the great promontory opposite the Calf. In ORK, *nes* is very common in the names of coastal promontories.

ofer, ufer OE ? 'tip of promontory, flat-topped ridge'. This word is not on record but has been conjectured to explain a considerable number of place-names, including about 40 major settlement-names, for which the recorded word *ōfer* 'bank, margin, shore', which would suit on formal grounds, was not considered appropriate topographically. The settlements are mostly on raised sites, and *ofer* has been considered to mean 'slope, hill, ridge', and to be related to the preposition *ofer* (modern *over*) and the comparative adjective *uferra* 'higher', and a place-name element **yfer** which is discussed below.

This is probably roughly correct; but study of the sites of settlements with names containing *ofer* reveals a high degree of topographical consistency, and this renders possible a more precise definition. In English settlement-names, *ofer* or *ufer*, is used for a site on the tip of a flat-topped hill-spur. There is frequently a level approach to the village along the high ground from which the spur projects, and there is often a steep drop on all other sides. The sites are constricted, and once a village has covered the flat top of such a spur it does not expand over the edges; this restriction causes the topographical evidence to survive on the modern map in a fairly high proportion of the examples. Before speculating on the likely origin of the term, it is desirable to support this statement about the way *ofer* is used in place-names by reference to examples. Eight sites may be instanced which fit the above prescription particularly well. These are:

1   Over CHE, S.W. of Winsford. As stated in the EPNS survey (3, p. 171): 'Over is on a pronounced ridge parallel to the R. Weaver.' There is now a straggling 2½ mile long settlement along the road which follows the ridge. Littler, near the N. end of this, was earlier *Little Overe*, clearly a distinct settlement. Over Hall and the district called Church Hill lie further S., near the 'nose' of the ridge.

2   English Bicknor GLO, N. of Coleford. This, rather than Welsh Bicknor HRE, is probably the original settlement called Bicknor, as it is the one which is entered in DB. The settlement is on the summit of a ridge which runs alongside the R. Wye. Below this summit the ridge has a long snout, and in view of this special characteristic the first element is likely to be the word *bica* 'point, bill', which is conjectured to explain some place-names.

3   Hunsingore YOW, N.E. of Wetherby. The village occupies the tip of a promontory made by the 100′ contour in the marshy land on the N. bank of the R. Nidd.

4   Southover SSX, on the southern outskirts of Lewes. A narrow ridge which runs between the Winterbourne stream and the marshes of the R. Ouse approaches Lewes from the S.W., and Southover is at the tip of this. Another possible SSX example is Southover Hall in the Weald, N.W. of Burwash, which stands at the tip of a narrow promontory between two brooks; there are, however, no early spellings available for this name.

5   Wellingore LIN, on the long escarpment which runs S. from Lincoln. There are other settlements with topographical names on this escarpment, but this is the only one for which the word *ofer* is used, so it is likely that *ofer* refers to a special feature to be found at this point on the escarpment. The 1st edition 1″ map shows the topography very clearly. There is a rounded promontory jutting out from the higher ground, and the village occupies most of this.

6   Wentnor SHR, S.W. of Church Stretton. This is perhaps the most perfect site with which to support my hypothesis about the meaning of *ofer*. The village occupies the flat top of an oval-shaped promontory which projects from a higher massif to the N. The church is on the tip of the level area, and the ground slopes away steeply all round the promontory. North of Wentnor is a farm called Overs; this is a DB manor, so an ancient name, and this also is situated on the tip of a hill-spur.

7   Ramshorn STF, 8 miles W. of Ashbourne. This was *Romesovere* in the 13th century. The settlement is on the tip of a long, narrow ridge.

8   Wychnor STF, N.E. of Alrewas. The 200′ contour makes a round-ended promontory jutting into the low ground (probably liable to flooding) by the R. Trent, and the church is on the edge of this promontory.

A number of other sites can be associated with the pattern set by the 8 examples described above. At Okeover and Tittensor STF there are appropriate ridges, but the settlements (only a Hall at Okeover) are not on top of the ridge, but on its lowest shelf. At Shotover OXF, Shotover Hill is an appropriate feature, but it is not certain that the early settlement stood on its tip. One of two places called Northover in SOM lies at the point of Wearyall Hill, which shoots out into the Moor from the high ground at Glastonbury; this is not a typical *ofer* site, however, as the top of Wearyall Hill is not flat. Bolsover DRB is an interesting variant: here, the spur does not jut out from the parent massif but runs at an oblique angle to it. The 1st edition 1″ map marks a long 'Intrenchment' round the higher, eastern side of the town. While there is no reason to think that *ofer* was specifically used of a defended settlement, it is obvious that the more typical *ofer* sites could have been easily defended by a short rampart cutting off the end of the promontory. The site of Bolsover, in addition to needing a longer rampart for defence, offered more room for expansion than the more constricted *ofer* sites. The only instance in HRT is a minor name, Highover Fm in Hitchin, which stands at the tip of a low hill-spur.

Remaining examples in major names may be discussed county by county. DRB, HRE, STF and SHR have most examples. In DRB, besides Bolsover, are Ashover, Birchover (N.W. of Matlock), Calver and Edensor (E. of Bakewell), Codnor and Heanor (S.E. of Ripley), and Littleover and Mickleover (S.W. of Derby). Ashover is on the tip of a small ridge. Birchover and Calver lie under the tip of their hill-spurs. Edensor was moved in the 19th century to improve the view from Chatsworth House, so no conclusions can be based on its present position. Codnor and Heanor are built up and the sites are difficult to evaluate, but both could probably be described as occupying hill-spurs. Littleover and Mickleover are on low ridges; Cameron (EPNS survey, p. 707) takes these and the minor name Rough Heanor to refer to the same broad ridge, but it is possible that distinct spurs of the massif are denoted. Another DRB minor name, Cobnar Wood N.W. of Chesterfield, is on the edge of a small rounded hill-spur.

In HRE, *ofer* occurs in the settlement-names Bircher, Chadnor, Eastnor, Hennor and Yazor. Bircher, N.W. of Leominster, occupies the top of a low ridge. Chadnor, S.E. of Dilwyn, is inexplicable from the modern map, as Chadnor Court is in flat ground by a minute stream. Eastnor, E. of Ledbury, which means '(place) east of the *ofer*', suggests that the spur now called Eastnor Hill was originally called *Ofer*. Hennor, E. of Leominster, lies just off the tip of a ridge. Yazor, N.W. of Hereford, has a slightly raised site on a long hill-slope. Old Radnor RAD may be considered together with the HRE sites, as it is the only certain example of an *ofer* name in Wales; it is on the tip of a low, oval-shaped hill, overshadowed by Old Radnor Hill, which is much higher and steeper.

SHR, like HRE, has five settlement-names containing *ofer*. Overs and Wentnor have been discussed; the others are Badger, N.E. of Bridgnorth, where the settlement lies to the E. of an appropriate hill-spur, Condover, S. of Shrewsbury, where the village occupies a low bluff in a bend of the R. Cound, and Gravenor near Wentnor, which lies beside a hill. STF also has five settlement-names of this type, four of which (Okeover, Ramshorn, Tittensor and Wychnor) have been discussed. The remaining STF name is Haselour, N. of Tamworth, where the Hall (which is the only surviving settlement-unit) is on low ground but has a low hill immediately to the N.

No other county has been noted which has more than three major settlement-names containing *ofer*. There are three in YOW: Hunsingore (already discussed), Thorner, and Northowram and Southowram (counted as one example of the name, which is the dat. pl. of *ofer*). At Thorner, N.E. of Leeds, the present settlement is in a dip between two peaks, but Northowram and Southowram, E. of Halifax, are situated more satisfactorily on flat-topped high ridges.

SOM has two instances of Northover, one of which is discussed above. The other is on the tip of a sharply-pointed low promontory, N. of Ilchester. Ekwall 1960 also lists Eastover (a Fm near Muchelney), and a Westover, which I have not located. GLO has Bicknor (already discussed) and Elmore, S.W. of Gloucester, which Smith (EPNS survey 2, p. 162) derives from the recorded word *ofer* 'bank', referring, in his view, to the bank of the R. Severn. There are so many settlements on the bank of the Severn, however, that this would not be a distinctive name. There are several hills in the great river-bend here, and it is possible that the original settlement was on one of these. There are some minor names in GLO, including two well-recorded examples of the simplex name Over. Over S.W. of Almondsbury has a slightly raised site on the lower slope of a long ridge running parallel with the Severn estuary. Over N.W. of Gloucester is (to quote EPNS survey 3, p. 159) 'at the end of an elevated tongue of land between the Leadon and the Severn.' This is close to Elmore, and strengthens the case for a more specific meaning that 'bank of the R. Severn' in the generic of that name.

In CAM *ofer* occurs only once, in the simplex name Over, N.W. of Cambridge. Here there is a broad wedge of raised ground with a number of settlements on it by the R. Ouse, and Over occupies a rounded knob jutting out from this into the fens. The nature of the site can be seen very clearly on the 1st edition 1″ map.

WOR and WAR have one certain example each, though there are some other possible ones in WAR. The WOR name is Hadzor, S.E. of Droitwich, where Hadzor House is on the tip of a low ridge. The WAR name is Haselor, E. of Alcester, by a small oval-shaped hill. RUT has Tixover, S.E. of Oakham, where the scattered parts of the settlement lie round the edges of a hill-spur which overlooks a bend of the R. Welland. NTP has one example, Tansor N. of Oundle, where the village runs along the side of a rounded spur in the marshes along the R. Nene.

North of Yorkshire, *ofer* is a very rare place-name element. It is not present at all in CMB, WML or LNC. NTB, however, has Wooler, which is on the edge of high ground overlooking the broad plain of the R. Till.

ofer is nowhere a common element, and the corpus discussed above is by far the greater part of the material bearing on the meaning of this term. The association with flat-topped ridges and with tongues of raised ground in marshy areas is clearly established. There is little reason to postulate a meaning 'slope'; settlements with *ofer* names are often situated above slopes, but they seldom lie on sloping ground. With this evidence in mind, it is time to look at the words recorded in OE which could be related to the place-name element, and to enquire whether the unrecorded *ofer*, which reference books translate 'slope, hill, ridge', is a sound conjecture. Recorded OE has:

1 *ōfer* (noun) 'margin, river-bank, sea-shore'. Ekwall 1960 (p. 348) considers this to be the word which occurs in some of the names discussed above. He instances Over CAM, Northover and Westover SOM, and Tansor NTP. He suggests that the same word may be involved in other names, but with a sense-development from 'border, margin' to 'edge, brae of hill'. He points out, however, that OE *ōfer* cannot be the source of those names which have *Ufre* among the early spellings, and instances Over CHE, DRB, and Owram YOW.

2 *ofer* (preposition and adverb) 'above, across', modern 'over'. This word is found in the name Overy OXF, which means '(place) across the river' (i.e. from Dorchester).

3 *ufer(r)a* (comparative adjective and adverb) 'upper, higher'. This is probably the word found in Overton (10 examples in Ekwall 1960) and in some
   instances of Orton (HNT, LEI(2), NTP, WAR, WML). Where OE
   spellings exist for this name, as *Uferantun* 909 for Overton HMP, it can be
   seen that the *U–* of the pre-Conquest spellings has become *O–* by the time
   of DB, so a run of spellings in ME sources like *Overton*, *Ovreton* is perfectly
   appropriate to derivation from *ufer(r)a*. This adjective occurs with other
   generics besides **tūn**, as in Overbury WOR. No attempt has been made
   here to distinguish instances of Overton/Orton which might belong with
   the corpus of names discussed above, and be named from their individual
   topographical situation, as opposed to being more elevated (or higher up a
   river) than some other settlement.

4 *ufor* (comparative adjective and adverb) 'higher'. This is presumably a
   variant form of *ufer(r)a*.

The last three words, though obviously not possible as place-name generics, should be borne in mind, because if the solution preferred by Ekwall and
Smith of an unrecorded noun *ofer*, *ufer* be adopted, then it is necessary to
explain why it seemed specially appropriate to such a site as Wentnor SHR.
The answer could be that the noun was associated with the preposition *ofer*
'above', and this led to the specialized use of the word for a settlement-site on
the tip of a projecting piece of ground. It would be possible to explain names
which have no *U–* spellings as containing the recorded word *ōfer* in Ekwall's
suggested developed sense 'brae of a hill', and only to postulate *ofer*, *ufer* for
names which do have *U–* spellings; but the body of material discussed here
seems to me to be so coherent that a single explanation for all the examples is
preferable. If there is to be a single explanation, only the postulated word *ofer*,
ufer will suit.

There was probably a certain amount of confusion in ME spellings between
ofer and *ōra*, but none of the place-names discussed in the next article has a
significant number of spellings in *–ofer*, and for the purpose of the present
exercise it has not seemed difficult to decide which names belong in each
category.

A few major settlement-names derive from a word **yfer**, which is generally
agreed to be related to *ofer*, *ufer*: these are Iver BUC, Rivar WLT, River SSX
and Hever KNT. For Bignor SSX, spellings such as *–evere* predominate, and
indicate derivation from *yfer*, but there is some interchange with *–overe*, *–ovre*
forms, which are appropriate to *ofer*. The nature of the sites of these 5
settlements suggests that *yfer* was used in place-names in the same way as *ofer*,
ufer. Bignor SSX (S. of Petworth) is at the end of a ridge, with a level approach
from the E. and a fairly steep drop to the N. and W. River SSX (N.W. of
Petworth) is on the tip of a hill-spur. The settlement at Hever KNT (S.E. of
Edenbridge) is at the tip of a spur overlooking the valley of the R. Eden, and
Iver BUC lies just off the tip of a low spur overlooking marshy ground. At

Rivar WLT (S. of Shalbourne) the lowest shelf of a steep escarpment broadens, with the settlement occupying the knob of land thus formed. There are some occurrences of *yfer* in charter boundaries; these have not been checked.

ōra OE 'shore, hill-slope, ? foot of a slope'. This word is used in place-names only in the parts of southern England where Jutish and West Saxon dialects were operative. It occurs in settlement-names in BRK (Bagnor, Boxford, Cumnor, Oare), BUC (Hedsor), DEV (Galsworthy, Loxhore), GLO (Batsford), HMP (Copnor, Ower, Rowner), HRE (Bradnor, Orcop), IOW (Bouldnor), KNT (Bicknor, Oare, Stonar), OXF (Chinnor, Clare, Golder, Lewknor, Stonor), SSX (Bognor, Itchenor), WLT (Oare, Wardour) and WOR (Pershore). Pershore WOR has long been recognized as the most northerly example, and this instance together with those in GLO and HRE is testimony to the part played by the West Saxons in the settlement of the territory which later formed the Mercian sub-kingdom of the Hwicce (see Fig. 8). In addition to the names listed above there are five certain and several possible examples of the compound *windelesōra*, and these are discussed below. There are some minor names in most of the counties listed. The element is probably best represented in HMP, but with no detailed surveys available for some of the southern counties the incidence in minor names and field-names cannot be accurately assessed.

ōra is one of a number of topographical terms (see **ānstiga, gelād, hop**) which are so poorly evidenced in literary OE that place-names constitute the main evidence for their meaning. It occurs once in a poem, where it refers to a position, *on hlithes oran*, from which a cuckoo can be heard calling in a grove. A different use occurs in the phrase *on oran his hrægles*, which is a translation of Latin *in oram vestimenti ejus*, but here OE *ōra* may be chosen as echoing the Latin word *ora*, so this does not constitute strong evidence for a sense 'border'. Holthausen 1934 suggests that *ōra* is related to OE *ōr* 'beginning', and lists related words in other languages which have the general sense 'mouth'. The Latin cognate shares with the OE word the sense-development which results in the meaning 'shore'.

There is a clear dichotomy between coastal settlements with names containing *ōra*, and inland examples, like the group in the Chilterns. It would be possible to treat as a third group some examples which stand on the banks of major rivers.

The main concentration of coastal names containing *ōra* is to be found in SSX and the adjacent part of HMP. Here are Bognor, Itchenor, Keynor Fm and Chalder Fm in Sidlesham, Honer in Pagham, and Marker in W. Thorney; and the series is continued into HMP by Ower near Southampton, Copnor by Portsmouth, and Rowner by Gosport. It is possible that a large stretch of low ground along the coast from Bognor to Southampton was called *Ōra*, 'the shore', and that the district-name was used by all these settlements. Off Selsey there is a series of banks called Malt Owers, The Middle Owers, The Outer Owers, and these may mark the ancient position of the coast-line. The traditional landing-place of the founders of the South Saxon dynasty, a place called *Cymenesora*, lay in this area. There are two coastal names in IOW: Bouldnor, on a flat stretch of coast at the foot of higher ground, and Gurnard, on a coastal bluff W. of Cowes. Ventnor IOW is probably not an example. In KNT, two of the three major names containing *ōra* are coastal: these are Stonar N.E. of Sandwich and Oare N.W. of Faversham, both overlooking marshes which were probably unreclaimed when the names came into use. The meaning 'coast' is found in some names in DOR, Ower, Fitzworth and Goathorn, which lie adjacent to each other on the marshy N. coast of the Isle of Purbeck.

The most notable concentration of inland names containing *ōra* is to be found in the Chilterns, in BUC and OXF. (These are shown on Fig. 2.) In the BUC section of the Chilterns are Ballinger, Courns Wood, Denner, Honor End and Pednor, and in OXF are Chinnor, Clare, Golder, Lewknor, Stonor and *Radnor* (the old name of Pyrton). It seems impossible to discern any individual topographical features to which *ōra* could apply in each of these names. A general sense 'hill-slope' is probably reasonable, but not very specific for any single instance. It may be suggested, very tentatively, that stretches of country on the lower slopes of the Chilterns were called *Ōra* 'edge', and that settlement-names like Clare and Golder are using the district-name with a distinguishing prefix.

There are some non-coastal SSX names in which 'hill-slope' seems to be the best meaning which can be offered for *ōra*. These include Oreham in Henfield, Rowner in Pulborough, and Warningore N.W. of Lewes, which is at the foot of the N. escarpment of the South Downs. Ore, N.E. of Hastings, however, has a hill-top site. The EPNS survey (2, p. 505) says 'the old church and manor house were on the top of the hill.' For Bicknor KNT the sense 'hill-slope' is appropriate. If the 500' hill to the W. was called *bica* (a word meaning 'beak' which has been conjectured on the basis of place-name evidence), Bicknor could be the slope under this.

The sense 'hill-slope' is the only one which seems possible for *ōra* in DEV, but here, as in OXF, it is difficult to see why the word is used in names of some settlements whose situations appear on the map, to have no significant difference from those of their neighbours. Loxhore, N.E. of Barnstaple, is about a third of the way up a steepish hill-side, in a position where there may be a fairly level shelf. Galsworthy, S.W. of Bideford, is on a hill-slope (but so is nearly every settlement for miles around). Some minor names—e.g. Nower Fm in Kilmington, Horner in Diptford, and Rora in Ilsington—are on, or at the foot of, hill-slopes.

WLT has Oare, N. of Pewsey, which lies on one side of Oare Hill. This settlement is alternatively called *Motenesora* in a charter of AD 934. The tip of Oare Hill is called Martinsell Hill, and Martinsell was earlier *Mattelesore*. This suggests that a strip of land along the S. side of the hill might have been called

Ōra, and two land-holdings in this strip might have been distinguished by the names of the landowners. Minor names in WLT are Brickworth House in Whiteparish, which is on a long hill-slope, and Oare in Wilcot, said in the EPNS survey to be below a steep hill. The odd man out in WLT is Wardour, in the S.W. of the county, which has a hill-top site; Wardour Castle crowns a hill-spur, and the use of *weard* 'watch, guard' as qualifier suggests that the name always referred to the top of the hill, not to an earlier settlement on the slope.

BRK names containing *ōra* include four instances in the area N. of New-bury. These are Bagnor, N.W. of Newbury, Boxford, the next village upstream on the R. Lambourn, Oare, N.E. of Newbury, and Woolver's Barn in E. Ilsley. Bagnor, Boxford and Oare may all be using a district-name *Ōra*. A smooth hill-slope runs from Bagnor to Boxford. It would be possible to see a sense 'river-bank' in these names, and an alternative one 'hill-slope' in Oare, but the three names are so close together that it seems likely that *ōra* has the same sense in all of them. Woolver's Barn is 4½ miles N.W. of Oare, on another smooth hill-slope. In the part of the county which lies in the great bend of the Thames W. of Oxford, *ōra* occurs in one major name, Cumnor, a lost name *Colmanora*, and two names in OE charter boundaries. Cumnor is cer-tainly a 'hill-slope' site. In the E. of the county there are Windsor, which is discussed below, and three lost names, *Upnore*, *Underore* and *Ortone*, all near Windsor.

The sense 'hill-slope', which is the usual one in BRK, is the probable one in SUR, where, however, the element only occurs in minor names. These include Nower Wood in Headley, Radnor House in Ewhurst, and Stanners Hill in Chobham. Pinner and the nearby Nower Hill in GTL are the only names containing *ōra* in the ancient county of MDX. Here the meaning seems to be 'hill' rather than 'slope'. Pinner occupies a curiously shaped low hill-spur (which is shown on Fig. 2), and Nower Hill is a separate small hill to the S. of this. Hedsor BUC (also on Fig. 2) stands apart from the Chiltern names discussed above. It is on a hill-top, overlooking the R. Thames.

The small corpus of names containing *ōra* which lie in the ancient ter-ritories of the Hwicce and the Magonsæte comprises Pershore WOR, Bradnor Hill (N.W. of Kington) and Orcop HRE, and Batsford GLO. Pershore is beside the R. Avon, and could be taken to contain *ōra* in the sense 'river-bank', but as it is one of many settlements on the bank of the Avon this does not yield a specific meaning. The town lies between the river and a modest hill. Batsford is on a steep hill-slope. Orcop is on the tip of a narrow ridge.

The foregoing topographical notes are offered without any pretence that they constitute a satisfactory explanation of the meaning of *ōra* in place-names; but the evidence they provide, however inconclusive, should be borne in mind in considering the significance of the recurring name *Windelesōra*, which has become Windsor BRK, WAR, Winsor DEV, HMP, Broadwindsor and Little Windsor DOR. Windsor PEM is probably a transferred name from the BRK example, rather than an independent instance (similarly Woodstock PEM is to be considered as a transferred use of the OXF name). In addition to the five certain examples of *Windelesōra* there are several possible late-recorded ones, including a lost *Windesore Mill* in Breadsall DRB, and Windsor in Nether Wasdale CMB. If these last two be accepted, it follows that the term *windelesōra* was current outside the area in which *ōra* was used as a free element in place-name formation.

The discussion of this name in Gelling 1978 (pp. 170–1) requires emendation. Professor Ekwall's etymology 'river-bank with a windlass for pulling up boats' was there accepted uncritically, but it has been pointed out to me by several readers that this explanation will not suit the HMP or DOR names. The stream at Broadwindsor can never have been navigable, and Winsor HMP (three miles W. of Eling, near Southampton) is between two minute streams, on a low hill, in an area which looks like ancient heath on the edge of forest. Even if Windsor BRK, Windsor in Stratford WAR, and Winsor in Yealmpton DEV are connected with river-traffic, the term *windelesōra* must have had a flexible significance which suited the DOR and HMP sites. A connection with boats is by no means certain in any of the names. It is suggested above that 'river-bank' is not a proven sense of *ōra*, whereas 'hill-slope' seems to be absolutely required as one of its meanings. Perhaps the term *windelesōra* 'windlass bank or slope' refers to some device by the roadside for helping laden carts along the steep, muddy stretches of road. Such devices might occur where land slopes up from a river. The lost names in Windsor BRK—*Upmore* and *Underore*—show that some higher ground in the area was called *Ōra*, and this may be the 'bank' of the place-name Windsor, rather than the low ground bordering on the Thames. The stream at Broadwindsor DOR has very steep banks, and carts crossing it might have needed help up the opposite slope. Windsor DEV is a quarter of a mile from the R. Yealm, and there is a fairly steep slope from the hamlet to the river.

penn PrW, PrCorn, PrCumb, **pen** Welsh, Cornish, 'head, hill; end; (as adjective) chief'. In Gaelic the word became *ceann*. This is one of the commonest Celtic words in English place-names, but its true frequency is difficult to assess because it is impossible to distinguish from OE *penn* 'pen for animals'. In some instances where the topography is highly appropriate to PrW *penn* (as, e.g. Pilsdon Pen DOR, Inkpen BRK) some doubt may be entertained because the high place is crowned by a hill-fort, and OE *penn* might have seemed appropriate to the Anglo-Saxons in naming the fort.

The British ancestor of PrW *penn* occurs once in the place-names recorded from Romano-British times, in *Pennocrucium*, now Penkridge STF, which is discussed under **crūc**. Pentridge DOR was once mistakenly considered to be the same name as Penkridge STF, and this error has been perpetuated (in e.g. Smith 1956, Gelling 1978, Rivet and Smith 1979), although Ekwall 1960 correctly explains Pentridge DOR, Pentrich DRB and Pentyrch GLA as 'hill of the boar', with the gen. of Welsh *twrch* as qualifying element.

The simplex name Penn occurs in BUC and STF, and Pendomer SOM is *Penne* in the earliest records. Pendle Hill LNC and the first part of Pendlebury LNC are tautological hybrids in which *penn* is glossed by OE **hyll**. The hills so named in LNC are referred to also in two instances of Pendleton. The compound with **hyll** also gives rise to Penhill YOW and Pen Hill SOM. There are some non-tautological hybrids with *penn*, including Pensnett STF. Penistone YOW may have as first element a hill-name *Penning*, formed by the addition of OE *–ing* to *penn*.

PrW or Brit compounds with *penn* which have survived as place-names in England include Pennard SOM and Penyard HRE (both probably 'high hill', but with influence from OE *geard* 'enclosure'), Pencraig HRE, and Penrith CMB (on which see Gelling 1970). Pensax WOR and Pennersax DMF (on which see Gelling 1978, pp. 99–100) mean 'hill of the Saxons'. Cornish names in *pen–* include Penare, Penryn and Penzance; and Penwith was the Cornish name of Land's End.

In addition to the names already mentioned in which *penn* means 'hill, end, headland', there is a notable group which derives from PrW *Penn-gēd*, which probably means 'wood's end'. Here belong Penge GTL, Pencoyd HRE, Penquit DEV, Penquite CNW, Penketh LNC; and the compound is the first part of Penkhull STF. Clarendon Forest WLT was called *Penchet* or *Paunchet* until the 15th century. Pengethly HRE is a similar name using another Welsh word for a wood.

pen is common in Welsh place-names, and Pembroke is British *Pennbrogā*, Welsh *Penfro* 'end land'.

ric OE, **ræc** OE ? 'raised straight strip'. Neither of these related words is recorded in literary OE. It is convenient to discuss them together because their use in place-names suggests that they were synonymous. Whether they are appropriately discussed in this chapter depends on the degree of credence given to my suggestion that both denote a raised feature.

The modern noun *reach* is not recorded till the 16th century, and is a new formation from the verb. The hypothetical OE *ræc* required for a few place-names in eastern England is a derivative of the OE verb *rǣcan*, the ancestor of the modern verb *reach*. The other hypothetical OE word, *ric*, which is more widespread in place-names, is considered to derive from the same stem. The intransitive sense of the OE verb 'to extend' is the one which is likely to be reflected in these derivative nouns. The idea of 'straightness' may fairly be considered appropriate to words connected with OE *rǣcan*. There is no 'built-in' significance which would lead to the use of the words for raised features, but if a linear feature is particularly striking in the landscape it is likely to stand above the surrounding ground level.

ræc has been noted in Reach CAM, BDF, and in two minor names, The Reaches in Eye NTP and Reach in Whittlesey CAM.

Reach CAM is at the end of the Devil's Dyke, a post-Roman earthwork of dramatic straightness which runs for 7 miles to the S.E. It would be perverse to see this name as anything other than a reference to the Dyke. Reach BDF is N. of Leighton Buzzard, where there is a straggling village called Heath and Reach. This village is a mile S. of Watling Street, but in spite of the distance I believe the name to refer to the Roman road. Margary 1955 (p. 157) says of the relevant stretch—'the road being much raised, up to 5 feet in parts'. It is suggested below that *ric* may also be used sometimes for the *agger* of a Roman road. The NTP minor name, The Reaches N.E. of Peterborough, is now applied to a short N./S. road which connects two longer E./W. roads to the E. of the village of Eye. Previous reference books take the meaning to be 'narrow road', but many roads in this area have the same character. The reference may rather be to the narrow ridge which is shown on the 1st ed. 1″ map running N.E. into the fens from Eye. The road called The Reaches starts near the tip of this. Reach in Whittlesey CAM, which is fairly close, may refer to a drainage channel with high banks. The EPNS survey (p. 136) says that it is 'a stretch of marsh-land near the King's Dyke, with nothing distinctive in the topography.'

Smith 1956 (2, p. 79) cites Reach in Bishop's Nympton DEV under *rǣc*, but it seems unlikely that this rare eastern term should occur again, just once, in DEV, and Reach may in this instance derive from a misdivision of OE *æt thǣre ǣc* 'at the oak tree'.

ric has a much more widespread distribution than *rǣc*. While being best represented in Yorkshire it also occurs in NTT, LIN, DRB, CAM, DOR and SSX.

It seems clear that *ric* could sometimes be used of a natural ridge if the feature was unusually straight and narrow. The most unequivocal example is probably to be seen in YOE, in the names Escrigg and Wheldrake, S.E. of York. There is a very narrow ridge formed by the 50′ contour which runs for 6 miles, with a road following it fairly closely; Escrigg is half-way along, Wheldrake at the eastern end of this. At Reighton, S. of Filey, also in YOE, Speeton Hills and Speeton Cliffs make a straight line running to the E. of the settlement. In YOW, Rastrick S. of Brighouse is on the side of a long, narrow ridge. At Chatteris CAM the *ric* is shown very clearly on the 1st. ed. 1″ map as a straight, narrow ridge beside the road which runs N.W. from the settlement. Kimmeridge DOR, in the Isle of Purbeck, is in a gap in a narrow ridge; this is more curving than the features described above, but there are straight lengths on either side of the village.

In Cookridge YOW, N.E. of Horsforth, it is probable that *ric* refers to the *agger* of a Roman road. Margary 1957 (p. 136) says of this road: 'a good stretch . . . is traceable for a mile, showing an *agger* 16 feet wide. The line goes past the north side of the fish pond in Cookridge Hall Fish Pond Plantation, and beyond it the *agger* is visible . . . on to Cocker Hill Farm.' This sense is possible in Lendrick Hills YOW, a minor name W. of Bramham (but see below). It may also be the meaning in Mouldridge DRB: the road from Derby to Buxton runs through Pikehall which is near Mouldridge Grange, and the *agger* is said by Margary 1957 (p. 44), to be visible in this stretch.

Ekwall 1960 confidently translates *ric* as 'stream, ditch'. This is not acceptable as the general sense, but there are some instances in which a meaning 'drainage channel' is indicated. There are instances in SSX and LIN which are in marshy land, and it may be that, as with modern drainage channels in East Anglia, such watercourses were bordered by long spoil banks. This would bring them within the scope of the interpretation suggested here for *ric*. The names are Glynde Reach SSX, E. of Lewes, which is a straight drainage channel, and *Riche* LIN, a lost village which was a DB manor, by the Wash, S.W. of Boston. In Yorkshire there is record of a number of streams or drainage channels called Skitterick, and these are listed in Ekwall 1928 (pp. 369–71). It was in this discussion that Ekwall arrived at the conclusion that 'stream, ditch' was the meaning of *ric*. It seems clear that Skitterick was a name for a stream or ditch which carried sewage, but it is not certain that it contains OE *ric*. It is more likely to be a derivative of OE *scitere*, which is well evidenced as a stream-name, with the OE suffix *–ic*.

Names containing *ric* noted in the course of the present investigation which cannot be slotted into the above categories are:

Askrigg YON, E. of Hawes. There is a long, steep hillslope above the R. Ure, but it might be fairly be objected that this is not an uncommon feature in the area, so did not obviously merit a distinctive name.

Lindrick YOW, W. of Ripon. This is on a gentle slope in a bend of the R. Laver, and nothing striking is to be seen on the 1″ map.

Lindrick NTT, which was a district on the NTT/YOW boundary. Carlton in Lindrick NTT retains the name as an affix, and it occurs in some minor names in South Anston YOW, over 3 miles away. Lindrick on the southern outskirts of Tickhill YOW perhaps marks the northern limit; if so, the district extended for 5 miles from N. to S. This was probably a forest name, and it could only be elucidated by analysing the medieval references to see whether a more precise local application could be obtained.

Lindridge DRB, a minor name in Stanton by Dale. This is not on the 1″ map. It is described as 'mons' in a Latin reference of 1240.

Another possible example is Lostrigg Beck CMB, but there seems to be no reason why this ordinary stream should have in its name a rare term otherwise unknown in the north west, and it would be preferable to seek another explanation for it.

It will be noted from a number of the examples given that, in modern forms, *ric* is liable to be replaced by the common word **hrycg**. There should be a preponderance of spellings in *–ric*, *–rich*, *–riche* (as *Cameric* 1086, *Kimerich* 1212 for Kimmeridge DOR) before a name is classified in this small category. Ekwall 1960 gives *ric* in Puckeridge HRT, but this is equally likely to contain **hrycg**.

The occurrence of 4 instances with *lind* 'lime-tree' as first element (3 listed above, and Lendrick YOW, tentatively associated with the 'Roman road' group) is noteworthy, but unexplained. A row of trees might be thought of as a raised linear feature, but why should lime-trees be specially likely to be planted in rows?

scelf (Anglian, Kentish), **sci(e)lf**, **scylf** (West Saxon), **scylfe** (Anglian, West Saxon), **scelfe** (Kentish) OE 'shelf'. The different forms of this word are discussed in Smith 1956 (2, pp. 104–6).

The validity of the translation 'shelf' requires some discussion because, although this meaning is clearly exhibited in about 50 major settlement-names, it is not considered to be evidenced in OE literary sources. In its modern sense the word *shelf* is first noted in Chaucer c. 1386, and NED regards this as a ME borrowing from Low German *schelf*, which it describes as a cognate of OE *scylfe*. This is echoed in Onions 1966. In OE glosses, the strong word *scelf* is used to render Latin words which mean 'rock, pinnacle, battlement'. The weak word *scylfe* is only recorded once in a passage about the building of Noah's ark, and commentators differ as to whether the *scylfan* of this reference were decks or compartments. A few of the occurrences of the strong word could perhaps be interpreted as references to ledges rather than pinnacles, but the general tenor of the glosses suggests that in literary OE a *scelf* was sharp or pointed. The place-name evidence, on the other hand, demonstrates that in the speech of the countryside a *scelf* was broad, level, and more likely to occur at a low altitude than at a high one. The meaning 'crag, pointed rock' is said in Smith 1956 to be evidenced in Shilstone (in Drewsteignton) DEV, which refers to a cromlech; but the EPNS survey (2, p. 433) states more correctly that in this name (of which there are several occurrences in DEV) the *scylf* is the horizontal stone supported by the standing stones.

The 'shelf' words occur most frequently as first elements. They are rare in minor names and field-names.

Sites of settlements with names containing *scelf* or *scylfe* can be divided into five categories. In the largest group the reference is to a broad area which is level or very gently sloping. Examples are Skelton S.E. of Ripon and Skelton S.E. of Leeds YOW, Skelton S.E. of Howden YOE, Shelton BDF, NTT, SHR, Sheldon and Shelfield WAR, Shelley ESX, SFK, Selly Oak WOR, Shelfanger NFK, Shelland SFK, Bothamsall NTT, Minshull CHE. About half of these are on the banks of major rivers. A typical site is that of Minshull CHE, which, as the EPNS survey (3, p. 155) says, 'occupies a broad shelving terrain between the river and the 150ft contour.'

Sometimes the area of level ground is remarkable because it is surrounded by hills. In this category belong Shelf YOW, Shelve and Shelvock SHR, Silton YON, Shildon DRH, Shilvinghampton DOR, Shulbrede SSX and Litchfield HMP. Shelf YOW is one of the most striking instances of this use, occupying a level area in the mountainous country S.W. of Bradford.

Occasionally the level ground could be described as a low plateau. Here belong Shelton NFK, Shelfield STF, Shilton OXF, WAR, Moxhull WAR, and possibly Shell WOR and Wadshelf DRB.

Sometimes the flat area projects from higher ground, or is at the end of a ridge. Here belong Earl Shilton LEI, Bashall and Hunshelf YOW, Oxhill WAR, Tibshelf DRB and Silpho YON. The last place, Silpho, is a very good instance. It is N.W. of Scarborough on a flat-topped ridge which projects from the narrow ridge of Suffield Moor. The site is a **hōh** because it is a long projection, but also a *scylfe* because it is flat-topped and rather broad for a **hōh**. In Bashall (W. of Clitheroe) the **bæc** is a narrow little ridge which broadens at its S.W. end, with Bashall Hall and Town standing on the *scelf* formed by this broad part.

A final category consists of sites on hill-sides. Some are on the lower slopes of the hill (as Skelton S.W. of Saltburn YON, Shelton under Harley and Bramshall STF, Gomshall SUR); others are on terraces, often poised above a steeper slope (as Skelton Hall W. of Richmond YON, Skelton CMB, Sheldon DEV, Shelley YOW and Shareshill STF).

Readers with local knowledge will probably wish to move some of these names from one category to another, but there can be little doubt that *scelf* and *scylfe* in major settlement-names can generally be translated by the modern word *shelf*, thus establishing that this sense belonged to the words in OE.

The corresponding ON word **skjalf** may be found in Ranskill NTT (N.E. of Blyth, on the edge of a broad low ridge overlooking marshland), Raskelf YON (N.E. of Boroughbridge, on a broad low ridge jutting out into marshland), Skutterskelfe YON (S. of Middlesbrough, on the broad, flat bank of the R. Leven) and Ulleskelfe YOW (S.E. of Tadcaster on the broad, flat bank of the R. Wharfe). It is possible, however, that in spite of the ON personal name found in Ulleskelfe and the ON stream-name possibly found in Skutterskelfe these are Scandinavian adaptations of earlier OE names.

sīde OE 'side', used of long hill-slopes, is fairly common in northern England, mostly in minor names. Examples include Birkenside DRH (W. of Consett), Facit LNC (N. of Whitworth), Fawcett Forest WML, Langsett YOW (S.W. of Penistone), and Whernside YOW (2 examples, one of which, on the boundary with YON, is a perfect specimen). Some north-country names with modern –side contain ON *sætr* 'shieling'.

sīde is rare in southern England and the midlands, but Syde GLO, S. of Cheltenham, is a good instance.

6

Trees, Forests, Woods and Clearings

The raison d'être of this book is the comparative neglect of topographical terms in previous works on place-names. The words collected in this chapter have, however, received more careful consideration than any other category of topographical elements, and the attention paid to them by scholars has made the chapter easier to write than the other six. From an early stage in English place-name studies it was recognized that woodland terms constituted the main evidence available for the distribution of surviving or regenerated woodland in the post-Roman period, and such terms have been consistently included on distribution maps when these were supplied with EPNS volumes.

In the main it has been possible in this chapter to follow the guidelines provided by my predecessors without feeling that important points have been missed by failure to locate names on maps or to think of them in relation to the landscape. Occasionally, as in the discussion of **fyrhth**, noting the position of ancient settlement-names suggests a modification of the traditional interpretation, and sometimes, as with **holt** and the 'grove' words, analysis of qualifying elements suggests a more precise definition of the generic.

Words for clearings deserve especially careful attention when they are used in settlement-names. The evidence they provide must be taken into account in the perennial debate about how many hamlets and villages are new foundations of the post-Roman period. It will be apparent from the tone of my discussion of **lēah**, **rodu** and **thveit**, especially the last, that I believe a good deal of new settlement in forest areas to have taken place relatively late in Anglo-Saxon times. In spite of the importance of 'clearing' terms, I have not included the group of words discussed in Smith 1956 under the headings *rōth*, *ryd*, *rydding* (an error for *ryding*) and *ryden*, because these have given rise to very few names of major settlements, and they could only be studied by examination of types of material which are not the main subject of this book.

The long essay on **trēow** is included on account of the interest of the problems posed by its use in settlement-names, rather than for any light it sheds on the state of the landscape before the Norman Conquest. As Dr Rackham observes (1976, p. 56): 'Tree (*trēow*) place-names tell us next to nothing about the landscape; many areas with no woodland nevertheless have plenty of trees.' The notes on individual tree-names appended to the discussion of **trēow** are, however, relevant to the study of pre-Conquest ecology, if not of woodland cover, and the use of words for individual tree-species as settlement-names poses intriguing questions about the state of the landscape. The occurrence of the word *elm* as the name of a large parish in the northern tip of CAM may indicate that the landscape was so flat and featureless that an elm tree was a major landmark. In most cases it is reasonable to assume that a species whose name is used as a settlement-name was not common in that area.

The British element in the naming of forests is greater than appears from the inclusion in the chapter of the single term **cęd**. A number of medieval forests had individual names which were adapted by Anglo-Saxons from names passed on to them by British speakers. Here may be instanced Arden WAR, Lyme LNC/CHE/STF/SHR, Kinver and Morfe STF, Wyre WOR, and Savernake WLT.

Four ON terms are included: **lundr, skógr, thveit** and **vithr**. The fact that **thveit** is by far the most commonly used of these seems to me to convey a clear message about the nature of the Scandinavian settlements.

bearu OE 'grove'. The gen. sg. is *bearwes*, dat. sg. *bearwe*, nom. pl. *bearwas*. There is evidence (for which see the EPNS survey pp. 107–8) that in DEV *bearu* developed an irregular dat. sg. *beara*, and this is likely to be the source of –beer, –bear, or Bere, Beere, Beare, Beara, Beera in the place-names of that county. When only ME spellings are available *bearu* may be difficult to distinguish from **beorg** 'hill' and **bǣr** 'swine pasture'. It is probable that most names containing *bearu* have been identified, but some in DOR—Bere Regis and Beer Hackett—and in SOM—Beer Crocombe and Beere (near Cannington)—could be from *bearu* or *bǣr*. In WLT, where Barrow usually comes from **beorg** and refers to tumuli, two instances— in Langley Burrell and Bishopstrow—are ascribed to *bearu* because they have ME spellings *Barwe*, *Barewe*, *Baruwe* instead of spellings like *Berewe* which are appropriate to **beorg**.

The way in which *bearu* is used in place-names suggests that it referred to a wood of limited extent and was not applied to forest areas. If there was a consistent difference of meaning between *bearu* and **grǣfe, grāf(a), grāfe**, it may have been related to the extent to which the wood was coppiced. The material discussed under the 'grove' words could be held to support a meaning 'coppice'.

bearu is commonest in the south west, and Smith 1956 cites four names—Bearah, Beer, Harrowbarrow, Ogbeare—in CNW. Among the counties for which detailed surveys are available it is only in DEV that *bearu* is common. There are some counties—CAM, CMB, ESX, HRT, NTP, NTT, OXF, SSX, WAR, WML, YOE, YON—in which it has not been noted at all, and others—BRK, MDX—in which it occurs only in a few minor names or field-names. It is comparatively frequent in CHE, GLO and YOW.

bearu is most frequent as a simplex name. There are 9 instances in which

Barrow from this source has become a major settlement-name. These are Barrow (E. of Chester) CHE, Barrow upon Trent DRB, Barrow (in Boddington) GLO, Barrow upon Soar LEI, Barrow upon Humber LIN, Barrow (E. of Much Wenlock) SHR, Barrow (between Newmarket and Bury St Edmunds) SFK, Barrow Gurney (S.W. of Bristol) SOM, and N. and S. Barrow (S.W. of Castle Cary) SOM. The simplex name has the modern form Bare in LNC (E. of Morecambe) and Beer(2) in DEV (W. of Seaton and N.W. of Barnstaple). As a first element, *bearu* is combined with **ford** in Barrasford NTB and Barrowford LNC. The absence of compounds with habitative words contrasts with the evidence discussed under **græ̈fe, graf(a)**.

As the second element of a compound, *bearu* occurs in Adber DOR, Haselbury DOR, SOM, Kigbeare DEV, Larkbeare DEV, Rockbeare DEV, Sedgeberrow WOR, Shebbear DEV and Timsbury SOM. There is insufficient material in major names for an analysis of first elements to be of much significance, but it is interesting that the compound with 'hazel' occurs again in a well-documented minor name, Hazlebarrow Fm on the S.E. outskirts of Sheffield. There are enough minor names in DEV for meaningful analysis.

Local historians will be able to say to what extent settlements with *bearu* in their names are in ancient forest country. Some are clearly not so situated, as Sedgeberrow WOR (S. of Evesham) and Timsbury SOM (S.W. of Bath). Others, such as Larkbeare and Rockbeare DEV (N.E. of Exeter), and Shebbear DEV (N.W. of Okehampton) may have been on the edge of heavily wooded country. Barrow upon Soar LEI and Barrow upon Humber LIN are both on the edge of areas called The Wolds, a district-name discussed under **wald**.

It seems likely that *bearu* refers to isolated woods, and the presence of forests at Bere Regis DOR and Bere Forest HMP should perhaps be taken to indicate that those names derive from *bǣr* 'swine pasture' rather than *bearu*.

cę̄d, coid PrW, PrCorn, PrCumb, **coed** W 'forest, wood', cognate with English *heath*. This is one of the commonest Celtic words in English place-names, though (as with **penn**) its British ancestor only occurs once in the names recorded from Roman Britain, the single instance being *Letocetum*, preserved in Lichfield STF. An adjective *cę̄diǫg* 'wooded' occurs in Chideock DOR and Dunchideock DEV.

In the forest-name Chute WLT/HMP, *cę̄d* is used alone. In another forest-name on this county boundary, Melchet, it is qualified by PrW *mę̄l* 'bare', perhaps used as a substantive meaning 'bare hill'. The compound found in *Letocetum*, which means 'grey wood', occurs also in Lytchett DOR, Litchett HMP, and there are a number of Cornish and Welsh instances of it. Other PrW names which have *cę̄d* as second element are Culcheth LNC and Culgaith CMB (variously explained as 'nook wood' or 'narrow wood'), and Morchard DEV. Morchard means 'great wood', and the two settlements so named doubtless refer to the same ancient forest. Penge, Penketh and Penkhull are discussed under **penn**.

In another group of names *cēd* has been glossed by an OE word for a forest. Cheadle CHE, STF have **lēah** added, and Chetwode BUC has **wudu**. Chithurst SSX may be a comparable formation with **hyrst**. In Chatham ESX, KNT and Cheetham LNC OE **hām** 'village' is combined with *cēd*. Cheetwood, situated in Cheetham LNC, may be a shortened version of *Cheethamwood*. Another hybrid name is Kesteven, one of the three divisions of LIN, explained in Ekwall 1960 as formed by the addition of ON *stefna*, used in the sense 'administrative district', to an ancient district-name from *cēd*.

The appropriate translation for most occurrences of *cēd* in English place-names appears to be 'forest', though in Wales and the Welsh Marches, and in CNW, the later forms *coed* and *côs*, *coys* may be used of smaller woods.

There are a number of English place-names beginning with Chat– or Chet– which are not usually derived from *cēd* because the ME spellings have *Chate–* or *Chete–*, and the *–e–* between the first and second elements is likely to indicate a genitive inflexion, suitable to derivation from the OE personal name *Ceatta*.

fyrhth, fyrhthe (a form *gefyrhth* is sometimes found in charter boundaries) OE ?'land overgrown with brushwood, scrub on the edge of forest'. The accepted translation is 'wood', but the definition suggested here suits the use of the term in settlement-names and the sense-development traced in NED under *frith*. It would also explain the adoption of *fyrhth* into Welsh, where in the 14th century *ffridd* meant 'barren land'. In modern Welsh toponymy *ffridd*, pl. *friddoedd*, is used of land at a certain altitude, above the belts of good arable. The sentence in Gospatric's writ in which *freyth* is contrasted with *wald* is discussed under **wald**.

fyrhth is much more common in minor names and field-names than it is in major settlement-names of the type examined here, and a full discussion would have to be based on a different collection of material. The usual modern forms are Frith and Thrift. In Kentish dialect the word became *fright*. The EPNS survey of CAM (pp. 179–80) notes that *frithfen* was a type of fen from which brushwood was obtained.

fyrhth occurs as the final element in Pirbright SUR, which lies in a vast expanse of heathland. As first element it is found in Firbank WML (in an area of rough grassland N.W. of Sedbergh), probably in Firbeck YOW (S.W. of Tickhill, perhaps on the edge of a forest area), and, in the gen., in Frithsden HRT (at the edge of Berkhamsted Common). It occurs as an affix in Chapel en le Frith DRB. Frithville LIN was a simplex name *Le Frith* in 1331, and here the word may have been used as in CAM of an area of fen where brushwood grew.

Ekwall 1960 considers the second element of Flyford WOR to be *fyrhth*. Flyford, which was a district-name in the 10th century, is preserved as a settlement-name in Flyford Flavell (Flavell being a Normanized version of Flyford) and an an affix in the neighbouring Grafton Flyford (*–juxta Flavell*,

– *sub Fleuarth*, – *souz Flavell* in 13th to 14th century references). The earliest reference to the district called Flyford is in a charter of AD 930, which mentions that woodland at *Fleferth* is attached to an estate at Dumbleton GLO. This property is the subject of a later grant, dated 1002, in which the woodland area is called *Fleferht*. Both charters say that the woodland is by the Piddle Brook, and Flyford Flavell and Grafton Flyford are beside this stream. There is also an estate called *Flæferth* in the foundation charter of Pershore Abbey (dated AD 972), and the boundary survey indicates that this is Flyford Flavell. The name *Fleferth* occurs again as a boundary-mark in an OE survey of Phepson, 3 miles N.W. of Grafton Flyford. In Ekwall 1928 (p. 160), the possibility of *Fleferth* being a pre-English river-name was mooted, but (as Ekwall observed) there is no stream which runs near Phepson and near Flyford Flavell, so it is much easier to explain *Fleferth* as a wood-name, and to think of –*ferth* as a reduced form of *fyrhth*. If this be accepted, it could be argued that here is evidence that *fyrhth* means 'wood' rather than 'scrub on the edge of forest'; but the area is at the southern edge of Feckenham Forest, between it and the open land of the Avon valley, and the wood may have been thinner there. The first element of Flyford presents difficulties. Ekwall 1960 suggests that it is a feminine personal name *Flæde*, a short form of *Ælflæde*, found in the lost settlement-name *Ælflædetun* which occurs (together with *Fleferth*) in the charter of 972 which lists the properties of Pershore Abbey. *Ælflædetun* clearly lay in the same vicinity, but it is unreasonable to postulate such different degrees of shortening in two names in the same charter, so there is probably no connection between *Ælflædetun* and *Fleferth*, and the first element of Flyford should be regarded as obscure.

græfe OE 'thicket, brushwood', **gráf, gráfa, gráfe** OE 'grove, copse'. It is convenient to consider these related words together. They are difficult to distinguish in place-names from *græf* and *grafa*, which are considered to mean 'digging, grave, trench'. Smith 1956 (1, p. 208), probably echoing NED, says that the 'grove' words are only found in OE with no known cognates in other languages. It would make good sense if the 'grove' words could be assigned to the same root as the 'grave' words, which are related to *grafan* 'to dig'. Rackham 1976 (p. 115) says: 'In lowland areas . . . nearly all woods more than 100 years old have some kind of earthwork round the edge. Typically this consists of a bank and ditch . . . boundary earthworks have been a feature of coppice woods since the Middle Ages.' Expert philological opinion would be required before the possibility of a connection between the word *grove* and the embanking of woods could be entertained; the long vowel of the 'grove' words, as opposed to the short *a* of *grafan*, *grafa*, may be against it. Even if accepted it would not obviate the difficulty of knowing whether, in some place-names, we are dealing with a 'grove' or a 'trench'. Bygrave HRT could mean '(place) by the grove' or '(place) by the trench'. In previous reference books some compound names are classified under *græf*, *grafa*, translated 'pit', because the first elements (e.g. 'chalk' in Chalgrave BDF, Chalgrove OXF, 'ore' in Orgrave LNC, Orgreave YOW) seem appropriate, others, including Filgrave BUC, Palgrave SFK and Palgrave NFK (different names), are considered ambiguous. Ekwall 1960 gives 'reed ditch' for Redgrave SFK, but 'red grove' seems at least as likely.

Development to modern –grove suggests association, at least, with the woodland term, but neither ME nor modern spellings can be conclusive in most instances. Only where the term occurs as first element with an –*es* genitive, as in Gravesend KNT, is it possible to say firmly that one of the 'grove' words, the strong form *grāf*, is indicated. It should be noted, however, that the usual word in place-names for a linear earthwork is *dīc*, and the usual one for a pit is *pytt* (*sēath*, evidenced in Orsett ESX, Roxeth GTL, perhaps went out of use at an early date). Orgrave LNC and Orgreave YOW are likely to mean 'ore pit', with reference to iron mining, but other place-names ending in –greave, –grave or –grove should probably be considered to refer to groves unless there is very strong topographical evidence which points to the contrary.

Major settlement-names usually considered to contain *græfe* include Congreave STF, Hargrave in Little Neston CHE, Orgreave STF (not the same name as Orgrave YOW), Ramsgreave LNC, Whitgreave STF and Youlgreave DRB. Some other names, including Bromsgrove WOR and Wargrave BRK, have occasional –*greve* forms among a preponderance with –*grave*. Although *græfe* is recorded in OE with the meanings 'thicket' and 'brushwood' it seems likely that in place-names there was no firm distinction of meaning between the words here being considered as a group, and it is probably safe to translate *græfe* by 'grove'. The distribution suggests that *græfe* was a dialect variant, used mainly in the N.W. midlands.

Grove occurs as a simplex name for a major settlement in BUC, BRK, and NTT, and there are other examples among minor names in various counties. As a first element one or other of the 'grove' words is compounded with **hām** in Grafham HNT and Graffham SSX, and with **tūn** in Grafton CHE, GLO, HRE, NTP(2), OXF, SHR, WAR, WLT WOR(2), YOW. These names may indicate that the settlements derived special advantages from their management of the grove. There are some compounds in which the second element is another word for wood; these include Graveley CAM, HRT, Groveley Wood WLT, Gravenhunger SHR and Gravenhurst BDF. Grayshott HMP belongs here according to the interpretation of *scēat* in Ekwall 1960 (p. 407).

As the second element of a compound, *græfe*, *grāf*, *grāfa* or *grāfe* occur in about 30 major names. The largest class of first elements consists of words describing the grove, most of these being adjectives of colour. Here belong Blagrave BRK (and several minor names of identical etymology), Hargrave CHE(2), NTP, SFK, Redgrave SFK, Whitgreave STF and Youlgreave DRB. Leagrave BDF, 'light grove', can be classed with these. Shape is referred to in Shortgrove ESX, and probably in Gargrave YOW and Orgreave STF.

Notgrove GLO is considered to mean 'wet grove'. There are 5 examples with a personal name as first element: Bromsgrove WOR, Copgrove YOW, Cosgrove NTP, Cotgrave NTT and Filgrave BUC; Palgrave NFK may be another. A similar-sized group has first elements which refer to a nearby feature, either natural or man-made: here belong Congreave STF, Howgrave YOW, Sulgrave NTP, Wargrave BRK and Warpsgrove OXF, and probably Potsgrove BDF. Only Boxgrove SSX and Ramsgreave LNC refer to vegetation, and only Gedgrave SFK and Musgrave WML to living creatures. Palgrave SFK probably produced poles, and Staplegrove SOM produced posts. In Walgrave NTP and Wingrave BUC the groves are defined by nearby places, Old and Wing. Walsgrave WAR was probably adjacent to an area called **wald**.

As mentioned above, Chalgrave BDF and Chalgrove OXF are usually rendered 'chalk pits'; but this is not certain to be correct. A Hampshire charter-boundary has a *cealc graf* in a context which is suitable for a grove, but not for a pit. Chalgrove OXF is not on chalk, though there are small patches in the vicinity. These names are an unsolved mystery.

The 'grove' words are better represented in minor names than in major names, but they are nowhere very common, and the proportion of examples which have become names of major settlements is much higher than for some other woodland terms, such as **fyrhth, hyrst, sceaga**. The material has not been thoroughly studied, and no systematic account has been taken of occurrences in charter boundaries, but some tentative conclusions can be drawn from the cursory analysis given above. It seems likely that a grove was a wood of limited size, which was a striking visual feature, able to be described by a colour adjective or a word referring to its shape, or to be defined by proximity to a single feature, such as a weir or a hill-spur. In spite of the limited size, a grove seems to have had some economic importance. Rackham 1976 (p. 56) says: 'The element *grove*, Anglo-Saxon *gráf*, has almost the opposite meaning [i.e. from **lēah**], a small, defined, and possibly managed wood, normally surrounded by non-woodland; its use therefore carries a presumption that there was not much Wildwood left when the name was formed.'

The names discussed here are fairly widely scattered, but there are some concentrations. The BDF names Leagrave, Chalgrave (not a certain example) and Potsgrove are by Watling Street, and two minor names in HRT, Mangrove Fm and Mortgrove, N.E. and N. of Luton, are quite close. Some distance to the N.W. but still near Watling Street are Cosgrove and Grafton Regis BUC. The nature of the woods referred to, and the relationship of Grafton to known ancient woodland, might be worth consideration by local historians.

hangra OE 'sloping wood'. This term is well evidenced in the boundary surveys of charters but is not otherwise on record in OE. It is usually translated 'wood on a steep slope', which is the sense in which *hanger* is recorded in the 18th century, and this may suit the charter boundary-marks. Those in BRK are listed in EPNS survey 3 (p. 779) and their positions can be ascertained from the accompanying notes and maps; they are on appreciable slopes. In settlement-names, however, the reference is to very gentle slopes, and it seems necessary to conclude that this is the earlier use. The word is a derivative of the verb *hang*, so it would be reasonable to expect a steep declivity in all instances, but the evidence of the settlement-names is firmly against this. There may be a special feature of the gentle slope—a slight concavity perhaps—which gave woods in this position a characteristic appearance.

Most of the settlement-names containing *hangra* refer to sites in relatively low areas. Here may be instanced Barnacle WAR (DB *Bernhangre*, N.E. of Coventry) which straddles the 350′ contour; Betteshanger (W. of Deal) which, together with the DB manor of Hartanger, is on the slopes of the foothills of E. KNT; Birchanger ESX (N.E. of Bishop's Stortford) on a gentle slope above the 300′ contour; Denshanger NTP (N.E. of Buckingham) on the banks of the R. Ouse; Goldhanger ESX (N.E. of Maldon) where the village lies athwart the slope of a low hill overlooking the R. Blackwater; Moggerhanger BDF (W. of Sandy) where there is a spot height of 152′ in the village; Oakhanger HMP (a hamlet S.E. of Alton) on gently rising ground with a spot height of 280′; Panshanger HRT (W. of Hertford) on a gentle slope above the R. Mimram; Polehanger BDF (a farm S.W. of Shefford) at the foot of a gentle slope; Rishangles SFK (S.E. of Eye) on very gently rising ground; Saniger GLO (earlier *Swanhangre*, a farm in Hinton) which, together with Oakhunger Fm, lies S. of Sharpness on slightly raised ground above the bank of the R. Severn; Shelfanger NFK (N. of Diss) on very gently rising ground; Shutlanger NTP (N.E. of Towcester) on a gentle slope between the 300′ and 400′ contours; Timberhanger WOR (a hamlet W. of Bromsgrove) on top of a low ridge; and Tyttenhanger Park and Fm HRT (S.E. of St Albans) where the park is below, and the farm above, the 250′ contour beside the R. Colne. Ekwall 1960 notes under Shelfanger NFK that 'there is not much of a hill here', but the site is not, in fact, atypical. Slightly more dramatically-sited examples are Cathanger SOM (a farm near Fivehead, S.W. of Langport), which stands above the long escarpment overlooking West Sedge Moor, and Gravenhunger Hall SHR (N.W. of Market Drayton), where the slope looks quite gentle on the map but the modern name Banktop suggests a noticeable feature. The only high site in the examples studied is that of Binegar SOM (N.E. of Wells), which is between the 700′ and 750′ contours. The recurring compound with *clǣg* 'clay' has become Clayhanger CHE, DEV, STF, Clehonger HRE, Clinger DOR, and Clingre GLO. The DEV village lies athwart a steepish slope, E. of Bampton, but some of the others have positions on gentle slopes, similar to those noted in the majority of settlement-names containing *hangra*.

Few compounds of *hangra* with a descriptive term other than Clayhanger and its variants have become settlement-names, but Goldhanger probably belongs in this category. Vegetation is referred to in Birchanger, Oakhanger, Oakhunger and Rishangles, and a wild creature in Cathanger, Hartanger and Saniger. The qualifier is a personal name in Denshanger and Tyttenhanger, and possibly in Binegar. Shelfanger and Polehanger refer to another topographical feature, Shutlanger and Timberhanger to a product. Barnacle refers to a building, as probably does Betteshanger. The first elements of Gravenhunger, Moggerhanger and Panshanger are obscure or uncertain. In minor names and field-names *hangra* is often used as a simplex name.

hangra is not found in every county. In the south and midlands no instances have been noted in CAM, DRB, IOW, SSX or SUR, though there are detailed place-name surveys for those counties. In the north, the element has not been noted in CMB, LNC, WML, YOE or YOW. The only possible instance in YON is the wapentake-name Hang, which has two early spellings with –*r*; the failure of the element to appear otherwise in Yorkshire makes this a very uncertain instance, and similar considerations tell against the interpretation of the first element of Hangleton SSX as a Normanized form of *hangra*.

A full study of this word would have to take account of minor names and field-names, and of all occurrences in OE charter-boundaries.

holt OE 'wood'. The place-name evidence suggests that this was to some extent a specialized term for a single-species wood. It is found in about 35 major settlement-names, more frequently in minor names and field-names, but not with the same disproportion as is noted for **hyrst**.

Among counties for which there are detailed surveys, *holt* is most frequent in CHE, ESX, GLO and SSX. It is not noted at all in OXF, or in the northern counties of LNC, CMB, WML, YOE and YON, but it is well represented in YOW. There are a few instances in Wales.

The simplex Holt occurs as a major name in DEN, DOR, HMP, LEI, NFK, SOM, STF, WLT and WOR, and there are other instances in minor names. *holt* is the first element of Haltham LIN and Howtel NTB. As a second element it is combined with tree-names in Acol KNT, Occold SFK, Knockholt and Knockhall KNT ('oak'); Alderholt DOR; Aisholt SOM and Esholt YOW ('ash'); Bircholt KNT; Buckholt HMP, SSX ('beech'); and Wiggenholt SSX ('wych elm'). A high proportion of the minor names containing *holt* are of this type. Wild creatures are referred to in Eversholt BDF and Wormwood Scrubs GTL (*Wormoltwode* 1437). No bird-names have been noted in major names, but Crowholt occurs as a minor name in CHE and there are two instances of Gledholt ('kites' wood') in YOW. Ramsholt SFK may refer to rams or to wild garlic. The only compound of *holt* with a personal name includes in Ekwall 1960 is Poulshot WLT, but there are a few others in minor names. Kensal Green GTL is 'king's holt', and Hainault Forest ESX is 'monastic community's holt'. Chittlehamholt DEV is 'wood of the people of Chittlehampton'.

The qualifying element refers to a product in Sparsholt BRK, HMP, Sparcell's Fm WLT and Throckenholt CAM. Bergholt ESX, SFK and Linkenholt HMP are defined by topographical features, and Southolt SFK by position.

hylte, a derivative of *holt*, is considered to be the final element of Salkeld CMB.

hyrst OE 'wooded hill'. Ekwall 1922 (p. 13) quotes a Welsh grammar of 1913 as stating that *hyrst* is cognate with Welsh *prys* 'brushwood', and this is echoed without comment by Onions (1966) and by Smith (1956). Occurrences in OE texts are ambiguous as between 'hillock' and 'wood'. Both senses are evidenced in ME and in modern English, sometimes combined, so 'wooded hill' seems the best rendering.

hyrst occurs as a simplex name or as the final element of a compound in some 70 major settlement-names in England, and is common in minor names in some areas. The distribution is heavily weighted towards SUR and the Weald of KNT and SSX. The word is fairly common (though not on the same scale as in KNT, SSX and SUR) in YOW, CMB and LNC. The 70 major names stand out from a much greater mass of minor names and field-names. In SSX, there are 17 major names out of a total of 70, and in SUR only 2 out of a similar total (excluding field-names). In GLO there are 3 major names and 8 minor names; in WAR the figures are 3 and 12, in YOW 2 and over 30. It seems likely that major settlements with names in –*hyrst* are of relatively late origin, and grew up in areas not immediately recognized by the Anglo-Saxons as appropriate to arable farming.

There are 10 major names in which *hyrst* is uncompounded. These are Herstmonceaux SSX, Hirst NTB, YOW, Hurst BRK, KNT, SOM, WAR, Hurstpierpoint SSX, Old Hurst and Woodhurst HNT (for which, see below). An analysis of first elements in some 60 compound settlement-names in –*hyrst* reveals an unusually even spread of a limited number of categories. There are 8 or 9 which have a personal name. Smith 1956 says 'not common with pers. ns. and other words denoting ownership', which may be true for the whole corpus, but personal names are well represented among the examples which became major settlements. Relevant names are: Bathurst SSX, Baughurst HMP, Billingshurst SSX, Borckenhurst HMP, Chippinghurst OXF, Penshurst KNT, Wadhurst SSX, and possibly Wheatenhurst GLO. Eleven examples have a tree or plant-name: Ashurst KNT, SSX, Buckhurst ESX, Ewhurst HMP, SSX, SUR, Fernhurst SSX, Holdenhurst HMP, Lindhurst NTT, Lyndhurst HMP, Salehurst SSX. Six refer to wild creatures: Brockhurst WAR, Crowhurst SUR, Deerhurst GLO, Hawkhurst KNT, Haycrust SHR, Henhurst KNT. Another 7 refer to domestic animals: Bolnhurst BDF, Gathurst LNC, Gayhurst BUC, Goathurst SOM, Lamberhurst KNT, Ticehurst SSX, Tickenhurst KNT, and it is noteworthy that 5 of these refer to goats. Some names incorporate a word describing the *hyrst* or its surroundings, 5 of these (Chislehurst KNT, Sandhurst BRK, GLO, KNT, Stonyhurst LNC) referring to gravelly, sandy or stony soil. Others are Collyhurst LNC, which Ekwall 1960 renders 'grimy with coal dust', and Madehurst SSX ('meadow hurst', a rare instance of OE **mǣd** as a first element; the compound occurs also as a minor name in KNT, Medhurst in Edenbridge). Midhurst SSX was probably surrounded by wooded hills. Longhirst NTB has a rare reference to shape. A few names refer to a product (Bredhurst KNT, Nuthurst SSX, WAR, Speldhurst KNT, Staplehurst KNT) or an industry (Kilnhurst YOW, Tilehurst BRK). Limehurst LNC refers to the forest of Lyme, and Chithurst SSX may refer to a wood known by the pre-English term cẹd. Four names contain –inga–; Bringhurst LEI, Doddinghurst ESX, Sissinghurst KNT and Warminghurst SSX. Growhurst SSX, Fingest BUC, Goudhurst KNT, Gravenhurst BDF, Penhurst SSX and Shadoxhurst KNT are not classified.

Of the simplex names the most interesting are Old Hurst and Woodhurst HNT. The prefixes **wald** and **wudu** were attached to the names at the dates of the first recording (1227 and 1209), but as the parishes adjoin, and were in the district of a people called the *Hyrstingas*, it can be assumed that both settlements were once called *Hyrst*. A rough stone seat called The Abbott's Chair on the boundary between the parishes was earlier called *Hurstingstone*, and was the marker for the meeting-place of Hurstingstone Hundred. The hundred belonged to Ramsey Abbey, and the Abbot held his court at the old meeting-place, thus causing the stone to acquire its modern name. It seems clear that there was a district called *Hyrst*, the people of which formed an administrative unit called *Hyrstingas*.

Old Hurst and Woodhurst lie on a broad, low ridge made by the 100′ contour. Deerhurst and Sandhurst GLO also give a good idea of the sort of low hill to which the term *hyrst* was felt appropriate.

lēah OE 'forest, wood, glade, clearing', later 'pasture, meadow'. This is certainly the commonest topographical term in English place-names. It is not, however, one of the commonest elements in names recorded by AD 730; Cox 1976 (p. 50) lists only seven examples, and this indicates that it must have been used much more frequently after 730 than it was before that date.

lēah is believed to be related to OE *lēoht*, modern *light*, and the senses 'glade, clearing' are more obviously appropriate to this ultimate etymology than 'forest', though it seems probable that 'forest' was the earlier sense in English place-names. The Weald of KNT and SSX is called both *Andredesweald* and *Andredesleage*. Cognate words in some other languages, including Latin *lucus*, are also used of woodland. Like a number of common place-name elements, *lēah* is infrequent in OE literary use, and some examples which do occur in literary sources are capable of different interpretations. The massive testimony provided by place-names, which is summarized well in Smith 1956, is the main evidence for the word's meaning.

No attempt is made here to provide a comprehensive survey of settlement-names containing *lēah*. Because of its importance as an indicator of Anglo-Saxon woodland the word has received more systematic attention from place-name scholars than any other topographical term. It is shown on distribution maps for many of the counties which have EPNS surveys, and there are detailed studies of its use in some areas, e.g. the Birmingham region in Gelling 1974, and Durham in Watts 1976. Occurrences of *lēah* in all types of name recorded before the Norman Conquest are painstakingly examined in Johansson 1975.

It may be regarded as established that *lēah* is an indicator of woodland which was in existence and recognized as ancient when English speakers arrived in any region; and in Rackham 1976 (p. 56) it is assumed that 'names, especially village names, ending in –ley or –leigh . . . imply that some of the Wildwood remained at the time they were formed'. In Gelling 1974 it is suggested that isolated names containing *lēah* (such as Elmley Castle WOR, in the circle of names in –**tūn** which surround Bredon Hill) are likely to refer to woods in open country, whereas clusters of settlement-names containing *lēah*, such as are found in N.WAR, may contain the word in a quasi-habitative sense, used by English speakers to denote sites where settlements in forest clearings were flourishing when they arrived.

Names which contain *lēah* in the late OE sense 'pasture, meadow' can often be identified from the topography, and from the nature of the first element, for example a word such as **wisce** 'marshy meadow' in Whistley BRK; this point is discussed in the EPNS BRK survey (p. 936). The sense-development was to some extent a natural one from 'clearing', but NED points out (under *lea*) that 'the sense has been influenced by confusion with LEAS *sb.*[1] (OE. *lǣs*), which seems often to have been mistaken for a plural, and also with LEA *sb.*[2]'. (NED's *lea* sb.[2] is the elliptical use of OE *lǣge* adj. 'fallow, untilled'.) The choice of meaning in any place-name containing *lēah* may fairly be left to the local historian.

The attention given to names containing *lēah* in existing studies is one reason why a comprehensive account is not attempted here. Another is that for a thorough study of *lēah*, more than for most topographical elements, it would be necessary to include names of farms and hamlets and of actual woods as well as the names of ancient administrative centres which are the material on which this book is based. The EPNS survey of BRK (p. 935) gives an analysis of the types of name, excluding field-names, in which *lēah* occurs in that county. Although, with 54 examples, it is the commonest element in BRK apart from **tūn**, only 14 of the examples are major names, while about 30 refer to farms and hamlets, and at least 13 are names of woods.

For these reasons, all that will be attempted is a regional survey of the country to show in which counties *lēah* is more or less frequent, and an analysis of the first elements of those compounds which occur more than once in the material included in Ekwall 1960.

In N.E. England, *lēah* is very common in parts of DRH, and there is an excellent distribution map and discussion in Watts 1976. No information is readily available for NTB, but it is clear from Macdonald 1941 that the element virtually dies out at the Scottish border. In WLO there is Parkly in Linlithgow parish, which Macdonald translates 'enclosed meadow', and a few late-recorded names, including Merrilees in Abercorn parish, which is 'marsh meadows', from **mōr**, with later influence from *merry*. Some examples in BWK, DMF, ROX are mentioned in Fraser 1982.

In the N.W., *lēah* is less common than it is in DRH. For CMB, LNC and YON the EPNS survey of CMB may be quoted. Here it is stated (p. 502) that: '*lēah* occurs but is not very common. It is very frequent indeed in LNC (though very few examples are north of the Sands) . . . and in YON . . . there are still nearly four times as many examples as in CMB.' The later EPNS survey of WML confirmed these findings, stating (2, p. 307) that: '*lēah* is by no means common in either place-names or field-names . . . it appears in only one parish name (Staveley). Its frequency agrees with that of CMB and the adjacent parts of YON; it is far commoner in LNC and YOW.'

The pattern discerned in these surveys of the most northerly English counties is continued to the south. The area of England in which *lēah* is a very common element runs on a N.E./S.W. alignment, sweeping in a broad band down the country from DRH. Only in the south midlands does it extend to the E. coast, in ESX. In most of YOW *lēah* is very common, and the distribution (which largely excludes the N.W. of the county) is shown on a map accompanying Part 7 of the EPNS survey. It is much less common in YOE. For CHE, there is as yet no distribution map or discussion of frequency, but *lēah* is certainly one of the commonest elements in the county. For DRB, the EPNS survey states (p. 707): '*lēah* is the commonest of all elements but, as compared with **tūn**, fewer examples are the names of important places. Of the 147 noted, 42 are parish-names, and 40 are mentioned in DB. Many of the others are the names of farmsteads. They are found in the main in the old woodland areas.' The distribution map with the survey (here reproduced as Fig. 4) shows the uneven distribution in the county. In NTT, which lies mostly to the E. of the north-midland area in which *lēah* is common, the element is much rarer than in DRB, the densest cluster being S.W. of Mansfield, near the DRB border.

There is as yet no published survey for LIN, but early-recorded settlement-names containing *lēah* are mapped in Fellows Jensen 1978 (p. 240), and it is clear that the term is infrequent there, as it probably is in NFK and SFK. For CAM there is a survey with a distribution map, and this confirms the close association of *lēah* with areas where ancient woodland is believed, on other grounds, to have survived into the Anglo-Saxon period. There are two clusters, one in the S.E. of the county to the E. of the Icknield Way, and the other in the S.W., adjacent to HNT. These are shown with some additional information on the map on p. 57 of Rackham 1976. In BDF and HNT *lēah* is an important, but not an overwhelmingly dominant, place-name element.

Moving W. from the fenlands, the EPNS survey of NTP states (p. 256) that *lēah* is 'fairly common, especially in the old Rockingham, Salcey and Whittlewood forests'. The map on p. 240 of Fellows Jensen 1978 shows a low frequency in LEI and RUT, however, and it is to the W. of these counties that

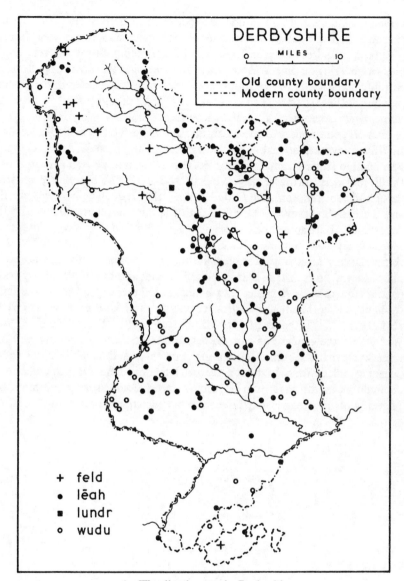

DERBYSHIRE

MILES
0   10

----- Old county boundary
-·-·- Modern county boundary

+   feld
●   lēah
■   lundr
○   wudu

4   Woodland terms in Derbyshire

lēah becomes an element of major importance. A large area with Birmingham as its centre was mapped in Gelling 1974. This map (reproduced as Fig.10 in Gelling 1978) includes WAR, WOR, S.STF, and part of HRE, SHR, DRB, LEI and OXF, and it shows names containing **tūn**, as well as those containing *lēah*. (This innovation was followed by Fellows Jensen 1978, but the results are difficult to assess because of the smallness of the map and the largeness of the symbols.) The reasoning behind the experiment in Gelling 1974 was that **tūn** and *lēah* predominate so heavily over all other elements in the area that the relationship between them deserves study. The map has proved a very useful one with bearing on several aspects of settlement-history. Moving W. from the Birmingham region, *lēah* continues to be very well represented in the western parts of SHR and HRE, but it is rare in Wales, though found in the areas immediately adjacent to the English border.

For all the counties of the south midlands, from GLO to ESX, there are EPNS surveys which enable precise statements to be made. In GLO *lēah* is very common indeed, and 29 examples are parish names; it is, however, rare in the E. and S.E. of the county. In OXF and BUC *lēah* is well represented, though not so common as in GLO. In HRT the frequency increases greatly, and the EPNS survey (p. 245) says that it is the commonest element in the county. There are some blank areas on the distribution map, but examples are more evenly distributed in HRT than in most counties. In MDX *lēah* is comparatively rare, but an unusually high proportion of the examples are major names. In ESX *lēah* is extremely common, and the EPNS survey states (p. 568) that of some 90 names, 34 are those of DB manors and 24 of parishes.

South of the Thames, statistics are only to hand for the counties of SUR, SSX, BRK, WLT and DEV. The EPNS survey of SUR states (p. 352) that: '*lēah* . . . is the element of most frequent occurrence in the county, but it is remarkable that it is entirely absent in the north-east, though there was a good deal of woodland here. In this it agrees with KNT, where this element is not as common as might have been expected.' In SSX *lēah* is very common, but unevenly distributed, as may be seen from the map accompanying the EPNS

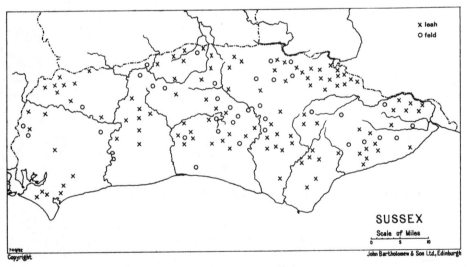

5   Woodland terms in Sussex

survey, here reproduced as Fig. 5. Figures for BRK, where *lēah* is of more modest frequency, are quoted above. In WLT, as in SSX, the frequency is high and the distribution very uneven; the map from the EPNS survey is Fig. 6. The WLT survey says (p. 417) that *lēah* is 'twice as common as in DOR, but only half as common as in HMP.' In DEV the element is extremely common, especially so as a simplex name.

lēah is frequently used alone as a place-name. Modern spellings from the nom. or dat. sg. are Lea, Lee, Leigh, Lye. The plural becomes Leece, Lees(e), or (from the dat.) Leam. There is no certain instance of a compound name with *lēah* as first element. The massive corpus in which it is the second element of a compound has not been systematically analysed, but some tentative conclusions are offered below, mainly from a study of recurrent compounds in Ekwall 1960.

The incidence of personal names with *lēah* is unassessed. In the corpus as a whole it is probably high, but it may vary a good deal between counties. In WOR, for instance, names containing *lēah* have personal names as first element more frequently than is the case in WAR. With such a quantity of material it is not surprising that some personal names should appear several times. Ekwall 1960 includes, e.g., Baddesley HMP(2), WAR(2), from *Bæddi*, Madeley SHR, STF(2), from *Māda*, and Offley HRT, STF, from *Offa*. The 5 apparent instances with *Cufa* which have become Cowley BUC, DEV(2), OXF, STF might, however, be considered beyond the bounds of coincidence. Among names of important places in which *lēah* is qualified by a personal name may be instanced Barnsley, Batley, Keighley, Otley YOW, Bletchley BUC, Dudley WOR and Hinckley LEI.

Leaving personal names aside, study of recurrent compounds in Ekwall 1960 suggests that the two largest categories of first elements used with *lēah* may be those which refer to specific trees or other types of vegetation, and those which describe the *lēah* by referring to its size or shape or some other physical characteristic.

Among references to specific types of tree, the most frequent are to oak, ash, willow and hawthorn. Oak occurs in Acklam YOE, YON, Akeley BUC, Oakle GLO, Oakleigh KNT, Ocle HRE and 12 instances of Oakley. Ash occurs in 14 instances of Ashley and in Ashleyhay DRB. Various words are used for 'willow'. OE *welig* occurs in Weeley ESX and in Willey CHE, HRE, SHR, WAR; OE *wīthig* in Widley HMP, Willey DEV and Withiel Florey SOM. The sallow willow, OE *salh*, is the first element of Sall NFK, Saul GLO, Sawley YOW(2) and an adjective derived from it occurs in Saltley WAR. The hawthorn is referred to directly in Hatherleigh DEV, Hatherley GLO, Thorley HRT, IOW, Thornley DRH, LNC, and indirectly in Hagley SHR, SOM, STF, WOR. Other trees recur, but less frequently: 'elm' in Almeley HRE, Elmley KNT, WOR(2); 'apple' in Apperley GLO, NTB, YOW, Apley IOW, LIN, SHR, SOM and Appley LNC; 'aspen' in Aspley BDF, STF, WAR and Espley NTB; 'birch' in Bartley HMP, WOR, Berkeley GLO, Berkley SOM;

'box' in Bexley GTL and Boxley KNT; 'hazel' in Haseley IOW, OXF, WAR, and perhaps, by implication, in Notley BUC, ESX.

Apart from trees, the commonest types of vegetation mentioned with *lēah* are bent-grass, in 16 instances of Bentley; ferns in Fairlight SSX, Farnley YOW(3), 7 instances of Farleigh and 5 of Farley; heath, in Hadleigh ESX, SFK, Hadley HRT, SHR, Headlam DRH, Heatley CHE, Hedley DRH(2),

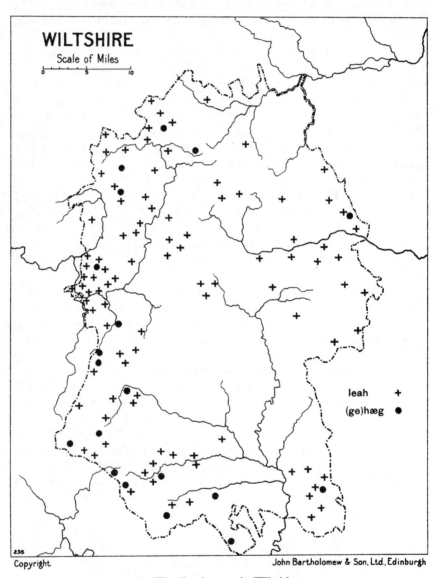

6 Woodland terms in Wiltshire

NTB, Hoathly SSX(2), and 4 instances of Headley; and broom, in 6 instances of Bramley and 5 of Bromley. The only other form of vegetation which occurs at all frequently with *lēah* among names in Ekwall 1960 is brushwood, OE *hrīs*, found in Riseley BDF, BRK and Risley DRB, LNC. Some other plants occur twice.

Among compounds in which a *lēah* is defined by its size or shape, the commonest adjectives are 'broad' and 'long'. Ekwall 1960 lists Bradle DOR and 20 instances of Bradley; and he gives 20 instances of Langley. A *lēah* could be 'small' as in Lutley STF and Lydley Hays SHR, or it could be of strip form, as Ripley DRB, HMP, SUR. Geological characteristics are described by 'stone' in 8 instances of Stanley and in Stoneleigh WAR, Stonely HNT, and by 'gravel' in Greasley NTT and Gresley DRB. A *lēah* could be 'hard' (Hardley HMP, IOW) or 'soft' (Softley DRH, NTB) or 'rough' (5 instances of Rowley). Scarle LIN, NTT were characterized by 'dung'. There are 8 major names in which a *lēah* is described as 'white' (Whitleigh DEV and 7 instances of Whitley), and 2 in which it was 'red' (Radley BRK, Raleigh DEV). In view of the bias of the material Shirley DRB, HMP, SUR, WAR are perhaps more likely to mean 'bright wood/clearing' than to refer to ownership or use by the shire.

Among recurrent compounds in which a *lēah* is characterized by reference to a living creature, wild things are commoner than domesticated ones. Commonest are various types of deer, in Darley DRB(2), Durleigh SOM, Durley HMP, Hartley BRK, DOR, HMP(3), KNT(2), Hurstley HRE, Hiendley YOW, Hindley CHE. Next commonest (curiously) are eagles (OE *earn*) in Areley WOR, Arley CHE, LNC(2), WAR, WOR, Earley BRK and Earnley SSX. Bagley BRK, SHR, SOM, YOW and Baguley CHE probably refer to badgers. Bees are mentioned in Beeleigh ESX and Beoley WOR, possibly in Bickleigh DEV(2), Bickley CHE, KNT, WOR, and by implication in Honiley WAR. Other animals are cats, in Catley HRE, LIN; boars (assumed in this context to be wild) in Everley WLT, YON, Eversley HMP and Yearsley YON; foxes in Foxley NFK, NTP, WLT; hares in Harley SHR, YOW(2); martens in Martley SFK, WOR; mice in Moseley WOR, Mowsley LEI; wolves in Woolley BRK(2), HNT, YOW. No birds are as frequently mentioned as eagles, but crows occur in 5 instances of Crawley, finches in Finchley GTL and Finkley HMP, bitterns in Purleigh ESX and Purley BRK. Insects and reptiles occur in Midgley YOW(2), Migley DRH (and other instances in minor names in northern counties); Wormley HRT, Wormsley HRE; and Wigley DRB, HMP.

Words for woodland products yield recurring compounds in Bordesley WAR, WOR, Bordley YOW; Cowley DRB(2); Pilley HMP, YOW; Stapeley CHE, Stapely HMP; Staveley DRB, LNC, WML, YOW; Tiley DOR, Tyley GLO; Yardley ESX, NTP(2), WOR, Yarley SOM. Stockleigh DEV(2), DRH, STF perhaps belongs in this category.

There are fairly numerous references to domestic creatures in compound names with *lēah*, and these are considered to indicate the meaning 'pasture'. Recurrent compounds of this type in Ekwall 1960 are Callaly NTB, Calveley CHE, Calverley YOW, Chawleigh DEV (all referring to calves, Cowley GLO refers to cows); Horsley DRB, GLO, NTB, STF, SUR and Hursley HMP, with which may be linked Stoodleigh DEV and Studley OXF, WAR, WLT, YOW; Lambley NTB, NTT and Lamesley DRH, with which may be linked 6 instances of Shipley. Some other domestic animals appear once with *lēah* in major names, as in Bulley GLO, Oxley STF, Gateley NFK, Stirchley SHR.

There are some recurrent references to crops which, like those to domestic animals listed above, must indicate a developed stage of settlement in the *lēah*. Here belong Barley LNC and Barlow DRB; Lindley YOW(2), Linley SHR(2) and Flaxley GLO, YOW; and 7 instances of Wheatley. The compound with 'butter' found in Bitterley SHR, Butterleigh DEV, Butterley DRB, HRE is a reference to rich pasture.

If the whole corpus were examined, instead of the fraction being studied here, it might be found that references to the appearance of the *lēah* or to things found in it were more frequent than references to its topographical setting. It may be that a *lēah*, unlike a 'grove', was too big to be characterized by an adjacent feature. The commonest of the topographical features which do occur with *lēah* in major names is **strǣt**, found in Streatlam DRH, Streatley BDF, BRK, Streetley ESX, Streetly CAM, WAR and Strelley NTT. Next commonest is **mōr**, in Moreleigh DEV and 4 instances of Morley. Selly Oak WOR and Shelley ESX, SFK, YOW contain **scelf**. Dickley ESX and Ditchley OXF were near, or were characterized by, ditches, and Hurley BRK, WAR were in corners. One common compound which perhaps belongs here is that with **burh** 'fort'. Bearley WAR, Birley HRE, Burghley NTP and 7 instances of Burley contain *burh*, and Bierley YOW, Birley DRB(3) probably contain the gen. *byrh*. If the reference be to ancient earthworks, these are names in which the *lēah* is characterized by a topographical feature.

There are some **-inga-** compounds—such as Billingley YOW, Chiddingly and Hellingly SSX, Hastingley KNT, Knottingley YOW, Oddingley WOR—but references to groups of people are rare with *lēah*. Chorley CHE(2), LNC, STF were 'of the *ceorls*', and Kingsley CHE, HMP, STF were royal property. Other classes of owner occur occasionally, as in Childerley CAM and Knightley STF. Burwardsley CHE and Broseley SHR may have belonged to an official called *burhweard*. Structures are rarely mentioned, Ansley WAR ('hermitage wood') being the sort of exception which proves the rule. Warleigh SOM and Warley ESX contain *wer* 'weir'.

The only remaining way of characterizing a *lēah* which is at all common in major place-names is to refer to its comparative position. Direction occurs in Astley (5 instances), Norley CHE, Nordley SHR(2), Soudley and Sudeley GLO, and Westley CAM, SFK. Marley DEV, DRH and Mearley LNC were on boundaries. Olney and Onley NTP were isolated. The commonest compound of this type, however, is with *hēah* 'high', found in the nom. in

Healaugh YON, YOW, Healey LNC(3), NTB(3), YON, YOW, Heeley YOW, and in the dat. in Handley CHE, DOR DRB(2), NTP, Hanley STF, WOR(2), Henley OXF, SFK, SOM(2), SUR, WAR. These are the examples included in Ekwall 1960; additional ones could doubtless be found. The likeliest meaning is perhaps 'high wood', and the frequency of the settlement-name may be due to the visual impact made by such a feature. The sites vary from those where the settlement is overlooked by very high hills (as in Healaugh W. of Reeth YOW) to those where the elevation is a modest one in very low ground (as in Handley N.E. of Farndon CHE). In a few instances, particularly Hanley Castle and Hanley Swan WOR, it is necessary to assume that the wood was at some distance from the modern settlements.

lundr ON 'small wood'. Smith 1956 stresses the Scandinavian use for a sacred grove, but although a 12th-century English writer apparently shows awareness of this in rendering the second element of Plumbland CMB as *nemus paci donatum*, there is little reason to suspect anything more than a simple topographical meaning for the term in place-names in England.

lundr is not common anywhere. It is best represented in Yorkshire, WML, NTT, NTP and DRB. The EPNS survey of NTT (p. 287) states that it was a common noun in that county till the late 12th century; and some names, especially late-recorded simplex ones, may have been formed with it after the Norman Conquest. It is rather rare in CHE and LNC, and rare or absent in CMB, CAM, ESX and WAR. The above named counties are those which had Norse settlements and for which detailed place-name surveys are available. The incidence is not precisely known for some other Danelaw counties, but it is unlikely that *lundr* is common in any of them. When it occurs in minor names *lundr* frequently refers to woods which are still extant. It occurs in two wapentake names—Aveland LIN and Framland LEI—and in *Naveslund* Hundred in NTP. This may indicate that woods designated *lundr* were particularly likely to stand on boundaries.

As a simplex name *lundr* becomes Lound (LIN, NTT, SFK), Lund (LNC, YOE, YON, YOW) and Lunt (LNC). The DRB parish of Heath was *Lunt* in DB, *Lowne alias Heeth* in 1535. As a first element *lundr* occurs in London-thorpe LIN and Lumby YOW.

As a final element *lundr* usually becomes –land. Craiselound and Eastlound LIN are exceptions, perhaps because they were simplex names at the time of DB. *lundr* is combined with a personal name in Boyland NFK, Natland WML, Snelland LIN, Swanland YOE and Toseland HNT, and in the three meeting-place names listed above. Toseland gave name to a hundred, as well as a settlement. *lundr* is said in several EPNS surveys to occur relatively often with a personal name in ME field-names, and this characteristic might indicate that it was used of plantations. Types of tree are referred to in Hasland DRB, Plumbland CMB, and possibly Shrubland SFK (which is not a certain instance of *lundr*). In Birklands NTT, *Birkelund* (1250) has been substituted for (or perhaps coexisted with) the synonymous English *Birchwude* (1188). Timberland LIN is 'timber grove'. References to topography are rare, but Morland WML is 'moor grove' and Swithland LEI 'burnt-clearing grove'. Kirkland LNC is 'church grove', and in Upsland YON *lundr* has been added to a place-name meaning 'higher hall'. The only reference noted in major names to living creatures is in Rockland NFK(2) and Ruckland LIN, probably the sites of rookeries. Rowland DRB probably contains ON *rá* 'boundary', and Shirland DRB OE *scīr* 'bright'.

rodu OE 'clearing'. This word has survived in the form *royd* in the dialect of LNC and YOW. In OE charter boundaries it is used of a linear clearing. Occurrences in minor names, field-names and charter boundaries are widespread in the county, showing that the word was generally available for use in place-name formation; but it is only common in LNC and YOW. It has not been noted at all in CMB or WML.

As a simplex name *rodu* has become Road SOM, Roade NTP, Rodd HRE, Rode CHE, and (in the dat. pl.) Roddam NTB. It is the final element of the major names Blackrod, Heyrod, Heyroyd, Huntroyde and Ormerod LNC, Mytholmroyd YOW.

sceaga (earlier **scaga**) OE 'small wood'. Literary references and occurrences in charter boundaries imply that a *sceaga* was of limited extent, and the use of some corresponding words in other Germanic languages suggest that it was likely to be projecting. In modern English, from the 16th to 19th centuries, *shaw* is recorded in the sense 'strip of wood or underwood forming the border of a field'. The word is related to ON **skógr**

Occasional names containing *sceaga* occur sufficiently widely in England to show that the term was generally available in the place-name-forming vocabulary; but the overall distribution is strikingly uneven. It is only common in a group of contiguous counties comprising WML, YOW, DRB, CHE and LNC, and detailed plotting of examples in those counties would probably reveal smaller areas within which the element was used fairly freely in all categories of place-names. In DRB there is a marked concentration in High Peak Hundred, and the word is well represented in the adjacent parts of YOW. It is possible that the frequency is due to regional methods of exploiting surviving woodland. The distribution in YOW was studied by A H Smith, and his conclusion (EPNS survey 7, p. 281) was that 'it seems very often to be peripheral to the main woodland areas'.

Outside the counties listed above *sceaga* is a rare place-name element. To the north of them it is a little more frequent in NTB and DRH than in CMB, where the EPNS survey only noted 2–3 minor names. To the south and east, *sceaga* occurs occasionally in SHR and STF, has only been noted in one minor name and a few field-names in NTT, is not noted at all in YON, and is only found in one late-recorded minor name in YOE. For LEI, LIN, NFK and

SFK there are as yet no detailed surveys, but the only major name containing *sceaga* in these counties appears to be Strumpshaw NFK. The word is rare in WOR, and probably in HRE, and also in NTP and WAR, though the last county has one major name. In all other counties *sceaga* is absent or rare, though better represented in GLO and WLT, and perhaps HMP, than in most.

The simplex name Shaw has become that of a major settlement in BRK, LNC, WLT, and another instance occurs in DEV in the form Shaugh. As a first element *sceaga* occurs in Shawbury SHR and Shawdon NTB. Analysis of first elements in settlement-names with *sceaga* as second element shows the largest category to consist of references to wild creatures. Here belong Bagshaw DRB, Crawshaw Booth LNC, Evershaw BUC, Fulshaw CHE, Hogshaw BUC, Ickornshaw YOW, Ottershaw SUR, and probably Buckshaw DOR and Huntshaw DEV. Fulshaw CHE has a doublet in the minor name Foulshaw in Witherslack WML, and Ickornshaw YOW is repeated in Icornshaw in Lupton WML. The first element refers to a species of tree in Appleshaw HMP, Birkenshaw YOW, Bramshaw HMP, Oakenshaw YOW, Wythenshawe CHE and probably Wishaw WAR. A descriptive term is used as qualifier in Balshaw LNC, Blackshaw YOW, Bradshaw DRB, LNC, YOW, Sansaw SHR and probably Strumpshaw NFK. The compound with 'broad' is repeated in minor names, and this strengthens the impression that a shaw was usually long and narrow. Personal names are only noted in Audenshaw LNC, Barnshaw CHE and Ellishaw NTB; in the first two the personal name is dithematic, which strengthens the impression that settlement-names containing *sceaga* are likely to belong to the late OE period. Bickershaw LNC is 'beekeepers' wood' and Frenchay GLO is 'wood by the R. Frome'.

sceaga can become Shay or Shave in minor names.

skógr ON 'wood', cognate with OE **scaga**. The word survived into ME; NED gives a few quotations under *scogh*, the latest of which is dated c. 1420. This suggests that some minor names, particularly the simplex forms Scaw(s), Sceugh, Schoose which occur in CMB, need not have been coined by ON speakers; but early-recorded settlement-names containing *skógr* are likely to be of ON origin, especially if they contain another ON word. Ekwall 1960 includes Aiskew YON, Briscoe CMB, YON, Burscough LNC, Haddiscoe NFK, Litherskew YON, Loscoe DRB, YOW, Myerscough LNC, Swinscoe STF and Thurnscoe YOW, in which *skógr* is the second element, and Scorbrough YOE, Skewsby YON, in which is used as a qualifier. Another name in the last category is Skewkirk Hall in Tockwith YOW, and among well-recorded minor names in the first category may be noted Haresceugh CMB.

In Aiskew YON, Briscoe CMB, YON and Thurnscoe YOW the first element is a tree-name, and other such compounds occur as minor names, as Hessleskew in Sancton YOE, Aldersceugh in Blennerhasset CMB and several instances of Askew in WML. It is possible that (like OE **holt**) *skógr* was considered especially appropriate to a single-species wood.

The compound found in Loscoe DRB and YOW is repeated as a minor name in Loscoe Fm in Repton DRB. There is also Loskay House in Kirkby Moorside YON (ME *Loftisco*) which is from ON *loft i skógi* 'lofthouse in a wood'. Fellows Jensen 1978 (p. 171) prefers Professor Cameron's interpretation (EPNS survey DRB, p. 434) 'wood with a lofthouse' to that in Ekwall 1960 'wood on a hill'. It is possible that *loft-skógr* denoted a wood with a building of an official character, rather as OE *wudu-hall* and *wudu-hūs* may refer to buildings with a special function in relation to woodland management.

skógr is best represented in minor names in LNC, CMB, YOW and WML. Outside these counties it is rare in all categories of names.

thveit ON 'clearing, meadow, paddock'. This element belongs to a group of words which share the general sense of cutting or being cut. Smith 1956 takes the view that the root meaning of *thveit* was 'something cut down' and that there was a sense-development from 'a felled tree' to 'a clearing'. In English place-names the translation 'clearing' is usually acceptable, but allowance must be made for the later senses of 'enclosed pasture' and 'meadow'. This later development resembles that of OE **lēah**, but for *thveit* there is no reason to suppose an earlier meaning 'wood'. The element occurs at least occasionally in most areas where there was substantial Norse settlement, but it is only frequent in the north west, particularly in CMB. It is also common in the part of S.W. Scotland adjacent to CMB, and examples there are mapped in Nicolaisen 1976 (p. 106). Since the word is, to quote Professor Nicolaisen, 'associated with the secondary development of less promising ground, usually on a higher level', allowance should be made for its being sometimes a borrowed appellative used by ME speakers rather than a term used in every instance by ON speakers. Compounds with ON first elements are, however, likely to be names coined by ON speakers for clearings made in the earlier stages of Norse settlement, and a high proportion of the major names discussed below are of this nature.

A full study of *thveit* would have to take account of minor names and field-names. The element does, however, occur in more than 60 names of places of sufficient importance to appear in Ekwall 1960, and this is a noteworthy total in view of its obvious connection with expansion of settlement during and after the Viking age.

Ekwall 1960 lists only 3 instances (NFK(2), SFK) of the simplex name Thwaite, but more occur in minor names. Analysis of the first elements of compound names in Ekwall 1960 yields the following results.

One of the two largest categories of first elements used with *thveit* consists of references to buildings or man-made structures, and here there is a direct contrast with OE **lēah**. The first elements are ON *búr* 'storehouse' in Bouthwaite YOW, *hús* in Husthwaite YON, *kirkja* in Curthwaite CMB, *loft* 'two-storey house' in Lowthwaite (in Uldale) CMB, *sætr* 'shieling' in Satterthwaite LNC. Particularly interesting are Nibthwaite LNC 'new-booth clearing' and

Waberthwaite CMB 'hunting-booth clearing'. There are a number of names with ON *kros* 'crucifix': Crosthwaite CMB, WML, YON, Crostwight and Crostwick NFK.

The other fairly large category of first elements consists of descriptive terms, and here there is a resemblance to the findings for lēah. In this class belong Braithwaite CMB(3), YON, Graythwaite LNC, Langthwaite LNC, YON, YOW, Longthwaite near Wigton CMB, Micklethwaite YOW, Southwaite (in Hesket in the Forest) CMB, Stainfield (earlier *Steynthweyt*) near Haconby LIN and Swinithwaite YON. Southwaite contains an OE word (*thōh* 'clay'), but all the other descriptive terms are certainly or probably ON.

There are 7 compounds with personal names: Allithwaite LNC, Austhwaite CMB, Bassenthwaite CMB, Finsthwaite LNC, Gunthwaite YOW, Hampsthwaite YOW and Yockenthwaite YOW. *Bastun* in Bassenthwaite is Anglo-French, *Eoghan* in Yockenthwaite is Old Irish, otherwise all the personal names are ON. That in Gunthwaite is feminine.

Other categories are small. Earlier place-names are found in Guestwick NFK, Radmanthwaite NTT, Subberthwaite LNC, Tilberthwaite LNC. Topographical features occur in Huthwaite NTT, YOW and Seathwaite LNC. Trees, tree-products or other types of vegetation occur in Applethwaite CMB, WML, Brackenthwaite CMB, Branthwaite CMB, Roundthwaite WML and Thornthwaite CMB, WML, YOW. Crops are mentioned in Haverthwaite LNC, Heathwaite LNC, YON, Linethwaite CMB and Linthwaite YOW, but the only reference noted to domestic animals is that in Calthwaite CMB. No references have been noted to wild creatures. Eastwood NTT is 'east' (perhaps E. of the R. Erewash). Armathwaite CMB had a hermit. The first element of Hunderthwaite YON is disputed. Slaithwaite YOW is probably 'clearing where timber was felled'.

Further examples of compounds in all the above categories can be found in the account of *thveit* in Smith 1956, where many minor names are listed.

trēow OE 'tree, post, beam'. As a first element *trēow* occurs in Treborough SOM, Treeton YOW, Trewick NTB, Trobridge DEV and Trowbridge WLT. In the last four of these the reference may be to the use of posts or beams in the building construction. Treyford SSX is defined in Ekwall 1960 as 'ford marked by a tree or provided with a tree-trunk to assist in crossing'. Trimdon DRH is from OE *trēo-mǣl-dūn*, which is thought to mean 'hill with a crucifix tree'. Names of this type are heavily outnumbered by compounds in which *trēow* is the second element, and it is this usage which renders the word of special interest.

It might be expected that the use of *trēow* as a second element would be mainly evidenced in field and minor names, but this is not the case. The word does occur in some minor settlement-names, but the bulk of the material falls into the two categories of major place-names, and names of hundreds and wapentakes.

Major settlement-names which have *trēow* as second element are: Aintree LNC, Allestree DRB, Appletree NTP, Austrey WAR, Aymestrey HRE, Bartestree HRE, Bishopstrow WLT, Braintree ESX, Cholstrey HRE, Collingtree NTP, Coventry WAR, Daventry NTP, Earnstrey SHR, Elmestree GLO (an estate in AD 962), Elstree HRT, Faintree SHR, *Fickenappletree* WOR, Goostrey CHE, Hallatrow SOM, Harptree SOM, Heavitree DEV, Hussingtree WOR, Langtree DEV, LNC, Manningtree ESX, Oswestry SHR, Ottery DEV, Pettistree SFK, Plumtree NTT, Plymtree DEV, Rattery DEV, Tiptree ESX, Wanstrow SOM, Warter YOE, Wavertree LNC, Willestrew DEV. In addition to these, Ayntree N.W. of Ludlow SHR, Cocktree in S. Tawton DEV and Vinnetrow in N. Mundham SSX are well-recorded minor names which may conveniently be included in the discussion.

Hundred and wapentake names with *trēow* as a second element are: *Alnodestreu* SHR, Becontree ESX, Brentry GLO, Brimstree SHR, *Condetre* SHR, Culliford Tree DOR, Doddingtree WOR, Edwinstree HRT, Gartree LEI, LIN, *Ghidenetroi* SSX, Gostrow SSX, Greytree HRE, *Helmestrei* KNT, *Hezetre* HRE, Holmstrow SSX, Langtree OXF, Longtree GLO, Pastrow HMP, Thedwestry SFK, Toltingtrough KNT, *Wandelmestrei* SSX, *Warmundestrou* CHE, Webtree HRE, *Wimundestreu* HRE, *Winburgetrowe* WOR, Winstree ESX, Whittery SHR, Wixamtree BDF, *Yarlestree* YON. It is assumed that in all these instances the tree was the marker for the assembly place of the wapentake or hundred.

This is a considerable body of material, with 38 names in the first list, and 30 in the second. When these 68 names are analysed to ascertain the nature of the first elements, a remarkably clear pattern emerges. The lists may be conflated for this purpose, as the two groups show the same predominant characteristics. Most of the first elements fall into two categories, the larger of which consists of personal names in the genitive, the other of words which describe the nature, appearance or function of the tree. Ascription of some names to the first category is complicated by problems which are discussed in Gelling 1978 (Chapter 7), and some names are included in the following list which are not certain to be derived from personal names.

Names which certainly or probably have as first element a personal name in the genitive are:

Allestree DRB (*Adelardestreu* DB, 'Æthelheard's tree')
Alnodestreu Hundred SHR ('Ælfnōth's tree')
Austrey WAR (*Aldulfestreo* 1002, 'Ealdwulf's tree')
Aymestrey HRE (*Elmodestreu* DB, *Ailmondestre* 1291, 'Æthelmund's tree')
Bartestree HRE (*Bertoldestreu* DB, 'Beorhtwald's tree')
Becontree Hundred ESX (*Beuentreu* DB, *Begetreowa*, *Begintre*, *Beghentro* 12th
    cent., 'Beohha's tree', with later influence from the word *beacon*)
Bishopstrow WLT (*biscop* 'bishop' was used as a personal name in OE)
Braintree ESX (*Branchetreu* DB, 'Branca's tree')

Brentry Hundred GLO (*Bernintreu* DB, probably 'Beorna's tree')

Brimstree Hundred SHR (*Brimestre* 1203, 'Brēme's tree')

Cholstrey HRE (*Cerlestreu* DB, 'Ceorl's tree')

Cocktree DEV (*Caketreu* 1248, *Kaketrewe* 1285, possibly 'Cæfca's tree')

Collingtree NTP (*Colentreu* DB, 'Cola's tree')

Condetre Hundred SHR (the name survived till 1317, as *Conditre*, in Walton near Stottesdon, 'Cunda's tree')

Coventry WAR (*Cofentreo*, *Cofantreo* c. 1060, ? 'Cōfa's tree', see below)

Culliford Tree Hundred DOR (*Cuferdestroue* c. 1086, *Culverdestre* 1228, probably 'Cylferth's tree', but the personal name is not on independent record)

Daventry NTP (*Daventrei* DB, ? 'Dafa's tree', see below)

Doddingtree Hundred WOR (*duddantreo* 11th cent., 'Dudda's tree')

Earnstrey SHR (*Ernestreu* 1172, 'Earn's tree')

Edwinstree Hundred HRT (*Edwinestreu* DB, 'Ēadwine's tree')

Elmestree GLO (*Elmondestreo* 1201, 'Æthelmund's tree')

Elstree HRT (*Tithulfes treow*, a. 1066, 'Tīdwulf's tree', see below)

Heavitree DEV (*Hefatriwe* c. 1130, probably 'Hefa's tree')

Helmestrei Hundred KNT ('Helm's tree')

Hussingtree WOR (*Husantreo* 972, 'Husa's tree')

Oswestry SHR (*Croesoswald* 1254, *Oswaldestre* 1272, 'Ōswald's tree' or 'St Oswald's cross', see below)

Ottery DEV (*Odetreu* DB, 'Oda's tree')

Pastrow Hundred HMP (*Pachetrewe* 1236, *Pachestrowe* 1280, 'Pæcci's tree')

Pettistree SFK (*Petrestre* 1253, 1254, 'Peohtrēd's tree')

Thedwestry Hundred SFK (*Theod Wardes Treo* DB, 'Thēodweard's tree')

Tiptree ESX (*Typpetre* c. 1225, possibly 'Tippa's tree')

Wandelmestrei Hundred SSX (probably 'Wændelhelm's tree')

Wanstrow SOM (*Wandestreow* DB, *Wandelestr'* 1225, 'Wændel's tree')

Warmundestrou Hundred CHE ('Wǣrmund's tree')

Webtree Hundred HRE (*Webetrie* 1159, 'Webba's tree')

Whittery Hundred SHR (*Witentreu* DB, *Wittintre* 1250, probably 'Hwīta's tree')

Willestrew DEV (*Wilavestreu* DB, 'Wīglāf's tree')

Wimundestreu Hundred HRE ('Wīgmund's tree')

Wimburntree Hundred WOR (*Winburgetrowe* DB, 'Wynburh's tree', see below)

Winstree Hundred ESX (*Wensistreu* DB, 'Wynsige's tree')

Wixamtree Hundred BDF (*Wichestanestou* DB, *Wykestanestre* 1247, 'Wihtstān's tree')

Yarlestree Wapentake YON ('Eorl's tree')

The material has been set out in this way, with a sample of early spellings, because it is felt to be important to establish the fact that many of the items indisputably contain OE personal names. Twenty-one settlements are listed, and twenty meeting-places. Bishopstrow, Brentry, Cholstrey, Earnstrey,

Whittery, *Yarlestree* could be considered to contain nouns—'bishop', 'warrior' (OE *beorn*), 'churl', 'eagle' (OE *earn*), 'white' and 'earl'; Oswestry could be considered to stand outside the series because of its traditional association with the death of St Oswald (see below); and some of the postulated personal names—e.g. *Cōfa*, *Dafa*, *Tippa*—are not evidenced independently of place-names. But this still leaves at least 30 place-names, nearly half of the total number of settlement-names and meeting-place names ending in *trēow*, for which derivation from a personal name is virtually unavoidable. Sixteen of the personal names are dithematic—e.g. *Æthelheard*, *Ealdwulf*, *Æthelmund*—and one—*Wynburh*—is feminine. Since some of the places in the list, such as Braintree, Coventry, Daventry, Elstree, Oswestry, have become major centres of population, it is of interest to consider the identity of the people from whom these trees were named. But first it is desirable to complete the analysis of first elements.

The second large category of names ending in *–trēow* has as first element a word which describes the tree. All the following names probably belong in this class:

Appletree NTP ('apple-tree')

Faintree SHR ('variegated tree')

Fickenappletree WOR (a lost estate in Hampton Lovett, 'thick apple-tree')

Gartree Wapentakes LEI, LIN (the most recent discussion, Fellows Jensen 1978 (p. 154), accepts derivation from ON *geiri* 'gore' used of a mark on a tree, perhaps made by stripping bark. The LIN name is wholly ON, the LEI name is a hybrid with OE *trēow*)

Goostrey CHE, Gostrow Hundred SSX ('gorse-tree', but OE *gorst* meant 'juniper' as well as 'gorse')

Greytree Hundred HRE (perhaps 'grey tree', but *Græga* could be a personal name)

Hallatrow SOM ('holy tree'). This compound occurs again as the first part of the minor name Hallytreeholme in Leven YOE

Hezetre Hundred HRE (probably 'hazel-tree')

Langtree DEV, LNC, Langtree Hundred OXF, Longtree Hundred GLO ('tall tree')

Plumtree NTT, Plymtree DEV ('plum-tree')

Rattery DEV ('red tree')

Toltingtrough Hundred KNT (possibly 'tottering tree')

Warter YOE ('gallows-tree')

Wavertree LNC ('wavering tree')

There are two names in which the first element is a numeral: these are Aintree LNC, which means 'solitary tree' and may be an ON coinage, and Twantry NTP, a late-recorded minor name which probably means 'at the two trees'. Manningtree ESX could mean 'many trees', or it could belong in the first category and mean 'Manna's tree'.

The following names are more difficult to classify:

Ayntree SHR (the spellings, the earliest of which are *Avenitre* 1255, *Avenetre* 1271, suggest the river-name Avon as first element. This would be an atypical compound, but is topographically possible, as the hill on which the hamlet stands overlooks an unnamed tributary of the R. Onny)

Ghidenetroi Hundred SSX (it has been suggested that this denotes a sacred tree, with a first element related to the word *god*)

Harptree SOM (first element possibly the word *harp*, but this is sometimes a shortened form of *herepæth* 'main road', and the parish of W. Harptree is bounded by a Roman road)

Holmstrow Hundred SSX (*Homestreu* DB, *Holmestre* 1193; it has been suggested that the first element is either an OE personal name *Holm*, cognate with the recorded ON *Hólmr*, or an unrecorded OE word meaning 'hill')

Vinnetrow SSX (this is *Feningetrowe* 12th cent., *Fenehetre*, *Fenegetrewe* 13th cent., *Feneghetrowe* 1327; perhaps 'marshy tree')

It emerges from this analysis that names in *-trēow* seldom have as first element words referring to the topography of their surroundings. The likeliest exceptions are Ayntree SHR and Harptree SOM, but in general a tree which forms the generic of a compound place-name is not defined by its situation. It is much more likely to be associated with a particular individual or distinguished by a special physical characteristic. Names meaning 'plum-tree', 'apple-tree' and 'hazel-tree' have been included in the last category on the assumption that they mean more than the name of a species like 'oak' or 'elm' used as a simplex name.

The limited range of first elements in the whole group is important when a decision has to be made about a particular example. Coventry WAR has been the subject of much speculation. One of the more sensible conjectures which have been advanced is derivation from OE *cofa*, modern 'cove'. This is recorded in literary use with the meanings 'inner chamber, den, cave'. In place-names it appears to be used of a slight valley (e.g. in Discove SOM) and of a wide place in an estuary (e.g. in Runcorn CHE, earlier *Rumcofa* 'wide bay'). In Coven STF which is from the dat. pl. it may refer to a now obscured feature of the R. Penk; it can hardly mean 'valleys' as suggested in Ekwall 1960. Coventry lies in a shallow basin and is beside the R. Sherbourne, which might well have formed pools, so the name might be considered to contain the dat. or gen. of the noun *cofa* referring to one of these features. The main objection is the extreme rarity of comparable compounds with *trēow*. For Daventry NTP Ekwall 1960 suggests a river-name identical with Dane CHE as an alternative to an unrecorded personal name *Dafa*; this would render the name comparable to Ayntree SHR, but in view of the overwhelming bias of the material, personal names, even if only conjectured to suit place-names, seem a safer assumption for Coventry and Daventry. There is an Old High German cognate for a personal name *Dafa*, and *Cōfa* is tentatively related in Ekwall 1960 (p. 115) to the recorded OE *Coifi*.

The nature of the whole corpus of place-names in –*trēow* should be remembered also when Oswestry SHR is considered. Here discussion is dominated by the ancient identification of Oswestry with *Maserfelth*, the name given by Bede for the site of the battle of AD 641 in which the Christian King Oswald of Northumbria was killed by the heathen King Penda of Mercia. This is discussed in Gelling 1970. The Welsh name of Oswestry, *Croesoswald*, is on record in 1254, earlier than the English name, which is first recorded in 1272. The Welsh name establishes that the popular interpretation as 'cross of St Oswald' was current in the mid 13th century; but it is likely that both the tradition and the church dedication to St Oswald arose from an English place-name meaning 'Oswald's tree' which was of the same type as all the others listed above. The type is well represented in the Welsh Marches.

Whatever opinion may be held about such examples as Coventry, Daventry and Oswestry, there is no doubt that names meaning 'x's tree' are fairly common, and are sometimes the names of important settlements. The next problem to be considered is the nature of the connection between the person and the tree, and for this topic it is necessary to bring into the discussion another class of names in which compounds with –*trēow* feature conspicuously. Such compounds are relatively common in the boundary-marks of the OE surveys attached to Anglo-Saxon charters. There is as yet no comprehensive analysis of these boundary surveys, but some sections of the material have been studied recently, and these will serve to demonstrate the use of trees as boundary-marks and the types of first element by which *trēow* is qualified in this context. The surviving OE surveys for BRK were analysed in EPNS survey 3. They contain 10 boundary-marks with names in –*trēow*, and seven of these certainly have personal names as first element, including one which is feminine. One is unexplained, another is the enigmatic *frigedæges treow* 'Friday's tree', and the remaining pair are a 'communal' tree (*gemænan treowe*) and another *langan treowe* identical with Langtree/Longtree discussed above. Hooke 1980 analyses OE boundaries for GLO, WAR and WOR and says (p. 171): '*Trēow* is usually confined to specimens associated with particular individuals and of 26 instances noted in pre-Conquest place-names and charters only one is not of this type—the "long tree" which gave its name to Longtree Hundred in Gloucestershire.'

The occurrence in boundary surveys of names in –*trēow* which are closely comparable to the settlement-names and hundred-names examined above may fairly be seen as providing the clue to the significance of most examples. Stenton 1924 made this point when he said (p. 40): 'There are many parallels among Old English boundary names to the Derbyshire village name Allestree, "Æthelheard's tree", and the Warwickshire village name Austrey, "Ealdwulf's tree".' But it was not possible in 1924 to appreciate the predominance of this type of compound in the whole corpus, and the comparison between settlement-names, hundred-names and boundary-marks needs stressing in order to bring it to the attention of modern students of settlement history.

The typical hundred or wapentake meeting-place was situated on a boundary between two or more Anglo-Saxon estates, so it is natural that objects which were suitable for boundary-marks should sometimes be the markers for assembly places. It has been suggested (Anderson 1934, 1939) that the personal names in the 'x's tree' type of hundred-name are those of prominent members of the community who presided over the assemblies; but it seems to me more probable that these personal names are to be explained in the same way as those in the charter boundary-marks. These last are certainly the names of estate owners on the boundary of whose land the tree stood. There are comparable boundary-marks, such as the *cincges thornas* ('king's thorns') of Kingston Lisle BRK, in which titles are used instead of personal names. Reasons were given in the BRK EPNS survey (p.828) for believing that in charter boundaries such compounds as *ælfheages gemære*, *ælfsiges mor*, *ælfthrythe dic*, *cyneeahes treow* are shorthand for 'boundary of the estate now or recently in the possession of a thegn called Ælfhēah', 'ditch on the boundary of the lady Ælfthrȳth's estate' etc.; and I consider that the frequent occurrence of the *cyneeahes treow* type of name as that of hundred and wapentake meeting-places arises from the holding of such meetings on boundaries, where these names were well represented, rather than from the formation of special names referring to the leading men of the hundred concerned.

The use of 'x's tree' names in hundred meeting-places and charter boundaries can be explained as aspects of the same phenomenon. The problem remains of how so many names of this type came to be applied to major settlements. The earliest reference to Elstree HRT is a crucial piece of evidence here.

The name which developed into Elstree occurs in a set of OE boundaries for the manor of Aldenham. This estate was bounded by the R. Colne on the west side and partly by Watling Street on the east, and one of the boundary points between these two lines, in the southern half of the area, is *Tithulfes treow*, which can be shown with the help of later spellings to have developed into Elstree. The boundary survey has not been worked out in detail and the exact position of the tree has not been established, but it is noteworthy that the village of Elstree is divided by a crossroads into four parts which lay in the parishes of Aldenham and Elstree HRT and Stanmore and Edgware MDX. It may fairly be postulated that the settlement grew up at a relatively late date in this boundary position, and that at the time of the Aldenham survey one of the estates which abutted there was in the possession of a man named Tīdwulf. The parish of Elstree is small and irregularly shaped.

It must be left to local historians to decide whether the hypothesis of late origin on a boundary between older estates suits some of the settlements with names meaning 'x's tree' which are listed above. Shape and size of parish is sometimes a valuable clue. Bartestree HRE is a small parish lying between the larger units of Lugwardine and Weston Baggard, and Bishopstrow WLT is similarly placed between the larger parishes of Warminster and Norton Bavant. These could well represent an infill of settlement.

Parishes with names meaning 'x's tree' are not all small, irregularly shaped units, however, and the hypothesis of late origin on the boundary between older estates does not suit such places as Coventry and Oswestry, or Aymestrey HRE, which is a large parish N.W. of Leominster. For such as these, it may be suggested that the estates contained a number of small settlements but had no nucleated centre until a relatively late stage of their history. A central settlement might have grown up on the boundary between township areas, and the trees of Coventry, Oswestry and Aymestrey might be internal boundary marks between the divisions of a large estate.

In some instances where the 'x's tree' settlement has not developed into a parish centre, the hamlet or village is still on a parish boundary. Notable examples are Ottery and Willestrew in DEV, which lie on the S. and N. boundaries of Lamerton parish. Cholstrey HRE is on the boundary between Leominster and Kingsland, and Cocktree DEV is near the boundary between N. and S. Tawton. The tiny hamlet of Ayntree SHR is also on a parish boundary.

The hypothesis that a tree named from a landowner was a boundary mark before it gave name to a settlement could be applied to names in the second main category of meaning: those which have as first element a word which describes the tree. The hypothesis is not so necessary for these, however, as a farm might reasonably be named from a nearby tree which was unusually tall or had some other outstanding physical characteristic.

This article is a convenient place for some notes on the specific types of tree which are mentioned in settlement-names. Commonest are **āc** 'oak', **æppel** 'apple', **æsc** 'ash', **alor** 'alder', **beorc** and **birce** 'birch', **elm** 'elm', **hæsel** 'hazel', **pirige** 'pear', **thorn** 'thorn', and **welig** and **wīthig**, which both mean 'willow'.

āc OE 'oak-tree' is a feminine noun, belonging to a declension which has a change of vowel in the dat. sing. and in the nom. and acc. pl. The nom. sg. is likely to give –oak or –ock in place-names, while the dat. sg. (*ǣc*) is likely to become –age. Each KNT means 'at the oak'. The dat.pl., *ācum*, has become Acomb NTB, YON, YOW, and Oaken STF.

āc is a common first element in various compounds, such as Oakford DEV, Oakmere CHE, Oxted SUR. The compound with **tūn** gives modern Acton (CHE(2), DEN, GLO, GTL, HRE, SHR(5), STF), Aighton (LNC) and Aughton (LNC, YOE, YOW). It is an open question what physical reality lies in this name; whether we should picture a farmstead sheltered by a single fine oak, a building made of oak, or an estate of which oak-trees are a conspicuous feature. Possibly the name has a technical sense, and these are settlements of component parts of large estates which were specially concerned with the production of building timber. It is not an early OE name, as examples are mainly in the west midlands, Acton GTL being an outlier; but Acton HRE is recorded in AD 727, so is one of the earliest **tūn** compounds. *āc* is fairly common with some second elements meaning 'wood' or 'clearing', and examples are cited under **hangra, holt, lēah**.

As a final element *āc* or *ǣc* is most often combined with a word describing the appearance or condition of the tree, as in Broadoak GLO etc., Fairoak SOM etc., Harrock LNC, Radnage BUC, Stevenage HRT, Whitnage DEV. Matlock DRB means 'council oak'. Cressage SHR means 'Christ's oak'. Personal names may occur occasionally, as probably in Tipnoak Hundred SSX, but they are not frequent.

Some place-names with modern spellings Noke, Noak, Rock, Roke are from the ME phrases *atten oke*, *atter oke*, which were misdivided to give *atte noke*, *atte roke*. Since *āc* is a feminine noun, *atter oke* is grammatically correct, *atten* for 'at the' being strictly appropriate to masculine and neuter nouns; but these grammatical niceties were not meticulously observed in Middle English.

The cognate ON *eik* occurs, e.g., in Eyke SFK, Aigburth LNC, Aiskew YON; and there is some interchange between the OE and ON words in areas of Norse settlement.

æsc OE 'ash-tree' is frequent as a simplex name, e.g. Ash and Nash in various counties, Ashe HMP, Esh DRH, Ashen ESX. It is common as a first element—e.g. in Ashbourne DRB, Ashtead SUR, Ashwell ESX—and especially common with words meaning 'wood', examples of which are cited under **holt, hyrst, lēah, wudu**. The corresponding ON word occurs with **skógr** and **vithr**.

The compound with **tūn** (Ashton CHE(2), GLO, LNC(4), NTP(2), SOM, WLT(3), Eshton YOW) is of similar frequency to that of **āc** with **tūn**, but for some reason *æsc* is also common with ON **bý**. Ashby occurs in the east midlands and East Anglia (LEI(3), LIN(6), NFK(2), NTP(5), SFK). The compound also occurs in the form Asby in CMB and WML, but it is not found in Yorkshire. Some Ashbys probably derive from the corresponding ON word *askr*, but some appear to be English/Norse hybrids. The limited distribution is curious, and as with Acton there may be a precise meaning which has not been ascertained. Perhaps Scandinavian colonists planted ash woods.

As a second element *æsc* sometimes occurs with a personal name, as in Avenage GLO (earlier *Abbenesse*), Butsash HMP, Franche WOR, Hamnish HRE, and some hundred-names, including Bromsash and Broxash HRE. Matlask NFK, like Matlock DRB, has *mæthel* 'speech' as first element.

æppel OE 'apple-tree' and **pirige** OE 'pear-tree' occur with **tūn** in Appelton BRK, CHE, CMB, KNT, LNC, NFK, YON(4), YOW and in Pirton HRT, WOR, Puriton SOM, Purton GLO, STF, WLT, Pyrton OXF. These names probably mean 'apple' and 'pear orchard', with **tūn** in its original sense 'enclosure'. Appleby occurs in LEI, LIN, WML, apparently with OE *æppel* rather than ON *epli*. Other compounds are noted under **ford, lēah, sceaga, thveit**. OE **appuldor** 'apple-tree' occurs in Apperley GLO, YOW, NTB, Appuldurcomb IOW, and as a simplex name in Appledore DEV, KNT. *pirige* occurs as a simplex name in Perry HNT, KNT, OXF, STF, and as a first element in Perivale GTL, Pirbright, Pyrford SUR, Purley GTL (but Pur–,

Pir– in place-names can have several other origins). *pirige* occasionally occurs as a final element, as in Buttsbury ESX (earlier *Botolvespirie*) and Hartpury GLO.

alor OE 'alder-tree' occurs by itself in Aller DEV, SOM, Arle, Awre GLO, and is fairly common as a first element: Alderford NFK, Allerford SOM(2), Alderholt DOR, Aldershot HMP, Alderton SHR, SFK, Allerton LNC, YOW(3), Ollerton CHE, NTT, Orleton HRE, WOR, Allerwash NTB, Alrewas STF, Aldridge STF. It occurs occasionally as a final element, as in Bicknoller SOM, Longner SHR and Longnor SHR, STF (the last two names meaning 'tall alder', or more likely, as suggested in Ekwall 1960, 'long alder-copse'). In DEV it is fairly frequent in minor names. The ON word *elri* occurs in High and Low Ellers YOW, Ellerton YOE, YON, YOW, Ellerbeck, Ellerburn YON.

beorc OE 'birch-tree' occurs as first element in some major names: Barkham BRK, SSX, Barkway HRT, Little Barford BDF, Bartley HMP, WOR, Berkeley GLO, Berkley SOM, Bartlow CAM, Berkesdon HRT. **birce**, another form of the word, occurs by itself in Much and Little Birch HRE, and as first element in Birchanger ESX, Bircher HRE, Birchover DRB, Birchill DRB, Birchills STF, Birchington KNT, Bircholt KNT. Some north-country names in Birk– contain either a Scandinavianized form of *birce* or the corresponding ON *birki*. Birkenhead CHE contains the adjective *bircen* 'overgrown with birch'.

elm OE 'elm-tree' occurs as a simplex name in Elm CAM, SOM, and is fairly common as a first element: Elmham NFK, SFK, Elmton DRB, Elmbridge WOR, Elmdon ESX, WAR, Almeley HRE, Elmley KNT, WOR, Elmore GLO, Elmsall YOW, Elmstead ESX, GTL, Elmswell SFK, Embleton DUR (earlier *Elmedene*). The adjective *elmen* occurs in Elmington NTP, as probably in the two Elmdons, and possibly some other names listed above.

hæsel OE 'hazel-tree' occurs once as a final element in Badsaddle NTP (earlier *Bateshasel*), and fairly frequently as a first element: Hasbury WOR, Haselbech NTP, Hazelbadge DRB, Haselbury DOR, SOM, Haseley IOW, OXF, WAR, Haselor WAR, Haselour STF, Hasfield GLO, Haslemere SUR, Hazelmere BUC, Haswell DUR, SOM, Hazlewood DRB, SFK, YOW. The adjective *hæslen* occurs in Haslingden LNC, Haslington CHE, Heslington YOE. ON *hesli* 'hazel grove' occurs as a simplex name in Hessle YOE, YOW and as a first element in Hessleskew YOE.

thorn OE 'hawthorn-tree' is one of the commonest tree-names in English place-names, and (like *trēow*) it is common in charter boundaries and in hundred-names. It occurs as a simplex name in Thearne YOE, Thorne CNW, KNT, SOM, YOW, and is very common both as a first and second element of compounds. As first element it occurs more than 30 times with **tūn**, mostly as Thornton, but also as Tarleton GLO and Thorington SFK. Ekwall 1960 lists one Thornton in BUC and one in DOR, otherwise the distribution is an east-midland and north-country one, with 3 in CHE, 2 in LNC, one in LEI, 4 in LIN, 2 in NTB and 16 in Yorkshire. Other compounds include Thorley HRT, IOW, Thornley DRH; Thornborough BUC, Thornbrough YON(2) (**beorg**); Thornbrough NTB, YOW, Thornbury GLO, HRE (**burh**); Thorncombe DOR; Thorndon SFK; Thornford DOR; Thorness IOW (*hege* 'hedge'); Thorney CAM, GTL, SFK, SOM, SSX (**ēg**); Thorney NTP, NTT (*haga* 'enclosure'); Thornham KNT, LNC, NFK, SFK (**hām**); Thornhill DOR, DRB, WLT, YOW; Thornthwaite, CMB, WML, YOW.

As a second element *thorn* is fairly frequently combined with a personal name or with a word which describes the tree, and here again there is a resemblance to the use of *trēow* in place-names. With personal names it occurs in Eythorne KNT (a fem. name), Kelstern LIN, Pitstone BUC, Rostherne CHE (ON), Scothern LIN, Sigglesthorne YOE (ON), Tedstone HRE, Wilstone HRT. Compounds with descriptive words include Langthorne YON, Pickthorn SHR and Rowthorn DRB. Other compounds are varied, e.g. Fretherne GLO (possibly 'sanctuary thorn'), Souldern OXF ('thorn tree in a gully'), Cropthorn WOR (possibly 'thorn by a hill called *Cropp*').

thyrne, another form of the word, occurs in Chawston BDF, Henthorn LNC, Lighthouse WAR, Stathern LEI; Thurnham LNC is the dat. pl. ON *thyrnir* is probably the source of some Danelaw names, e.g. Thirn YON, Thurne NFK, Thrimby WML, Thrintoft YON, Thurnscoe YOW.

wīthig OE is probably the commonest of the words for 'willow-tree'. It occurs as a simplex name in Widey (in Egg Buckland) DEV, and in the pl. in The Wergs (near Wolverhampton) STF. As a first element it occurs with **tūn** in Weeton LNC, YOE, YOW, Little Weighton (but not Market Weighton) YOE. Some settlement-names including Widdington ESX, Winton LNC, Withington CHE, HRE, LNC, SHR (but not Withington GLO), contain either the derivative noun *wīthegn* 'willow holt' or the adjective *wīthigen*. Other compounds are noted under **cumb, ford, halh, hamm, lēah.**

welig (W. Saxon), **wilig** (Anglian), another OE term for 'willow-tree', occurs as a simplex name in Wellow WLT, and in the dat. pl. in Willen BUC, Willian and Welwyn HRT. It is the first element of Weeley ESX, Willey CHE, HRE, SHR, WAR, Welford BRK, Wilbury HRT, Willicote GLO, Willitoft YOE. Combined with **tūn** it gives Willington BDF, DRB, Willoughton LIN, and probably some instances of Wilton (those in CMB, HRE, NFK, YOE, YON). The surprising frequency, especially in the east midlands, of Willoughby (LEI, LIN(4), NTT(3), WAR) and Wilby (NFK, NTP, SFK) has led to the suggestion that in some of them the final element is not ON **bý** but OE *bēag* 'ring', and the spellings for Wilby SFK lend some support to this.

salh (W. Saxon **sealh**) OE 'sallow-willow-tree' is used as a simplex name in Sale CHE, Zeal Monachorum DEV, and Zeals WLT; but some similar or identical modern names such as Seal KNT, Seale SUR, South Zeal DEV may be from OE *sele* 'hall'. Salhouse NFK may be 'sallows'. As a first element *salh* occurs with **tūn** in Saighton CHE, Salton YON, and with **wīc** in Salwick LNC. Other compounds are noted under **brycg, denu, ford, halh, hyrst, lēah, wudu.**

Tree-names which occur less frequently in major names include:

æspe OE 'aspen-tree' (several times with lēah, Aspall SFK)

bēce OE 'beech-tree' (Beech Hill BRK, Beech STF, Bitchfield NTB)

bōc OE 'beech-tree' (Bookham SUR, some instances of Boughton, Buckholt HMP, SSX, Buckhurst ESX)

box OE 'box-tree' (Box GLO, HRT, WLT, Boxford BRK, Boxford SFK, Boxgrove SSX, Boxley KNT, Boxted SFK, Boxwell GLO)

byxe OE 'box-tree', perhaps 'box-wood' (Bix OXF, Bexhill SSX, Bexley GTL)

ellern OE 'elder-tree' (Elstead SSX, SUR, Elstob DRH)

īw OE 'yew-tree' (Ewhurst HMP, SSX, SUR, Ewshott HMP, Iwode HMP, Uley GLO)

lind OE 'lime-tree' (Lyne SUR, Lindal, Lindale LNC, Lindley near Otley YOW, Lindridge KNT(2), WOR, Linwood HMP, LIN(2), Lyndhurst HMP, and 4 compounds with ric)

mapul OE 'maple-tree' (Maplebeck NTT, Maplestead ESX, Mappleton DRB, YOE)

mapuldor OE 'maple-tree' (Mappowder DOR, Mapledurham HMP, OXF, Mapledurwell HMP, Mapperley DRB, Mapperton DOR(2), Maperton SOM, Mappleborough WAR)

wice OE 'wych-elm-tree' (Horwich LNC, Wichenford WOR, Wishford WLT, Witchford and Witcham CAM)

vithr ON 'wood', cognate with OE **wudu**, is a rather rare element in ON names in England. Ekwall 1960 includes Askwith YOW, Blawith LNC, Hartwith YOW, Rookwith YOW and Witherslack WML. In Menwith YOW, Skirwith CMB and Yanwath WML, Ekwall considered that *vithr* was a replacement of OE **wudu**. This is certainly the case in Beckwith YOW, which is *Becwudu* c. 972; but Menwith, Skirwith and Yanwath may be OE/ON hybrids. In Bubwith YOE, Cottingwith YOE, Skipwith YOE and Tockwith YOW Ekwall considered that *vithr* had replaced OE **wīc**, and the evidence supports this for three of the names. Fellows Jensen 1972 (p. 106), however, takes Tockwith to be a wholly ON name meaning 'Tóki's wood'.

vithr does not occur in all counties where there were Scandinavian settlements. It has not been noted in DRB, NTP, NTT, for all of which there are detailed surveys. YON and YOW have some well-documented additional examples in minor names and field-names, and there are a few in YOE and WML, but it seems clear that *vithr* should not lightly be adduced to account for –*with* in modern minor names and field-names.

wald OE 'forest'. In Kentish and West Saxon *wald* became *weald*.

NED gives 'wilderness' as one of the senses of some cognates in other Germanic languages, and Holthausen 1934 makes a tentative association with the OE adjective *wilde* 'waste'. The ON cognate *vǫllr* means 'untilled land, plain'. EPNS GLO survey (4, p. 8) says 'the original meaning of OE **wald** . . . was "an area of woodland on high ground" '.

Smith 1956 gives an account of the senses in which *wald* is used in literary OE and ME. As with other topographical terms the literary contexts do not always indicate a precise translation, but 'forest' is clearly the predominant sense before the date (c. 1205) of the poem known as Layamon's *Brut*, in which *wald* seems to mean 'open downland'. The meanings 'downland' and 'forest' are both found after that date in literature. The sense 'wood' is probably found in the mid-11th-century document known as Gospatric's writ, which deals with land tenure in CMB. This mentions rights *on weald, on freyth, on heyninga*, which could be translated 'in forest, in heathland, in enclosed arable'; a *weald* at Caldbeck is one of the boundaries of the area defined. As regards modern usage, NED says: 'After the early 16th cent., the word ceased to be in general use and became restricted to localities in which it entered into the proper designation of characteristic tracts of country, probably at one time thickly wooded.' NED also catalogues instances later than 1600 of what it terms a 'vague poetical use' of *wold*.

Place-name specialists have explained the change of meaning from 'forest' to 'open high ground' by saying that the term was specially applied to high forest land, and that when the forest had been cleared the survival of the names of such areas as the Cotswolds and the Lincolnshire and Yorkshire Wolds caused the word to be newly interpreted in accordance with the late Saxon appearance of the landscape.

The original connotation of woodland was discussed by Professor Alan Everitt in an article about settlement patterns in Kent (Everitt 1977). This study postulates an early Anglo-Saxon landscape in east KNT in which ancient settlements in river valleys were bordered by woodland pasture in the downland. Professor Everitt believes that the forests of the Kentish Downs began to be cleared in the early part of the Anglo-Saxon period, and that *wald* in the names of some settlements in the newly-broken-in arable (such as Womenswold, Sibertswold, Southwold, Ringwould) refers to the woodland which covered the downs when the English first saw the country. The Weald of KNT and SSX is the portion of the great south-eastern forest which survived till a much later date. The meaning 'forest' is clearly found in some other region-names, in particular Bromswold in NTP/HNT/BDF, but Professor Everitt says he is uncertain whether the word is employed in this sense in the Yorkshire and Lincolnshire Wolds.

The occurrence in the east KNT names of the form *–wold* (as opposed to *–weald*, the modern spelling for the normal Kentish and West Saxon form) was noted by Ekwall, who comments (1960, pp. 491–2): 'Owing to influence from Standard English the form *wold* has often replaced original *weald* in later times, as in Ringwould, Sibertswold, Womenswold K.' An alternative explanation, however, is that these names were formed before *wald* became *weald* in the dialects of KNT and SSX, and that the original form was preserved in local speech. Some of them have OE spellings with *-weald*, but this may be because Kentish scribes felt that this was the correct form of the word. The later form, *weald*, becomes Weald or Wild in modern names.

In his prefatory remarks to the 1977 paper Professor Everitt asked 'Did other areas of wold, now largely woodless, such as the Cotswolds and Lincolnshire Wolds, also originate as the outlying wood-pasture of early river-peoples?' This question was taken up by Dr Della Hooke (1978) in a paper which assembled evidence from place-names and Anglo-Saxon charter boundaries for the presence of woodland in substantial quantities in the northern Cotswolds at a very early date in the post-Roman period. A third paper by Mr Terry Slater (1979) examined the evidence for the southern Cotswolds, which he describes as 'an area in which intensive settlement during the Roman period might be expected to have brought open downland landscapes into being well before the Saxon settlement.' Here *wald* only occurs in two names: Wiggold in the N.E. extremity of the ancient Cirencester parish, and Barnsley Wold in the N.W. corner of Barnsley parish. These, and the woodland referred to in a few other names such as Barnsley, indicate the whereabouts of the last remnants of the ancient forest.

From these studies it appears that *wald* or *weald* in an ancient settlement-name is likely to indicate the presence of woodland when the name arose; though Rackham 1976 does not include the term in the brief but important discussion (pp. 56–8) of the place-name elements which have this significance.

There have not yet been studies of the Lincolnshire and Yorkshire Wolds comparable to those of the Cotswolds. For LIN the evidence of Domesday Book suggests that the Wolds were clear of wood in the 11th century, though one of the three concentrations of woodland in the county, which is on the clay S.E. of Louth, extends on to the margin of the high ground.

In Yorkshire, Domesday Book records woodland immediately east of the Wolds, in the neighbourhood of Beverley. This area is known to have been forested at an earlier date; the monastery afterwards called Beverley is named *Inderauuda* 'in the wood of Deira' by Bede, and this is rendered *Deirewald* in a later source. DB also mentions underwood in its account of some estates on the western side of the southern tip of the Wolds.

For the Yorkshire Wolds, there is also the EPNS survey of YOE, which enables the place-name evidence for woodland to be taken into account. The distribution map of OE and ON woodland terms in Smith 1936 is complicated by the inclusion of a symbol for *wald* in each instance where the district-name is used as an affix (as in Middleton-on-the-Wolds) or occurs in a minor name (like Warter Wold) which designates one community's share of the upland pasture. These are not relevant to any discussion of woodland. There are only two names containing *wald* on the Yorkshire Wolds which are relevant, these being Wauldby and a minor name, Hawold, in Huggate parish. When the map is emended by excluding all the others it becomes clear that there is a concentration of woodland terms between Scorborough ('booth in a wood') and Swanland Hall ('Svan's wood') in North Ferriby. Some of the woodland terms are on the southern tip of the Wolds, and there are a sufficient number to make it clear that there was woodland at the southern extremity of the higher ground in the Anglo-Saxon period, and that some of it survived till the period of the Norse settlements. In the northern part of the Wolds, place-names indicating woodland are very scarce. In the central portion there are a parish named Lund and a minor name containing lēah (Bealeys Plantation in Lockington); but north of that there is only Oldleys Plantation in Tibthorpe and Lund Wood in Wharram le Street. Acklam, which means 'at the oak woods', lies off the crest of the wolds. It seems clear that there were only small fragments of woodland in the main area of the Yorkshire Wolds when the OE and ON names of the region arose, and in fact archaeologists believe that in the northern half of the area the higher ground had been virtually denuded of trees from a much earlier time. Here, as in the southern Cotswolds, there was intensive settlement during the Roman period.

In the case of the Yorkshire Wolds, if the district-name is a pre-Conquest one, it should probably be presumed to have been applied originally to the southern tip of the Wolds, where place-names and the Domesday Survey show the late survival of woodland. Wauldby in this area is in DB, and probably incorporates the earliest recorded use of the district-name. Since it is more likely that *wald* would be used of a wooded area before the Viking period than after, Wauldby could be seen as evidence that *Wald* was the established name of the southern Wolds when the Vikings arrived. The district-name as such is first recorded in Norse sagas of the 13th century. Hawold, a minor name in the parish of Huggate, is first recorded in the 12th century, and may incorporate the earliest evidence for the district-name *Wald* as extended to include the northern part of the high ground. The etymology of Hawold is uncertain as regards the first element.

The distinction between *wald* and lēah is probably a matter of date rather than meaning. There is good reason to regard lēah as a term which did not become fashionable in place-name formation until the mid 8th century. The use of *wald* for large stretches of ancient woodland is likely to have been relatively early, and the term would not be sufficiently fashionable after c. AD 750 to acquire the developed senses which characterize lēah.

Other district-names containing *wald/weald* include Bromswold (mentioned above), the Wolds in NTT/LEI, and two districts in CAM, one extending N. from Croydon Wilds to Dry Drayton (formerly *Wold Drayton*), and touching the boundary with HNT, where the hamlet of Weald, E. of St Neots, is named from it, the other extending over the claylands of the Isle of Ely. The last name survived in Witchford in the form *Wold* till the end of the 18th century. The main concern of the present discussion, however, is with settlement-names derived from or incorporating *wald/weald*.

As a simplex name *wald* has become Old NTP. This name may have been conferred in recognition of the situation of the village at a junction of wood and open land. There is a cluster of names in **lēah** to the N. of Old, but no sign of **lēah**, or any other woodland term, in the settlement-names to the S., between Old and Northampton.

The Kentish/West Saxon form *weald* has given rise to simplex settlement-names in ESX, OXF and HMP. South Weald ESX (N.E. of Romford) is in an area marked by a cluster of names referring to woodland, and North Weald Bassett is at the N. end of Epping Forest. Wield HMP has a high situation, over 500′, on the north edge of heavily wooded country. In these instances 'wooded upland' is a satisfactory translation. Odd man out as regards simplex names is Weald near Bampton OXF, which is on a low promontory overlooking flat ground by the R. Thames. The nature of most of the settlement-names here suggests open country. There are, however, some minor names, like Barleypark in Ducklington, and some early field-names in –**hyrst**, which support the evidence of Weald for the former presence of wood, and it is probably necessary to assume a survival of forest here into the early Anglo-Saxon period, continuing long enough for this name to assume the West Saxon dialect form. Clanfield, which adjoins Weald, may be named in contrast to this wood.

wald is fairly common as a first element, but in some names it is a reference to a district called Wold or Weald, rather than a free use of the place-name element. Waldron SSX and Woldingham SUR refer to The Weald. Waldershare KNT contains *wald-ware* 'wold dwellers', to which has been added *scearu*, probably meaning 'district'; Professor Everitt considers these 'wold dwellers' to be the people of the forest which bordered the river-territories of east Kent. Great and Little Waldingfield SFK incorporate the name of a *Wold* which probably covered the area between Lavenham and Sudbury, and which does not seem to be recorded otherwise.

'Settlement on a wold' is one of the possible etymologies for the Waltons which do not have *Waleton* spellings in ME. Only a topographical study could identify examples for which this etymology is appropriate. Waltham, on the other hand, is a name which can always be interpreted 'wold estate'. Mrs Rhona Huggins has studied all the examples of Waltham, and argues convincingly that they form a coherent group, and that the name was used in the first century of the Anglo-Saxon period for royal administrative centres in forest areas (Huggins (1975). The name occurs in BRK, ESX(2), HMP(2), KNT, LEI, LIN, SSX(2). Some of these estates have been split up, so that there are two villages bearing the name, as White Waltham and Waltham St Lawrence in BRK.

As a final element, *wald* is combined with a personal name in Coxwold YON, Cuxwold LIN, Sibertswold KNT, Stixwould LIN and Wymeswold LEI, as well as in some of the district-names discussed above. Easingwold YON, Horninghold LEI and Womenswold KNT are –**inga**– compounds. Descriptive terms are very rare with *wald*, but Hammill KNT is probably 'broken wold', from *hamela* 'maimed', found most commonly in Hambledon. Hockwold NFK contains a rare reference to vegetation. Prestwold LEI was owned by priests. Studdall KNT makes the only reference noted to animals. In NFK and SFK some names refer to the position. Methwold NFK is 'middle wold' with reference to its situation betwen Hockwold and Northwold. There is an isolated Southwold in SFK. Harrold BDF, Hawold YOE and Ringwould KNT are of uncertain etymology.

It is probable that *wald* was only considered appropriate to districts, and was not used freely as the second element of individual settlement-names. Coxwold and Easingwold YON are less than 5 miles apart, and may refer to portions of a single forest called *Wold*. Wymeswold and Prestwold LEI are near the southern end of a district called The Wolds. Harrold BDF is perhaps not too far south to be named from the great forest of Bromswold. The few names which appear to be isolated, such as Stixwould LIN, Horninghold LEI and Southwold SFK, may be the only surviving records of vanished *Wolds*, rather than being instances of *wald* used for a wood of more limited extent. Compounds of *wald* with personal names should probably be interpreted as 'Swīthbeorht's/ Stígr's/ Wīgmund's part of the district called *Wold*' rather than 'Swīthbeorht's forest' etc.; though, for brevity's sake, the latter type of etymology has been given in the Glossarial Index.

wudu, earlier **widu**, OE 'wood'. This is probaably the most colourless OE term for a collection of trees. It is very common in minor names and field-names. Major settlement-names in which it occurs number about 225; about 90 of these have it as first element, 33 of them being compounds with **tūn**. Woodham DRH, from the dat. pl., is the only simplex example noted among major names.

The compound with **tūn** is sufficiently frequent to deserve consideration as a name which may have an economic, as well as a topographical, significance. Settlements so named perhaps had a special function in relation to the wood and its products. The appropriate topographical meaning of the compound would be 'settlement near a wood', as **tūn** is very rarely used for a place lying within a forest area. The name has the modern form Wootton in BDF, BRK, DOR(3), HMP(2), IOW, KNT, LIN, NFK, NTP, OXF, SHR (sometimes spelt Wooton), SOM(2), STF(2), WAR(3), WLT(2). It has become Wotton in BUC, GLO(2) and SUR, and Woodton in NFK. Some instances of Witton contain the early form *widu*, as Witton le Wear DRH and Witton NFK, NTB(2), YON, but this name can have other origins. Four instances of Woodhouse (LEI and YOW(3)) are listed in Ekwall 1960, and many others occur in minor names. Woodsome and Wothersome YOW are from the dat. pl. of this compound. Woodhall HRT, LIN, YOE, YOW is a similar compound, also repeated in minor names. It is possible that 'wood house' and 'wood hall' originally denoted establishments with an official function in relation to an area of woodland.

In Woodham ESX(3) and SUR, *wudu* is combined with **hām**; and in

Woodcote, HMP, OXF, SHR, SUR, WAR and Woodcott CHE, HMP it is combined with *cot*. Other habitative terms occur in Woodstock OXF and Woodthorpe DRB, LIN. Woodbridge SFK, Woodchurch CHE, KNT and Woodkirk YOW are probably 'bridge/church near the wood', but they could refer to the material of the structure.

Compounds in which *wudu* is combined with a second element of topographical significance include Woodbarrow SOM and Woodborough WLT; Woodborough NTT and Woodbury DEV; Woodburn NTB; Woodchester GLO; Woodford CHE(2), CNW, ESX, NTP(2), WLT; Woodhorn NTB; Woodleigh DEV and Woodley BRK; Woodrow WLT, WOR. (**burh** in Woodborough NTT and Woodbury, and *ceaster* in Woodchester, are here regarded as referring to ancient landscape features.) In Woodcroft NTB, Woodgarston HMP and Woodsetts YOW the second element is a word for an enclosure. The name Woodland(s) is discussed under **land**.

Analysis of the first elements of about 130 major settlement-names in which *wudu* is the second element reveals that the commonest type of qualifier is a descriptive term, a characteristic noted in compounds with some other generics, such as **ford**, which did not have a highly specialized meaning. Here belong Blackwood YOE, YOW; Brandwood, Brantwood LNC, Brentwood ESX and Burntwood STF; Broadwood DEV(2), SOM; Evenwood DRH; Fulwood LNC, NTT; Harewood HMP, Horwood BUC; Marshwood DOR; Stobswood NTB; Stowood OXF; Weetwood NTB, Wetwood STF; Whitwood YOW. Yanwath WML may be a Scandinavianized doublet of Evenwood. In the next largest group the qualifying term refers to the relative position of the wood. Here belong Astwood BUC, WOR, Eastwood ESX, Heywood LNC, Melwood LIN, Middlewood HRE, Northwood GTL, IOW, Norwood GTL, Southwood NFK, Upwood HNT, Westwood WAR, WLT, WOR. Marwood DEV and Ringwood HMP may be 'boundary wood'. A smaller group defines the wood by reference to a nearby topographical feature, as Brookwood SUR, Downwood HRE, Dunwood HMP, Ewood LNC(2), Holmwood SUR (**hamm**), Lingwood NFK, Lipwood NTB (perhaps containing *lippa* 'lip'), Lythwood SHR. An earlier place-name, wood-name or river-name is used in Brewood STF, Charnwood LEI, Chetwode BUC, Halewood LNC, Hockerwood NTT, Kentwood BRK, Portswood HMP, Stockwood DOR, and possibly in Crewood CHE.

Wild creatures mentioned in compounds with *wudu* are mostly birds, as in Arnwood HMP and Earnwood SHR, Cawood LNC, YOW, Coquet NTB, Cornwood DEV, WOR and Hanwood SHR. But hares are probably referred to in Harewood HRE, YOW and Harwood LNC(2), NTB(2), YOW. No compounds have been noted with words for domestic animals. Species of trees have only been noted in Ashwood STF, Beckwith YOW, Hackwood HMP (which implies hawthorn), Iwode HMP, Linwood HMP, LIN(2) and Selwood SOM; and other types of vegetation only in Bestwood NTT and Marchwood HMP.

Personal names are rare with *wudu*, but here belong Barnwood GLO, Goodwood SSX (from the feminine *Gōdgiefu*), Intwood NFK, Packwood WAR, Simonswood LNC and Woolstanwood CHE. Specific categories of owners or inhabitants are mentioned in Bushwood WAR, Charlwood SUR, Henwood WAR, Inglewood CMB, Kingswood GLO(2), SUR, WAR, Ratchwood NTB. Wychwood OXF may be 'wood on the boundary of the Hwicce' rather than indicating that it lay within their territory. Sherwood NTT and Skirwith CMB were presumably owned by the shire or district. Scrainwood NTB may be 'of the villains' or 'of the shrews'; the former seems more likely, as small mammals do not otherwise appear in this material. Words for products are rare, though more examples could be found in minor names. Bowood DEV perhaps produced wood for bows, and Walkwood WOR may have supplied building material. Saltwood KNT perhaps produced fuel for salt boiling. Needwood STF may mean 'refuge wood'. Threapwood CHE was probably subject to disputed ownership. Haywood HRE, SHR, STF, Heywood WLT and Lockwood YOW contained enclosures. Hopwood WOR may have been near some enclosed arable land.

Bowood DOR and WLT, Underwood DRB and NTT, and Westwood KNT are phrases meaning '(place) above/under/west of the wood'. Belwood LIN, Bernwood BUC, Garswood LNC, Marwood DRH, Whittlewood NTP and Wicklewood NFK have not been classified.

7

Ploughland and Pasture

Chapters 1, 3, 4 and 5 of this book are concerned with what were, for medieval farmers, immutable factors of their landscape. They could not alter the contours or turn dry land into wet. They could only assess the possibilities which the landscape offered for desirable amenities such as shelter, ease of access, dry ground to build on, safety from floods, convenience of water-supply, and decide on the siting of their villages so as to obtain the best conditions possible within the given framework. Chapter 6, however, dealt with woodland, which is to a considerable extent subject to human control; and the theme of human control and manipulation is even more to the front in the present chapter.

Three types of land were essential for the practice of subsistence agriculture. There had to be arable to produce crops, meadow to provide hay, and somewhere for the animals to be pastured. Woodland was a highly desirable extra, and the standard of living of peasants in forest areas was always higher than that of their contemporaries whose villages lay in open country; but it must have been possible to manage without, in some areas at any rate, by the later Anglo-Saxon period.

In this chapter we are concerned with the words used in place-names for the three indispensable types of land. The most valuable, because the most limited, was meadow, which was to a great extent an immutable factor to the medieval farmer, though the creation and maintenance of drainage systems enabled him to make the maximum use of the potential supply. Meadow is not often mentioned in settlement-names, probably because its presence could be assumed, and boundaries between settlements were drawn so as to ensure that each community had its share. Some names containing OE **mǣd** are listed, however, and a few containing the rare element **wisce**, which was perhaps used of meadow-land that was only just on the right side of the dividing line with swamp. Abundance of meadow was one of the characteristics implied by some of the words discussed in Chapter 3. In late OE, **lēah** developed the meaning 'meadow'; but **lēah** is primarily a woodland term, so has been included in Chapter 6. The rare word *winn* 'meadow, pasture' occurs as first element in some names discussed under their final elements.

Pasture and arable were much more flexible. A great deal of land could be one or the other according to how farmers decided to use it. Obviously there was a limit to the height at which arable farming was practicable, but heathland

and some marsh could with diligence be converted to ploughland, and the proportions of arable and pasture within the area which was available to a community could be varied to meet changing circumstances.

I believe that by studying the use in settlement-names of some of the words discussed here—particularly **æcer**, **feld** and **land**—we can observe part of the process by which the arable steadily increased at the expense of the rough ground available for communal pasturing of stock. The evidence set out in the chapter suggests to me that settlements whose names contain the word **feld** represent the breaking-in for arable of ancient rough pasture-land, some by the earliest Anglo-Saxon settlers, some at a much later date. The coining of village-names containing **feld** in areas of arable encroachment on pasture probably went on till the end of the 9th century. Other encroachments, some by Scandinavian settlers, may be indicated by names containing **land**, and a still later stage of the process perhaps resulted in names containing OE **æcer** or ON **akr**. There must have been considerable pressure on land resources when English-speaking farmers decided to plough at Cliviger and Norse-speaking farmers broke in land at Muker. A temporary climatic amelioration could have played a part.

The question of whether any settlements were new during the Anglo-Saxon and Viking period is hotly debated, and it would be difficult, even if one wished it, to avoid taking sides on this matter. I am an unrepentant believer in the more or less continual expansion of settlement from the neolithic period to the present day, and my belief that a considerable number of new arable communities were founded during the Anglo-Saxon settlements and after the Viking invasions has obviously coloured my interpretation of **æcer**, **feld** and **land**, as well as influencing the discussion of some 'clearing' terms in Chapter 6.

The chapter does not include all the OE and ON words for newly-broken-in land, because a number of such terms are characteristically employed in field-names, and seldom or never enter into the settlement-names which are the material of this book. Such terms include OE *ēcels* 'land added to an estate', which occurs mainly in minor names in the north midlands in such forms as Etchells CHE, DRB, Neachill, Nechells STF, and ON *afnám* 'intake', found occasionally in north-country field-names in such forms as Avenam, Annums, Onnams, Aynam, Yannam. OE *innām*, ON *innám* are similar terms, also found in minor names and field-names. ME words which refer to land-reclamation include OFr *assart*, *essart*, used of woodland clearances, and *intake*, derived from ON *intak*, which was used of land enclosed from a moor. A detailed study of the colonization of a limited area would have to take careful account of such terms, but they are not so essential to the broad picture which is sketched out here.

Another dimension would be added to the subject by the inclusion of words used to denote enclosures and specialized types of settlements in pasture land, but it seems better that these should be reserved to form part of a study of habitative place-name elements, rather than appended to this study of the main topographical words. For the same reasons some words used for woodland enclosures were omitted from Chapter 6.

æcer OE 'plot of cultivated land, measure of land which a yoke of oxen could plough in a day'. It is the first sense, 'cultivated land', which is relevant to the study of settlement-names, and a development of the second sense, modern *acre*, which is found in field-names. A combination of the meanings may have caused *æcer* to seem specially appropriate to pieces of arable land which were surrounded by rough pasture. The use made of the word in settlement-names indicates that it was one of the terms used for farms on the edges of cultivation, probably new establishments of the Anglo-Saxon or Viking periods. Instances of ON *akr* may conveniently be discussed with names from OE *æcer*. Both words may have developed a sense 'piece of marginally cultivable land of limited extent'.

OE *æcer* and ON *akr* occur in about 25 major settlement-names, and in a fair number of minor names, a few of which are included in the following study. Examples can be grouped according to proximity to heath, marsh or high moorland.

Acre NFK is the name of three settlements, distinguished as Castle, South and West, which are beside the R. Nar, with expanses of heathland to north and south. Alsager CHE, E. of Crewe, is almost surrounded by heath. Bicknacre ESX, S.W. of Maldon, is adjacent to a large area of rough pasture. Gatacre SHR is in heath country on the SHR/STF border. There was a lost *Linacre* in Horseheath CAM. Ridgeacre WOR, by the Birmingham to Halesowen road, was probably in heathland. Sandiacre DRB is on the DRB/NTT border, on the edge of ancient woodland, where heath often occurs. Weddiker CMB, E. of Whitehaven, and Wheatacre NFK occupy similar situations to each other, most of the land attached to the settlements being on dry ridges enclosed by rivers. Wheatacre is in a great bend of the R. Waveney, Weddiker at the junction of the R. Keekle and Dub Beck. Whitacre WAR, E. of Birmingham, is at the edge of ancient forest. Chadacre SFK, N.W. of Lavenham, probably belongs in this group; the meaning is not obviously suitable to the area as shown on modern maps, but the first element of Chadacre is OE *ceart* 'rough common'.

A similar-sized category of settlement-names containing OE *æcer* or ON *akr* refers to cultivated land on the edge of marsh. Three names E. of Garstang LNC, Barnacre, Stirzaker and Woodacre, overlook the meanders of the Rivers Wyre and Calder, and Tarnacre S. of Garstang is beside the R. Wyre. Benacre SFK (S.E. of Wheatacre NFK) occupies a tongue of land between two marshes. Bessacar YOW is in the marshes S.E. of Doncaster. Some LNC names in Liverpool—Fazakerley, Gateacre and Linacre—may be in marshy land; it is difficult to evaluate them from modern maps, but this sense certainly seems appropriate to Waddicar, N.E. of Aintree. Handsacre STF is on a low hill jutting into the marshes of the R. Trent, S.E. of Rugeley. Roseacre LNC, E. of Blackpool, may be in a drained marsh.

The remaining settlement-names whose sites have been studied lie on the edge of high moorland. Here belong Cliviger LNC, S.E. of Burnley; Dillicar WML, which has Langdale Fell and Whinfell to N.E. and N.W.; Minsteracres DRH, N.E. of Consett; and Muker YON, by the Pennine Way. Stainsacre YON, S.E. of Whitby, perhaps belongs in the category; it is at the junction of coastal plain with the lower slopes of moorland.

Acre NFK is the only simplex name noted. As a second element *æcer/akr* occurs four or five times with personal names—in Alsager CHE, Handsacre STF, Stainsacre YON, Stirzaker LNC, and probably Bicknacre ESX. There are references to position or to topographical features in Chadacre SFK, Cliviger LNC, Fazakerley LNC, Ridgeacre WOR and Roseacre LNC: Bicknacre ESX belongs here if it contains *bica* 'point'. Descriptive terms are used as qualifiers in Muker YON, Sandiacre DRB and Whitacre WAR. Crops are mentioned in Benacre SFK, Dillicar WML, Linacre CAM, LNC, Waddicar LNC and Wheatacre NFK, and wild vegetation in Bessacar YOW, Woodacre LNC and Weddiker CMB. Goats are mentioned in Gatacre SHR and Gateacre LNC, cranes in Tarnacre LNC. Barnacre LNC has a barn, and Minsteracres DRH was near a source of millstones.

Some of the compounds, especially the first part of Fazakerley ('border acre'), Muker ('narrow acre'), and the two 'weed acre' names, seem very appropriate to the interpretation suggested here.

OE *erth* 'plough land', which occurs in Eartham SSX, Cornard SFK and Horningsheath SFK, may have a similar meaning.

brēc (Anglian, Kentish), **bræc** (W. Saxon) OE 'breach'. This word, which clearly refers to newly-broken-in land is manifested mainly in ME field-names, most of which probably derive from ME *breche*, rather than being of OE origin. The OE word is, however, found as the first element of a few settlement-names. Ekwall 1960 gives this derivation as certain for Bircham and Breckles NFK and for Bratton DEV(2), SOM, WLT, as probable for Bretton DRB, YOW(2), and as possible for Braxted ESX. The Bretton names are interpreted in EPNS surveys of YOW and DRB as 'settlement of Britons', and Braxted is derived in the ESX survey from *bracu* 'fern', so these names are best left aside. The others seem convincing examples of OE *brēc*, *bræc*.

At Bircham NFK, N.E. of King's Lynn, the name belonged in the first instance to Great Bircham. The nearby villages of Bircham Newton and Bircham Tofts were called *Niwetuna* in DB and *Toftes* in 1205, and both names suggest that expansion of settlement was still taking place at the end of the Anglo-Saxon period. Bircham itself, however, probably contains **hām** 'village', and may well be a new, relatively early, Anglo-Saxon foundation in heathy country. Breckles NFK, W. of Attleborough, is at the edge of a large area of heath.

The two DEV Brattons, Bratton Clovelly S.W. of Okehampton and Bratton Fleming N.E. of Barnstaple, and Bratton W. of Minehead SOM, do not have situations markedly different from that of their neighbours, though in all three areas it is easy to believe that there was ground to be broken in from moorland. Bratton WLT, N.E. of Westbury, is easily understood as a settlement formed by encroachment on downland pasture.

denn OE 'woodland pasture, especially for swine'. This is the usual source of –den in place-names in SSX and KNT, and confusion with **denu** is to some extent obviated by the frequent development of **denu** to –dean in those counties. There are a few minor names containing *denn* in SUR, but Smith 1956 is probably mistaken in saying that it occurs in ESX. This last statement must be based on p. 556 of the EPNS survey of ESX, where *denn, dænn* is included in the list of elements found in ESX names, and Danbury, *Danegris* and Dengie are ascribed to it. Under Dengie, the ESX survey accepts a suggestion made by Zachrisson that the three names contain an –**ingas** formation with *denn* which would mean 'people of the forest pastures'. This is ignored in Ekwall 1960, and it seems much more likely that the basis of these names is a personal name *Dene*. There was probably no need for the hypothetical E. Saxon form *dænn* to be included in the heading to Smith's article on *denn*. The word may have had some currency outside KNT, SSX and SUR; there are a few names in OE charter boundaries, like *ælfredes denn* in Taynton OXF, *ea denn* in Donnington GLO, which could contain it. But OE *denn* which became modern *den* ('hiding place')—and which may ultimately be the same word as the 'pasture' term—may be involved in the charter names. At all events, *denn* 'swine-pasture' need not be considered as a possible element in settlement-names outside the Weald of KNT and SSX and areas bordering that forest.

  denn can be accorded summary treatment here because it has been discussed in recent articles: Brandon 1978 (*passim*) and Everitt 1979 (pp. 103–6). The use of the word in settlement-names implies that swine pastures belonging to settlements outside the forest evolved into agricultural establishments and acquired independent status. Everitt 1979 says: 'They might be situated at almost any distance from the parental settlement, and in a few cases were as much as 45 miles away, as at Tenterden, the pasture of the men of Thanet, though usually between about eight miles and 20 miles.'

  Only a small number of the names containing *denn* belong to settlements of sufficient status to appear in Ekwall 1960. These include the SSX names Danehill (earlier *Denne*), Iden, Playden, and the KNT names Benenden, Chillenden, Cowden, Pinden, Smarden, Tenterden.

ersc OE 'ploughed field'. This is a southern English term which, like **æcer**, is likely to refer to newly broken-in land. It is nowhere common, but it is well represented in minor names in DEV, KNT, SSX and SUR. It occurs in E. BRK (which has ancient connections with SUR), but not in the W. half of the county, and it is only found in two ME field-names in WLT. The distribution is not, however, exclusively a S.E. one, as the term is fairly common in minor names in DEV. It is only manifested N. of the Thames in Pebmarsh ESX and in a lost name (*Oakhurst*) in Shenley HRT. It is most unlikely to occur further N. than HRT and ESX. The EPNS survey of CHE ascribes several field-names to it, but none is convincing. It occurs in a single field-name in GLO.

ersc had the sense 'stubble-field' in OE, as well as 'ploughed field', and this translation is sometimes given for place-names. Stubble would be a recurrent feature of permanent arable land, not a distinguishing permanent characteristic such as might be expected to be noted in a place-name. But a suggestion made in Brandon 1978 (p. 148) that *ersc* might refer to an early stage of shifting agriculture is interesting here. If reaping of crops was not followed by plough-ing of the same area, the stubble would be visible for some time. In the sense 'stubble, aftermath' *ersc* survived into south-country dialect in the forms *earsh*, *arrish*. NED, under these forms, wrongly suggests derivation from OE *edisc* 'enclosed park'—also a place-name element, but not included in this study.

Names containing *ersc* which belong to places of sufficient status to be included here are Burwash, Hazelhurst, Lagness and Socknersh SSX, Great-ness, Ryarsh and Sundridge KNT, *Oakhurst* HRT, Pebmarsh SSX, Winnersh BRK and Wonersh SUR.

Burwash, Hazelhurst and Socknersh SSX are fairly close together in the Weald, N.W. of Battle. The other SSX name, Lagness in Pagham, is in marshy coastland N.W. of Bognor Regis. Greatness and Sundridge KNT are near Sevenoaks, and Ryarsh is E. of Wrotham; none of these is in an obviously disadvantageous situation. The lost HRT name, *Oakhurst* in Shenley, was in ancient woodland. Pebmarsh SSX is N.E. of Halstead, and there is no obvious reason why this name should contain a term not otherwise found in the county. Winnersh BRK lies on the R. Loddon, between places with names containing **feld** and **hyrst**. Wonersh SUR, S.E. of Guildford, is almost surrounded by heath.

The examples are too few for an analysis of first elements to be useful, but it should be noted that the compound of *ersc* with a word for a crop found in Ryarsh KNT is a type which recurs in minor names and field-names. BRK has minor names Ryehurst, Ryeish, and field-name compounds with 'rye', 'oat' and 'wheat'. The BRK hundred-name Beynhurst is a compound of *ersc* with *bēan* 'bean'. In addition to some compounds with cereal-names SUR has a *Lynerssh*, from *līn* 'flax'. The solitary GLO field-name is a compound with 'oat'. Sundridge KNT, 'separate arable land', has a doublet in a SUR field-name.

feld OE 'open country'. The word is used in literary texts to describe unen-cumbered ground, which might be land without trees as opposed to forest, level ground as opposed to hills, or land without buildings. In many references there is a contrast between *feld* and areas which are difficult of access or passage. The contrast most often recorded is that with woodland, but contrast with hills is also well evidenced, and one text, an agreement dated 852 about land at Sempringham and Sleaford LIN, says that the estate is given 'mid felda and mid wudu and mid fenne', which suggests that *feld* might be contrasted with marsh as well as with woodland and hills. In charter boundaries the phrase 'ut on thone feld' is quite frequent on the edge of woodland. The general tenor of the passages in which *feld* occurs in OE texts clearly indicates that for most of the pre-Conquest period it was used indifferently of land which might or might not be under the plough. It certainly had no special connotation of arable.

It seems likely that *feld* came to mean arable land, particularly the communally-cultivated arable which characterized the open-field farming system, in the second half of the 10th century (which is the date at which the open-field system is now thought likely to have arisen). There is evidence for this use of *feld* in WOR charters dated 966 and 974 (Hooke 1981, p. 179, Fox 1981, p. 84), and the new sense appears in literature at the end of the century. Ælfric's colloquies, written about then, include a statement by a ploughman that he drives his oxen 'to felda' at dawn, and yokes them to the plough. The natural interpretation is that the *feld* is the area being ploughed, the implement having been left there at the close of the previous day's work. But at an earlier date, and at least till the middle decades of the 10th century, Anglo-Saxon charters use a term variously spelt *irthland*, *yrthland*, *ierthland*, *earthland*, *eorthland* in this sense, whereas *feld* is used of common pasture. The two words occur in a BRK charter dated AD 961 which has instead of boundary clause the statement: 'Thas nigon hida licggead on gemang othran gedal lande feldlæs gemane and mæda gemane and yrthland gemæne' (These nine hides lie intermingled with other lands held in shares: open pasture common, and meadow common, and plough-land common). Here the arable land of the community is *yrthland*, 'ploughland', while *feldlæs*, 'field leasow', is generally taken to refer to land used for pasturing stock. The use of *yrthland* is well illustrated by some bounds of Sotwell BRK, which are attached to a charter of 957. These run 'swa be Maccaniges wirthland swa swa oxa went' (so by the ploughland of Mackney just as the ox turns).

There is one text in which *yrthland* glosses Latin *agros*, and it might have been expected that these English and Latin terms, *irthland* and *ager*, would be used in post-Conquest surveys for the open fields. But in fact the terms which emerge in regular use after the Conquest are *feld* and *campus*.

The semantic change in *feld* is dramatic, and one would expect it to be due to a sudden change in the pattern of farming. It is argued below that there must have been an early phase of Anglo-Saxon encroachment on pasture land which gave rise to the numerous ancient settlement-names in –*feld*. This did not cause the word to develop a new meaning, however, and the next likely period for such a development is at the end of the ninth and the beginning of the tenth centuries, when the influx of Scandinavian farmers must have led to a great increase of arable land in the east and north of England. As the rough pasture was converted to arable, the grazing available on the old arable—on fallow fields and balks—would become even more important, so there could have been a period when the plough was commonly to be seen on the *feld*, and the cattle were grazing on parts of the *irthland*. By the middle of the tenth century there were some areas, notably north-west BRK, where a number of estates had very little or no rough grazing or woodland inside their borders, so the only types of open land to be seen must have been meadow and ploughland, and *feld* 'open land' may have come to seem the appropriate term for the larger of these two divisions.

It is clear at any rate that the sense 'arable land' need not be reckoned with in ancient settlement-names. As a term employed in the naming of villages *feld* probably means 'open land previously used for pasture', and it may be an indicator of areas which were converted from rough pasture to arable in the Anglo-Saxon period. In some instances the contrast implied may be partly between pasture and arable. Some isolated names, such as Clanfield OXF and Watchfield BRK, are in areas where woodland is likely to have disappeared at an early date in the Anglo-Saxon period, and it might be suggested as a hypothesis that the land covered by these parishes was at a very early period of English name-giving reserved for communal pasture by the people of the surrounding villages. A farmer who studied the layout of the open fields at Clanfield OXF (Pocock 1968) thought that he could detect the breaking-in of the furlongs by five groups of people working from different directions. It is possible that what he observed was the taking in of former common pasture by the communities of the surrounding villages.

There are areas, such as central BRK, where names in *feld* occur on the edge of forest, and there are others, not so common, where the contrast is probably with marsh. Three names in YOE—Cavil, Kelfield and Duffield— which are on the north bank of the R. Humber, fit this last category, and it is the obvious explanation of Feldom in the parish of Marske near the coast of YON, since Feldom means 'at the open lands' and Marske probably means 'at the marshes'. A fourth type of contrast, that with hilly land, deserves emphasis, as it has not been clearly appreciated in previous books. The map in Fig. 7 has been drawn to illustrate this. It shows all the ancient settlement-names in *feld*, together with some district-names, in the section of England between the Tyne and the Wash. Land over 500′ has been stippled, and it can be seen that there is a large category of settlement-names in *feld* which shows a marked relationship to the 500′ contour, particularly on the east side of the Pennines, where the towns of Sheffield and Huddersfield lie on the edge of the higher ground. If the map were continued to the south, the same relationship could be discerned round the edges of the Birmingham Plateau, where Northfield and Sutton Coldfield adjoin land over 500′.

Among English place-names recorded by AD 730 (Cox 1976) there are 10 instances of *feld*. This indicates that it was a prolific name-forming term in the

7   Major names containing *feld* between the R. Tyne and The Wash

early Anglo-Saxon period, and it is of interest to consider whether there were
settlements at these places. Three—Hatfield YOW, *Hefenfeld* and
Maserfelth—were the sites of battles. Austerfield YOW and Hatfield HRT
were the sites of synods, and it is possible that tented accommodation on
heathland should be envisaged. Lichfield STF was the site chosen by St Chad
for his cathedral. The unlocated *Bedesfeld* and *Mirafeld* were certainly settlements, and Bradfield BRK and another unlocated place, *Widmundesfelt*, were
estates granted to monasteries. From this it appears that in at least 4 out of the
10 places an estate with a settlement had been formed in the 7th century. If *feld*
is an indicator of previously uncultivated grazing land which was broken in by
the Anglo-Saxons, some of this expansion of cultivation and settlement is likely
to have happened soon after the arrival of the first English colonists, and it may
be more than a coincidence that Driffield YOE is known from archaeological
evidence to have been the focal point of one of the major 6th-century settlement areas on the southern side of the Yorkshire Wolds (Faull 1974,

pp. 12–13). In addition to being in use at an early date, *feld* may have remained active as a place-name-forming term until after AD 900, as it is compounded with an ON word in Scrafield LIN (*skreith* 'landslip') and possibly in Holmesfield DRB.

There are about 250 major settlement-names which contain *feld*. The potential historical importance of the term has not been fully appreciated. The word deserves a monograph, but for the time being all that can be attempted is a region by region survey of its distribution and a classification of the first elements with which it is compounded.

feld is not a common element in major names in KNT. It is more common in SSX, occurring mainly in the eastern half of that county. A recent study of settlement in SSX, Brandon 1978, concludes that the SSX evidence is consistent with the hypothesis (put forward in Gelling 1976) that the word indicates areas used for common grazing in the early Anglo-Saxon period. Rotherfield means 'cattle pasture', and Brandon says: 'the name of Rotherfield was probably bestowed by cattle drovers from East Blatchingdon, near Seaford . . . All the coastal communities probably sent up cattle with swine to the detached swine pastures in this way.' Brandon also points to the etymology of Ninfield, which means 'newly taken-in *feld*'.

In SUR, *feld* is less common in major names than it is in SSX. There is a broad strip of the county running north east/south west where the element is not evidenced, and only in the south east is it used in parish-names (Tatsfield, Limpsfield, Lingfield, Nutfield); in this area was the great DB estate of *Cherchefelle*, usually identified with Reigate. In HMP and IOW, as in SUR, *feld* is used more in minor names than in names of parishes and Domesday manors. Heckfield and Stratfield in north-east HMP continue the belt of names in *feld* which is one of the most conspicuous features of BRK. These BRK names have been discussed in Gelling 1976. There are eight contiguous parishes (Bradfield, Englefield, Burghfield, Shinfield, Wokefield, Stratfield, Swallowfield, Arborfield) occupying a belt of country on the outskirts of Windsor Forest. There is much heathland in the southern part. This may have been a border territory between West Saxons and Middle Saxons, and was perhaps used for common pasture while it was on a boundary. In west BRK, on the other hand, as in the adjacent county of WLT, ancient names in *feld* occur singly, not in clusters or belts. The element is comparatively rare in major names in WLT, and very rare in DOR and SOM.

In DEV, the use of *feld* is characterized by the frequent recurrence of some compounds. There are thirteen instances with **hæth**, ten with *myrig* 'merry', and five with *hwīt*. The compound with *myrig* (which occurs also in Marvell, IOW) is found mainly in west DEV, and Merryfield is fairly common in CNW. English penetration into the south-west peninsula was probably too late for much use of *feld* in name-formation, but the use of an element in certain compounds often continues after the word has ceased to be freely employed.

Moving north from Wessex into the territory of the Hwicce and

Magonsæte, GLO has 10 parish-names in *feld*. Some of these (Driffield, Brimpsfield, Haresfield, Hasfield) are isolated examples, but there is a notable cluster in the south-west projection of the county, east of the Severn estuary. This consists of Falfield, Charfield, Marshfield, Mangotsfield and Horfield, with Nympsfield as an outlier. This group is clearly to be associated with adjacent woodland (shown by names in lēah). There is no such cluster by the Forest of Dean, however, the only example in that part of GLO being Hewelsfield.

In WOR, the element appears to be associated with high ground. Northfield and Houndsfield lie on the edge of the ridge which runs from West Heath to Headley Heath, and Madresfield and Woodsfield lie close together at the northern end of the Malvern Hills. Eldersfield on the south-west boundary is a relatively isolated example. In HRE, besides the district-name Archenfield, *feld* occurs in the names of five Domesday manors. These are isolated examples, some of them (Brimfield, Broadfield, Hatfield) on the edge of high ground, but Sarnesfield is probably named by contrast to surrounding woodland. Mawfield in Allensmore is surrounded by marshy commons. In SHR, the word seems sometimes to be used of areas at a junction of hill and plain. Cheney Longville and Longville in the Dale are both good examples of this, and Morville is overlooked by a steep escarpment. Felton Butler lies under Nesscliff. Ightfield, on the other hand, stands in marshy ground on the SHR/CHE border, and in Worfield the contrast is probably with woodland. In CHE, as can be seen from Fig. 7, four names (Macclesfield, Hurdsfield, Hulme Walfield and Dukinfield) are on the western edge of the Pennines, while Hoofield in Clotton lies in marshy ground by the R. Gowy.

The frequency and situation of ancient names in *feld* in most of northern England can be ascertained from Fig. 7. It is much less common in the north west than in the north east. The Fylde LNC is from a related word *(ge)filde* 'plain'.

Turning from CHE east into the central parts of Mercia, there are only a few names in *feld* in the northern half of STF. Three of these are marked on Fig. 7: two of them (Mayfield near Ashbourne and Field west of Uttoxeter) show the characteristic relationship to the 500′ contour, while Alstonfield is high up in Dovedale. Blithfield, south of Field, is well away from high ground, as, in the southern half of the county, are Lichfield and Chesterfield, but other examples in south STF (Wednesfield and Finchfield in Tettenhall) lie close to the Birmingham plateau, and Sutton Coldfield in north WAR belongs with this group. Enville, west of Stourbridge, has a similar relationship to the Enville-Trimpley upland, which is separated from the Birmingham plateau by the Stour valley. Enville means 'level plain', and is an apt description of the level valley overlooked by the church, which stands on a sharp rise.

The position of names in *feld* in NTT and north DRB, and the relationship of some of them to the eastern edge of the Pennines, can be seen from Fig. 7. Most DRB examples are in the northern half of the county. Fairfield near

Buxton has been described by Professor Cameron as 'the finest pasturage in Peak Forest'.

In LEI and LIN *feld* is rare. LEI examples are Glenfield, on the western outskirts of Leicester, Marefield E. of Leicester, and Markfield on the edge of Charnwood Forest. Marefield and Markfield both lie very close to the 500' contour.

In WAR *feld* is very rare in ancient settlement-names, but occurs in two district-names. Coldfield, surviving as the affix in Sutton Coldfield, is in the extreme north of the county. The name Feldon, which refers to the southern part of the county as contrasted with the Forest of Arden, may be the same name as Feldom YON, 'at the open lands', from the dat. pl. *feldum*. The only parish-name is Snitterfield, north of Stratford, 'open land of the snipe', possibly at an early period an isolated area of uncultivated grazing land. Cryfield Grange in Stoneleigh lies at the southern edge of the Forest of Arden.

In OXF there are eight parish-names in *feld*. Four (Caversfield, Clanfield, Elsfield and Wheatfield) are relatively isolated. Two (Leafield and Stonesfield) are on the edge of Wychwood Forest. Rotherfield is on the edge of the Chilterns, and Nuffield near the crest. There are four BUC parishes. Turville (like Nuffield OXF) is high up on the Chilterns, and Beaconsfield lies against the eastern scarp. The others (Brayfield and Luffield) are on the BUC/NTH boundary, by Yardley and Whittlewood Forests. In NTP several parish-names in *feld* (Brafield, Benefield, Byfield, Tiffield and Whitfield) are to be associated with forest. The affix of Field Burcote, in the same region as Tiffield, contrasts with that of Wood Burcote three miles to the south east.

In HRT and MDX the parish-names in *feld* are a feature of the county boundaries. Enfield lies near the MDX/HRT border, Harefield near the junction of BUC, MDX and HRT. Therfield HRT lies in heathland on the CAM/HRT boundary, and Broadfield HRT is in the same region. Bramfield, however, is in the centre of the county, N.W. of Hertford. Hatfield is not far from the south boundary of HRT.

In the part of the south-east Midlands occupied by BDF, HNT and CAM *feld* is very rare in ancient settlement-names, but it becomes common again to the east, in ESX, NFK and SFK.

In ESX the parish-names in *feld* include two remarkable concentrations. There is a large area in the north, where Bardfield, Finchingfield, Toppesfield, Wethersfield, Gosfield and Panfield adjoin each other, and Canfield and Hatfield Broad Oak lie a little to the south west. Felsted, which is a compound of *feld* and **stede**, lies at the south end of this concentration. The other group is about in the centre of the county, where Springfield, Hatfield Peverel and the three Hanningfield parishes are to be found. There are some isolated examples in addition to these groups. Any serious study of the history of settlement and land-use in ESX should take account of these names.

In SFK, there is a wide belt of *feld* names running north/south through the county, from Homersfield and Ringsfield on the NFK/SFK border to

Westerfield north of Ipswich. As in ESX there are a number of names in
–*ingafeld*, Great and Little Waldingfield being 'open land of the dwellers in the
wold'. Some of the *feld* names in SFK adjoin, but mostly they are interspersed
with names of various other types, and they do not form a continuous chain like
the *feld* names of central BRK. The main characteristic of the areas of SFK
where *feld* names predominate may be comparative dryness. Many of them are
beside very small streams, whereas the villages beside major rivers have names
with different final elements.

In NFK there are some *feld* names in the interior of the county (e.g.
Blofield, Stanfield, Westfield), but the main concentration is fairly near the
coast, running from Bayfield to Catfield, and including the cluster of Bradfield,
Suffield and Swafield. Catfield refers to wild cats, and Edgefield has *edisc*
'enclosed pasture' as first element. In Field Dalling and Wood Dalling the
contrast is explicitly with woodland.

The final topic requiring consideration is that of the types of compound in
which *feld* occurs. The word could be used as a simplex name, as in Field STF,
Leafield OXF (with French definite article), and Feldom YON (from the
dative plural), but this is very rare. As a first element (also rare) it occurs with
tūn in Felton HRE, NTB, SHR (two examples) and SOM (Felton in Win-
ford). There are single examples with **hām** or **hamm** (Feltham MDX), with
brycg (Felbridge SUR), and with *stede* (Felsted ESX), but the commonest use
is as the final element of a compound name.

Analysis of the first elements of major settlement-names in which *feld* is the
generic brings out some interesting points. Much the commonest type of
qualifier is a word describing the *feld*. There are more than 50 names which I
would place in this category. The qualities described are, however, of varying
kinds, and a different analyst might not see these names as a coherent group.

In some the reference is to size or shape. Here belong Bradfield BRK, ESX,
NFK, SFK, YOW, Broadfield HRE, HRT; Longville SHR(2); and Mickle-
field YOW. Enville STF ('level open space') might be included with these.

In others the descriptive term refers to the surface of the *feld*. Examples are
Charfield GLO; Clanfield HMP, OXF, Clanville HMP, SOM, Glenfield LEI
(all 'clean'); Driffield GLO, YOE, Horfield GLO (all 'dirty'); Henfield SSX,
Stainfield LIN, Stanfield NFK (characterized by rocks or stones); Kelfield
LIN, YOE ('chalk'); Nuffield OXF; Therfield HRT, Turville BUC (both
'dry'). I would include in this sub-group all the names with 'heath' as first
element, since they probably refer to poor land with a rough surface, rather
than primarily to the growth of heather. The 'heathfield' names are Hadfield
DRB, Heathfield SOM, SSX, Hatfield ESX(2), HRE, HRT, NTT, WOR,
YOE, YOW, and Hothfield KNT.

Aesthetic qualities or colour are referred to in Fairfield DRB, KNT;
Falfield GLO (and possibly Fallowfield LNC, NTB); Marvell IOW, Mirfield
YOW; Shenfield ESX; Sherfield HMP(2); Wheatfield OXF, Whitefield IOW,
LNC, Whitfield DRB, KNT, NTB, NTP.

A few other names may have descriptive first elements. Bramfield HRT may contain OE *brant* 'steep'; Bredfield SFK contains OE *brǣdu* 'breadth' the sense of which is never perfectly clear in place-names; Swafield NFK and Swayfield LIN contain OE *swæth*, modern *swathe*, another rare place-name element whose precise sense has not been ascertained.

Personal names constitute the second largest category of first elements used with *feld*. There are more than 30 instances among major names, and a few others for which a personal name is one of the possible etymologies. Reasonably certain instances are Alstonfield STF, Bayfield NFK, Beauxfield KNT, Bedfield SFK, Brimpsfield GLO, Brushfield DRB, Canfield ESX, Caversfield OXF, Chelsfield KNT, Cratfield SFK, Cuckfield SSX, Ellisfield HMP, Elsfield OXF, Framfield SSX, Haresfield GLO, Hewelsfield GLO, Homersfield SFK, Howfield KNT, Huddersfield YOW, Isfield SSX, Luffield BUC, Macclesfield CHE, Mangotsfield GLO, Matfield KNT, Mountfield SSX, Pakefield SFK, Sedgefield DRH, Stonesfield OXF, Tatsfield SUR, Toppesfield ESX, Uckfield SSX, Wethersfield ESX, Winkfield BRK, Wokefield BRK. Eight, at least, of the personal names are dithematic.

Place-names which may have a personal name as first element include Arborfield BRK, Hellifield YOW, Houndsfield WOR, Manfield YON, Stansfield SFK, Wattisfield SFK, Winkfield WLT. Arborfield may contain the only feminine name noted with *feld*, and Hellifield the only ON name.

No other category of first elements used with *feld* approaches the size of the two already discussed. There are, however, four categories of similar size to each other. These are earlier place-names or river-names, words for a topographical feature in or near the *feld*, references to vegetation, and references to wild creatures.

Earlier place-names or river-names are used to define a *feld* in about 20 major settlement-names. Here belong Blithfield STF, Cantsfield LNC, Dogmersfield HMP, Eaglesfield CMB, Ecclesfield YOW, Edenfield LNC, Holmesfield DRB, Hundersfield LNC, Lichfield STF, Limpsfield SUR, Mansfield NTT, Morville SHR, Nympsfield GLO, Panfield ESX, Sheffield YOW, Swallowfield BRK, Tanfield DRH and Worfield SHR. Possible examples are Charsfield SFK and Ightfield SHR.

Topographical features are referred to in a slightly smaller group comprising Beaconsfield BUC, Brafield/Brayfield NTP/BUC, Broxfield, NTB, DOR, Burghfield BRK, Chesterfield DRB, STF, Crowfield SFK, Cruchfield BRK, Cryfield WAR, Hilfield DOR, Marshfield GLO, Sarnesfield HRE, Stratfield BRK/HMP, Walfield CHE, Washfield DEV, Wightfield GLO, Winchfield HMP. Nosterfield CAM, YON probably belong to this class.

The first element refers to vegetation in Benfieldside DRH, Bentfield ESX, Binfield BRK (all 'bent-grass'); Bitchfield NTB; Bramfield SFK, Bromfield ESX, KNT, SOM (all 'broom'); Brimfield HRE; Dockenfield HMP; Farnsfield NTT; Hasfield GLO; Ifield KNT, SSX; Lindfield SSX; Mayfield STF; Nutfield SUR. Eldersfield WOR, Hemingfield YOW and Tanfield YON are less certain members of this category. Edgefield NFK and Wingfield DRB, which have as first elements OE *edisc* and *wynn*, both meaning 'pasture', can be roughly classified here, as can Metfield SFK. Five of these names refer to trees.

Wild creatures are mentioned in Catfield NFK, Catsfield SSX, Cavil YOE, Cranfield BDF, Darfield YOW, Dronfield DRB, Duffield DRB, YOE, Finchfield STF, Froxfield HMP, WLT, Marefield LEI, Netherfield SSX, Padfield DRB, Snitterfield WAR, Yarnfield STF, WLT. The ducks of Dukinfield CHE and the geese of Gosfield HMP could be domestic, but the bias of the material is in favour of their being classed as wild.

There are no certain references to crops, and surprisingly few to domestic creatures. Enfield MDX may refer to lambs; Sheffield SSX certainly refers to sheep. Fairfield WOR (*Forfeld* 817) is thought to contain OE *fōr* 'hog'. Nesfield YOW may have the gen. of *nēat* 'cattle' as first element. Warmfield YOW may refer to stallions, but wrens are equally likely. The only firm reference to domestic animals which is repeated is that in Rotherfield HMP, OXF, SSX.

The number of names in which *feld* is added to the gen. of a group-name in –ingas is a noteworthy feature of the corpus. The clearest examples are Atherfield IOW, Bedingfield SFK, Benefield NTP (*Beringafeld* c. 970), Finchingfield ESX, Hanningfield ESX, Haslingfield CAM, Huntingfield SFK, Itchingfield SSX, Lingfield SUR, Shinfield BRK, Springfield ESX, Waldingfield SFK and Waldringfield SFK. Possible examples are Bingfield NTB, Fressingfield SFK and Wingfield SFK. In Haslingfield, Lingfield, Springfield and Waldingfield, –ingas may have been added to an earlier place-name, rather than to a personal name. Other groups of people are rare with *feld*, but 'Angles' are referred to in Englefield BRK and 'Mercians' in Markfield LEI, Markingfield YOW. Otherwise the only name noted in which a *feld* is associated with a particular category of person is Madresfield WOR, which might mean 'open land of the mower'.

Only a few names with *feld* refer to man-made structures. Austerfield YOW had a sheep-fold, Hoofield CHE a hovel, Hurdsfield CHE a hurdle, Sheffield BRK a shelter, Stalisfield KNT a stall. Only Warfield BRK is named from a more permanent structure—a weir. The only reference noted to a product is that to charcoal in Coldfield WAR.

In a few names the direction of a *feld* is mentioned: here belong Northfield WOR, Suffield NFK, YON, Westerfield SFK, Westfield NFK, SSX. Byfield NTP is probably '(place) beside open land'.

There are a few names which cannot without undue violence be pushed into any of the above categories. Aldfield YOW was 'old', and Ninfield SSX was 'newly reclaimed'. Wakefield NTP, YON were the scenes of festivities. Wednesfield STF was a centre of Wōden worship.

The number of compounds with *feld* in which the first element is too obscure or ambiguous for classification is relatively small. I have failed to reach a conclusion about Bardfield ESX, Blofield NFK, Harefield MDX, Heckfield

HMP, Mawfield HRE, Ringsfield SFK, Shedfield HMP, Sternfield SFK, Tiffield NTP, Wingfield BDF, Woodsfield WOR.

hǣth OE (**hāth** in KNT and SSX) 'heather, tract of uncultivated land'. The use of a plant-name for a type of country is analogous to that discussed under **mos**. Ekwall 1960 (p. 210) considers that *hǣth* generally referred to vegetation when used as a first element, and Smith 1956 concurs about this except when the second element is a habitative term. It is possible, however, that as a qualifier for some topographical terms, especially **feld**, *hǣth* referred to the quality of the ground rather than primarily to the plant. The senses are not, of course, mutually exclusive. In this book, perhaps inconsistently, *hǣth* has been considered a descriptive term with **feld**, and a plant-name with **lēah**, **dūn** and **hyll**. The use of *hǣthfeld* in OE charter boundaries suggests that it was a compound appellative for the sort of land which later became a common.

hǣth is much more frequent as a first element than as a second. Compounds with topographical terms are listed elsewhere, under **dūn**, **hyll** and **lēah**. Among habitative terms, *hǣth* occurs most frequently with **tūn**. Ekwall 1960 lists nine examples of Hatton, in CHE(2), DRB, LIN, MDX, SHR(2), STF, WAR. Heathcote occurs in DRB and WAR.

A few compounds with *hǣth* as second element have become settlement-names. These include Blackheath GTL, Crickheath SHR and Horseheath CAM. Simplex names from *hǣth* include Heath BDF, HRE, SHR, YOW, Hethe OXF, Hoath KNT.

hǣth may have been to some extent interchangeable with **mōr**.

land OE, ON 'land, estate, ?new arable area'. This term occurs in about 100 names in Ekwall 1960, excluding those from *bōcland* and *sundorland* (discussed below). A distinction should be recognized between the significance of *land* in ancient settlement-names and the more casual use of it in minor names and field-names. In the last two categories of place-names it sometimes has the specialized sense 'strip in a field-system', but usually it is to be understood as having the same connotations as the modern word, i.e. 'ground, part of the earth's surface'. In settlement-names, however, it is reasonable to expect a more specific meaning. This will sometimes be 'estate', in which sense *land* probably overlapped with **tūn** in the late OE and early post-Conquest periods. Earlier than this *land* may have been one of the terms used in place-names to denote new settlements of the Anglo-Saxon period in areas colonized or reclaimed in response to an increasing need for arable. It is because of this possibility that the word is included in this chapter. The evidence set out below, which includes 5 East Anglian names with –inga–, a number of northern names with ON first elements, and some post-Conquest formations, suggests that *land* had this sense from c. AD 600 to c. AD 1150. It is reasonable to regard the ON word *land* as subsumed in the use of the OE term.

The sense 'estate' is probably seen in some names in the south west in which *land* replaces **tūn**, or is added to an earlier place-name. In Hartland DEV, the name with –*land* appears in records later than an alternative name with –**tūn** (*Heortigtun* 880–5, *Hertitone* DB) with which it coexisted from 1167 to 1566. As the EPNS survey (p. 72) suggests, the name with –*land* may have seemed more appropriate to the very large manor and parish which centres around the settlement. Stoke Climsland CNW contains a settlement called Climson (*Climestone* DB). In Portland DOR, *land* has been added to the earlier name *Port*, and 'estate attached to Port' seems a sensible rendering; the full name is recorded in the 9th century, suggesting that *land* was occasionally used in the sense 'estate' at a relatively early date. Buckland (BRK, BUC, DEV(8), DOR(2), GLO, HMP, HRE, HRT, KNT(2), LIN (lost), SOM(4), SUR) is from OE *bōcland* 'estate granted by royal charter'. Redland GLO ('third land') is interpreted in EPNS survey 3 (p. 143) as referring to the third part of an estate which had been divided up for some reason. Kirkland CMB is probably 'church estate'.

Copeland CMB and Coupland NTB are from ON *kaupland* 'purchased land', and here also *land* should be translated 'estate'. Copeland CMB was a barony, as was Gilsland CMB; the last is named from Gille son of Bueth who is mentioned in the Lanercost foundation charter of AD 1169, so this is a ME coinage. A more general sense than 'estate' is found in some district-names, such as Bowland Forest LNC/YOW, Cleveland YOW, Holland LIN, Kidland Forest NTB, and in the three most northerly county-names of England. On a smaller scale, the general sense occurs in Threapland CMB ('disputed land'), which is on the boundary of its parish.

A more precise meaning than 'estate', the suggested 'new arable area', is obviously appropriate to Newland. This occurs as a major name in BRK, GLO, LNC, WOR, YOW, and the variant Newlands is found in CMB and NTB. None of these is recorded before the 13th century, and all of them probably refer to land brought into cultivation after the Norman Conquest. In the BRK and GLO examples the reclamation was demonstrably by clearance of forest. Pre-Conquest colonization may be referred to in names in which *land* is combined with varying first elements, especially when groups of such names occur in areas where relatively late colonization is geographically likely. It is probable that in some areas a close correlation could be demonstrated between *land* and some other terms discussed in this chapter, such as **feld**, **æcer**, **ersc**. Some of the names mentioned below may contain ON *land*. This is most likely to be the case in Litherland, of which there are two examples in LNC, since this has as first element ON *hlithar*, gen. of **hlíth** 'slope'.

The most striking concentration of names containing *land* is to be found in YOW, on sheet 102 of the O.S. 1″ map. The county has 13 such names. Six of them—Barkisland, Elland, Greetland, Norland, Soyland and Stainland—are bunched together in the area between Halifax and Huddersfield, and another 6—Crosland, Thurstonland, 3 instances of Hoyland, and Thurgoland— extend in an arc S. and S.E. from this group. The remaining name, Newland near Wakefield, is an outlier, but is close enough to appear on the same 1″ map. It would be easy to make a case, based on archaeology, type of landscape, and incidence of ON names, for the late arable exploitation of this area.

Another county in which names containing *land* are concentrated in one area is NFK, where, with the exception of Thorpland near Fakenham, the examples are in a rough line stretching from N.W. to S.E. of Norwich. Irmingland is the most northerly, then Haveringland, Ringland and Poringland, with Sisland (W. of Loddon) the most southerly. In this region reclamation would be from heath. All except Sisland are –**inga**– names, and Kessingland SFK, another –*ingaland*, is not far away, S. of Lowestoft, on the other side of the Hundred River from Benacre.

Examples from other counties of names in which 'new arable' seems a likely meaning for *land* may conveniently be grouped according to the type of reclamation appropriate to their sites.

For Woodlands DOR, David Mills (EPNS survey 2, p. 284) suggests 'land cleared for cultivation near or within a wood', and this seems the appropriate sense for the compound in all instances in which it was a settlement-name in the early medieval period. In addition to the DOR name, Ekwall 1960 lists Woodland DEV (a parish S.E. of Ashburton) and Woodlands KNT and SOM. He comments 'self-explanatory', presumably meaning that the sense is that of modern England *woodland*; but this is only appropriate for minor names of later origin. Leaveland KNT is in heavily wooded country S. of Faversham, but apart from Woodland(s) and some instances of Newland(s), compounds with *land* do not often have a clear relationship to forest. Relation to heath, high moorland and marsh is much easier to demonstrate.

Most of the NFK and SFK names containing *land* are in areas which were probably heathland. This applies to Shelland and Swilland SFK, in addition to the 6 names listed above. Other instances of heathland sites are:

1. Burland W. of Nantwich CHE, said in EPNS survey 3 (p. 134) to be a district of ancient common land
2. Cadland, on the W. bank of Southampton Water, HMP
3. Cooksland, N.W. of Stafford, STF
4. Curland, S.E. of Taunton, SOM
5. East Donyland, S. of Colchester, ESX
6. Studland, on the Isle of Purbeck, DOR
7. Welland, E. of the Malvern Hills, WOR

A number of settlements with names containing *land* are at the limits of cultivable land on the edge of high moors. Here may be instanced:

1. Blackland, S.E. of Calne, WLT
2. Buteland, S.E. of Bellingham, NTB
3. Byland, beside Hambledon Hills, YON
4. Dotland, S. of Hexham, NTB

5   Goathland, S.W. of Whitby, YON
6   Hulland, E. of Ashbourne, DRB
7   Rusland, in Furness Fells, LNC
8   Spotland, N. of Rochdale, LNC
9   Strickland, N. of Kendal, WML
10 Swarland NTB, between the significantly-named settlements of Newton-on-the-Moor and Felton
11 Upholland LNC

Some of the DEV names containing *land* perhaps belong in this category; possibly examples are Allisland, Marland and Dowland, all S.E. of Bideford, Molland and Stockland in the E. of the county, and in the S. of the county Membland S. of Yealmpton. Some hesitation in categorizing the DEV names arises, however, from doubt as to whether a situation near the edge of high moorland would have been considered noteworthy there.

Names containing *land* which may refer to the reclamation of coastal or riverine marsh are:

1   Brookland KNT, in Walland Marsh
2   Burland YOE, N.E. of Howden
3   Crowland LIN
4   Downholland LNC, E. of Formby
5   Ealand LIN
6   Holland, on the ESX coast
7   Snodland KNT, overlooking marshy ground by the R. Medway
8   Stockland Bristol SOM, overlooking coastal marsh near the estuary of the R. Parrett
9   Yaverland IOW, near marshland in the estuary of the R. Yar
10 Yealand LNC, where the settlements are on raised ground with marsh on either side.

It is hoped that in the foregoing discussion a reasonable case has been established for a meaning 'land broken in from marsh/moor/heath/wood', but no claim is made that all ancient settlement-names containing *land* can be easily slotted into these categories after a cursory examination of the 1″ map. No obvious explanation suggests itself for Leyland LNC, Ponteland NTB, North Sunderland ('southern land') S. of Bamburgh NTB, Thurland in Tunstall LNC, Willand DEV or Woolland DOR. Willand DEV, however, has *wilde* 'waste' as first element, and this may indicate that the Anglo-Saxons found a deserted settlement here. For Wigland CHE, on the SHR border, the surrounding place-names suggest a mixture of wood, heath and fen.

In Oldland GLO the sense is certainly 'arable land', here probably 'primary area of cultivation'. The compound is fairly common as a minor name or field-name, but only the GLO instance has achieved the status of DB manor and parish. In minor names, Oldland (like Oldfield) can mean either 'primary area of cultivation' or 'abandoned arable on the outskirts of settlement'.

OE *sundorland*, for which Smith 1956 gives 'land set apart for some special purpose, private land, detached land', occurs in the form Sunderland in CMB, DRH, LNC, WOR and YOW, and as Sinderland in CHE. There is also a Sunderlandwick in YOE, and the term occurs in minor names and field-names. This name is considered to have a tenurial, rather than a geographical, significance.

It remains to analyse the first elements of those names in which *land* is most likely to mean 'cultivated area'. One of the largest categories consists of personal names, a significant number of which are ON. In this category are Allisland DEV, Barkisland YOW (ON), Buteland NTB, Byland YON, Cadland HMP, Cooksland STF, Donyland ESX, Dotland NTB (ON), Leaveland KNT, Rusland LNC, Sisland NFK, Snodland KNT, Thurgoland YOW (ON), Thurland LNC (ON), Thurstonland YOW (ON) and Wigland CHE. The category in which the first element is a topographical term is slightly larger, but this is because several compounds recur. Here belong Brookland KNT; Ealand LIN, Elland YOW, Ponteland NTB (all with ēa 'river'); Holland ESX, LNC, Hoyland YOW(3), Hulland DRB (all with hōh 'hill-spur'); Litherland LNC(2); Marland DEV; Shelland SFK; Woodland DEV, Woodlands DOR, KNT, SOM; and Woolland DOR.

The first element is a descriptive word in Blackland WLT, Greetland YOW, Leyland LNC, Soyland YOW, Stainland YOW, Swarland NTB, Willand DEV and Yealand LNC. Spotland LNC, with an OE or ON noun meaning 'small piece', perhaps belongs by implication in this group, and Newland(s) and Oldland can be roughly classified here. The nature of some of the descriptive terms—'gravel', 'stone', 'mud', 'heavy', 'waste'—supports the interpretation suggested for *land*. The 5 –inga– compounds of NFK and SFK are also consistent with the hypothesis of colonization in the Anglo-Saxon period. Apart from these group-names, the only reference to a specific type of owner or occupier noted is that in Burland CHE. For Burland YOE the EPNS survey (p. 248) suggests 'land with a byre', and this appears to be the only example with a building term. Direction is referred to in Norland YOW and Sunderland North NTB.

The first element is certainly or probably an earlier place-name or river-name in Curland SOM, Stockland DEV, SOM, Thorpland NFK and Welland WOR. Membland and Molland DEV may contain a river-name and a hill-name. These names should be interpreted differently from Portland DOR (discussed above), as the sites offer scope for late development of arable land which is lacking at Portland. The first elements of Strickland WML, Studland DOR and Swilland SFK refer to domestic animals, and in this context it seems best to take the boars of Yaverland IOW as domestic rather than wild. Strickland recurs several times as a minor name in WML. There is a notable absence of references to wild creatures, and to vegetation.

Crowland LIN and Dowland DEV are obscure.

mǣd OE 'meadow'. The declension of nouns to which *mǣd* belongs takes a *–w–* in the oblique cases, and modern *meadow* is from the OE dat. *mǣdwe*. The word is related to *mow*, and it refers to land from which hay-crops could be obtained. It is rare in settlement-names, probably because the presence of such land was taken for granted as a condition of settlement.

mǣd is the first element of Madehurst SSX, Medhurst KNT; Meaburn WML, Medbourne LEI, WLT; and Metfield SFK. It is the second element of Breightmet LNC, Bushmead BDF, Denmead HMP, Hardmead BUC, Hormead HRT, Shipmeadow SFK and Whiteoxmead SOM. In Runnymede SUR it has been added to an earlier place-name meaning 'council island'.

Presteigne RAD is OE *hemm-mǣd* 'border meadow' with 'priest' prefixed. This etymology was put forward in Charles 1938, but has been subsequently ignored. The town overlooks a large triangle of flat ground in the confluence of the R. Lugg and a tributary. There are steep hills all round, which makes this area a noteworthy feature, and it is on the RAD/HRE border. OE *hemm* is used in border-names in the Welsh Marches. Ekwall 1960 (besides ascribing Presteigne partly to SHR) offers a fanciful etymology involving OE *hǣmed* 'marriage, sexual intercourse'. Smith 1956 takes the name to be simply 'priests' mead', but early spellings such as *Presthemede* 1291, 1341 accord very well with B G Charles's etymology.

wisce, wixe OE 'marshy meadow'. The word survives in SSX dialect as *wish*. It is the first element of Wisborough Green SSX. Wisley SUR and Whistley BRK are from OE *wisclēah*, which was probably a compound appellative as it is repeated in a number of minor names and field-names which are listed in EPNS survey of BRK (pp. 100–1). *wisce* is the second element of Cranwich NFK and Dulwich GTL. Hautbois NFK (earlier *Hobwiss*, *Hobwise*) may contain *wisce* or a related word *wisse*. The latter is a possible first element for Wisbech CAM.

8   The Anglo-Saxon kingdoms and peoples

References

Anderson, O S 1934: *The English Hundred-Names*, Lund. 1939: *The English Hundred-Names; The South-Western Counties*. Lund.

Brandon, P 1978: The South Saxon *Andredesweald*. *The South Saxons*, ed. P. Brandon. Chichester, 138–59.

Cameron, K 1965: *Scandinavian Settlement in the Territory of the Five Boroughs: The Place-Name Evidence*. Inaugural lecture, University of Nottingham.

Charles, B G 1938: *Non-Celtic Place-Names in Wales*. London.

Coates, R 1980: Methodological reflexions on Leatherhead. EPNS *Journal* XII, 70–73. 1981: The slighting of Strensall. EPNS *Journal* XIII, 50–53.

Cole, Ann 1982: Topography, hydrology and place-names in the chalklands of southern England: *cumb* and *denu*. *Nomina* VI, 73–87.

Cox, B 1973: The significance of the distribution of English place-names in –*hām* in the Midlands and East Anglia. EPNS *Journal* V, 15–73. 1976: The place-names of the earliest English records. EPNS *Journal* VIII, 12–66.

Davis, R H C 1962: Brixworth and Clofesho. *Journal of the British Archaeological Association*, Series 3, XXV, 71. 1973: The ford, the river and the city. *Oxoniensia* XXXVIII, 258–67.

Dodgson, J M 1967–8: The –*ing*– in English place-names like Birmingham and Altrincham. *Beiträge zur Namenforschung*, neue folge, Band II, Heft 3, 222–45. Various forms of Old English –*ing* in English place-names. *ibid.*, Heft 4, 325–96. Various English place-name formations containing Old English –*ing. ibid.*, Band III, Heft 2, 141–89. 1973: Place-names from *hām*, distinguished from *hamm* names, in relation to the settlement of Kent, Surrey and Sussex. *Anglo-Saxon England* II, 1–50. 1978: Place-names in Sussex: the material for a new look. *The South Saxons*. ed. P Brandon. Chichester, 54–88

Duignan, W H 1902: *Notes on Staffordshire Place Names*. London.

Ekwall, E 1922: *The Place-Names of Lancashire*. Manchester. 1928: *English River-Names*. Oxford. 1960: *The Concise Oxford Dictionary of English Place-Names*. (1st ed. 1936, 4th ed. 1960). 1962: *English Place-Names in –ing*. (1st ed. 1923, 2nd ed. 1962).

Emery, F 1974: *The Oxfordshire Landscape*. London.

Everitt, A 1977: River and wold: reflections on the historical origin of regions and pays. *Journal of Historical Geography* III (1), 1–19. 1979: Place-names and pays: the Kentish evidence. *Nomina* III, 95–112.

Faull, Margaret L 1974: Roman and Anglian settlement patterns in Yorkshire. *Northern History* IX, 1–25.

Fellows Jensen, Gillian 1972: *Scandinavian Settlement Names in Yorkshire*. Copenhagen. 1978: *Scandinavian Settlement Names in the East Midlands*. Copenhagen.

Forsberg, R 1950: *A Contribution to a Dictionary of Old English Place-Names*. Uppsala.

Förster, M 1921: Keltisches Wortgut im Englischen. *Texte und Forschungen zur englischen Kulturgeschichte, Festgabe für Felix Liebermann*. Halle, 119–242.

Fox, H S A 1981: Approaches to the adoption of the midland system. *The Origins of Open Field Agriculture*, ed. T Rowley. London, 64–111

Foxall, H D G 1980: *Shropshire Field-Names*. Shrewsbury.

Fraser, I A 1982: The Scottish border—an onomastic assessment. *Nomina* VI, 23–30.

Gelling, Margaret 1960: The element *hamm* in English place-names: a topographical investigation. *Namn och Bygd* XLVIII (1–4), 140–62. 1961: Place-Names and Anglo-Saxon Paganism. *University of Birmingham Historical Journal* VIII, 7–25. 1970: English entries in M Gelling, W H F Nicolaisen and M Richards, *The Names of Towns and Cities in Britain*. London. 1973: Further thoughts on pagan place-names. *Otium et Negotium: Studies in Onomatology and Library Science Presented to Olof von Feilitzen*, ed. F Sandgren. Stockholm, 109–28. 1974: Some notes on Warwickshire place-names. *Transactions of the Birmingham and Warwickshire Archaeological Society* LXXXVI, 59–79. 1976: Introduction to 'The Place-Names of Berkshire'. EPNS BRK survey, 800–47. 1978: *Signposts to the Past: Place-Names and the History of England*. London. 1982: Some meanings of *stōw*. *The Early Church in Western Britain and Ireland: Studies presented to C.A.R. Raleigh Radford*, ed. S M Pearce. British Archaeological Reports, British Series 102, 187–96.

Hald, K 1978: A-mutation in Scandinavian words in England. *The Vikings*, ed. T Andersson and K I Sandred. Uppsala, 99–106.

Holthausen, F 1934: *Altenglisches Etymologisches Wörterbuch*. Heidelberg.

Hooke, Della 1978: Early Cotswold woodland. *Journal of Historical Geography* IV, 333–41. 1981: *Anglo-Saxon Landscapes of the West Midlands: the Charter Evidence*. British Archaeological Reports, British Series 95.

Huggins, R 1975: The significance of the place name 'Wealdhām'. *Medieval Archaeology* XIX, 198–201.

Jackson, K 1953: *Language and History in Early Britain*. Edinburgh.

Johansson, C 1975: *Old English Place-Names and Field-Names containing lēah*. Stockholm.

Kökeritz, H 1940: *The Place-Names of the Isle of Wight*. Uppsala.

Löfvenberg, M T 1942: *Studies on Middle English Local Surnames*. Lund.

Macdonald, A 1941: *The Place-Names of West Lothian*. Edinburgh.

Margary, I D 1955: *Roman Roads in Britain*, Vol. I. London. 1957: *Roman Roads in Britain*, Vol. II. London.

Marwick, H 1952: *Orkney Farm Names*. Kirkwall.

Mawer, A 1920: *The Place-Names of Northumberland and Durham*. Cambridge.

Maynard, Helen 1974: The use of the place-name elements *mōr* and *mersc* in the Avon valley. *Transactions of the Birmingham and Warwickshire Archaeological Society* LXXXVI, 80–4.

Nicolaisen, W H F   1976: *Scottish Place-Names: their study and significance*. London.

Noble, F   1983: *Offa's Dyke Re-Viewed*. British Archaeological Reports, British Series 114.

Onions, C T   1966: *The Oxford Dictionary of English Etymology*.

Padel, O J   1981: Welsh **blwch** 'bald, hairless'. *The Bulletin of the Board of Celtic Studies* XXIX (2), 523–6.

Pocock, E A   1968: The first fields in an Oxfordshire parish. *The Agricultural History Review* XVI (2), 85–100.

Pool, P A S   1973: *The Place-Names of West Penwith*. Penzance.

Rackham, O   1976: *Trees and Woodland in the British Landscape*. London.

Rivet, A L F and Smith, C   1979: *The Place-Names of Roman Britain*. London.

Rumble, A R   1980: HAMTVN *alias* HAMWIC (Saxon Southampton): the place-name traditions and their significance. *Excavations at Melbourne Street, Southampton, 1971–6*. Council for British Archaeology Research Report 33, 7–20.

Sandred, K I   1976: The element *hamm* in English place-names: a linguistic investigation. *Namn och Bygd* LXIV (1–4), 71–87.

Slater, T R   1979: More on the Wolds. *Journal of Historical Geography* V, 213–8.

Smith, A H   1956: *English Place-Name Elements*. EPNS XXV, XXVI.

Stenton, F M   1911: *The Place-Names of Berkshire: An Essay*. Reading. 1924: The English Element. *Introduction to the Survey of English Place-Names*. EPNS I, Part 1, 36–54. 1943: *Anglo-Saxon England*, first edition. Oxford.

Thomas, C   1980: *Christianity in Roman Britain to AD 500*. London.

Thompson, T R F   1978: Early Cricklade. *Cricklade Historical Society's Bulletin* II (3), 28–34.

Watts, V E   1976: Comment on 'The Evidence of Place-Names' by Margaret Gelling. *Medieval Settlement: Continuity and Change*, ed. P H Sawyer. London, 212–22.

Glossarial Index

Most of the place-names listed in this index can be accorded an etymology which only the most argumentative critic would wish to dispute, but for a substantial minority a greater or lesser degree of doubt or obscurity must be admitted. All the names have been included in the book because they contain (or have been considered in the past to contain) a word for a feature of the landscape, and this means that for most of the compound names the nature of one of the components is beyond doubt. The landscape term may be the first element in a compound, as in Compton and Houghton; but more frequently it is the final element. When a landscape term is qualified by a first element there is often a degree of uncertainty as to the nature of the qualifier, and only detailed discussion could do justice to the possibilities. Here, since the main concern is with the landscape term, summary treatment has been meted out to a considerable number of qualifying elements. Degrees of doubt which are mainly subjective are indicated by 'prob.', 'poss.', '?' and 'partly uncertain/ obscure'. More detailed discussions can be found in Ekwall 1960, and more detailed ones still in EPNS surveys; and by turning to the pages indicated in this index readers will obtain information about the general class to which a name belongs, and this should influence their choice between the various possible etymologies offered by other reference books.

If no comment is made on the language, place-names in the glossarial index may be assumed to be in Old English. Where the name is not OE, some statement is offered, using the abbreviations—PrW, ON, ME etc.—employed in the rest of the book. River-names compounded in OE or ON settlement-names have been treated as items in the language of the people who coined the settlement-names, so in this context no account is taken of whether they are of pre-English origin.

Some of the main settlement terms used in OE and ON place-names are entered in the glossary with a rough translation, to enable them to be referred to without constant explanation in the text of the book.

As regards the translations offered here, no attempt has been made to achieve perfect consistency. For the most part different modes of translation, such as 'thorn wood' and 'wood where thorn-trees grow', 'fort clearing' and 'clearing of the fort', 'lambs' pasture' and 'lamb stream', are deliberate variants, reflecting the grammatical structure revealed by early spellings. This policy is, however, difficult to maintain when the main element in a compound requires two words for translation into modern English. The grammatical structure of Hawkhurst KNT and Hawkridge BRK, SOM is identical, but Hawkhurst is translated 'wooded hill frequented by hawks' because 'hawk wooded hill' seems unsatisfactory. Similarly, Henfield SSX has been rendered 'open land characterized by rocks' because 'rock open land' sounds odd, and 'rocky open land' might be taken to indicate that the first element is an adjective, which is not the case.

Where personal names are involved, the translations take account of the distinction between use of the genitive inflection, as in Abney and Addlestone, and the connective particle -*ing*-, as in Aldingbourne and Ballinger.

It must be emphasized that many of the translations represent a compromise between the conflicting claims of brevity, accuracy and acceptability as modern English phrases. I have felt obliged to follow the advice given by the Good Duke Alfred to his princely friends in Norman Douglas's novel *South Wind*: 'One knock to each nail. And keep smiling.' I hope, however, that nothing offered in the glossary will be seriously misleading, and that over-simplifications will be to some extent offset by more detailed discussions in the text of the book.

Glossarial Index

á ON 'river', 11, 20

Abbotsham DEV 'enclosure'; 'abbot's' prefixed, 45

Abenhall GLO 'Abba's nook', 103

Aberford YOW 'Ēadburh's ford', 69

Abingdon BRK 'Æbba's hill', 147

Abloads Court GLO 'Abba's river-crossing', 73, 75

Abney DRB 'Abba's island', 36, 38

Abridge ESX 'Æffa's bridge', 65

Absol ESX 'Abba's spring', 20

Aby LIN 'river settlement' (ON), 11

āc OE 'oak-tree', 12, 218–19

Acklam YOE, YON '(place) at the oak woods', 203, 225

Acol KNT 'oak wood', 196

Acomb NTB, YON, YOW '(place) at the oak-trees', 218

Acre NFK 'newly-cultivated land', 232, 233

Acton var. cos. 'oak-tree settlement', 218, 219

Adber DOR 'Ēata's grove', 190

Addlestone SUR 'Ættel's valley', 98

Adel YOW 'filthy place', 61

Adeney SHR 'Ēadwynn's island', 37

Adgarley LNC 'Ēadgār's slope', 165

Adlingfleet YOW 'prince's stream', 21

Adwell OXF 'Eadda's spring', 31

Agden HNT 'Acca's valley', 98

Agden YOW 'oak-tree valley', 98

æcer OE 'plot of cultivated land', 231, 232–3, 234, 246

æppel OE 'apple-tree', 218, 219–20

æsc OE 'ash-tree', 218, 219

Æscesdun BRK ?'hill of the ash-tree', 147, 154

æspe OE 'aspen-tree', 222

ǣwell OE 'river-source', 12

ǣwelm OE 'river-source', 12

Agneash IOM 'edge ness' (ON), 173

Aigburth LNC 'oak-tree hill' (ON), 219

Aighton LNC 'oak-tree settlement', 218

Ainderby Mires YON 'Eindrithi's village' (ON); 'in the marsh' added, 57

Ainsdale LNC 'Ægenwulf's valley', 96

Ainstable CMB 'bracken slope' (ON), 167

Ainsty Cliff YOW ?'linking road', 64

Aintree LNC 'solitary tree' (?ON), 212, 214

Airmyn YOW 'mouth of R. Aire' (ON), 11

Aiskew YON 'oak wood' (ON), 209, 219

Aisholt SOM 'ash wood', 196

Akeld NTB 'oak-tree slope', 162

Akeley BUC 'oak wood', 203

akr ON 'plot of cultivated land', 231, 232–3

Albourne SSX 'alder stream', 18

Aldbourne WLT 'stream associated with Ealda', 18

Aldcliffe LNC, prob. 'Alda's cliff', 134, 135

Alderford NFK 'alder-tree ford', 70, 220

Alderholt DOR 'alder wood', 196, 220

Aldersceugh CMB 'alder wood' (OE/ON), 209

Aldersey CHE ?'Ealdhere's island', 35

Aldershot SUR 'projecting land with alders', 220

Alderton SHR, SFK 'alder-tree settlement', 220

Alderwasley DRB 'wood/clearing/pasture belonging to alluvial land with alders', 60

Aldfield YOW 'old open land', 244

Aldford CHE 'old ford', 69

Aldingbourne SSX 'stream associated with Ealda', 18

Aldon SHR 'river-source hill', 12, 145, 154

Aldreth CAM 'landing-place by alders', 62, 76, 77

Aldridge STF 'alder-tree settlement', 220

Alford SOM 'Ēaldgyth's ford', 69

Allensmore HRE 'marsh'; owner's name prefixed, 54

Aller DEV, SOM 'alder-tree', 220

Allerdale CMB 'valley of R. Ellen' (ON), 94, 95

Allerford SOM(2) 'alder-tree ford', 70, 220

bæce, bece OE 'stream in a valley', 11, 12–13, 14, 125, 126
bæth OE 'bath', 13–14
Bagendon GLO 'valley of Bæcga's people', 99
Bageridge DOR, STF, Baggridge SOM 'badger ridge', 169
Bagley BRK, SHR, SOM, YOW 'badger wood', 205
Bagnor BRK 'badger slope', 179, 181
Bagpath GLO 'badger path', 79
Bagshaw DRB 'badger shaw', 209
Bagslate LNC, prob. 'badger valley', 122
Baguley CHE 'badger wood', 205
Baildon YOW, prob. 'round hill', 142, 143, 157
Bain, R., LIN, YON ? 'helpful' (ON), 11
Bakewell DRB 'Badeca's springs', 31
Baldon OXF 'Bealda's hill', 53, 150
Bale NFK 'bath wood/clearing', 13
Balkholme YOE 'ridge island', 51, 52
Balking BRK 'playful stream of the pools', 13
Ballidon DRB 'bag valley', 98
Ballingdon SFK 'rounded hill', 143
Ballinger BUC 'hill-slope connected with Beald', 120, 180
Ballingham HRE, prob. 'river-bend land of the people of Badela', 47
Balsall WAR 'Bælli's nook', 105
Balsdean SSX 'Beald's valley', 98
Balshaw LNC 'rounded shaw', 209
Baltonsborough SOM 'Bealdhūn's hill', 128
Bamford DRB, LNC 'tree-trunk ford', 69
Bampton (near Morebath) DEV 'settlement of the bath-dwellers', 13
Bandon SUR 'bean hill', 144
Bannisdale WML 'Bannandi's valley' (ON), 94
Banwell SOM 'Bana's spring', 31
Bapchild KNT 'Bacca's spring', 20
Barbon WML 'bear stream', 18
Barbourne WOR 'beaver stream', 18
Barden YON, prob. 'valley where barley grows', 98
Barden YOW, 'barley valley', 98
Bardfield ESX, partly uncertain, 241, 244
Bardney LIN 'Bearda's island', 38
Bardon LEI ? 'tumulus hill', 142, 156
Bardsea CRN 'Bárthr's island' (ON), 36

Bardsea LNC, Bardsey YOW 'Beornræd's island', 35, 36, 38
Bare LNC 'grove', 190
Barford (Little) BDF 'birch-tree ford', 220
Barford var. cos. 'barley ford', 71
Barforth YON 'barley ford', 71
Barham CAM, HNT, SFK 'hill village', 127
Barhaugh NTB 'barley nook', 108
Barholm LIN 'hill village', 127
Barkham BRK, SSX 'birch-tree meadow', 43, 49, 220
Barkisland YOW 'Barkr's newly-cultivated land' (ON), 246, 249
Barkway HRT 'birch-tree way', 83, 220
Barley LNC, prob. 'barley clearing', 206
Barleyhill NTB 'barley hill', 163
Barlow DRB, prob. 'barley clearing', 206
Barmer NFK ?'bear pond', 26, 27
Barmoor NTB 'berry moor', 55
Barnacle WAR 'sloping wood by a barn', 195, 196
Barnacre LNC 'newly-cultivated land with a barn', 232, 233
Barnhill YOE 'Beorn's hill', 170
Barnsdale RUT 'Beornheard's hill', 170
Barnshaw CHE 'Beornwulf's shaw', 209
Barnsley YOW 'Beorn's clearing', 203
Barnwell NTP, partly uncertain, 32
Barnwood GLO, 'Beorna's wood', 229
Barpham SSX 'hill village', 127
barr PrW 'top', 124, 127
Barr STF 'hill' (Brit), 127
Barrasford NTB 'ford of the grove', 70, 190
Barrock Fell CMB 'hilly place' (Brit); 'fell' added, 127
barrǫg PrW 'hilly', 127
Barrow var. cos. 'grove', 190
Barrow RUT, SOM 'hill', 127
Barrow-in-Furness LNC 'promontory island' (Brit/ON), 40, 127
Barrowden RUT 'hill of the tumuli', 127, 156
Barrowford LNC 'grove ford', 70, 190
Bartestree HRE 'Beorhtwald's tree', 212, 217
Bartley HMP, WOR 'birch wood', 204, 220
Bartlow CAM 'birch-tree tumuli', 220
Barugh YON 'hill', 127
Barway CAM 'tumulus island', 37, 39, 127

Belsay NTB 'Bill's hill-spur', 167, 168

Belwood LIN, partly uncertain, 229

Bembridge IOW '(place) inside the bridge', 66

Benacre SFK 'newly-cultivated land used for beans', 232, 233

Benefield NTP 'open land of Bera's people', 241, 244

Benenden KNT 'woodland pasture associated with Bionna', 234

Benfieldside DRH 'hill-slope by the bent-grass open land', 243

Benfleet ESX 'tree-trunk creek', 22

Bengeo HRT 'hill-spur of the dwellers by the R. Beane', 169

Bengeworth SUR, 'enclosed settlement connected with Beonna', 120

Benhall SFK 'nook where beans grow', 110

Benham BRK 'Benna's meadow', 43, 49

Benhilton SUR 'bean hill'; 'in Sutton' added, 171

Bentfield ESX 'bent-grass open land', 243

Benthall SHR 'bent-grass nook', 104

Bentley var. cos. 'bent-grass clearing', 204

Beobridge SHR 'bee bridge', 66

Beoley WOR 'bee wood/clearing', 205

beorc OE 'birch-tree', 218, **220**

beorg, berg OE 'hill, mound', **127–8**, 129, 189, 221

Bere DEV 'grove', 189

Bere Regis DOR, Bere Forest HMP ?'swine pasture'; 'of the king' added, 189, 190

Bergholt ESX, SFK 'hill wood', 127, 196

Berkeley GLO 'birch wood', 204, 220

Berkesdon HRT 'birch-tree valley', 98, 220

Berkley SOM 'birch wood', 204, 220

Berkswell WAR 'Beorcol's spring', 31

Bermondsey GTL 'Beornmund's island', 38

Bernwood BUC, partly uncertain, 229

Berrier CMB 'hill shieling' (ON), 127

Berrington NTB 'fort hill', 144, 158

Berrow SOM, WOR 'hill', 127

Bessacar YOW 'newly-cultivated land where bent-grass grows', 232, 233

Bestwood NTT 'rush-clump wood', 228

Betchcott SHR 'stream-valley cottages', 12

Betchton CHE 'stream-valley settlement', 12

Bethnal Green GTL, prob. 'nook by R. *Blythe*'; 'village green' added, 111

Betteshanger KNT, prob. 'sloping wood by a building', 195, 196

Bettiscombe DOR 'Betti's coomb', 92

Bevendean SSX 'Beofa's valley', 89, 98

Beversbrook WLT 'beaver's brook', 16

Bexhill SSX 'box wood', 222

Bexley GTL 'box wood', 204, 222

Beynhurst Hundred BRK 'ploughed field used for beans', 235

Bickenhill WAR ?'projecting hill', 154, 170

Bicker LIN ?'(place) by a marsh' (OE/ON), 52–3

Bickershaw LNC 'beekeepers' shaw', 209

Bickerstaffe LNC 'beekeepers' landing-place', 80

Bickleigh DEV (2), Bickley CHE, KNT, WOR ?'bees-nests' wood/clearing', 205

Bickmarsh WAR, partly uncertain, 53

Bicknacre ESX, prob. 'Bica's newly-cultivated land', 232, 233

Bicknoller SOM 'Bica's alder-tree', 220

Bicknor KNT ?'slope near a hill called The Beak', 176, 179, 180

Bicknor GLO/HRE 'ridge with a point', 174

Bidden HMP 'tub-shaped valley', 89

Biddenham BDF ?'Bīeda's land in a river-bend', 47

Biddick DRH '(place) by a ditch', 53

Biddlesden BUC, Biddlestone NTB 'valley of the building', 99

Biddulph STF '(place) by a quarry', 53

Bidna CNW, DEV 'tub-shaped valley', 89

Bidwell BDF 'vessel spring', 32

Bierley YOW 'wood/clearing of the fort', 206

Biggleswade BDF 'Biccel's ford', 83

Bignor SSX ?'Bica's ridge-tip', 178

Bigrigg CMB 'barley ridge' (ON), 169

Bilbrook SOM, STF 'watercress brook', 15

Billesdon LEI 'Bill's hill', 156

Billingford NFK 'ford of Billa's people', 70

Billingley YOW 'clearing of Billa's people', 206

Billingshurst SSX 'Billing's wooded hill', 197

Billington BDF 'Billa's hill', 151

Billington LNC 'sword-shaped hill', 142, 143, 144, 145, 157

Bilney NFK(2) 'island of/at a beak', 38, 39

Bilsdale YON 'Bild's valley', 96

Bincombe DOR 'bean coomb', 93

Bindon DOR '(place) within the down', 147

Binegar SOM ?'Bēage's sloping wood', 195, 196

Binfield BRK 'bent-grass open land', 243

Bingfield NTB ?'open land of Bynna's people', 244

Binley WAR 'island of/at a beak', 36, 38, 39

Binsey OXF 'Byni's island', 38

birce OE 'birch-tree', 218, **220**

Birch HRE 'birch-tree', 220

Bircham NFK 'village by newly-cultivated ground', 233

Birchanger ESX 'birch wood on a slope', 195, 200

Bircher HRE 'birch-tree ridge', 176, 220

Birchill DRB, Birchills STF 'birch-tree hills', 171, 220

Birchington KNT 'settlement where birch-trees grow', 220

Bircholt KNT 'birch wood', 196, 220

Birchover DRB 'birch-tree ridge', 175–6, 220

Birdbrook ESX 'birds' brook', 15

Birdforth YOW 'brides' ford', 70

Birdsall YOE 'Bridd's nook', 108

Birkdale LNC 'birch valley' (ON), 94, 95

Birkenhead CHE 'headland where birch-trees grow', 161, 220

Birkenshaw YOW 'shaw where birch-trees grow', 209

Birkenside DRH 'long hill-slope where birch-trees grow', 187

Birklands NTT 'birch grove' (ON), 207–8

Birley HRE 'ford wood/clearing', 206

Birley DRB(3) 'wood/clearing of the fort', 206

Birlingham WOR 'river-bend land of the people of Byrla', 43, 47, 49

Birmingham WAR, prob. 'village of Beorma's people', 49

Birstwith YOW 'landing-place of the fort', 80, 81

Bishopdale YON 'bishop's valley', 96

Bishopsbourne KNT 'stream'; 'bishop's' prefixed, 17, 19

Bishopstrow WLT 'Biscop's tree', 189, 212, 213–14, 217

Bishopton WAR 'bishop's hill', 145, 154

Bitchfield NTB 'beech-tree open land', 222, 243

Bitterley SHR 'butter pasture', 206

Bitteswell LEI ?'spring of the broad valley', 32, 87

Bittiscombe SOM 'Bitel's coomb', 92

The Bittoms GTL 'broad valley', 87

Bix OXF, prob. 'box wood', 222

Blackberry Hill LEI 'black hill'; 'hill' added, 128

Blackborough DEV, NFK 'black hill', 128

Black Brook var. cos. 'black brook', 15

Blackden CHE 'black valley', 98

Blackdown DOR black hill', 142, 143, 147

Blackford SOM(2) 'black ford', 68

Blackfordby LEI 'black-ford village' (OE/ON), 68

Blackheath GTL 'black heath', 245

Blacklache LNC 'black boggy stream', 25

Blackland WLT 'black newly-cultivated land', 247, 249

Blackmoor DOR 'black moor', 55

Blackmoor HMP 'black pond', 27

Blackmore ESX, WLT, WOR 'black marsh', 55

Blackmore HRT 'black pond', 27

Blackpool LNC 'black pool', 28

Blackrod LNC 'black clearing', 208

Blackshaw YOW 'black shaw', 209

Blackwell DRB(2), DRH, WOR 'black spring', 31

Blackwood YOE, YOW 'black wood', 228

Bladon OXF, pre-English river-name, 21, 74

blaen Welsh 'point, end, top', **128**

Blagdon NTB 'black valley', 98

Blagdon DEV, DOR, SOM(2) 'black hill', 143, 147

Blagrave BRK 'black grove', 193

blain PrW, PrCumb 'point, end, top', 124, **128**

Blaisdon GLO 'Blecci's hill', 143, 149

Blakeney GLO, NFK 'black island', 39

Blakenhall CHE 'black nook', 106, 110

Bowdon CHE 'curved hill', 143, 155
Bowland LNC/YOW 'district characterized by bends', 246
Bowler's Green SUR '(place) above the slope', 165
Bowness CMB 'rounded ness', 172
Bowness WML 'bull ness', 173
Bowood DEV 'bow wood', 229
Bowood DOR, WLT '(place) above the wood', 229
box OE 'box-tree', 222
Box GLO, HRT, WLT 'box-tree', 222
Boxford BRK 'box-tree slope', 5, 72, 179, 181, 222
Boxford SFK 'box-tree ford', 222
Boxgrove SSX 'box grove', 194, 222
Boxley KNT 'box wood', 204, 222
Boxted SFK 'box-tree place', 222
Boxwell GLO 'box-tree spring', 31, 222
Boyland NFK 'Boia's grove' (OE/ON), 207
Brabourne KNT 'broad stream', 18
Bracebridge LIN, partly obscure, 66
Bracewell YOW 'Breith's spring' (ON/OE), 31
Brackenborough LIN 'bracken hill', 128
Brackenthwaite CMB 'bracken clearing' (?ON), 211
Bracknell BRK 'Bracca's nook', 101
Bradbourne DRB 'broad stream', 18
Bradda IOM 'steep headland' (ON), 162
Bradfield var. cos. 'broad open land', 238, 239, 242
Bradford var. cos. 'broad ford', 67, 68
Bradiford DEV 'broad ford', 68
Bradle DOR 'broad clearing', 205
Bradley var. cos. 'broad clearing', 205
Bradmore NTT 'broad lake', 27
Bradney SOM 'broad island', 39
Bradnop STF 'broad valley', 115, 116
Bradnor HRE 'broad slope', 179, 181
Bradpole DOR 'broad pool', 28
Bradshaw DRB, LNC, YOW 'broad shaw', 209
Bradsole KNT 'broad muddy place', 58
Bradwall CHE 'broad spring', 31
Bradway DRB 'broad way', 83
Bradwell var. cos. 'broad spring', 31
Brafield NTP 'open ground by a raised area', 241, 243
Braintree ESX 'Branca's tree', 212, 214
Braithwaite CMB(3), YON 'broad clearing' (ON), 211
Brambridge HMP 'broom bridge', 65

Bramdean HMP 'broom valley', 98
Bramfield SFK 'broom open land', 243
Bramfield HRT ?'steep open land', 241, 243
Bramhill CHE 'broom nook', 106, 110
Bramhope YOW 'broom valley', 115, 116
Bramley var. cos. 'broom clearing', 205
Bramshall STF 'broom shelf', 187
Bramshaw HMP 'bramble shaw', 209
Brancepeth DRH, prob. 'Brant's path', 78, 79
Brandon var. cos. 'broom hill', 142, 153, 154, 157
Brandon LIN ?'hill by R. *Brant*', 145, 156
Brandwood LNC 'burnt wood', 228
Branscombe DEV 'Branoc's coomb', 92
Bransdale YON 'Brand's valley', 96
Bransty CMB 'steep path' (ON), 81
Branthwaite CMB(2) 'bramble clearing' (ME/ON), 211
Brantwood LNC 'burnt wood', 228
Brathay. R., LNC/WML 'broad river' (ON), 11
Bratton DEV(2), SOM, WLT 'settlement by newly-cultivated ground', 233, 234
Brauncewell LIN 'Brand's spring' (ON/OE), 31
Brawith YON 'broad ford' (ON), 82
Braxted ESX ?'fern place', 233
Bray BRK 'marsh' (OFr), 34, 129
Bray DEV 'hill' (Brit), 129
Braybrooke NTP 'broad brook', 15
Brayfield BUC 'open ground by a raised area', 241, 243
Breadsall DRB 'Brægd's nook', 107
Breamore HMP 'broom moor', 55
brēc, brǣc OE 'breach', 233–4
Breckles NFK 'meadow by newly-cultivated ground', 233
Bredfield SFK ?'open land characterized by breadth', 243
Bredhurst KNT 'wooded hill where boards are obtained', 198
Bredon WOR, Breedon LEI 'hill called *Bre*' (Brit/OE), 129, 142, 145, 154, 156
breȝ. PrW, PrCorn, PrCumb 'hill', 124, **128–9**
Breightmet LNC 'bright meadow', 250
Breighton YOE 'bridge settlement', 65
brekka ON 'slope', **129**

Frenchmoor HMP ?'French marsh', 55

Fressingfield SFK ?'open land of the Frisians', 244

Fretherne GLO ?'sanctuary thorn-tree', 221

Frilford BRK 'Frithela's ford', 67, 69

Frith var. cos. ?'scrub on the edge of the forest', 191

Frithsden HRT 'valley of the scrubland', 99, 191

Frithville LIN 'brushwood'; modern -ville (from French *ville*) added, 191

Frizenham DEV 'Frisian's enclosure', 45

Frizinghall YOW 'nook associated with a Frisian', 108

Frodsham CHE ?'Frōd's promontory', 48

Frogmore var. cos. 'frog pond', 26

Frome, R., DOR, HRE, SOM 'brisk' (Brit), 21

Frostenden SFK, poss. 'frogs' valley', 98

Froxfield HMP, WLT 'frogs' open land', 244

Fryup YON, partly uncertain, 116

Fulbeck LIN 'dirty brook' (OE/ON), 14

Fulbourn CAM 'bird stream', 18

Fulbrook BUC, OXF, WAR 'dirty brook', 15

Fulford DEV, SOM, STF, YOE 'foul ford', 68

Fulham GTL 'Fulla's land in a river-bend', 42, 43, 49

Fulmer BUC 'bird pond', 26

Fulready WAR 'foul stream', 29

Fulshaw CHE 'bird shaw', 209

Fulwell DRH, OXF 'foul spring', 31

Fulwood LNC, NTT 'foul wood', 228

funta OE 'spring', **22**, 32

Funtley HMP 'spring wood', 22

Furness LNC 'ness at the island called *Futh* (posterior)' (ON), 173

Furtho NTP 'ford spur', 68, 168

The Fylde LNC 'plain' 240

fyrhth, fyrhthe OE ?'scrub on the edge of forest', 188, **191–2**, 194

Gabwell DEV 'Gabba's spring', 31

Gad Bridge BRK 'goats' bridge', 66

Gaddesden HRT 'Gǣte's valley', 98

Gagingwell OXF 'kinsmen's spring', 32

Gaisgill WML 'valley of geese' (ON), 99

Galgate LNC, poss. 'Galloway road' (ON), 73

Galsworthy DEV ?'slope of bog-myrtle', 179, 180

Gamlingay CAM 'Gamela's enclosure', 37

Gappah DEV 'góats' path', 78

Garford BRK, Garforth YOW 'gore ford', 67, 70

Gargrave YOW 'spear-shaped grove', 193

Garmondsway DRH 'Gārmund's way', 83

Garsdale YOW 'grass valley', 96

Garsdon WLT 'grass hill', 144

Garsington OXF 'hill where grass grows', 144, 150

Garswood LNC, partly obscure, 229

Gartree Wapentake LEI, LIN 'marked tree' (ON/OE) (ON), 212, 214

gata ON 'road, street', 73

Gatacre SHR 'newly-cultivated land where goats are kept', 232, 233

Gatcliff IOW 'goats' cliff', 130, 136

Gatcombe IOW 'goats' coomb', 90, 93

Gateacre LNC 'newly-cultivated land where goats are kept', 232, 233

Gateford NTT, Gateforth YOW 'goats' ford', 71

Gate Helmsley YON 'Hemele's island'; 'road' prefixed, 38

Gateley NFK 'goats' pasture', 206

Gateshead DRH 'goat's head', 160, 161

Gathurst LNC 'goats' wooded hill', 197

Gatley CHE 'goats' cliff', 136

Gattertop HRE, partly obscure, 113

Gaunless, R., DRH 'useless' (ON), 11

Gauxholme LNC 'Gauk's island' (ON), 52

Gayhurst BUC 'goats' wooded hill', 197

Gazegill YOW 'valley of geese' (ON), 99

Gedgrave SFK 'goats' grove', 194

Gedney LIN 'Gydda's island', 38

gelād OE ?'difficult river-crossing', 7, 23, 62, 73–6, 179

Georgeham DEV 'well-watered valley'; church dedication prefixed, 44, 50

gewæd OE 'ford', 62, **83**

Ghidenetroi Hundred SSX ?'sacred tree', 212, 215

Gibsmere NTT 'Gyppi's pond', 26

Giddinge KNT 'Gydda's place', 119

gil ON 'deep, narrow valley', **99**

Gilcrux CMB 'retreat by a hill' (PrCumb), 138

Gillcamban CMB 'Kamban's valley' (ON), 99

Gilsland CMB 'Gille's estate' (ME), 246

Girtford BDF 'gravel ford', 68

Gisburn YOW, partly uncertain, 19

Givendale YOE 'valley of R. *Gifl*', 96

Givendale YOW, poss. 'hollow associated with Gȳthla', 94

Glaisdale YON 'valley of R. *Glas*', 96

Glandford NFK 'merriment ford', 72

Glanford Brigg LIN 'merriment ford'; 'bridge' added, 72

Glanton NTB, partly uncertain, 158

gleann Gaelic 'valley', **99–100**

Gledholt YOW(2) 'kites' wood', 196

Glen, R., LIN, NTB 'clean' (Brit), 99

Glen LEI, prob. 'valley' (Brit), 99

Glencoyne CMB/WML 'valley of R. *Coyne*' (PrCumb), 100

Glendon NTP 'clean hill', 144, 153

Glendue NTB 'dark valley' (PrW), 100

Glenfield LEI 'clean open ground', 241, 242

glennos Brit 'valley', **99–100**

Glenridding WML, poss. 'fern valley' (PrW), 100

glin Corn 'valley', **99–100**

Glossop DRB 'Glott's valley', 115, 116

Glusburn YOW 'shining stream', 18

glyn Welsh 'valley', **99–100**

Glynde Reach SSX 'drainage channel at Glynde', 185

Gnatham DEV 'gnat-infested enclosure', 45

Gnosall STF, partly obscure, 105, 111

Goathill DOR 'goat hill', 171

Goathland YON 'Gōda's newly-cultivated land', 248

Goathorn DOR 'goat shore', 180

Goathurst SOM 'wooded hill frequented by goats', 197

Godington OXF 'Gōda's hill', 149

Godney SOM 'Gōda's island', 38

Golborne CHE, LNC 'marsh-marigold stream', 18

Golder OXF 'marigold slope', 179, 180

Goldhanger ESX 'golden sloping wood', 195

Gomeldon WLT 'Gumela's hill', 149

Gomersal YOW 'Gumer's nook', 107, 110

Gomshall SUR 'Guma's shelf', 187

Goodwood SSX 'Gōdgiefu's wood', 229

Goosey BRK 'goose island', 5, 6, 37, 39

Goostrey CHE 'gorse-tree', 212, 214

Gopsall LEI, partly uncertain, 171

Gornal STF 'mill nook', 105, 111

Gosbrook STF 'goose brook', 15, 16

Gosfield ESX, HMP 'open land of geese', 241, 244

Gosford DEV, OXF, WAR, Gosforth CMB, NTB 'ford of geese', 71

Gostrow Hundred SSX 'gorse-tree', 212

Goudhurst KNT, partly uncertain, 198

Gowdall YOW 'marigold nook', 107

græfe OE 'thicket, brushwood', prob. 'grove', 189, **192–4**

grāf, grāfa, grāfe OE 'grove, copse', 167, 189, **192–4**

Graffham SSX, Grafham HNT 'grove village', 193

Grafton var. cos. 'grove settlement', 193, 194

Grandborough BUC, WAR 'green hill', 128

Gransden CAM/HNT 'Grante's valley', 98

Gransmore YOE 'Grente's marsh', 55

Grappenhall CHE 'nook of the drain', 106, 111

Grasmere WML 'lake with grassy shores', 26

Grassendale LNC 'pasture valley', 96

Graveley CAM 'grove wood', 193

Gravenhunger SHR ?'hanging wood with a coppice', 193, 195, 196

Gravenhurst BDF ?'wooded hill with a coppice', 193, 198

Gravenor SHR, prob. 'grove ridge', 176, 193

Gravesend KNT 'grove's end', 193

Grayrigg WML 'grey ridge' (ON), 169

Grayshott HMP ?'projecting coppice', 193

Graythwaite LNC 'grey clearing' (ON), 211

Grazeley BRK 'badger wallowing-place', 58

Greasley NTT 'gravel clearing', 205

Greatford LIN 'gravel ford', 68

Greatness KNT ?'ploughed field by a gravelly stream', 235

Greenford GTL 'green ford', 68

Greenhaugh NTB 'green nook', 108, 110

Greenhill WOR, partly uncertain, 171

Greenhithe KNT 'green landing-place', 76, 77

Greetland YOW 'newly-cultivated land with rocks' (ON), 246, 249

Grendon HRE 'green valley', 98

Henmarsh GLO 'wild-birds' marsh', 53

Hennor HRE 'high ridge', 176

Henny ESX 'wild-bird island', 39

Hensall YOW 'Hethīn's nook', 107

Hensborough Hill WAR 'hill of the stallion', 128

Henshaw NTB 'Hethīn's nook', 108

Henstridge SOM 'stallion's ridge', 169

Henthorn LNC 'wild-bird thorn-tree', 221

Henwood WAR 'religious community's wood', 229

Hepple NTB 'hip nook', 108

Hereford HRE(2) 'army ford', 67, 71

Hernhill KNT, prob. 'grey hill', 170

Heronbridge CHE 'bridge at a river-bend', 66

Heronshead SUR 'eagle's head', 161

Herriard HMP 'army enclosure', 50

Herringfleet SFK 'stream of Herela's people', 22

Herringswell SFK, partly uncertain, 32

Herstmonceaux SSX 'wooded hill'; surname suffixed, 197

Herteshede HRT 'hart's headland', 160

Hertford HRT 'hart ford', 67, 71

Hertfordlythe YOE 'goat-ford slope' (OE/ON), 167

Hescombe SOM 'witch coomb', 93

Hesket Newmarket CMB 'ash-tree headland' (ON/OE); 'new market' added, 161

Hesleden DRH 'hazel valley', 98

Heslington YOE 'settlement where hazel-trees grow', 220

Hessay YOW, prob. 'hazel-tree island', 35, 39

Hessle YOE, YOW 'hazel grove', 220

Hessleskew YOE 'hazel wood' (ON), 209, 220

Hestercombe SOM 'bachelor's coomb', 93

Heswall CHE 'hazel-tree spring', 31

Hethe OXF 'heath', 245

Hethel NFK 'heath hill', 171

Hetton DRH 'hip hill', 157

Heugh DRH, NTB 'hill-spur', 167

Hever KNT 'high promontory-tip', 178

Hewelsfield GLO 'Hygewald's open land', 240, 243

Heybridge ESX 'high bridge', 66

Heydon CAM 'hay valley', 98

Heydon NFK 'hay hill', 144, 152

Heyford NTP, OXF 'hay ford', 71

Heyop RAD 'high valley', 114, 116

Heyrod LNC, Heyroyd LNC 'high clearing', 208

Heywood LNC 'high wood', 228

Heywood WLT 'enclosure wood', 229

Hezetre Hundred HRE 'hazel-tree', 212, 214

Hidden BRK 'landing-place valley', 77, 99

Hiendley YOW 'hinds' wood', 205

Highbridge SOM 'high bridge', 66

Highlaws NTB 'high hill', 163

Highnam GLO 'river-meadow'; 'of the monks' prefixed, 43

Highover HRT 'high promontory-tip', 175

Highway WLT 'hay way', 83

Hilfield DOR 'open land by a hill', 170, 243

Hilgay NFK, prob. 'island of Hȳthla's people', 39

Hill var. cos. 'hill', 170

Hillam YOW '(place) at the hills', 170

Hillbeck WML 'cave stream' (ON), 14

Hillersdon DEV 'Hildhere's hill', 148

Hillesden BUC 'Hild's hill', 150

Hillhampton WOR 'hill settlement', 170

Hillingdon GTL 'Hilda's hill', 152

Hillmorton WAR, two place-names; 'hill' and 'moor settlement', 170

Hillsea HMP, partly obscure, 39

Hilton DOR, WML 'slope settlement', 162, 166

Hilton DRB, HNT, STF, YON 'hill settlement', 170

Hinckley LEI 'Hȳnca's clearing', 203

Hindhead SUR 'hind headland', 160

Hindley CHE 'hinds' wood', 205

Hindon WLT 'religious community's hill', 145, 149

Hinksey BRK, prob. 'stallion's island', 37, 39

Hinxhill KNT 'stallion's hill', 171

Hippenscombe WLT ?'stepping-stones coomb', 93

Hirst NTB, YOW 'wooded hill', 197

Hitcham BUC 'Hycga's village', 2

Hithe Bridge OXF 'landing-place', 76

Hive YOE 'landing-place', 77

Hixon STF 'Hyht's hill', 155

hlāw, hlǣw OE 'tumulus, hill', 124, 162–3

hlenc OE 'hill-slope', 163

hlinc OE 'bank, ledge', 125, 163–5

Marlborough WLT, partly uncertain, 128

Marlbrook SHR 'boundary brook', 16

Marlcliff WAR, prob. 'Mearna's cliff', 131, 136

Marldon DEV 'gentian hill', 148

Marley DEV, DRH 'boundary clearing', 206

Marlingford NFK, partly uncertain, 70

Marnhull DOR ?'Mearna's hill', 170

Marple CHE 'boundary pool', 27–8

Marr YOW, 'marsh' (ON), 34

Marrick YON 'boundary ridge', 169

Marsden LNC, YOW, prob. 'boundary valley', 99

Marsh SHR 'marsh', 53

Marsham NFK 'marsh village', 53

Marshfield GLO 'open land by a marsh', 53, 240, 243

Marsh Gibbon BUC 'marsh'; surname added, 53

Marshwood DOR 'marsh wood', 53, 228

Marske YON(2) 'marsh', 53, 237

Marston var. cos. 'marsh settlement', 34, 53

Marten WLT, Martin var. cos. 'pond settlement', 26

Martindale WML 'Martin's valley', 96

Martinhoe DEV 'hill-spur of Matta's people', 169

Martinsell WLT 'Mæthelhelm's hill-slope', 180–1

Martley SFK, WOR 'marten wood', 205

Marton var. cos. 'pond settlement', 26

Marvell IOW 'pleasant open land', 239, 242

Marwell DEV, HMP 'boundary spring', 32

Marwood DEV, prob. 'boundary wood', 228

Marwood DRH, partly uncertain, 229

Mason NTB 'Mærheard's fen', 41

Matfen NTB 'Matta's fen', 41

Matfield KNT 'Matta's open land', 243

Matlask NFK 'council ash-tree', 219

Matlock DRB 'council oak-tree', 219

Matson GLO, partly uncertain, 149

Matterdale CMB 'madder valley', 96

Mattersey NTT 'Mæthelhere's island', 38

Maulden BDF 'crucifix hill', 145, 151

Mawfield HRE, partly obscure, 240, 245

Maxey NTP 'Maccus's island' (ON/OE), 37

Mayfield STF 'open land where madder grows', 240, 243

Meaburn WML 'meadow stream', 18, 250

Meaford STF 'stream-junction ford', 11, 70

Meare SOM 'lake', 26

Mearley LNC 'boundary clearing', 206

Mease, R., LEI/DRB/STF 'mossy river', 56

Meathop WML, partly uncertain, 112, 117, 118

Meaux YOE 'sand-bank lake' (ON), 29

Medbourne LEI, WLT 'meadow stream', 18, 250

Meddon DEV 'meadow hill', 144, 148

Medhurst KNT 'wooded hill near meadowland', 198, 250

Medlock, R., LNC 'meadow stream', 23

Medmerry SSX 'middle island', 39

Meend GLO 'waste ground in forest', 172

Meerbrook STF 'boundary brook', 16

Meersbrook DRB 'brook of the boundary', 16

Meertown STF 'lake'; 'town' added, 26

Meesden HRT 'moss hill', 56, 152

Meese, R., STF/SHR 'mossy river', 56

Meeth DEV, Meethe DEV 'stream-junction', 11

Melbourn CAM, partly uncertain, 19

Melbourne YOE 'middle stream', 18

Melchbourne BDF 'milch stream', 18

Melchet HMP, prob. 'forest at the bare hill' (Brit), 190

Melcombe DOR(2) 'milk coomb', 93

Meldon NTB 'crucifix hill', 145, 158

Meldon DEV, WML 'multi-coloured hill', 143, 157

Meldreth CAM 'mill stream', 29

Melford SFK 'mill ford', 72

Mellor DRB, LNC, YOW 'bare hill' (Brit), 129

Melplash DOR 'mill pool', 27

Melverley SHR 'wood/clearing/pasture by a mill-ford', 72

Melwood LIN 'middle wood', 228

Membland DEV, partly uncertain, 248, 249

Mendip SOM, obscure, 172

meneth Corn 'hill', 172

Mentmore BUC 'Menta's moor', 55

Menwith YOW 'common wood' (OE/ON), 222

pirige OE 'pear-tree', 218, **219–20**
Pirton HRT, WOR 'pear orchard', 219
Pishill OXF 'peas hill', 171
Pishiobury HRT 'peas hill-spur'; 'manor' added, 168
Pitchcombe GLO 'pitch coomb', 93
Pitney SOM 'Pytta's island', 38
Pitsea ESX 'Pīce's island', 38
Pitstone BUC 'Pīcel's thorn-tree', 221
Pittington DRH 'hill associated with Pytta', 157
plæsc OE 'shallow standing water', 27
Plaish SHR 'shallow pool', 27
Plaitford HMP 'playing ford', 72
Plash SOM 'shallow pool', 27
Playden SSX 'play pasture', 234
Playford SFK 'play ford', 72
Plenmeller NTB ?'bare-hill summit' (PrW), 128, 129
Plowden SHR 'play valley', 99
Plumbland CMB 'plum-tree grove' (OE/ON), 207
Plumtree NTT 'plum-tree', 212, 214
Plush DOR 'shallow pool', 27
Plymtree DEV 'plum-tree', 212, 214
Podmore STF 'frog marsh', 55
pōl OE 'pool', 26, 27–8
Polden Hills SOM, partly obscure (prob. Brit/OE), 147
Polebrook NTP 'pouch brook', 15
Polehanger BDF 'sloping wood by a pool', 195, 196
Polesden SUR 'Pāl's valley', 98
Polperro CNW, partly uncertain (Corn), 28
Polruan CNW, partly obscure (Corn), 28
Polscoe CNW 'boat pool' (Corn), 28
Polsloe DEV 'pool slough', 28, 58
Polstead SFK 'pool place', 28
Poltimore DEV, partly obscure, 54, 55
Ponteland NTB ?'newly-cultivated land by a river'; river-name prefixed, 248, 249
Pontesford SHR 'ford on R. *Pant*', 72
Pool DEV, YOW, Poole CHE, DOR, GLO 'pool', 28
Poolham LIN '(place) at the pools', 28
Poringland NFK, partly obscure, 247
Portisham DOR, ?'well-watered valley near a market town', 44
Portishead SOM 'ridge of the harbour', 161
Portland DOR 'estate attached to *Port*, 246, 249

Portnall SUR 'Podda's nook', 101
Portslade SSX ?'river-crossing of the Roman harbour', 73, 74–5
Portswood HMP 'wood of the market town', 228
Posenhall SHR 'nook where peas grow', 104, 110
Postlip GLO ?'leaping-place of the pool', 57
Potlock DRB 'pot-hole channel', 23
Potsgrove BDF ?'grove of the pot-hole', 194
Poughill CNW, DEV ?'pouch-shaped hill', 170
Poulshot WLT 'Paul's wood', 196
Poultney LEI 'Pulta's island', 38
Poulton CHE(2), GLO, LNC(3) 'pool settlement', 28
Poundisford SOM 'pinder's ford', 70
Poundon BUC, partly obscure, 150
Powderham DEV 'promontory in reclaimed marshland', 43, 49
Pownall CHE, prob. 'Pohha's nook', 106
Prawle DEV, partly uncertain, 171
Preesall LNC 'brushwood headland' (PrW/ON), 161, 162
Pressen NTB 'priest fen', 41
Presteigne RAD 'boundary meadow belonging to priests', 250
Presthope SHR 'priests' valley', 113, 117
Prestwold LEI 'priests' forest', 227
Priestcliffe DRB 'priests' cliff', 131, 136
Princelett IOW 'Prim's stream', 22
Prudhoe NTB 'Prūda's hill-spur', 168
Puckeridge HRT ?'goblin ridge', 185
Pudleston HRE 'mouse-hawk's hill', 144
Pudsey YOW, uncertain, 35
Pulborough SSX 'hill of the pools', 28, 128
Puleston SHR 'Pēofel's hill', 142, 154
Pulford CHE 'pool ford', 28
Pulham DOR, NFK 'village of the pools', 28
pull OE 'pool', 27–8
Pulloxhill BDF 'Pulloc's hill', 170
Pulverbatch SHR ?'valley of R. *Pulre*', 12
Purbrook HMP 'puck brook', 16
Purfleet ESX 'Purta's creek', 22
Puriton SOM 'pear orchard', 219
Purleigh ESX, Purley BRK 'bittern wood', 205
Purley GTL 'pear-tree wood', 219
Purton GLO, STF, WLT 'pear orchard', 219

Raydon SFK 'rye hill', 144, 152

Rea. R., var. cos, 'at the river' (ME), 20

Reach BDF 'raised Roman road', 183–4

Reach (in Whittlesey) CAM ?'raised drainage channel', 183–4

Reach CAM 'linear earthwork', 183–4

Reach DEV ?'(place) at the oak-tree', 184

The Reaches NTP ?'ridge', 183–4

Read LNC 'female roe-deer headland', 160

Reading BRK 'Rēada's people', 2

Reagill WML 'fox valley' (ON), 99

Redbridge HMP 'reed bridge', 65

Redcar YON 'reed marsh' (OE/ON), 52

Redcliff GLO 'red cliff', 135

Redgrave SFK 'red grove', 193

Redhill SUR 'red slope', 162

Redland GLO 'third land', 246

Redlynch WLT 'red bank', 164

Redmarley WOR 'reed-pond wood/clearing/pasture', 26

Redmarshall DRH 'reed-pond hill', 26, 171

Redmire YON 'reed pond', 26

Rednal WOR, partly uncertain, 103, 111

Rednal SHR, poss. 'red nook', 105

Reed YON, obscure, 29

Reedness YOW 'reed ness', 172–3

Reighton YOE 'settlement by a straight cliff', 184

Rendcombe GLO 'valley of R. *Hrinde*', 93

Renhold BDF 'roe-deer nook', 111

Repton DRB 'hill of the tribe named *Hreope*', 145, 155

Retford NTT 'red ford', 68

Reydon SFK 'rye hill', 142, 144, 153

Rhydd WOR(2) ?'clearing', 79

Ribby LNC 'ridge settlement' (ON), 169

rīc OE ?'raised straight strip', 125, 183–6, 222

Riccall YOE 'Rīca's nook', 108

Rice Bridge Fm., Ricebridge ESX, SSX, SUR 'brushwood causeway', 66

Riche LIN ?'drainage channel', 185

Ricklinghall SFK 'nook of Rīca's people', 110

Riddlesden YOW 'Rēthal's valley', 98

Ridge HRT 'ridge', 169

Ridgeacre WOR, prob. 'newly-cultivated ground on a ridge', 169, 232, 233

Ridgebridge Hill SUR 'brushwood causeway', 66

Ridgewell ESX 'reed spring', 31

Ridgwardine SHR 'ridge settlement', 169

Ridware STF, prob. 'ford dwellers' (Brit/OE), 79, 80

Rigsby LIN 'settlement of the ridge' (ON), 169

Rigton YOW(2) 'ridge settlement', 169

Ringland NFK ?'newly-cultivated land of Rȳmi's people', 247

Ringmer SSX 'circle pond', 27

Ringmore DEV(2) 'reedmoor', 55

Ringsfield SFK, partly uncertain, 241, 245

Ringshall BUC 'Hring's nook', 102

Ringwood HMP, prob. 'boundary wood', 228

Ringwould KNT, partly uncertain, 145, 223, 227

Ripley DRB, HMP, SUR 'strip-shaped clearing', 205

Rippingdale LIN 'nook of Hrepa's people', 103, 110

Ripponden YOW 'valley of R. Ryburn', 99

Risborough BUC 'hills where brushwood grows', 128

Risebridge DRH, ESX, Risebrigg YOW 'brushwood causeway', 66

Riseley BDF, BRK 'brushwood clearing', 205

Rishangles SFK 'sloping wood characterized by brushwood', 195

Risingbridge NTP 'brushwood causeway', 66

Risley DRB, LNC 'brushwood clearing', 205

Rissington GLO 'hill where brushwood grows', 149

rīth, rīthig 'small stream', 11, 29

Ritton NTB, partly obscure, 29

ritu- Brit 'ford', 62, 79–80

Rivar WLT '(place) at the promontory', 178, 179

Rivenhall ESX, prob. 'rough nook', 102, 110

River SSX '(place) at the promontory-tip', 178

Riverhead KNT 'cattle landing-place', 77, 78

Road SOM, Roade NTP 'clearing', 208

Roborough DEV 'rough hill', 128

Rochford ESX, WOR 'hunting-dog's ford', 71

Stratfield BRK, HMP 'open land by a Roman road', 239, 243

Stratford var. cos. 'Roman-road ford', 62, 67, 70, 82

Stratton var. cos. 'settlement on a Roman road', 82

Streat SSX 'Roman road', 82

Streatham GTL 'village on a Roman road', 82

Streatlam DRH '(place) at clearings by a Roman road', 206

Streatley BDF, BRK 'Roman-road clearing', 82, 206

Street HRE, KNT, SOM(2) 'Roman road', 82

Streetley ESX, Streetly CAM, WAR 'Roman-road clearing', 82, 206

Strefford SHR 'Roman-road ford', 62, 70, 82

Strelley NTT 'Roman-road clearing', 82, 206

Strensall YON ?'lovers' nook', 109–10

Strete DEV(2) 'Roman road', 82

Stretford HRE, LNC 'Roman-road ford', 62, 70, 82

Strethall ESX 'nook by a Roman road', 102, 110

Stretton var. cos. 'settlement on a Roman road', 82

Strickland WML 'newly-cultivated land where stirks are kept', 248, 249

Stroat GLO 'Roman road', 82

strōd OE 'marshy land overgrown with brushwood', 34, 58–9

Strood KNT, Stroud GLO 'brushwood', 58

Strumpshaw NFK 'stump shaw', 209

Studdall KNT 'horse-herd forest', 227

Studland DOR 'newly-cultivated land where horses are kept', 247, 249

Studley OXF, WAR, WLT, YOW 'stud pasture', 206

Stuntney CAM 'steep island', 37, 39

Sturford WLT 'steers' ford', 71

Sturmer ESX 'pool on R. Stour', 27

Styal CHE, prob. 'nook by a path', 81, 106, 110

Styford NTB 'path ford', 70, 81

Subberthwaite LNC 'clearing belonging to *Sulby* (?pillar settlement)' (ON), 211

Sudbourne SFK 'south stream', 18

Sudbrooke (near Lincoln) LIN 'south brook', 16

Sudbrooke (in Ancaster) LIN 'sparrows' brook', 15

Sudeley GLO 'south clearing', 206

Suffield NFK, YON 'south open land', 242, 244

Sugdon SHR, prob. 'Sucga's hill', 154, 155

Sugnall STF 'sparrow's hill', 171

Sugwas HRE 'alluvial land frequented by sparrows', 59–60

Sulgrave NTP 'gully grove', 194

Sunderland, North NTB 'southern newly-cultivated land', 248, 249

Sunderland var. cos. 'detached estate', 249

Sunderlandwick YOE ?'dairy farm on a detached estate', 249

Sundon BDF 'Sunna's hill', 151

Sundridge KNT 'separate ploughed field', 235

Sunningwell BRK 'spring of Sunna's people', 32

Surfleet LIN 'sour stream', 22

Sutcombe DEV 'Sutta's coomb', 92

Swafield NFK 'open land characterized by swathes', 242, 243

Swalcliffe OXF 'swallow cliff', 131, 136

Swalecliffe KNT, Swallowcliffe WLT 'swallow's cliff', 131, 132, 136

Swallowfield BRK 'open land on R. Swale', 239, 243

Swalwell DRH 'swallow spring', 31

Swanbourne BUC 'swans' stream', 18

Swanland YOE 'Svein's grove' (ON), 207, 225

Swanmore HMP 'swans' pond', 26

Swarcliffe YOW 'black cliff', 132, 135

Swarland NTB 'heavy newly-cultivated land', 248, 249

Swarling KNT ?'sword-shaped ridges', 164

Swarthmoor LNC 'black marsh', 55

Swavesey CAM 'Swabian's landing-place', 62, 76, 78

Swayfield LIN 'open land characterized by swathes', 243

Sweethope NTB 'sweet valley', 116

Swell GLO 'swelling hill', 124

Swilland SFK 'newly-cultivated land where pigs are kept', 247, 249

Swimbridge DEV 'bridge'; owner's name prefixed, 65

Swinbrook OXF 'swine brook', 16

Swinburn NTB 'swine brook', 18

Thornborough BUC, Thornbrough YON(2) 'thorn-tree hill', 128, 221

Thornbrough NTB, YOW, Thornbury GLO, HRE 'thorn-tree fortified place', 221

Thorncombe DOR(2) 'thorn-tree coomb', 93, 221

Thorndon SFK 'thorn-tree hill', 152, 221

Thorne CNW, KNT, SOM, YOW 'thorn-tree', 220

Thorner YOW 'thorn-tree ridge', 176

Thorness IOW 'thorn hedge', 221

Thorney CAM, GTL, SOM, SSX 'thorn-tree island', 37, 39, 221

Thorney NTP, NTT 'thorn-tree enclosure', 221

Thornford DOR 'thorn-tree ford', 221

Thornham KNT, LNC, NFK, SFK 'thorn-tree village', 221

Thornhill DOR(2), DRB, WLT, YOW 'thorn-tree hill', 171, 221

Thornley DRH 'thorn wood', 203, 221

Thornley LNC 'wood where thorn-trees grow', 204

Thornthwaite CMB, WML, YOW 'thorn-tree clearing' (ON), 211, 221

Thornton var. cos. 'thorn-tree settlement', 220–1

Thorpland NFK 'newly-cultivated land near hamlets' (ON), 247, 249

Threapland CMB 'disputed land', 246

Threapwood CHE 'disputed wood', 229

Threlkeld CMB 'thralls' spring' (ON), 22

Thrift var. cos. ?'scrub on the edge of forest', 191

Thrimby WML 'thorn-tree settlement' (ON), 221

Thrintoft YON 'thorn-tree homestead' (ON), 221

Throckenholt CAM 'wood where beams are obtained', 196

Throckley NTB, partly uncertain, 163

Throphill NTB 'hamlet hill', 171

Thrybergh YOW 'three hills', 128

Thurgoland YOW 'Thurgar's newly-cultivated land' (ON), 246, 249

Thurland LNC 'Thorolf's newly-cultivated land' (ON), 248, 249

Thurne NFK 'thorn-tree' (ON), 221

Thurnham LNC '(place) at the thorn-trees', 221

Thurnscoe YOW 'thorn wood' (ON), 209, 221

Thurrock ESX, prob. 'dirty marsh', 34

Thursford NFK 'giant ford', 70

Thurnstonland YOW 'Thurstan's newly-cultivated land' (ON), 246, 249

thveit ON 'clearing, meadow, paddock', 167, 188, 189, 210–11, 219

Thwaite var. cos. 'clearing/meadow/paddock' (ON), 210

thyrne OE 'thorn-tree', **221**

Tibshelf DRB 'Tibba's shelf', 187

Ticehurst SSX 'wooded hill frequented by kids', 197

Tickenhurst KNT 'wooded hill of the kids', 197

Tickford BUC 'kid ford', 71

Tickhill YOW ?'kid hill', 171

Ticknall DRB 'kid nook', 107, 111

Tiddington OXF 'Tytta's hill', 150

Tideford CNW 'ford on R. Tiddy', 72

Tidenham GLO 'Dydda's enclosed land', 44–5, 49

Tideswell DRB 'Tīdi's spring', 31

Tidmarsh BRK 'nation marsh', 53

Tiffield NTP, partly uncertain, 241, 245

Tilberthwaite LNC 'clearing near *Tillesburg* (Tilli's fort)' (OE/ON), 211

Tilbrook HNT 'Tila's brook', 15, 16

Tilehurst BRK 'wooded hill where tiles are made', 5, 198

Tiley DOR 'wood/clearing where tiles are made', 205

Tillingdown SUR 'hill of Tilla's people', 145

Tiln NTT, Tilney NFK ?'useful island', 38, 102

Timberhanger WOR 'sloping wood where timber is obtained', 195, 196

Timberland LIN 'timber grove' (OE/ON), 208

Timberscombe SOM 'timber coomb', 93

Timsbury SOM 'grove of timber', 190

Tingrith BDF 'assembly stream', 29

Tintinhull SOM ?'Tinta's hill', 170

Tinwell RUT, partly uncertain, 32

Tipnoak Hundred SSX, prob. 'Tippa's oak-tree', 219

Tiptree ESX, prob. 'Tippa's tree', 212, 213

Titchmarsh HMP 'Ticcea's marsh', 53

Titchwell NFK 'kid's spring', 31

Titsey SUR 'Tydic's island', 38

Uckfield SSX 'Ucca's open land', 243

Udimore SSX, poss. 'woody pond', 26

Uggeshall SFK 'Uggeca's nook', 102

Ughill YOW 'Ugga's hill', 170

Ulcombe KNT 'owl's valley', 89, 93

Uldale CMB, prob. 'wolves' valley' (ON), 94

Uley GLO 'yew wood', 222

Ullenhall WAR 'Ulla's nook', 105

Ulleskelfe YOW 'Ulf's shelf' (ON), 187

Underley HRE '(place) under the slope', 165

Underore BRK '(place) under the slope', 181, 182

Underwood DRB, NTT '(place) under the wood', 229

Uphill SOM '(place) above the creek', 28

Upleatham YON '(place) at the upper slopes', 165

Upnore BRK '(place) upon the slope', 181, 182

Upsland YON 'higher-hall grove' (ON), 208

Upwell CAM 'spring'; 'upper' prefixed, 30

Upwood HNT 'higher wood', 228

Urchfont WLT 'Eohrīc's spring', 22

Urpeth DRH 'wild-cattle path', 78

Uxbridge GTL 'bridge of the *Wixan* tribe', 66

Vandlebury CAM 'Wændel's fort', 136

Vange ESX 'fen district', 40

vath ON 'ford', **82**, 83

vatn ON 'lake', **30**

Velly DEV 'wheel-rim', 87

Ventnor IOW, poss. named from a family called *Vintner*, 180

Vinnetrow SSX ?'marshy tree', 212, 215

vithr ON 'wood', 82, 189, 219, 222

Viveham DEV 'five enclosures', 45

Waberthwaite CMB 'hunting-booth clearing' (ON), 210–11

Wadborough WOR 'woad hills', 128

Wadden Hall KNT 'nook where woad grows', 100

Waddesdon BUC 'Weott's hill', 150

Waddicar LNC 'newly-cultivated land used for woad', 232, 233

Waddington GTL 'hill where wheat grows', 146

Waddon DOR, SUR 'woad hill', 144

Wade KNT, SFK 'ford', 83

Wadebridge CNW 'ford'; 'bridge' suffixed, 83

Wadenhoe NTP 'Wada's hill-spur', 168

Wadhurst SSX, prob. 'Wada's wooded hill', 197

Wadshelf DRB 'Wada's shelf', 187

wæsse OE 'riverside land which floods and drains quickly', 7, 34, 59–**60**, 86

wæter OE 'water, river, lake', **30**

wæterscipe OE ?'conduit, reservoir', **30**

wagen OE 'quaking bog', 34, **60**

Wainfleet LIN 'waggon stream', 22

Wainforth Wood YOW 'waggon ford', 72

Wainlode GLO 'waggon crossing', 73, 75

Waithe LIN 'ford' (ON), 82

Wakefield NTP, YON 'open land of festivities', 244

Walbrook GTL 'brook of the Britons', 16

Walburn YON 'stream of the Britons', 18

wald, weald OE 'forest', 191, **222–7**

Walden ESX, HRT, YON 'valley of the Britons', 99

Waldershare KNT 'district of the forest-dwellers', 1, 226

Walderslade KNT 'forest valley', 123

Waldingfield SFK 'open land of the forest people', 226, 242, 244

Waldridge BUC 'Wealda's ridge', 169

Waldridge DRH 'wall ridge', 169

Waldringfield SFK 'open land of Waldhere's people', 244

Waldron SSX 'forest building', 226

Walfield CHE 'open land by a spring', 240, 243

Walford (near Ross) HRE 'Briton ford', 70

Walford HRE, SHR 'spring ford', 30, 70

Walgrave NTP 'grove belonging to Old', 194

Walkwood WOR 'work wood', 229

Wallasey CHE 'island of *Waley* (Britons' island)', 39

Wallhope GLO 'spring valley', 30, 112, 113, 116

Wallingford BRK 'ford of Wealh's people', 67, 70

Wallop HMP, SHR 'spring valley', 30, 112, 113, 114, 116

Walltown SHR 'spring'; Modern English 'town' added, 30